HANDBOOK OF RESEARCH METHODS FOR ORGANISATIONAL CULTURE

T0327655

Handbook of Research Methods for Organisational Culture

Edited by

Cameron Newton

Professor, School of Management, Queensland University of Technology, Australia

Ruth Knight

Postdoctoral Research Fellow, Australian Centre for Philanthropy and Nonprofit Studies, Queensland University of Technology, Australia

EE **Edward Elgar**
PUBLISHING

Cheltenham, UK • Northampton, MA, USA

Published by
Edward Elgar Publishing Limited
The Lypiatts
15 Lansdown Road
Cheltenham
Glos GL50 2JA
UK

Edward Elgar Publishing, Inc.
William Pratt House
9 Dewey Court
Northampton
Massachusetts 01060
USA

Paperback edition 2023

A catalogue record for this book
is available from the British Library

Library of Congress Control Number: 2022930864

This book is available electronically in the **Elgar**online
Business subject collection
http://dx.doi.org/10.4337/9781788976268

ISBN 978 1 78897 625 1 (cased)
ISBN 978 1 78897 626 8 (eBook)
ISBN 978 1 0353 1340 2 (paperback)

Printed and bound by CPI Group (UK) Ltd, Croydon, CR0 4YY

Contents

Contributors

Kamarul Zaman Bin Ahmad, Dubai Business School, University of Dubai, United Arab Emirates

Karen Becker, School of Business and Creative Industries, USC Moreton Bay, Queensland, Australia

John B. Bingham, Marriott School of Business, Brigham Young University, USA

Adelle J. Bish, Willie A. Deese College of Business and Economics, North Carolina Agricultural and Technical State University, USA

Stefano Calciolari, Department of Economics, Management and Statistics, Università degli Studi di Milano "Bicocca", Italy, and Institute of Public Health, Università della Svizzera Italiana, Switzerland

Roslyn Cameron, Centre for Organisational Change and Agility, Torrens University, Adelaide, Australia

Jenna Campton, School of Business and Creative Industries, USC Sippy Downs, Sunshine Coast, Queensland, Australia

Tristan W. Casey, Safety Science Innovation Lab, School of Humanities, Languages and Social Science, Griffith University, Nathan, Brisbane, Australia

Jennifer A. Chatman, Haas School of Business, University of California, Berkeley, USA

Andrew Choi, Haas School of Business, University of California, Berkeley, USA

Niel J. Christensen, Marriott School of Business, Brigham Young University, USA

Shelby Danks, ARKEN Academy, Texas, USA

Maria Cristina Ferreira, Department of Psychology, Salgado de Oliveira University (UNIVERSO), Niterói, Rio de Janeiro, Brazil

Ronald Fischer, School of Psychology, Victoria University of Wellington, New Zealand

Frank W. Guldenmund, Safety Science & Security Group, Delft University of Technology, Netherlands

Xiaowen Hu, School of Management, Faculty of Business and Law, Queensland University of Technology, Brisbane, Australia

Bernd Irmer, School of Management, Faculty of Business and Law, Queensland University of Technology, Brisbane, Australia

Johannes Karl, School of Psychology, Victoria University of Wellington, New Zealand

Alireza Javanmardi Kashan, Middlesex University, Business School, London, UK

Ruth Knight, Australian Centre of Philanthropy and Nonprofit Studies, Queensland University of Technology, Brisbane, Australia

Nathanael J.N. Lee, Marriott School of Business, Brigham Young University, USA

Cameron Newton, School of Management, Faculty of Business and Law, Queensland University of Technology, Brisbane, Australia

Anna Prenestini, Università degli Studi di Milano, Department of Economics, Management and Quantitative Methods, and Center of Research and Advanced Education in Health Administration (CRC HEAD), Italy

Julian Randall, Heriot-Watt University/Edinburgh Business School, Edinburgh, UK

Jay Rao, Babson College, Babson Park, Massachusetts, USA

Chantelle Reid, Safety Science Innovation Lab, School of Humanities, Languages and Social Science, Griffith University, Nathan, Brisbane, Australia

Gerard Janse van Rensburg, School of Psychology, Victoria University of Wellington, New Zealand

Sonja A. Sackmann, EZO Institute for Developing Viable Organizations, Department of Economics and Organizational Science, University Bw Munich, Germany

Leesa Taylor, Torrens University, Australia

Phuong Anh Tran, School of Management, Faculty of Business and Law, Queensland University of Technology, Brisbane, Australia

Angela J. Ward, Denver Seminary, Littleton, Colorado, USA

Anna Wiewiora, School of Management, Faculty of Business and Law, Queensland University of Technology, Brisbane, Australia

Penny Williams, School of Management, Faculty of Business and Law, Queensland University of Technology, Brisbane, Australia

Athena Xenikou, Department of Aeronautical Sciences, Hellenic Air Force Academy, Athens, Greece

Acknowledgments

We gratefully acknowledge the incredible work of Alison Brodie who has judiciously and always happily responded to the many requests associated with putting this collection of work together. We also acknowledge Alison's thoughts and intellectual considerations as we glued together a book that is substantially about organisational glue.

1. Introduction to the *Handbook of Research Methods for Organisational Culture*

Cameron Newton

Organisational culture continues to be the pervasive force in organisations of all types, sizes, and objectives. If it is misaligned with organisational strategic objectives, the chances of achieving those objectives are greatly diminished. Schein (1996) referred to organisational culture as an influential force: stable and powerful. Over the years, organisational culture has been defined in hundreds of different ways, some more sophisticated than others. Schein (1985) contributed greatly to the debate around definitions of organisational culture, describing it as a layered phenomenon composed of inter-related levels of meanings. These can range from meanings that are mostly invisible, to those that are observable, and include basic assumptions that people share, values (governing rules and beliefs), and artefacts (the visible or tangible aspects). However, from here, researchers have diverged and used different methods and tools to explore and understand organisational culture. This *Handbook* highlights the varied approaches and challenges associated with researching and measuring organisational culture. Moreover, this collection of works from talented researchers highlights the need to continue to unpack and understand organisational culture, to meaningfully influence the future effectiveness and efficiency of organisations of all types across the globe.

OUTLINE OF THE *HANDBOOK*

This *Handbook* has been arranged in three parts representing the conceptual and definitional issues, measurement approaches, and contextual issues surrounding research of organisational culture.

PART I: CONCEPTUAL ISSUES RELATING TO ORGANISATIONAL CULTURE

In Chapter 2, Penny Williams explores the definitions, distinctions and functions of organisational culture, unpacking the values, norms and deeply held beliefs of employees, and the artefacts visible in corporate practices, statements, and symbols. She explores the value of organisational culture and its links to varied organisational outcomes. In Chapter 3, Athena Xenikou focusses on the role of leaders in organisational culture. She examines the nature of the relationship between leadership and organisational culture by initially delving into the mechanisms that leaders have at their disposal to formulate, reinforce, and change their organisation's culture depending on its developmental stage. Further exploring leadership as an antecedent of culture, and the mediating effect of culture in the leadership–organisational outcomes link, she examines culture as a social process activated by leaders to influence various aspects of organisational behaviour. In Chapter 4, Kamarul Zaman Bin Ahmad looks at the research relating to fit and congruence with organisational culture, and the definitional and measurement issues from this perspective. Last in Part I, Ronald Fischer, Johannes Karl, Gerard Janse van Rensburg, and Maria Cristina Ferreira explore multi-level issues in organisations and culture. They examine the complex phenomenon of cultures embedded within larger cultural systems, including national culture. Further, they explore the theoretical and methodological issues of culture at both organisational and national level and how they are interlinked.

PART II: QUANTITATIVE AND QUALITATIVE APPROACHES

Part II of the *Handbook* examines the varying methodological approaches to research of organisational culture. In Chapter 6, Stefano Calciolari and Anna Prenestini take a values-based perspective, analysing two different types of approaches – typological and dimensional – looking closely at the Competing Values Framework and the Organizational Culture Inventory®. In Chapter 7, Jennifer Chatman and Andrew Choi focus on establishing field-wide construct validity for measures of organisational culture, addressing the challenge of defining organisational culture and evaluating measurement options that, considered in conjunction, can increase construct validity and accessibility to relevant data while reducing various biases. In Chapter 8, Alireza Javanmardi Kashan and Anna Wiewiora take an extensive look at the commonly used qualitative approaches to researching organisational culture as well as the analytical and theory-building approaches used in qualitative studies. The chapter highlights the importance of alignment between assumptions about organisational culture and the methods and approaches used for studying it, and guides the researcher through the steps of designing qualitative studies on organisational culture, data collection methods and analysis, coding methods and theory-building approaches. Last in this part, Roslyn Cameron and Leesa Taylor focus on the use of mixed-methods research in measuring organisational culture, exploring definitional and methodological issues.

PART III: SPECIAL TOPICS OF ORGANISATIONAL CULTURE MEASUREMENT

Given the complexity associated with organisational culture, it is not surprising that the special topics part of the book is significant, including ten distinct chapters. In Chapter 10, Julian Randall addresses the difficult and contentious topic of cultural change, examining models and then taking a more qualitative and case-based perspective in exploring change. In Chapter 11, Adelle Bish explores more closely the multiple challenges involved with defining and measuring high-performance culture, concluding with a proposed framework that identifies questions to consider as part of the research design phase. In Chapter 12, Jay Rao and Shelby Danks take a detailed look at an enterprise culture of innovation. The authors overview some key instruments from the literature that define and assess an organisational culture of innovation, and present the InnoQuotient Model as an example of a practitioner-oriented measurement model for such assessment. Following on from this, Jenna Campton's Chapter 13 addresses the challenges associated with researching, measuring, and building corporate entrepreneurship cultures and the process of entrepreneurial activity within an organisation. She takes a critical look at research in this emerging area and the challenges associated with conceptualising and measuring this construct.

Niel Christensen, Nathanael Lee, and John Bingham, in Chapter 14, explore the measurement and development of ethical organisational culture. The authors examine current methods and research approaches to the study of ethical climate and propose a nomological categorization of existing antecedents as well as suggesting tools for practitioners and researchers seeking to measure ethical climate. In Chapter 15, Ruth Knight examines various issues particularly related to nonprofit organisational cultures, including the role and impact of nonprofit organisational culture on organisational and employee outcomes, measurement issues, and the emerging topic of philanthropic culture. Continuing the nonprofit theme, in Chapter 16, Adelle Bish, Karen Becker, and Bernd Irmer take a comparative case study approach to exploring the role of leadership capabilities in the context of nonprofit organisational culture influence.

Perhaps the most resilient of our contributors, Sonja Sackmann, in Chapter 17 ventures into the depths of deciphering bad organisational cultures. She discusses the critical issues associated with analysing 'bad' cultures in terms of being corrupt or unethical, before exploring various data collection methods that can be used for deciphering corrupt or unethical cultures, including their strengths and challenges. In Chapter 18, Angela Ward examines the issues around measurement of organisational culture in Christian churches, including the unique organisational qualities of the church, how these qualities affect the measurement of organisational culture, and how these may be quantified to aid culture measurement.

Last, in Chapter 19, Tristan Casey, Xiaowen Hu, Chantelle Reid, Phuong Anh Tran, and Frank Guldenmund discuss the often studied, yet poorly understood (or measured) concept of safety culture. The authors bring conceptual and methodological clarity with a particular focus on definitional-methodological alignment. A safety culture 'manifesto' is presented in the hope that it can guide future research on safety culture by advancing commitments that researchers can uphold.

Overall, this *Handbook* represents a valuable opportunity to reflect on the complexity and the advancement of organisational culture research over time, and the new ways and contexts that we need to be aware of as we continue to create meaningful impact.

REFERENCES

Schein, E. H. (1985). *Organizational Culture and Leadership: A Dynamic View*. San Francisco: Jossey-Bass.

Schein, E. H. (1996). Culture: The missing concept in organization studies. *Administrative Science Quarterly, 41*, 229–240.

PART I

CONCEPTUAL
ISSUES RELATING TO
ORGANISATIONAL CULTURE

2. Organisational culture: definitions, distinctions and functions

Penny Williams

The organisational culture literature is extensive and contentious. What is culture, how it is defined, and the most effective way to measure it, remain provocative issues despite decades of scholarly research. Yet the importance of culture in the operation of organisations is widely recognised by scholars and managers alike. The culture of an organisation, embodied in the organisations' values, norms and deeply held beliefs of employees, underpins the operation and approach to conducting business in an organisation. A distinct culture can be a source of competitive advantage for some organisations (Barney, 1986; Cameron & Quinn, 2011). For example, the success of Starbucks in the competitive coffee chain industry has been attributed to an organisational culture of belonging and inclusion where close bonds between employees facilitate strong customer service (Marques et al., 2015). Companies such as Walmart, IBM, Google and Apple have also been lauded for having distinct organisational cultures that have contributed to the market dominance of these firms (Flamholtz & Randle, 2012; Kaul, 2019). Equally, the literature is littered with cases where dysfunctional or toxic organisational cultures have damaged the reputation and value of firms. A widely publicised example can be found in the American Energy giant Enron, whose collapse in 2001 was at least partially attributed to a corporate culture of extravagance, ruthlessness and risk-taking (Cruver, 2002; Spector & Lane, 2007).

The belief that culture is fundamental to the success of an organisation is succinctly expressed in the statement "culture eats strategy for breakfast", attributed, rather contentiously, to management guru Peter Drucker and adopted by leaders in organisations such as Ford and the Giga Information Group (Anders, 2016; Kaul, 2019). A respected scholar in the field, Edgar Schein (1985, p. 33) more directly stated that "culture determines and limits strategy". Exactly how organisational culture influences strategy and impacts upon firm performance, what type of organisational cultures are advantageous, and whether an organisation should only have one unified culture, are some of the questions that sustain the interest of organisational culture researchers. The answers to these questions remain disputed, not the least because of the rich and varied approaches to studying the concept, but also due to the complex, inimitable and organic characteristics that comprise an organisation's culture. This chapter presents many of the inter-related debates about organisational culture such as a lack of unified definition; confusion between related constructs; and the influence of culture in organisations. The chapter begins by discussing the historical development of organisational culture as a concept, and considering the question of *what is organisational culture?* Alternate models and frameworks for measuring culture are presented and the idea of culture being functional or dysfunctional and made up of sub-cultures is examined. Definitions of organisational culture cannot be discussed without distinguishing culture from what it is not. Accordingly, the chapter discusses the distinction between culture and the related concept of organisational climate. Finally, the function of culture within organisations, and its relationship to organisational outcomes is considered in light of methodological and conceptual debates.

THE EMERGENCE OF ORGANISATIONAL CULTURE

Organisational culture gained momentum as a management concept in the early 1980s, when the economic success of Japan inspired research into the management practices of Japanese companies. Researchers such as Ouchi (1981), and Lincoln and Kalleberg (1985) identified distinct rituals, practices and structures that influenced employee commitment in Japanese firms. For subsequent decades, the utility of organisational culture as a means to explain observed patterns and variations in organisational behaviour and the potential influence of organisational culture on firm performance drove significant interest from scholars and managers alike.

The study of cultures within organisations began earlier however, emerging from the study of communities and societies in the disciplines of anthropology and sociology (Cameron & Ettington, 1988; Schein, 1990). Andrew Pettigrew (1979) was one of the first to suggest concepts from sociology and anthropology could be applied to understand organisational behaviour, arguing that people within organisations create meaning through "symbols, languages, beliefs, visions, ideologies, and myths" (p. 572). Pettigrew defined cultures as "the system of such publicly and collectively accepted meanings operating for a given group at a given time" (ibid.). While Pettigrew drew from both anthropology and sociology, current differences in perspectives on organisational culture can arguably be traced back to the differences between these disciplines. Mapping early organisational research into anthropological and sociological perspectives, two perspectives are considered to underlie the study of organisational culture (Smircich, 1983). The anthropological "functionalist" view focuses on how practices, beliefs and values maintain control within an organisation and suggests culture is something an organisation *has*. Culture can therefore be studied as an independent variable using quantitative methods that assess the presence of culture in elements such as norms or espoused values (Chatman & O'Reilly, 2016; Smircich, 1983). From this functionalist perspective, organisational cultures can be compared and the impact of culture on performance can be measured. In contrast, socio-cultural anthropologists argue that symbolic relationships, unique shared meanings, unconscious assumptions and deeply held beliefs of people within organisations *is* culture, which can only be studied through immersive qualitative research and cannot be compared between organisations (Cameron & Ettington, 1988; Chatman & O'Reilly, 2016). From the socio-cultural standpoint, organisational culture exists either in the social system manifested in organisational behaviours, or in the perspectives, cognitive frame and behaviour of the individuals who comprise the organisation (Cameron & Ettington, 1988). These fundamental differences, often termed the "culture wars" (Martin & Frost, 2011), have created significant debate on how to define and measure culture.

DEFINING ORGANISATIONAL CULTURE

Although the relevance of organisational culture to management theory and practice is widely acknowledged, a definition of the concept has not been agreed upon. Many scholars have enumerated the various definitions of organisational culture. For example, Cameron and Ettington (1988) identified 18 definitions, and Ott (1989) identified 73 definitions. While by no means an exhaustive list, some often-cited definitions are summarised chronologically in Table 2.1 below.

Table 2.1   Definitions of organisational culture

Definition of Organisational Culture	Author
"[A] system of publicly and collectively accepted meanings operating for a given group at a given time."	Pettigrew, 1979, p. 574
"Sets of symbols and myths."	Ouchi, 1981
"The set of meanings that evolves gives a group its own ethos, or distinctive character, which is expressed in patterns of belief (ideology), activity (norms and rituals), language and other symbolic forms through which organization members create and sustain their view of the world and image of themselves in the world."	Smircich 1983 p. 56
"The pattern of shared beliefs and values that give members of an institution meaning, and provide them with the rules of behaviour in their organization."	Davis, 1984, p. 1
"Culture is the set of important understandings (often unstated) that members of a community share in common."	Sathe, 1983, p. 6
"The shared beliefs and values guiding the thinking and behavioural styles of members."	Cooke & Rousseau, 1988, p. 245
"A common frame of reference or a shared recognition of relevant issues."	Feldman, 1991, p. 154
"The collective programming of the mind which distinguishes the members of one organization from another."	Hofstede, 1991, p. 262
"Culture is constituted by manifestation, realization, symbolization and interpretation processes. … organizational culture [is] the dynamic construction and reconstruction of cultural geography and history as contexts for taking action, making meaning, constructing images and forming identities."	Hatch, 1993, pp. 661, 686
"The taken for granted values, underlying assumptions, expectations, collective memories, and definitions present in an organization. It represents 'how things are done around here'."	Cameron & Quinn, 2011, p. 16
"The values, beliefs and assumptions that are held by members of an organization and which facilitate shared meaning and guide behaviour at varying levels of awareness."	Denison et al., 2014, p. 146

Indeed, organisational culture has often been used as a *catch all* to explain every aspect of an organisation that cannot be understood as separate from it (Denison, 1996). To bring clarity to the field, Schein (1985) proposed a framework that conceptualised culture as a layered phenomenon which manifests itself at three basic levels: deeply held underlying assumptions and beliefs; values and behavioural norms; and observable artefacts. Frequently illustrated as a pyramid (Figure 2.1), or metaphorically as an onion or an iceberg, Schein's framework remains one of the most widely accepted models, perhaps because it encompasses both the implicit and explicit components of organisational culture.

Artefacts: Artefacts are the visible symbols and signs of organisational culture. Material artefacts might include written documents, company records, annual reports and products. Artefacts also include observable facets of the environment such as the dress code, furnishings, the technology used or the physical office layout. Artefacts represent and reinforce an organisation's specific culture, and thus can also be seen in the language used in an organisation, the stories that are told and ceremonies held, and the routines and rituals of employees (Dailey & Browning, 2014; Smith & Stewart, 2011). Artefacts, however, do not always accurately portray deeper elements of culture. Annual reports, for example, are an organisational artefact developed to describe organisational performance to an external audience and thus may not accurately represent all aspects of the organisation's internal culture.

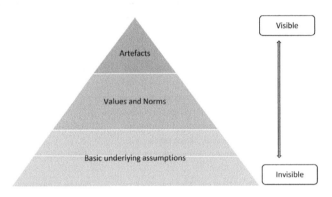

Source: Based on Schein (1985).

Figure 2.1   Three levels of organisational culture

Values: The behaviours and norms in organisations are a representation of shared values. Values have been defined as conscious, stable, enduring beliefs that a particular behaviour, outcome or course of action is preferable to an opposing behaviour, outcome or course of action (Hitlin & Piliavin, 2004). Values guide a person's evaluation of appropriate behaviour across different situations (Bourne & Jenkins, 2013). Organisational values are often explicitly stated and developed into a visible artefact such as a "values statement" that appears in annual reports, websites or other documents. E-commerce company Alibaba Group, for example, reinforces company culture with six publicised core values: customer first, teamwork, embrace change, integrity, passion and commitment (Alibaba Group, n.d.; Dolan & Bao, 2012).

The values shared and practised as part of organisational culture may, however, vary from the values articulated in documents. Rather enacted values are a manifestation of the underlying basic assumptions that commonly, and often implicitly, guide the decisions and behaviours of individuals within the organisation (Bourne and Jenkins, 2013; Schein, 1985). While values can become so ingrained within an organisation that they are hard to distinguish from underlying basic assumptions, they are usually less abstract and more measurable than basic assumptions, and they provide justification of behaviour. For this reason, values are often the focus in organisational culture research (Bourne & Jenkins, 2013; Deal & Kennedy, 1983; Ott, 1989).

Assumptions: Basic underlying assumptions are the deepest element of organisational culture and represent non-conscious, taken-for-granted beliefs that guide how individuals in an organisation think, act, feel and behave toward a given situation. These shared assumptions are deeply ingrained and are only visible through intense clinical observation, questioning and self-reflection (Hatch, 1993; Schein, 1990).

It is the simultaneous existence of all three components, and the interaction between them, that Schein defines as organisational culture:

> A pattern of shared basic assumptions that the group learned as it solved its problems of external adaptation and internal integration, that has worked well enough to be considered valid and, therefore, to be taught to new members as the correct way to perceive, think and feel in relation to those problems. (Schein 1985, p. 9)

> In analyzing the culture of a particular group or organization it is desirable to distinguish three fundamental levels at which culture manifests itself: (a) observable artefacts, (b) values, and (c) basic underlying assumptions. (Schein 1990, p. 111)

Inherent within Schein's definition is the idea that organisational culture is socially constructed, learned behaviour and beliefs that are shared between members of the organisation. The social construction of organisational culture through shared values, beliefs and norms, is common across most definitions of culture, and can be seen in the number of definitions presented in Table 2.1 that include these elements. As Chatman and O'Reilly (2016, p. 214) explain, most researchers, at least to some extent, agree with Schein's conceptualisation of culture as including cultural artefacts, supported by norms and values, beneath which exist assumptions and beliefs. A further point of agreement is that organisational culture serves as a social control mechanism that influence individual employee behaviour and collective organisational outcomes (Chatman & O'Reilly, 2016).

THEORIES AND MODELS OF ORGANISATIONAL CULTURE

As a construct, organisational culture is abstract, and there is continued debate about the appropriateness of qualitative versus quantitative methodologies to study organisational culture. As Martin (2001), however, suggests, rather than emphasising a researcher's definition of organisational culture, it may be more relevant to examine how they operationalise it. Proponents of qualitative approaches argue that the deep, unconscious elements of culture cannot be uncovered using quantitative methods, and further, that each culture is unique to an organisation and thus cannot be compared or measured along *a priori* categories (Denison et al., 2014; Schein, 1992). The more conscious elements of culture such as observable artefacts, shared values and behaviours can, arguably, be more readily measured quantitatively (Ashkanasy et al., 2000; Xenikou & Furnham, 1996). Consequently, several models have been developed and surveys are popularly used to measure, manage, characterise or change organisational culture. The following section provides a brief summary of some of the most prominent models applied in research and in organisational practice over time.

The Corporate Culture Survey (CCS)

One of the earliest questionnaires developed to measure organisational culture was the Corporate Culture Survey (CCS), developed by Glaser (1983). The CCS assesses four sub-dimensions that are based on the distinctive elements of culture identified by Deal and Kennedy (1982). Deal and Kennedy (1983, p. 501) suggest that while "implicit and taken for granted" culture consists of tangible elements that can be seen in the *shared values*; the *heroes and heroines* that embody those shared values; the *rituals and ceremonies* that are the physical manifestation of the values; and the *cultural network* that upholds the culture. The sub-dimensions of the CCS are closely related and because of the emphasis on observable elements of culture, some argue that the CCS measures cultural artefacts rather than values (Xenikou and Furnham, 1996).

The Culture Gap Survey (CGS)

Developed around the same time as the CCS, the Kilmann–Saxton Culture-Gap Survey (CGS) measures behavioural norms (Kilmann & Saxton, 1983). Developed by Kilmann and Saxton (1983), the CGS aims to measure differences between desired and actual behavioural norms in an effort to identify cultural gaps that might be impeding organisational success. This model seeks to measure behavioural norms against a matrix of four sub-scale pairs; *Technical versus Human Concerns, Short versus Long-term Orientation, Task Support versus Task Innovation*, and *Social Relations versus Personal Freedom* (Figure 2.2,). Used most often at the team or work group level, the model compares observed behaviours against the expectations of work group members.

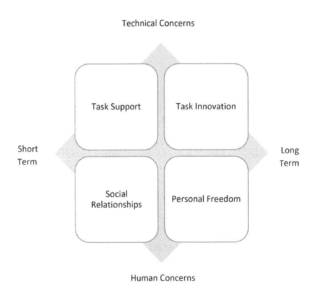

Source: Adapted from Kilmann and Saxton (1997, p. 21).

Figure 2.2   *The four culture gaps*

Organisational Beliefs Questionnaire (OBQ)

Based on Peters et al.'s (1982) work on excellence in organisations, Sashkin (1984) developed the Organisational Beliefs Questionnaire (OBQ) to measure the degree to which organisational beliefs or values are consistent with those held by successful organisations. The OBQ thus assesses organisational values across ten subscales, or "Pillars of Excellence" (Sashkin, 1984) which are:

1. Work should be fun
2. Being the best
3. Taking (thoughtful) risks
4. Attention to detail
5. The worth and value of people
6. Quality
7. Communicating to get the job done
8. Growth, profit and other indicators of success
9. Hands-on management; and
10. The importance of a shared philosophy.

The OBQ conceptually measures similar dimensions to other surveys, yet as a diagnostic tool for organisational culture, has not proved as popular (Denison et al., 2014; Xenikou & Furnham, 1996).

Organisational Culture Inventory (OCI)

More commonly applied, the Organisational Culture Inventory (OCI) was developed by Cooke and Lafferty (1989) to measure behavioural norms. The OCI is frequently used to assess culture as part of an organisational change process and uniquely considers the pressures on organisational members to behave in dysfunctional ways (Balthazard et al., 2006; Chatman & O'Reilly, 2016). The OCI uncovers the existing norms that guide the behaviour required for individuals to conform to co-worker expectations. By clustering interrelated behavioural norms, such as affiliation, approval, power or dependence along two dimensions that distinguish between task or people orientation and security versus satisfaction needs, the OCI can compare organisations or work groups against three organisational culture styles (Cooke & Lafferty, 1989; Cooke & Szumal, 2000):

1. Constructive cultures – characterised by interaction with others and an approach to tasks that will facilitate members meeting their higher-order satisfaction needs. This style features norms related to achievement, self-actualising, humanistic-encouraging and affiliative behaviours.
2. Passive/defensive cultures – characterised by norms associated with approval, conventional (or conforming), dependency and avoidance. In such a culture, members interact in ways that limit any threat to their own security.
3. Aggressive/defensive – described by oppositional, power, competitive and perfectionistic norms. In aggressive/defensive cultures members forcefully approach tasks to raise their status and security.

Similar to the CGS, the OCI also includes dimensions that range from task to person focussed, and while it too is subject to some limitations (see Chatman & O'Reilly, 2016), it is considered to be one of the most internally reliable instruments for measuring organisational culture (Xenikou & Furnham, 1996).

Competing Values Framework (CVF)

One of the most popular approaches to diagnosing organisational culture is to use the Competing Values Framework (CVF) (Chatman & O'Reilly, 2016; Quinn & Rohrbaugh, 1983). Like prior models, the CVF also emerged from studies on organisational effectiveness and received the name "competing values" because the four cultural dimensions described by the CVF appear to be conflicting. The CVF maps an organisation's preference for either flexibility and discretion or, conversely, stability and control, and the organisation's orientation either toward internal systems and integration or the external environment and differentiation, resulting in four models of organisational effectiveness; *Human Relations*, *Open Systems*, *Internal Process* and *Rational Goal Model*. These four models have subsequently been translated to four types of organisational cultures; *Clan*, *Adhocracy*, *Market* or *Hierarchy* (Quinn & Rohrbaugh, 1983; Cameron & Quinn, 2011). The Organizational Culture Assessment Instrument (OCAI) is a survey instrument used to gather data to compare the organisation's cultural values against the four models of organisational effectiveness, and define the type or culture within the organisation.

Organised according to the human relations model of organisational effectiveness, *clan* cultures can be distinguised by their shared values and goals, cohesiveness and participation, and reflect a sense of family or belonging. In an *adhocracy*, the open systems model of organising is adopted and innovation, creativity, adaptability and entrepreneurial qualities are valued. Reflecting traditional modes of operating (the internal process model), *hierarchy* cultures emphasise order, rules and regulations, efficiency and clear lines of authority and decision-making. The rational goal model leads to *market* cultures characterised by competitiveness, a focus on profit and the customer, decisiveness and goal accomplishment.

The Competing Values Framework has been widely used to differentiate and describe organisational cultures; however, some consider the typology to be too narrow to adequately capture the diversity of characteristics that make organisational cultures unique (Hartnell et al., 2011; Ostroff & Schulte, 2014).

Denison Organisational Culture Survey (DOCS)

As is the case with earlier approaches, the Denison Organisational Culture Survey (DOCS) was developed through an examination of the cultural characteristics of high performing organisations (Denison et al., 2014). Similar to the CVF, the framework that underpins DOCS is based on the notion that effective organisations must simultaneously balance the tensions between external adaptation and internal integration. The dimensions of stability and flexibility and internal and external focus create a framework for profiling organisations according to four characteristics (Denison & Mishra, 1995; Denison et al., 2014):

- *Involvement* – the empowerment and engagement of individuals in an organisation

- *Consistency* – the consistency of behaviours, processes and actions with the organisation's core values
- *Adaptability* – the ability to translate the demands of the organisational environment into action
- *Mission* – the existence of a clear sense of purpose and direction.

Denison (1990) argues that the most effective organisations display high levels of all four traits, however critics counter that traits such as mission are constructs distinct from organisational culture rather than reflective of behavioural norms or values implicit in the culture (Chatman & O'Reilly, 2016).

The models presented here do not represent an exhaustive list of all methods for understanding culture (for further examples refer Chatman & O'Reilly, 2016; Denison et al., 2014; Xenikou & Furnham, 1996), however, they do illustrate a key distinction between models. Existing approaches intend to measure either *values* – the preferences and priorities of individuals within in an organisation; or *behavioural norms* – the shared expectations regarding how individuals should behave (Xenikou & Furnham, 1996), as summarised in Table 2.2.

Table 2.2   *Organisational culture instruments measuring values and behavioural norms*

Measuring Values	Measuring Behavioural Norms
Corporate Culture Survey (CCS)	Culture Gap Survey (CGS)
Organisational Beliefs Questionnaire (OBQ)	Organisational Culture Inventory (OCI)
Organizational Culture Assessment Instrument (OCAI)	Denison Organizational Culture Survey (DOCS)

The wide variety of frameworks and instruments used to measure culture also illustrate the divergent views on how organisational culture should be studied. Quantitative measures of organisational culture are limited by their emphasis on behavioural norms or values, to the exclusion of other facets of culture such as shared assumptions and by the potential to oversimplify the wide diversity of cultural values that may exist in organisations. Frequently, the purpose of measuring organisational culture is to assist leaders to understand, and if necessary, improve an organisation. A dialogic approach which engages the leader and their employees in processes that reveal cultural dimensions, is thus also valid (Schein & Schein, 2017). In this respect qualitative approaches such as observation or individual and group interviews or facilitated group activities might prove more useful than quantitative frameworks in uncovering shared assumptions (Schein & Schein, 2017). Additionally, when used to diagnose the current organisational culture, most frameworks assume there is one unified culture across the organisation that can be readily identified and described, if not categorised. It is now widely recognised however that organisations consist of many sub-cultures.

ORGANISATIONAL SUB-CULTURES

Much of the early work on organisational culture reflected a view that the values, behavioural norms and artefacts of an organisation's culture were shared by all within the organisation and were distinct from other organisations. These studies posited that a single culture was shaped by senior management and, when strong, would provide a shared sense of direction and consensus on appropriate behaviours for all members of the organisation (Alvesson, 2012, p. 5). While organisations may have a dominant culture, sub-cultures have been found to exist across geographic locations, divisions or occupational groups. Sub-cultures reflect group-based cultural variations that may emerge from unique patterns of interaction, related to the type of work performed or the composition of group members (Hofstede, 1998). Studies, for example, have identified the influence of different sub-cultures in a police department (Rose & Unnithan, 2015); between doctors and nurses (Fitzgerald & Teal 2004); and across different divisions in an investment bank (Huang et al., 2002).

Some sub-cultures will share the dominant organisational values, other sub-cultures may display some variations but align with the dominant culture, while other sub-cultures may have values that directly oppose the dominant culture. Termed *counter-cultures*, these mis-aligned groups may cause cultural rifts or inter-cultural conflicts that negatively impact on organisational performance (Hofstede, 1998; Park & Lunt 2018). Yet subcultures, even counter-cultures, can play an important role in questioning the prevailing culture. In changing environments, subcultures can be the source of new ideas or new values that help organisations to develop and respond to shifting demands or emerging markets. Organisational culture can thus be measured at the whole-of-organisational level or using sub-cultures as the unit of analysis (Cameron & Quinn, 2011; Hofstede, 1998).

CULTURE STRENGTH

The existence of sub-cultures or counter-cultures points to another dimension of organisational culture – culture strength. Culture strength refers to how deeply entrenched the values, norms and assumptions are within the organisation, and the extent to which they guide the behaviour of employees. In strong cultures the goals of the organisation are understood and shared (Deal & Kennedy, 1983; Sathe, 1983). Employees tend to embrace the dominant values which are institutionalised through well-established artefacts, such as routines, stories, rituals and visible symbols (Smith & Stewart, 2011). The success of high-performing organisations has been attributed to the existence of strong organisational cultures in which the values are positive, and where participation is valued (Alvesson, 2012; Deal & Kennedy, 1982; Denison, 1984). For example, the continued success of the Walt Disney Company has been widely attributed to a strong culture of commitment to people, customer service and creative excellence that is commonly referred to both inside and outside the company as "The Disney Way". At Disney, customers are guests and employees are cast members trained at a Disney University so that they might create the "magic" that is a Disney experience (Capodagli & Jackson, 2016). Apparent in Disney, a strong organisational culture acts as a form of social control that steers employee behaviour, provides a sense of belonging and a frame of reference for employee decision-making (Alvesson, 2012). All of these aspects can help in the achievement of organisational goals.

Yet, strong cultures can also be problematic. Deeply held assumptions and beliefs may make it difficult for organisations to adapt to changes in the external environment or implement new approaches internally. Strong values may restrict decision-making or be counter-productive by suppressing constructive criticism, new ideas or potentially beneficial sub-cultures (Spector & Lane, 2007). Balthazard et al. (2006), in a study on culture in four government departments, found that strong cultures can, at times, be dysfunctional and constrain organisational effectiveness. New opportunities or problems may be missed if the culture limits organisational decision-making to established ways of doing things. Even failed company mergers have been attributed to the inability to integrate or align two strong organisational cultures (Bauer & Matzler, 2014; Stahl and Voigt, 2008). In recent times, negative employee behaviour and even illegal activity has been attributed to strong but dysfunctional organisational cultures. The Australian banking sector, for example, has been heavily criticised for engendering an industry-wide culture where rogue trading, greed and dishonesty proliferated, with attention drawn to particularly toxic cultures in certain banking organisations (Middlemiss, 2016). Globally, poor governance and corporate cultures that valued risk and cultivated unethical behaviour featured in the US- and UK-based finance companies at the centre of the 2007–2008 global financial crisis (Mellor, 2015).

These examples point to the importance of culture in achieving organisational outcomes and the function of culture in contributing to organisation performance.

THE FUNCTION OF CULTURE

Schein (1985) describes organisational culture as learned behaviour, evolving and emerging (Schein & Schein, 2017). That is, culture is cultivated from the ways in which organisations adapt to the external environment and the patterns of behaviour that employees learn as they interact with the organisation and its environment. The function of culture is to align the actions of employees with the desired organisational direction so that the organisation may successfully adapt to its environment (Korte & Chermack, 2007). Beliefs and assumptions collectively shared cue acceptable behaviour and provide a shared mental model that reduces ambiguity. Espoused values further reduce uncertainty by promoting commitment to higher order goals such as the company's values, direction, strategy or vision. Through these mechanisms of social control, culture directs and shapes individual employee behaviour in ways that can and do affect organisational performance (Chatman & O'Reilly, 2016).

The question of exactly how organisational culture influences firm performance has formed the basis of copious studies which either consider the effect of organisational culture on organisational outcomes (such as financial performance or value), function-specific outcomes (such as quality or innovation) or employee-level outcomes (such as commitment and satisfaction). These varying perspectives reflect how culture is deeply embedded and thus can shape performance and outcomes at multiple levels within an organisation.

Early research by Crémer (1993) demonstrated how an organisation's market reputation and the opinions of key stakeholders are shaped by perceptions of the organisation's culture. More recent research has taken this further to empirically measure the impact of organisational culture (or perceptions of culture) on shareholder value. For example, in an analysis of employee reviews on Glassdoor.com, Moniz (2017) found that shareholder value increased when the organisational culture and strategic goals were aligned. Popadak (2013) found that strong shareholder governance that emphasised a results-oriented corporate culture may produce short-term profits but reduces overall firm value, by virtue of a culture that de-emphasises collaboration, integrity and customer service. Popadak's (2013) study demonstrates a commonly explored link between organisational culture types and outcomes. For example, Yeung et al. (1991) tested the four culture types described in the CVF and found that organisations with high scores across all four culture quadrants experienced the best financial performance, and organisations with human relations cultures also had higher levels of financial performance. Similarly, other studies have tested the financial performance (or related measures) of organisations adopting various culture types. In dynamic markets, market-oriented cultures are related to strong financial performance (Denison, 1984; Homburg & Pflessor, 2000), while innovative cultures have been found to produce higher sales growth and bureaucratic cultures are more efficient (Berson et al., 2008; Chatman et al., 2014).

Within organisations, function-specific outcomes are frequently shaped by organisational culture. For example, the effectiveness of a manager's human resource role has been shown to be greater in market-based cultures (Teo et al., 2003). Yeung et al.'s (1991) study also demonstrated that organisational culture impacted on the implementation of human resource practices such as staffing, development, performance and reward. In a study of US hospitals, Shortell et al. (2000) found a relationship between organisational culture and the implementation of quality improvement processes. Innovation within a workforce is also shaped by culture (Naranjo-Valencia et al., 2017).

To result in superior financial performance and thus provide a source of sustained competitive advantage, Barney (1986, p. 658) argues that organisational culture must be *rare*, *valuable* and *imperfectly imitable*. That is, the culture must have characteristics that are not commonly found in other organisations, must lead to financial value for the firm (through, say, low costs or high sales), and must not be easily imitated by other organisations resulting in the same degree of success. Further, to ensure success, culture and strategy must be aligned (Kaul, 2019).

Organisational performance is generally considered to be derived from the collective performance of individual employees. Consequently, much of the organisational culture research has investigated the perceptions of the culture held by employees, and the impact of culture on employee-level outcomes. A wide range of employee-level outcomes are affected by organisational culture, including: employee performance (Pool, 2000); absences (Kangas et al., 2017); turnover/intention to leave (Kangas et al., 2018; Sturman et al., 2012); job satisfaction, commitment and employee engagement (Belias & Koustelios, 2014; Parent & Lovelace, 2018); and employee stress and well-being (Newton, 2006, Newton & Jimmieson, 2009). Recent studies have even demonstrated a link between smoking, workplace health and organisational culture (Kava et al., 2019). Cultures that value recognition, innovation, flexibility and collaboration result in higher levels of job satisfaction, organisational commitment and performance (Lok and Crawford, 2001). Cultures where employees feel supported also reduce employee stress, turnover, absenteeism, and occupational health and safety incidents, which in turn all have a positive impact on organisational outcomes (Newton, 2006). Regardless of the analytical perspective, there is ample evidence of the correlations between organisational culture, employee-level outcomes and organisational performance, and this is perhaps why there is consensus on the importance of culture despite a lack of definitional or epistemological agreement.

DISTINGUISHING CULTURE FROM CLIMATE

Some of the definitional debate on organisational culture emerges from the overlap and, at times, confusion between organisational culture and organisational climate. Prior to the emergence of organisational culture as a construct, Litwin and Stringer (1968) had proposed the concept of *organisational climate* to explain how employees' perceptions of structures and processes within their work environment influenced their attitudes and behaviour. Litwin and Stringer's (1968) views of climate are founded in Lewin's (1951) field theory in which individual behaviour is a function of the interaction between the person and the social environment. Organisational climate explains how employees perceive observable aspects of their work environment, such as the support received from management, the structure of the organisation or team, and the processes and levels of autonomy in decision-making and has been defined as "the shared perceptions of and the meaning attached to policies, practices and procedures employees experience" (Schneider et al., 2013, p. 362).

Organisational climate and culture share similarities, in that they both emphasise social control mechanisms and the organisation's social context in an attempt to understand behaviour in the workplace (Schneider et al., 2013). Both constructs also seek to uncover "shared meaning" of organisational phenomena. Climate, however, focuses on employees' conscious perceptions of overt structures and systems which are often able to be controlled, directed or manipulated. Climate, therefore, is considered somewhat temporary and able to change. For example, a change in leadership or an organisational restructure may alter employees' perceptions of and attitude toward their work environment, re-shaping the organisational climate for a period of time. In contrast, organisational culture is far more enduring. The values and assumptions that underpin culture are deeply held and therefore more difficult to discern, relatively stable over time, and much more difficult to change.

One common distinction is that unlike culture which is considered pervasive, climate can apply to a specific aspect of the work environment that might be required to achieve a specific outcome at a particular point in time (Chatman & O'Reilly, 2016; Denison, 1996). For example, to address legislative requirements or reduce accidents an organisation might take specific managerial actions that create a climate where employee safety is considered a priority (Zohar & Luria, 2005). Similarly, to address industry competition, organisational strategy might, for a short time, dictate a service climate to attract market share (Walumbwa et al., 2010).

Despite the occasional confusion, organisational culture and climate are complementary constructs that exist in organisations simultaneously and can be studied together (Denison, 1996; Ostroff & Schulte, 2014). For example, research demonstrated how both work-group climate and organisational culture at PepsiCo are shaped by HR processes (Church et al., 2014). Culture can be viewed as a foundation that underlies organisational climate, or perhaps, as some have suggested, organisational culture provides the normative context within which organisational climate develops (Ostroff & Schulte, 2014, Schneider et al., 2017).

FUTURE DIRECTIONS FOR ORGANISATIONAL CULTURE

This chapter set out to chart the development of the theories of organisational culture and present a summary of the various debates and the points of consensus on the concept of organisational culture. Having outlined the key methodological frameworks and dimensions of organisational culture and highlighted the significance of the concept to management and organisational theory and practice, it is also worth considering the role of culture in new organisational structures that present new ways of working.

When the concept of organisational culture was first articulated, work was primarily undertaken through traditional employer–employee relationships performed in organisations defined by a location-based workplace setting. Individuals *went to* work in a building, an office, a factory, hospital or other specific setting where they interacted with their colleagues, supervisors and managers. These place-based social interactions enabled the development and propagation of an organisation's culture. Indeed, most of the research on organisational culture has been undertaken in such settings. Social and technological changes have, however, fundamentally changed how and where people work. Facilitated by technology, employees can now work from an alternate office, from home, a shared workspace or even from a cafe or park. Flexible work arrangements are now commonplace in organisations and studies have shown that employee access and use of flexibility is dependent upon a supportive organisational culture (Williams et al., 2018).

Further, globalisation has presented opportunities for firms to expand new locations or access talented labour in other geographies who may work remotely or in satellite offices. Flatter, leaner organisational structures have changed traditional hierarchical decision-making processes and seen the rise of new forms of collaborative and supportive leadership, and smaller organisational sizes. As they respond to market variability, firms more frequently outsource or turn to contingent workers to fill temporary labour needs. In some industries, new innovative organisations have emerged which rely entirely on a contracted workforce. This new form of organisation is perhaps best represented in the gig economy where digital platforms facilitate the provision of labour and services through websites that connect independent contractors with purchasers of those services. Exemplified by Uber, those services might be provided in person, or negotiated and completed entirely online, as occurs on platforms such as Freelancer and Upwork (McDonald et al., 2019). Other examples, such as Amazon Mechanical Turk decouple and distribute tasks to an invisible "crowd" of online workers on behalf of other organisations. These new forms of working suggest that organisational culture cannot be bounded by physical infrastructures or location. They present new opportunities for studying the existence of culture in organisations where employees do not frequently, if ever, interact. When supervision is remote or when it is provided by an algorithm, how then is culture inculcated? What becomes of the links between organisational strategy, culture and performance? It is these questions that present exciting future directions for research into organisational culture.

REFERENCES

Alibaba Group (n.d.). Culture and values. Retrieved July 26, 2019 from https://www.alibabagroup.com/en/about/culture

Alvesson, M. (2012). *Understanding Organizational Culture*. London: Sage.

Anders, G. (2016), Did Peter Drucker actually say "culture eats strategy for breakfast" – and if so, where/when? Available at: www.quora.com/Did-Peter-Drucker-actually-say-culture-eatsstrategy-for-breakfast-and-if-so-where-when (accessed June 2019).

Ashkanasy, N.M., Broadfoot, L., & Falkus, S. (2000). Questionnaire measures of organizational culture. In N.M. Ashkanasy, C. Wilderom, & M. Peterson (Eds.), *The Handbook of Organizational Culture and Climate* (2nd ed., pp. 131–162). Thousand Oaks, CA: Sage.

Balthazard, P.A., Cooke, R.A., & Potter, R.E. (2006). Dysfunctional culture, dysfunctional organization. *Journal of Managerial Psychology*, *21*(8), 709–732. doi: 10.1108/02683940610713253

Barncy, J.B. (1986). Organizational culture: Can it be a source of sustained competitive advantage? *Academy of Management Review, 11*(3), 656–665.

Bauer, F. & Matzler, K. (2014). Antecedents of M&A success: The role of strategic complementarity, cultural fit, and degree and speed of integration. *Strategic Management Journal, 35*(2), 269–291.

Belias, D. & Koustelios, A. (2014). Organizational culture and job satisfaction: A review. *International Journal of Management and Marketing, 4*(2), 132–149.

Berson, Y., Oreg, S., & Dvir, T. (2008), CEO values, organizational culture and firm outcomes. *Journal of Organizational Behavior, 29*: 615–633. doi: 10.1002/job.499

Bourne, H. & Jenkins, M. (2013). Organizational values: A dynamic perspective. *Organization Studies, 34*(3), 495–514. doi: 10.1177/0170840612467155

Cameron, K.S., & Ettington, D.R. (1988). The conceptual foundations of organizational culture. In J.C. Smart (Ed.), *Higher Education: Handbook of Theory and Research* (vol. 4, pp. 356–396). New York: Agathon.

Cameron, K.S. & Quinn, R.E. (2011). *Diagnosing and Changing Organizational Culture: Based on the Competing Values Framework*. John Wiley & Sons.

Capodagli, B. & Jackson, L. (2016). *The Disney Way: Harnessing the Management Secrets of Disney in Your Company* (3rd edition). McGraw-Hill.

Chatman, J.A., Caldwell, D.F., O'Reilly, C.A., & Doeer, B. (2014). Parsing organizational culture: How the norm for adaptability influences the relationship between culture consensus and financial performance in high-technology firms. *Journal of Organization Behaviour, 35*(6), 785–808. doi: 10.1002/job.1928

Chatman, J.A., & O'Reilly, C.A. (2016). Paradigm lost: Reinvigorating the study of organizational culture. *Research in Organizational Behavior, 36*, 199–224.

Church, A.H., Rotolo, C.T., Shull, A.C., & Tuller, M.D. (2014). Understanding the role of organizational culture and workgroup climate in core people development processes at PepsiCo. In B. Schneider & K. M. Barbera (Eds.), *The Oxford Handbook of Organizational Climate and Culture* (pp. 793–820). Oxford, UK: Oxford University Press, Inc.

Cooke, R.A. & Lafferty, J.C. (1989). *Organizational Culture Inventory*. Plymouth, MI: Human Synergistics International.

Cooke, R.A. & Rousseau, D.M. (1988). Behavioral norms and expectations: A quantitative approach to the assessment of organizational culture. *Group & Organization Studies, 13*(3), 245–273. doi:10.1177/105960118801300302

Cooke, R. & Szumal, J. (2000). Using the organizational culture inventory to understand the operating cultures of organizations. In R. Cooke & J. Szumal (Eds.), *Handbook of Organizational Culture and Climate* (pp. 147–162). Sage Publications.

Crémer, J. (1993). Corporate culture and shared knowledge. *Industrial and Corporate Change, 2*(3), 351–386. https://doi.org/10.1093/icc/2.3.351

Cruver, B. (2002). *Anatomy of Greed: The Unshredded Truth from an Enron Insider* (1st edition). New York: Carroll & Graf Publishers.

Dailey, S.L. & Browning, L. (2014). Retelling stories in organizations: Understanding the functions of narrative repetition. *Academy of Management Review, 39*(1), 22–43.

Davis, S.M. (1984). *Managing Corporate Culture*. Cambridge, MA: Ballinger.

Deal, T.E. & Kennedy, A.A. (1982). *Corporate Cultures* (pp. 110–134). Reading, MA: Addison Wesley.

Deal, T.E. & Kennedy, A.A. (1983). Culture: A new look through old lenses. *Journal of Applied Behavioral Science, 19*(4), 498–505.

Denison, D.R. (1984). Bringing corporate culture to the bottom line. *Organizational Dynamics, 13*(2), 5–22. doi: 10.1016/0090-2616(84)90015-9

Denison, D.R. (1990). *Corporate Culture and Organizational Effectiveness*. New York: Wiley.

Denison, D.R. (1996). What is the difference between organizational culture and organizational climate? A native's point of view on a decade of paradigm wars. *Academy of Management Review, 21*(3), 619–654.

Denison, D.R. & Mishra, A.K. (1995). Toward a theory of organizational culture and effectiveness. *Organization Science, 6*(2), 204–223.

Denison, D., Nieminen, L., & Kotrba, L. (2014). Diagnosing organizational cultures: A conceptual and empirical review of culture effectiveness surveys. *European Journal of Work and Organizational Psychology, 23*(1), 145–161.

Dolan, S.L. & Bao, Y. (2012). Sharing the culture: Embedding storytelling and ethics in the culture change management process. *Journal of Management & Change, 29*(1).

Feldman, J. (1991), The meaning of ambiguity: Learning from stories and metaphors. In P. Frost, L. Morre, M. Moore, M. Louis, C. Lundberg & J. Martin (Eds.), *Reframing Organizational Culture* (pp. 145–156). Newbury Park, CA: Sage.

Flamholtz, E. & Randle, Y. (2012). Corporate culture, business models, competitive advantage, strategic assets and the bottom line. *Journal of Human Resource Costing & Accounting, 16*(2), 79–94. doi: 10.1108/14013381211284227

Fitzgerald, A. & Teal, G. (2004). Health reform, professional identity and occupational sub-cultures: The changing interprofessional relations between doctors and nurses. *Contemporary Nurse, 16*(1–2), 71–79. doi: 10.5172/conu.16.1-2.9

Glaser, R. (1983). *The Corporate Culture Survey*. Bryn Mawr, PA: Organizational Design and Development.

Hartnell, C.A., Ou, A.Y., & Kinicki, A. (2011). Organizational culture and organizational effectiveness: A meta-analytic investigation of the competing values framework's theoretical suppositions. *Journal of Applied Psychology, 96*(4), 677–694.

Hatch, M.J. (1993). The dynamics of organizational culture. *Academy of Management Review, 18*(4), 657–693.

Hitlin, S. & Piliavin, J.A. (2004). Values: Reviving a dormant concept. *Annual Review of Sociololgy, 30*, 359–393.

Hofstede, G. (1991). *Cultures and Organizations: Software of the Mind*. London: McGraw-Hill UK.

Hofstede, G. (1998). Attitudes, values and organizational culture: Disentangling the concepts. *Organization Studies, 19*(3), 477–493.

Homburg, C. & Pflesser, C. (2000). A multiple-layer model of market-oriented organizational culture: Measurement issues and performance outcomes. *Journal of Marketing Research, 37*(November), 449–462.

Huang, J.C., Newell, S. & Galliers, R.D. (2002). The impact of organizational sub cultures on the implementation of component based development: A case study of an international investment bank. *ECIS 2002 Proceedings*, 66.

Kangas, M., Muotka, J., Huhtala, M., Mäkikangas, A. & Feldt, T. (2017). Is the ethical culture of the organization associated with sickness absence? A multilevel analysis in a public sector organization. *Journal of Business Ethics, 140*(1), 131–145. doi: 10.1007/s10551-015-2644-y

Kangas, M., Kaptein, M., Huhtala, M., Lämsä, A. & Pihlajasaari, P. (2018). Why do managers leave their organization? Investigating the role of ethical organizational culture in managerial turnover. *Journal of Business Ethics, 153*(3), 707–723. doi:10.1007/s10551-016-3363-8

Kaul, A. (2019). Culture vs strategy: Which to precede, which to align? *Journal of Strategy and Management, 12*(1), 116–136. https://doi.org/10.1108/JSMA-04-2018-0036

Kava, C.M., Parker, E.A., Baquero, B., Curry, S.J., Gilbert, P.A., Sauder, M., & Sewell, D.K. (2019). Associations between organizational culture, workplace health climate, and employee smoking at smaller workplaces. *Tobacco Use Insights, 12*. https://doi.org/10.1177/1179173X19835842

Kilmann, R.H. & Saxton, M.J. (1983). *The Kilmann–Saxton Culture-Gap Survey*. Pittsburgh: Organizational Design Consultants.

Kilmann, R.H. & Saxton, M.J. (1997). *Kilmann–Saxton Culture-Gap Survey Instrument*. Tuxedo, New York: Xicom, Incorporated.

Korte, R.F. & Chermack, T.J. (2007). Changing organizational culture with scenario planning. *Futures, 39*(6), 645–656.

Lewin, K. (1951). *Field Theory in Social Science*. New York: Harper & Rowe.

Lok, P. & Crawford, J. (2001). Antecedents of organizational commitment and the mediating role of job satisfaction. *Journal of Managerial Psychology, 16*(8), 594–613. doi: 10.1108/EUM0000000006302

Lincoln, J.R. & Kalleberg, A.L. (1985). Work organization and workforce commitment: A study of plants and employees in the U.S. and Japan. *American Sociological Review, 50*(6), 738–760.

Litwin, G.H. & Stringer, R.A. Jnr. (1968). *Motivation and Organizational Change*. Boston: Division of Research, Graduate School of Business Administration, Harvard University.

Marques, J., Camillo, A.A., & Holt, S. (2015). The Starbucks culture: Responsible, radical innovation in an irresponsible, incremental world. In Handbook of Research on Business Ethics and Corporate Responsibilities (pp. 302–312). IGI Global.

Martin, J. (2001). *Organizational Culture: Mapping the Terrain*. Thousand Oaks: SAGE Publications.

Martin, J. & Frost, P. (2011). The organizational culture war games: A struggle for intellectual dominance. In S. Clegg & C. Hardy (Eds.), *Studying Organization: Theory and Method* (pp. 315–336). Thousand Oaks, CA: Sage Publications.

McDonald, P., Williams, P., Stewart, A., Mayes, R., & Oliver, D. (2019). *Digital Platform Work in Australia. Preliminary Findings from a National Survey*. Melbourne (June). Available at: https://research.qut.edu.au/work-industry-futures-research-program/wp-content/uploads/sites/35/2019/06/Report-of-Survey-Findings_18-June-2019_PUBLISHED.pdf

Mellor, J. (September 30, 2015). Regulation and culture change in banks. *World Financial Review*, retrieved July 2019 from https://www.worldfinancialreview.com/regulation-and-culture-change-in-banks-2/

Middlemiss, N. (January 15, 2016). Major bank denies caustic culture claims. *Human Resources Director*, accessed June 2019 at https://www.hcamag.com/au/news/general/major-bank-denies-caustic-culture-claims/144731

Moniz, A. (January 17, 2017). Inferring employees' social media perceptions of corporate culture and the link to firm value. http://dx.doi.org/10.2139/ssrn.2768091

Naranjo-Valencia, J.C., Jimenez-Jimenez, D., & Sanz-Valle, R. (2017). Organizational culture and radical innovation: Does innovative behavior mediate this relationship? *Creativity and Innovation Management, 26*(4), 407–417.

Newton, C. (2006). An exploration of workplace stressors and employee adjustment: An organisational culture perspective. (Thesis). Available from National Library of Australia.

Newton, C.J. & Jimmieson, N.L. (2009). Subjective fit with organizational culture: An investigation of moderating effects in the work stressor–employee adjustment relationship. *International Journal of Human Resource Management, 20*(8), 1770–1789.

Ostroff, C. & Schulte, M. (2014). A configural approach to the study of organizational culture and climate. In B. Schneider & K.M. Barbera (Eds), *The Oxford Handbook of Organizational Climate and Culture* (pp. 724–752). Oxford, UK: Oxford University Press, Inc.

Ott, J.S. (1989). *The Organisational Culture Perspective*. Pacific Grove, California: Brooks/Cole Publishing Company.

Ouchi, W. (1981). Theory Z: How American business can meet the Japanese challenge. *Business Horizons, 24*(6), 82–83.

Parent, J.D. & Lovelace, K.J. (2018). Employee engagement, positive organizational culture and individual adaptability. *On The Horizon, 26*(3), 206–214.

Park, S. & Lunt, N. (2018). Productive resistance within the Korean public sector: Exploring organisational culture. *Public Organization Review, 18*(3), 279–297. doi: 10.1007/s11115-017-0381-7

Peters, T.J., Waterman, R.H., & Jones, I. (1982). *In Search of Excellence: Lessons from America's Best-Run Companies*. New York, NY: Warner Books.

Pettigrew, A.M. (1979). On studying organizational cultures. *Administrative Science Quarterly, 24*(4), 570–581. doi: 10.2307/2392363

Pool, S.W. (2000). Organizational culture and its relationship between job tension in measuring outcomes among business executives. *Journal of Management Development, 19*, 32–49.

Popadak, J. (2013). A corporate culture channel: How increased shareholder governance reduces firm value. Available at SSRN, 2345384.

Quinn, R.E. & Rohrbaugh, J. (1983). A spatial model of effectiveness criteria: Towards a competing values approach to organizational analysis. *Management Science, 29*(3), 363–377.

Rose, T. & Unnithan, P. (2015). In or out of the group? Police subculture and occupational stress. *Policing: An International Journal of Police Strategies & Management, 38*(2), 279–294. https://doi.org/10.1108/PIJPSM-10-2014-0111

Sashkin, M. (1984). *Organizational Beliefs Questionnaire: Pillars of Excellence*. Organization Design and Development.

Sathe, V. (1983). Implications of corporate culture: A manager's guide to action. *Organizational Dynamics, 12*, 5–23.

Schein, E.H. (1985) *Organizational Culture and Leadership*. San Francisco: Jossey-Bass. Schein, E.H. (1990). Organizational culture. *American Psychologist, 45*(2), 109–119.

Schein, E.H. (1992). *Organizational Culture and Leadership* (2nd edition). San Francisco: Jossey-Bass.

Schein, E., & Schein, P. (2017). *Organizational Culture and Leadership* (5th edition). Hoboken: Wiley.

Schneider, B., Ehrhart, M.G., & Macey, W.H. (2013). Organizational climate and culture. *Annual Review of Psychology, 64*, 361–388.

Schneider, B., González-Romá, V., Ostroff, C., & West, M. (2017). Organizational climate and culture: Reflections on the history of the constructs in the Journal of Applied Psychology. *Journal of Applied Psychology, 102*(3), 468–482. https://doi.org/10.1037/apl0000090

Shortell, S.M., Jones, R.H., Rademaker, A.W., Gillies, R.R., Dranove, D.S., Hughes, E.F., Budetti, P.P., Reynolds, K.S., & Huang, C.F. (2000). Assessing the impact of total quality management and organizational culture on multiple outcomes of care for coronary artery bypass graft surgery patients. *Medical Care, 38*(2), 207–217. doi: 10.1097/00005650-200002000-00010

Smircich, L. (1983). Concepts of culture and organizational analysis. *Administrative Science Quarterly, 28*(3), 339–358.

Smith, A.C., & Stewart, B. (2011). Organizational rituals: Features, functions and mechanisms. *International Journal of Management Reviews, 13*(2), 113–133.

Spector, B. & Lane, H. (2007). Exploring the distinctions between a high performance culture and a cult. *Strategy & Leadership, 35*(3), 18–24. https://doi.org/10.1108/10878570710745794

Stahl, G.K., & Voigt, A. (2008). Do cultural differences matter in mergers and acquisitions? A tentative model and examination. *Organization Science, 19*(1), 160–176.

Sturman, M.C., Shao, L. & Katz, J.H. (2012). The effect of culture on the curvilinear relationship between performance and turnover. *Journal of Applied Psychology, 97*(1), 46–62. doi: 10.1037/a0024868

Teo, S.T.T., Ahmad, T., & Rodwell, J.J. (2003). HR role effectiveness and organizational culture in Australian local government. *Asia Pacific Journal of Human Resources, 41*, 298–315.

Walumbwa, F.O., Hartnell, C.A., & Oke, A. (2010). Servant leadership, procedural justice climate, service climate, employee attitudes, and organizational citizenship behavior: A cross-level investigation. *Journal of Applied Psychology, 95*(3), 517.

Williams, P., Cathcart, A., & McDonald, P. (2018). Signals of support: Flexible work for mutual gain. *International Journal of Human Resource Management, 32*(3), 738–762. https://doi.org/10.1080/09585192.2018.1499669

Xenikou, A. & Furnham, A. (1996). A correlational and factor analytic study of four questionnaire measures of organizational culture. *Human Relations, 49*, 349–371.

Yeung, A., K.O, Brockbank, J.W., & Ulrich, D.O. (1991). Organizational culture and human resources practices: An empirical assessment. In W.A. Pasmore & R.W. Woodman (Eds.), *Research in Organisational Change and Development*. Greenwich, CT: JAI Press.

Zohar, D. & Luria, G. (2005). A multilevel model of safety climate: Cross-level relationships between organization and group-level climates. *Journal of Applied Psychology, 90*(4), 616.

3. Leadership and organizational culture

Athena Xenikou

INTRODUCTION

An essential aspect of leadership is to influence the shared cognitions and behavioral norms that organizational members hold, and therefore, effective leaders put a lot of effort into culture formation, maintenance, and change. There are two different schools of thought with regard to the connection between leadership and organizational culture. The functionalist approach puts forward the proposition that leaders are key agents in the process of culture management (Schein, 2010; Trice & Beyer, 1993). There are various mechanisms that leaders can utilize in order to manage organizational culture, such as communicating a clear and powerful vision, the allocation of resources and rewards, organizational design and systems, and formal statements of an organization's philosophy. On the other hand, the anthropological approach conceptualizes culture as something the organization is, rather than something the organization has, treating culture as a root metaphor and not as a critical variable. In this approach leaders are considered to be part of culture, and not in a position to manage the culture of their organizations (Smircich, 1983; Hatch, 1993). Therefore, culture is not driven by organizational leaders, and cultural management is impossible to accomplish.

Most of empirical research in the organizational culture literature takes a functionalist approach demonstrating that (a) organizational culture has a strong impact on key organizational outcomes, such as performance, innovation, commitment to and identification with organizations, and job satisfaction (Abbott et al., 2005; Berson et al., 2008; Boyce et al., 2015; Finegan, 2000; Liu et al., 2013; Sorensen, 2002; Taylor et al., 2008; Vandenberghe & Peiro, 1999; Xenikou, 2014), and (b) leadership and organizational culture jointly exert an influence on organizational phenomena (Lim, 1995; Lok et al., 2005; Ogbonna & Harris, 2000; Sarros et al., 2008; Xenikou & Simosi, 2006). Specifically, organizational culture, manifested in the shared assumptions, values, behavioral norms, and practices that characterize an organization, affects the way organization members interpret aspects of their work environment and create meaning in any given situation at work. Organizational culture has been studied as a contextual variable that sets constraints and boundary conditions for organizational phenomena to occur, that is, organizational members are more sensitive and responsive to the presence and absence of stimuli and behaviors that are indicators of their organization's core values (Erdogan et al., 2006).

Even though sharedness of cultural elements is a feature of any definition of organizational culture (Ostroff et al., 2003), individual employees, and different groups in the organization, may substantially differ in their perceptions of their organization's culture. Indeed the differentiation theoretical approach to the study of organizational culture has put emphasis on the diversity in the internalization and enactment of organizational assumptions, values, and behavioral tendencies by various groups within organizations. Newcomers, for instance, are likely to have a less accurate perception of organizational values, practices, and behavioral norms compared to employees who have been employed by the organization for longer periods of time. Therefore, working with organizational culture at different levels of analysis, that is, the organization, the group, and the individual employee, is imperative to unravel the relation between leadership and culture.

DEVELOPMENTAL STAGES OF ORGANIZATIONS AND THE LEADERSHIP–ORGANIZATIONAL CULTURE LINK

Schein (2010) has argued for the importance of the developmental stages organizations go through for understanding the relation between leadership and organizational culture. In the founding stage, organizational culture is the creation of the organization's founder or founding team who, along with their successors, shape a culture of shared assumptions and beliefs to successfully deal with issues of internal integration and external adaptation. In the early growth stage of organizations, founders and leadership teams initiate the culture formation process by teaching their assumptions and values to the new group. The articulation and reinforcement of the leaders' values occur through the use of a number of primary and secondary mechanisms that leaders, as founders, have at their disposal. A way for leaders to create culture is by charisma that entails communicating their assumptions and values in an attractive, clear, and vivid manner. Other primary mechanisms that can be used by leaders to create culture involve:

- what leaders pay attention to, measure, and control on a regular basis
- how leaders react to critical incidents and organizational crises
- the allocation of scarce resources
- deliberate role modeling, teaching, and coaching
- observed criteria for allocating rewards and status
- observed criteria by which leaders recruit, select, promote, retire, and terminate members

There are also secondary mechanisms that founders can use to articulate and reinforce their values and assumptions. For example, founders have the capacity to (a) shape the design and structure of their organizations, and (b) build systems and procedures that reflect their basic value priorities. The secondary mechanisms are considered to be effective only given that they are consistent with the primary mechanisms, whereas in mature organizations secondary mechanisms become primary in embedding the core values that characterize a specific organization.

As the organization matures its structures and procedures, and practices become well-formulated and stable, the organization undergoes a process of differentiation, and the units, divisions, and departments that emerge may facilitate the creation of various subcultures. Differentiation within organizational settings does also occur in terms of many other factors, such as hierarchical levels, organizational tenure, functional lines, occupations, and demographics. At this stage organizational culture defines leadership more than leadership determines culture, that is, culture is a salient contextual variable that has an impact on the emergence and effectiveness of leadership. In mature organizations leaders have the responsibility to coordinate and integrate organizational subcultures for organizations to function smoothly.

With regard to the different tools leaders have at their disposal to change their organization's culture, Schein has proposed that these tools and opportunities for culture change also depend on the developmental stage an organization goes through. Specifically, in the early growing stage, an external crisis of survival may trigger the culture change process in order to deal with problems of successful external adaptation. Another mechanism that founders can use to achieve culture change is bringing about evolution through the promotion of insiders whose values and objectives are better adapted to environmental demands. In mature organizations, leaders can possibly change organizational culture by systematically promoting employees from selected subcultures, who reinforce the leader's value priorities and behavioral norms; this mechanism is an extension of the promotion of insiders taking place in the founding stage. Finally, in the last stage of organizational development, that is, maturity and possible decay, a tool for organizational change is coercive persuasion, which involves the dissemination of information to employees about organizational ineffectiveness, while making it very hard for them to resign.

The seminal work of Schein (2010) on leadership and organizational culture has greatly contributed to our understanding of organizational life taking a culture perspective. Additional future research, however, is needed to clarify how leaders influence culture and vice versa, especially research focusing on the effects of Schein's culture-embedding mechanisms (Schneider et al., 2013).

THEORIES OF LEADERSHIP AND ORGANIZATIONAL CULTURE

In the following two sections the research literature on the relation between organizational culture and (a) transformational/charismatic leadership, and (b) leader–member exchange (LMX) is reviewed. Among the theoretical approaches to organizational leadership which put emphasis on the leader's context or situational factors, the transformational/charismatic leadership and LMX theories are the research streams that have primarily investigated the interplay between leadership and organizational culture.

TRANSFORMATIONAL/CHARISMATIC LEADERSHIP AND ORGANIZATIONAL CULTURE

Organizational founders and their teams often exhibit transformational/charismatic leadership qualities in their efforts to shape their organization's policies, behavioral norms, and values that dominate its culture. The personality and the core values of the founders are reflected in the organization as it develops. The set of values the founders articulate and reinforce, their personal assumptions and vision of the future, become embedded in the emerging organizational culture. But it is also quite common that the transformational leader who firmly establishes and improves the organization's culture is far removed in time from the founding team.

During the past 30 years or so transformational leadership theory (Avolio et al., 1999; Bass, 1985; Bass & Riggio, 2006; Walumbwa et al., 2008) has stimulated an intense empirical investigation of how transformational and transactional leadership styles are related to performance (Walumbwa et al., 2008; Wang et al., 2011), organizational commitment and identification (Avolio et al., 2004; Bycio et al., 1995; Dvir et al., 2002; Simosi & Xenikou, 2010; Walumbwa et al., 2004; Xenikou, 2017), employee satisfaction (Bycio et al., 1995), leader effectiveness (Judge & Piccolo, 2004; Lowe et al., 1996), and organizational citizenship behaviors (Podsakoff et al., 2000). Bass and his colleagues have argued for the complementary relation between the two leadership styles as leaders typically exhibit a variety of patterns of transformational and transactional leadership; most leaders do both but in different amounts (Box 3.1).

BOX 3.1   DESCRIPTION OF TRANSFORMATIONAL AND TRANSACTIONAL LEADERSHIP STYLES

Transformational leaders

- are charismatic in the sense that they are seen by their subordinates as self-confident, competent, energetic, and optimistic about the future
- provide subordinates with intellectual stimulation to think about problems or to do things in novel ways
- reframe the situation and give creative insight to deal with environmental challenges
- offer individual consideration for each of their subordinates showing interest in followers' needs, ambitions, and individual growth

Transactional leaders

- recognize existing needs and desires in subordinates, and fulfill those needs and desires on the basis of the performance evaluation
- exchange effort for rewards and promises of rewards
- clarify task and role requirements for subordinates and offer direction
- give subordinates sufficient confidence to exert the required effort
- criticize negative work behaviors and punish unreasonably low performance

---

For organizations to maintain or gain a sustainable advantage, their culture has to work in concert with a mixture of both transformational and transactional leadership patterns (Bass, 1999). Transformational leadership aims at changing or improving at least some dimensions of culture, whereas transactional leadership works primarily within the culture as it exists. Bass and Avolio (1993) have put forward the idea that transformational/transactional leadership and organizational culture are so well interconnected that it is possible to describe an ideal transactional and an ideal transformational organizational culture. The prototypical transformational culture promotes creative change and growth by exhibiting a sense of vision and purpose, while the prototypical transactional culture promotes a metaphor of the organization as a 'marketplace' where performance indicators matter.

Empirical research on transformational/charismatic leadership and organizational culture has provided evidence for the associations between specific cultural dimensions and transformational/charismatic leadership (Table 3.1). Specifically, Block (2003) in examining the leadership–culture connection found that employees who rated their immediate supervisor high in transformational leadership were more likely to perceive the culture of their organization as involving, integrating, adaptive, and mission-oriented. In similar lines, Sarros et al. (2002) demonstrated that transformational leadership style best predicted cultures with an emphasis on supportiveness, whereas a mixture of transformational and transactional leadership styles best predicted cultures with an emphasis on rewards.

Table 3.1　　*Research that empirically supports the positive relationships between specific dimensions of organizational culture and transformational leadership (TFL)*

Empirical Studies	Dimensions of organizational culture positively associated with TFL, and grouped in terms of content similarity			
	Support	Innovation	Goal	Competition
Block (2003)	Involvement	Adaptation	Mission	
	Integration			
Sarros et al. (2002)	Supportiveness		Rewards	
Xenikou & Simosi (2006)	Humanistic		Achievement	
Sarros et al. (2008)			Performance-oriented	Competitive
Jung et al. (2003)		Learning-oriented		
Elenkov & Manev (2005)			Performance-oriented	Competitive
Xenikou (2017)		Innovation	Goal	
Simosi & Xenikou (2010)	Humanistic		Achievement	
	Affiliative			
	Self-actualizing			
Xenikou (2014)	Support			

Moreover, the relevant research literature has focused on how transformational and transactional leadership styles and culture dimensions have a joint effect on focal organizational outcomes, such as, performance, innovation, and commitment/identification. In a study of 32 business units of a large financial organization, Xenikou and Simosi (2006) showed that transformational leadership style and a humanistic culture orientation had an indirect positive effect on business unit performance via an achievement culture orientation. In other words, transformational leadership was shown to work in concert with participative, collaborative, supportive, and self-actualizing organizational cultures to bring about a culture focus on task and goal achievement, which, in turn, led to high performance of business units.

With regard to the transformational leadership–culture effects on innovation, Sarros et al. (2008) investigated the relationships between transformational leadership, organizational culture, and climate for innovation in a sample of managers and senior executives working for private sector organizations. Their findings showed that a competitive and performance-oriented culture was strongly related to climate for innovation, and it also mediated the link between three of the four transformational leadership factors, namely, vision articulation, provision of individual support, and high performance expectations, and climate for organizational innovation. Additionally, the study of Jung et al. (2003) in a large number of corporations showed that transformational leadership was positively associated with organizational innovation, and this link was mediated by a culture where members are encouraged to openly discuss and implement innovative suggestions and ideas. Finally, Elenkov and Manev (2005) examined the influence of transformational leadership in top and middle management on innovation and found evidence that the link between transformational leadership and innovation was mediated by performance-oriented and competitive organizational cultures.

There is also a stream of empirical research on the transformational leadership–culture impact on organizational identification and commitment. Xenikou (2017) examined transformational/transactional leadership styles and culture as antecedent factors of organizational identification, and found evidence that transformational leadership was more strongly related to cognitive identification via the perception of innovation culture, whereas transactional leadership style was more strongly related to affective identification via goal cultural orientation. Similarly, in a cross-sectional study Simosi and Xenikou (2010) demonstrated that four culture orientations, namely, achievement, support, affiliation, and self-actualization served as mediators in the relationship between leader behavior (i.e., transformational leadership, transactional contingent reward) and affective/normative commitment. Finally, Xenikou (2014) showed that organizational support values, as an indicator of culture, were positively associated with both cognitive and affective dimensions of identification with the organization. The findings also showed that there was an interaction between charismatic leadership and support values; specifically, the positive effect of charismatic leadership on affective identification was mitigated when employees thought of their organization as a place where support was valued.

In sum, a question that has recently received some attention in relevant research involves the association between specific dimensions of organizational culture and transformational/ transactional leadership styles. Adaptive and innovative cultures with an emphasis on supportiveness and goal achievement have been repeatedly shown to be related to transformational leadership, and to mediate the effect of transformational leadership on organizational performance, innovation, employee commitment to and identification with the employing organization. There is also some empirical evidence of the role competitive cultures may play in the leadership–organizational outcomes link, but it rather involves inter-organizational rather that intra-organizational competition.

LEADER–MEMBER EXCHANGE AND ORGANIZATIONAL CULTURE

Another line of research that emphasizes the interplay between leadership and organizational culture has been conducted within the leader–member exchange (LMX) theoretical framework of leadership. LMX theory concentrates on the interactions between leaders and subordinates, and states that leaders develop different relationships and act differently towards their subordinates. Subordinates fall into one of two groups, that is, the in-group characterized by a high-quality relationship with the leader and the out-group characterized by a low-quality relationship with the leader (Graen & Uhl-Bien, 1995). Several studies have examined the role of organizational culture as an antecedent factor or a moderator variable in the link between LMX and various work outcomes, such as organizational identification, perceptions of interactional and distributive justice, and job and career satisfaction.

In a multi-level study of high school teachers, Erdogan et al. (2006) investigated the role of the value systems in Turkish schools, measured at the organizational level of analysis, as a moderator of the link between perceptions of interactional and distributive justice and teachers' report of LMX relationships with their immediate supervisors, namely, each school's principal. The results indicated that organizational cultures putting emphasis on team orientation were related to higher levels of LMX quality. Moreover, in schools where respect for people was valued, the relation between interactional justice and LMX quality was stronger. On similar lines, for schools with a culture high in aggressiveness, the relation between distributive justice and LMX quality was stronger, indicating that members try to outperform each other and focus on tangible resources. On the other hand, when organizational culture was characterized by a high team orientation, the teachers' evaluations of LMX quality were not based on justice perceptions. Therefore, organizational culture was found to moderate the relationship between justice perceptions and LMX quality in the case of cultures that promote respect for people and aggressiveness, but not in the case of cultures that cultivate team orientation. In other words, organizational culture was found to influence the type of justice perceptions that become relevant for LMX quality.

The moderating role of organizational culture in the link between LMX quality and organizational identification was examined by Liu et al. (2013). These authors investigated whether employees' perceptions of collectivism-oriented Human Resource Management (C-HRM) moderated the relation between LMX quality and organizational identification. C-HRM was operationalized at the individual level of analysis and defined as a set of organizational practices that emphasize maintaining harmonious relationships with co-workers, and pursuing collective interests, goals, and objectives. The empirical findings showed that C-HRM moderated the positive relationship between LMX quality and organizational identification. Specifically, the relationship between LMX quality and organizational identification was stronger when C-HRM was high than when it was low.

Another study that investigated the link between perceptions of organizational culture and LMX quality was carried out by Joo (2010) with a diverse sample of employees from various industry sectors. The results pointed out that the perception of an organizational learning culture described as a working environment that encourages participation, dialogue, and team learning, and more importantly where leaders model and support learning, is positively associated with high-quality LMX relationships.

In a multi-level study of the relationship between work–family culture and LMX relationships Major et al. (2008) defined work–family culture as the shared assumptions, beliefs, and values an organization cultivates with regard to the importance of work–family integration, operationalizing culture at the organizational level of analysis. Their findings showed that work–family culture was positively associated with LMX relationships, indicating that organizations that value the integration of work and family lives tend to have high-quality LMX relationships characterized by mutual trust, support, and understanding.

Finally, Erdogan et al. (2004) examined work value congruence defined as the correlation between teachers' personal values and schools' organizational values. They found that LMX quality served as a moderator of the relationship between value congruence and career satisfaction supporting the compensatory role of leadership. Specifically, value congruence was related to career satisfaction in the case of low, rather than high, LMX quality. Therefore, high LMX quality seems to provide employees with the affective and resource-based support to deal with the potential negative effects of low value congruence.

To sum up, previous research examining the association between organizational culture and LMX relationships has pointed out that supportive and organizational learning cultures tend to coexist with high-quality relationships between leaders and their subordinates. Organizational cultures were also shown to set constraints in the relationship between perceptions of justice and LMX quality, indicating that culture drives attention to stimuli informative of its content; in other words, in cultures with an emphasis on respect for people, perceptions of procedural justice were related to high LMX, while in competitive cultures, perceptions of distributive justice were associated with high LMX quality.

THE NATURE OF THE RELATIONSHIP BETWEEN LEADERSHIP AND ORGANIZATIONAL CULTURE

Leadership and organizational culture are in a constant interplay and the examination of the nature of their relationship is of primary importance for understanding their joint effects on organizational phenomena (Bass & Avolio, 1993; Berson et al., 2008; Hartnell et al., 2011, 2016; Ogbonna & Harris, 2000; Sarros et al., 2008; Schein, 2010; Trice & Beyer, 1993; Waldman & Yammarino, 1999; Xenikou & Furnham, 2013; Xenikou & Simosi, 2006). There is a stream of culture research that investigates the interactive effect between organizational culture and leadership, and empirically tests the moderator role of culture or leadership in how the two constructs relate with key organizational outcomes. The bulk, however, of empirical studies that examine how leaders and organizational cultures work in concert to affect organizational outcomes consider leadership as a hypothetical antecedent of organizational culture. The vast majority of these studies have obtained cross-sectional data ruling out inferences about causal relationships. In this line of research there is a considerable number of studies that investigate the mediating effect of organizational culture in the connection between leadership and focal organizational outcomes, such as performance, innovation, and commitment/ identification.

THE INTERACTIVE EFFECT OF LEADERSHIP AND ORGANIZATIONAL CULTURE ON ORGANIZATIONAL OUTCOMES

The fit or interactional effect between leadership and organizational culture was studied with CEOs and their top management teams (TMTs) of corporations in the high-technology sector by Hartnell et al. (2016). Their aim was to examine the point of congruence between leadership and culture, specified in terms of similarity or dissimilarity in the task and relationships metathemes. They focused on the interaction between leadership and culture while refraining from identifying a primary determinant as in traditional applications of moderation. The findings demonstrated that the dissimilarity of values between CEOs, rated by their TMT, and organizational cultures, assessed by both CEOs and TMT, was associated with enhanced organizational performance. Therefore, organizational performance improves when levels of corresponding leadership and culture dimensions (i.e., task and relationships) are dissimilar such that leadership is high when culture is low or leadership is low when culture is high. In other words, leadership that aligns and reinforces the current culture may generate redundant resources and unnecessary guidance that fails to enhance performance.

In this line of thinking Schneider (1987) argues that excess homogeneity and myopic perspectives may result from high consistency in environmental cues within organizations, eventually leading to negative organizational outcomes. The 'right amount' of leadership behavior, therefore, might be necessary to enhance organizational performance depending on a given organization's existing culture.

An important question to be addressed in future research is whether the positive effect of dissimilarities and the negative effect of similarities between leadership and culture reported by Hartnell et al. (2016) generalize across levels within organizations. Leaders higher in the organizational hierarchy have more power and greater impact than middle- and lower-level managers. Senior management has the means and responsibility for culture management by formulating strategic goals and implementing strategic plans. Moreover, front-line employees may require more informational consistency from their immediate supervisors to channel their attention and effort to existing organizational rules, procedures, and goals. Therefore, the positive effect of incongruence between leadership and culture on organizational performance needs to be further tested taking into account the differences across levels of leadership within organizational settings.

The compensatory role of leadership has been demonstrated in two other studies that have investigated the interactive effect of leadership and organizational culture. Erdogan et al. (2004) found that high LMX quality compensated for the negative relation between value incongruence – the gap between school values and teachers' personal values – and teachers' career satisfaction. Moreover, charismatic leadership, as attributed by subordinates, was found to compensate for the lack of organizational support in enhancing employees' affective identification with their organization (Xenikou, 2014).

Finally, Erdogan et al. (2006) demonstrated how organizational culture directs attention and enhances cognitive elaboration of contextual stimuli that are informative of an organization's culture. These researchers found evidence that specific dimensions of culture, namely, respect for people, and aggressiveness, moderate the relation between employees' perceptions of justice and LMX quality. In cultures with an emphasis on respect for people, the social context makes perceptions of procedural justice predictors of the quality of the leader–subordinate relationship, whereas in cultures with an emphasis on aggressiveness, the work environment makes perceptions of distributive justice predictors of LMX quality (Table 3.2).

Table 3.2   *The interactive effects in leadership and organizational culture research on focal organizational outcomes*

Empirical studies	Main variable (1)	Main variable (2)	Focal outcomes
Hartnell et al. (2016)	Task leadership	Task culture	Organizational performance
	Relationships leadership	Relationship culture	
Erdogan et al. (2006)	Perceptions of procedural/	Culture of respect for people	LMX quality
	distributive justice	Aggressive culture	
Erdogan et al. (2004)	Value congruence	LMX quality	Career satisfaction
Xenikou (2014)	Charismatic leadership	Support culture	Cognitive/affective
			identification

Besides the fruitful findings of research on the interaction between leadership and culture there is also great value in the investigation of leadership as an antecedent variable in the leadership–culture link. This latter line of research provides insights into the mechanisms that leaders have at their disposal in order to influence (a) their subordinate perceptions of their organization's culture, and (b) their organization's culture as a group- and organizational-level variable.

LEADERSHIP AS AN ANTECEDENT OF ORGANIZATIONAL CULTURE

The personal values of top executives and how they relate to organizational performance were studied by Berson et al. (2008). Their findings provided empirical support for the hypothesis that the process through which top executives' dispositions relate to organizational outcomes involves different dimensions of organizational culture. Specifically, they found that CEOs' personal values were indirectly related to corporate performance (sales growth, efficiency, and employee satisfaction) via organizational culture. CEOs' personal values of self-direction, benevolence, and security were related to innovative, supportive, and bureaucratic cultures, respectively. Moreover, innovative, supportive, and bureaucratic culture orientations were associated with sales growth, employee satisfaction, and organizational efficiency.

In another study of top-level and middle management, Tsui et al. (2006) found that leadership substantially contributed to organizational culture. Their findings highlighted that cultural values were developed over time through member interactions and institutional processes or created in a short period of time as a result of the deliberate actions of leaders. Therefore, Tsui et al. (2006) put emphasis on the process by which leaders shape culture rather than the impact of leader's attributes on culture development. Overall, they concluded that culture cannot be sustained without systems and procedures that guide employees' behavior.

Finally, Sarros et al. (2002) and Block (2003), in examining leadership as a hypothetical antecedent of culture, showed that organization members who rated their immediate supervisor high in transformational leadership were more likely to perceive the culture of their organization as supportive, integrative, adaptive, and mission-oriented. Moreover, Sarros et al. found that a mixture of transformational and transactional leadership styles best predicted cultures with an emphasis on rewards (Table 3.3).

Table 3.3   *Empirical research treating leadership as a hypothetical antecedent of organizational culture*

Empirical studies	Leadership styles	Culture dimensions	Focal outcomes
Berson et al. (2008)	Leader's personal values:	Innovative culture	Organizational performance
	Self-direction	Supportive culture	
	Benevolence	Bureaucratic culture	
	Security		
Block (2003)	Transformational leadership	Involving culture	
		Integrative culture	
		Adaptive culture	
		Mission-oriented culture	
Sarros et al. (2002)	Transformational/	Supportive culture	
	Transactional leadership	Reward-oriented culture	

THE MEDIATING EFFECT OF CULTURE ORIENTATIONS IN THE LEADERSHIP–ORGANIZATIONAL OUTCOMES LINK

In the stream of research that examines leadership as an antecedent of organizational culture there is, more recently, a substantial number of empirical studies that investigate how different culture orientations jointly serve as mediators in the link between leadership styles and organizational outcomes, such as performance, employees' commitment, organizational identification, and innovation (Chong et al., 2018; Elenkov & Manev, 2005; Lok et al., 2005; Ogbonna & Harris, 2000; Sarros et al., 2008; Simosi & Xenikou, 2010; Xenikou, 2017; Xenikou & Simosi, 2006).

In a sample of nurses working at hospital settings, Lok et al. (2005) found evidence for the mediating role of innovative and supportive subcultures in the relation between consideration leadership and commitment. In similar lines, Simosi and Xenikou (2010) showed that achievement, support, affiliation, and self-actualization served as mediators in the link between leadership style (i.e., transformational leadership, transactional contingent reward) and affective/normative commitment.

Moreover, Ogbonna and Harris (2000) demonstrated that supportive and participative leadership were positively associated with performance via innovative and competitive organizational cultures. In a study examining the business unit performance of a large financial organization, Xenikou and Simosi (2006) found that transformational leadership and humanistic culture orientation had a positive indirect effect on business unit performance through culture that puts emphasis on achievement.

The study of Sarros et al. (2008) on transformational leadership, organizational culture, and climate for innovation in a sample of managers and senior executives from the private sector showed that competitive and performance-oriented culture mediated the link between three of the four transformational leadership factors – that is, vision articulation, provision of individual support, and high performance expectations – and climate for organizational innovation. Similarly, Jung et al. (2003) showed that the link between transformational leadership and innovation was mediated by a culture where members openly discuss and implement innovative suggestions and ideas. Another study by Elenkov and Manev (2005) provided evidence that the link between transformational leadership and innovation was mediated by performance-oriented and competitive organizational cultures.

Chong et al. (2018) studied the mediating role of leadership and influence strategies in the link between organizational culture and work outcomes (i.e., commitment, satisfaction, and performance) as well as the mediating role of organizational culture in the relation between leadership styles and work outcomes. Their findings showed that there is little evidence of the mediating role of leadership in the link between organizational culture and work outcomes. They studied three leadership styles, namely, detail, support, and change leadership, and found that only change leadership mediated the effect of innovative culture on work outcomes. Moreover, the findings with regard to the mediating effect of organizational culture in the link between leadership and work outcomes showed a similar pattern.

Finally, Xenikou (2017) investigated leadership styles and culture orientations as antecedent factors of cognitive and affective organizational identification using both cross-sectional and experimental designs. The findings supported the mediating effect of organizational culture in the link between leadership styles and identification. Specifically, when controlling for the effect of transactional contingent reward, transformational leadership was more strongly related to cognitive identification-perceived similarities between organizational members via innovation culture. On the other hand, when controlling for the effect of transformational leadership, transactional contingent reward was more strongly related to affective identification – emotional attachment to organization – via goal culture. Thus, transformational style led subordinates to focus on their similarities with their fellow co-workers through the process of an innovative culture, while transactional style led their subordinates to become emotionally attached to the organization via the experience of a goal culture (Table 3.4).

Table 3.4   *The joint mediating effect of organizational culture dimensions in the link between leadership and focal organizational outcomes*

Empirical studies	Leadership styles	Organizational culture dimensions	Focal outcomes
Chong et al. (2018)	Detail leadership	Detail culture	Organizational commitment
	Support leadership	Team culture	Employee satisfaction
	Change leadership	Innovation culture	Organizational performance
Lok et al. (2005)	Consideration leadership	Innovative culture Supportive culture	Commitment
Ogbonna & Harris (2000)	Supportive leadership Participative leadership	Innovative culture Competitive culture	Organizational performance
Sarros et al. (2008)	Transformational leadership	Performance-oriented culture Competitive culture	Climate for innovation
Elenkov & Manev (2005)	Transformational leadership	Performance-oriented culture Competitive culture	Innovation
Xenikou (2017)	Transformational leadership/ Transactional contingent reward	Innovative culture Goal culture	Cognitive/affective identification
Simosi & Xenikou (2010)	Transformational leadership/ Contingent reward	Humanistic culture Achievement culture Affiliative culture Self-actualizing culture	Affective/normative commitment
Xenikou & Simosi (2006)	Transformational leadership	Achievement culture Humanistic culture Adaptive culture	Business unit performance

The mediating effect of organizational culture in the link between leadership styles and focal organizational outcomes has been empirically supported in numerous studies. In this line of research both leadership and organizational culture are treated as antecedent factors of organizational outcomes, while at the same time leadership impact on outcomes is at least partly channeled via subordinates' perceptions of their organization's culture. Research on the mediating effect of culture has examined and provided evidence for the joint effect of numerous organizational culture dimensions and leadership styles on organizational performance, innovation, employee commitment, and identification with the organization, whereas research on the interactive effect between leadership and culture has examined the combined effects of leadership and culture on outcomes testing for one culture dimension at a time. This issue is of particular importance because the coexistence of apparently competing organizational values and beliefs, such as cooperation and individual development, has been systematically emphasized for effective organizational functioning (Hartnell et al., 2011, 2016; Miron et al., 2004; Quinn, 1988; Van Muijen et al., 1999; Xenikou & Furnham, 2013).

CONCLUSIONS

The study of organizations as cultures holding value beliefs, behavioral norms, and practices with regard to how they treat their members and make the most of the challenges set by external environment has offered a lot in understanding the complexities of organizational behavior, including leadership and performance.

Founders and their teams play a profound role in the creation of their organization's culture as they are often characterized by strong beliefs about the choices they have to make for their organization to successfully adapt to its environment and thrive. Founders and other leaders have at their disposal numerous mechanisms to communicate, establish, and reinforce their values and basic assumptions, such as role modeling, coaching, or the allocation of rewards and status. Different tools have also been identified that leaders can utilize in order to create opportunities for cultural change, as, for instance, the promotion of insiders from selected subcultures, the infusion of outsiders, technological seduction, or organizational development.

The diverse mechanisms leaders can set in action to manage their organization's culture need to be further studied in future research. Besides research on the tools of culture management, it is important to investigate the incongruence (dissimilarity) perspective in culture management that has already provided some empirical evidence on the positive effect of the dissimilarity in terms of culture content (i.e., task and relationships dimensions) between leadership and organizational culture on organizational performance. The incongruence approach to culture management argues for the complementary role of leadership to cultivate and enhance aspects of an organization's culture that have been disregarded or overlooked. For long the organizational culture literature has showed that apparently competing organizational values and practices tend to coexist and work in concert for an organization to run efficiently. It has systematically, for example, been demonstrated that collaboration and cooperation has to be equally promoted with an emphasis put on self-actualization and individual development for organizations to have high performance and promote their employees' well-being. Moreover, the incongruence approach to culture management reflecting on the complementary role of the leader needs to be tested across levels of hierarchy within organizational settings because front-line managers might have to provide more consistent guidance to their subordinates compared to senior management.

The coexistence and activation of apparently diverse cultural forces within organizational settings has for long been acknowledged as a key element for organizational efficiency. Leaders have the power to balance apparently competing demands set on organizations, such as a focus put on tasks or relationships, by utilizing numerous culture embedding mechanisms.

REFERENCES

Abbott, G. N., White, F. A., & Charles, M. A. (2005). Linking values and organizational commitment: A correlational and experimental investigation in two organizations. *Journal of Occupational and Organizational Psychology*, **78**, 531–551.

Avolio, B. J., Bass, B. M., & Jung, D. I. (1999). Re-examining the components of transformational and transactional leadership using the Multifactor Leadership Questionnaire. *Journal of Occupational and Organizational Psychology*, **72**, 441–462.

Avolio, B. J., Zhu, W., Koh, W., & Bhatia, P. (2004). Transformational leadership and organizational commitment: Mediating role of psychological empowerment and moderating role of structural distance. *Journal of Organizational Behavior*, **25**, 951–968.

Bass, B. M. (1985). *Leadership and performance beyond expectations*. New York: Free Press.

Bass, B. M. (1999). Two decades of research and development in transformational leadership. *European Journal of Work and Organizational Psychology*, **8**, 9–32.

Bass, B. M., & Avolio, B. J. (1993). Transformational leadership and organizational culture. *Public Administration Quarterly*, **17**, 112–121.

Bass, B. M., & Riggio, R. E. (2006). *Transformational leadership*. Mahwah, NJ: Lawrence Erlbaum.

Berson, Y., Oreg, S., & Dvir, T. (2008). CEO values, organizational culture and firm outcomes. *Journal of Organizational Behavior*, **29**, 615–633.

Block, L. (2003). The leadership–culture connection: an exploratory investigation. *Leadership and Organization Development Journal*, **24**, 318–334.

Boyce, A. S., Nieminen, L. R. G., Gillespie, M. A., Ryan, A. M., & Denison, D. R. (2015). Which comes first, organizational culture or performance? A longitudinal study of causal priority with automobile dealerships. *Journal of Organizational Behavior*, **36**, 339–359.

Bycio, P., Hackett, R. D., & Allen, J. S. (1995). Further assessments of Bass's (1985) conceptualisation of transactional and transformational leadership. *Journal of Applied Psychology*, **80**, 468–478.

Chong, M. P. M., Shang, Y., Richards, M. & Zhu, X. (2018). Two sides of the same coin? Leadership and organizational culture. *Leadership and Organization Development Journal*, **39** (8), 975–994.

Dvir, T., Eden, D., Avolio, B. J., & Shamir, B. (2002). Impact of transformational leadership on follower development and performance: A field experiment. *Academy of Management Journal*, **45**, 735–744.

Elenkov, D. S., & Manev, I. M. (2005). Top management leadership and influence on innovation: The role of sociocultural context. *Journal of Management*, **31**, 381–402.

Erdogan, B., Kraimer, M. L., & Liden, R. C. (2004). Work value congruence and intrinsic career success: The compensatory roles of leader–member exchange and perceived organizational support. *Personnel Psychology*, **57**, 305–332.

Erdogan, B., Liden, R. C., & Kraimer, M. L. (2006). Justice and leader–member exchange: The moderating role of organizational culture. *Academy of Management Journal*, **49**, 395–406.

Finegan, J. E. (2000). The impact of person and organizational values on organizational commitment. *Journal of Occupational and Organizational Psychology*, **73**, 149–169.

Graen, G., & Uhl-Bien, M. (1995). Relationship-based approach to leadership: Development of leader–member exchange (LMX) theory of leadership over 25 years: Applying a multi-level multi-domain perspective. *Leadership Quarterly*, **6**, 219–247.

Hartnell, C. A., Kinicki, A. J., Lambert, L. S., Fugate, M., & Corner, P. D. (2016). Do similarities or differences between CEO leadership and organizational culture have a more positive effect on firm performance? A test of competing predictions. *Journal of Applied Psychology*, **101**, 846–861.

Hartnell, C. A., Ou, A. Y., & Kinicki, A. (2011). Organizational culture and organizational effectiveness: A meta-analytic investigation of the competing values framework's theoretical suppositions. *Journal of Applied Psychology*, **96**, 677–694.

Hatch, M. J. (1993). The dynamics of organizational culture. *Academy of Management Review*, **18**, 657–693.

Joo, B. K. (2010). Organizational commitment for knowledge workers: The roles of perceived organizational learning culture, leader–member exchange quality, and turnover intention. *Human Resource Development Quarterly*, **21**, 69–85.

Judge, T. A., & Piccolo, R. F. (2004). Transformational and transactional leadership: A meta-analytic test of their relative validity. *Journal of Applied Psychology*, **89**, 755–768.

Jung, D. L., Chow, C., & Wu, A. (2003). The role of transformational leadership in enhancing organizational innovation: Hypotheses and some preliminary findings. *Leadership Quarterly*, **14**, 525–544.

Lim, B. (1995). Examining the organizational culture and organizational performance link. *Leadership and Organization Development Journal*, **16**, 16–21.

Liu, Z. Q., Cai, Z. Y., Li, J., Shi, S. P., & Fang, Y. Q. (2013). Leadership style and employee turnover intentions: A social identity perspective. *Career Development International*, **18**, 305–324.

Lok, P., Westwood, R., & Crawford, J. (2005). Perceptions of organizational subculture and their significance for organizational commitment. *Applied Psychology: An International Review*, **54**, 490–514.

Lowe, K. B., Kroeck, K. G., & Sivasubramaniam, N. (1996). Effectiveness correlates of transformational and transactional leadership: A meta-analytic review of the MLQ literature. *Leadership Quarterly*, **7**, 385–425.

Major, D. A., Fletcher, T. D., Davis, D. D., & Germano, L. M. (2008). The influence of work–family culture and workplace relationships on work interference with family: A multilevel model. *Journal of Organizational Behavior*, **29**, 881–897.

Miron, E., Erez, M., & Naveh, E. (2004). Do personal characteristics and cultural values that promote innovation, quality, and efficiency compete or complement each other? *Journal of Organizational Behavior*, **25**, 175–199.

Ogbonna, E., & Harris, L. C. (2000). Leadership style, organizational culture and performance: Empirical evidence from UK companies. *International Journal of Human Resource Management*, **11**, 766–788.

Ostroff, C., Kinicki, A. J., & Tamkins, M. M. (2003). Organizational culture and climate. In W. C. Borman, D. R. Ilgen, & R. J. Klimoski (eds.), *Handbook of psychology: Industrial and organizational* (vol. 12, pp. 565–593). Hoboken, NJ: John Wiley.

Podsakoff, P. M., MacKenzie, S. B., Paine, J. B., & Bachrach, D. G. (2000). Organizational citizenship behaviours: A critical review of the theoretical and empirical literature and suggestions for future research. *Journal of Management*, **26**, 513–565.

Quinn, R. E. (1988). *Beyond rational management: Mastering the paradoxes and competing demands of high performance.* San Francisco: Jossey-Bass.

Sarros, J. C., Gray, J., & Desten, I. L. (2002). Leadership and its impact on organizational culture. *International Journal of Business Studies*, **10**, 1–26.

Sarros, J. C., Cooper, B. K., & Santora, J. C. (2008). Building a climate for innovation through transformational leadership and organizational culture. *Journal of Leadership and Organizational Studies*, **15**, 145–158.

Schein, E. H. (2010). *Organizational culture and leadership* (4th edition). San Francisco, CA: Jossey-Bass.

Schneider, B. (1987). The people make the place. *Personnel Psychology*, **40**, 437–453.

Schneider, B., Ehrhart, M. G., & Macey, W. H. (2013). Organizational climate and culture. *Annual Review of Psychology*, **64**, 361–388.

Simosi, M., & Xenikou, A. (2010). The role of organizational culture in the relationship between leadership and organizational commitment: An empirical study in a Greek organization. *International Journal of Human Resource Management*, **21**, 1598–1616.

Smircich, L. (1983). Concepts of culture and organizational analysis. *Administrative Science Quarterly*, **28**, 339–358.

Sorensen, J. B. (2002). The strength of corporate culture and the reliability of firm performance. *Administrative Science Quarterly*, **47**, 70–91.

Taylor, S., Levy, O., Boyacigiller, N., & Beechler, S. (2008). Employee commitment in MNCs: Impacts of organizational culture, HRM and top management orientations. *International Journal of Human Resource Management*, **19**, 501–527.

Trice, H. M., & Beyer, J. M. (1993). *The cultures of work organizations.* Englewood Cliffs, NJ: Prentice Hall.

Tsui, A. S., Zhang, Z.-X, Wang, H., Xin, K. R., & Wu, J. B. (2006). Unpacking the relationship between CEO leadership behavior and organizational culture. *Leadership Quarterly*, **17**, 113–137.

Van Muijen & associates (1999). Organizational culture: The Focus Questionnaire. *European Journal of Work and Organizational Psychology*, **8**, 551–568.

Vandenberghe, C., & Peiro, J. M. (1999). Organizational and individual values: Their main and combined effects on work attitudes and perceptions. *European Journal of Work and Organizational Psychology*, **8**, 569–581.

Waldman, D. A., & Yammarino, F. J. (1999). CEO charismatic leadership: Levels-of-management and levels-of-analysis effects. *Academy of Management Review*, **24**, 266–285.

Walumbwa, F. O., Avolio, B. J., & Zhu, W. (2008). How transformational leadership weaves its influence on individual job performance: The role of identification and efficacy beliefs. *Personnel Psychology*, **61**, 793–825.

Walumbwa, F. O., Wang, P., Lawer, J. J., & Shi, K. (2004). The role of collective efficacy in the relations between transformational leadership and work outcomes. *Journal of Occupational and Organizational Psychology*, **77**, 515–530.

Wang, G., Oh, I. S., Courtright, S. H., & Colbert, A. E. (2011). Transformational leadership and performance across criteria and levels: A meta-analytic review of 25 years of research. *Group and Organization Management*, **36**, 223–270.

Xenikou, A. (2014). The cognitive and affective components of organizational identification: The role of perceived support values and charismatic leadership. *Applied Psychology: An International Review*, **63**, 567–588.

Xenikou, A. (2017). Transformational leadership, transactional contingent reward, and organizational identification: The mediating effect of perceived innovation and goal culture orientations. *Frontiers in Psychology: Organizational Psychology*, **8**, 1754.

Xenikou, A., & Furnham, A. (2013). *Group dynamics and organizational culture: Effective work groups and organizations*. Hampshire, UK: Palgrave-Macmillan.

Xenikou, A., & Simosi, M. (2006). Organizational culture and transformational leadership as predictors of business unit performance. *Journal of Managerial Psychology*, **21**, 566–579.

4. Fit and congruence with organisational culture: definitions and measurement issues

Kamarul Zaman Bin Ahmad

4.1 INTRODUCTION

The extent to which a person is congruent with the organisation's culture is related to important job outcomes (Kristof, Zimmerman & Johnson, 2005). Organisational culture can be viewed as one aspect of the work environment. If the organisation's culture dictates that people should behave in certain ways, and the person behaves in ways that are preferred by the culture, then a state of harmony or congruence is said to exist. Similarly, if culture is a set of values and beliefs, then if the worker has the same set of values and beliefs as the organisation, this will lead to that state of harmony or congruence.

A vast body of knowledge has studied the extent to which the worker is congruent with organisational culture and other aspects of the work environment. This subject area is popularly known among academics and practitioners alike as person–environment fit or PE fit. PE fit is linked to positive work outcomes such as job performance, satisfaction, organisational commitment, organisational citizenship behaviour and intention to stay (Kristof et al., 2005). For those reasons, studying PE fit is vital for both practitioners and academics alike.

4.2 DEFINITION AND HISTORICAL DEVELOPMENT OF PERSON–ENVIRONMENT FIT

PE fit was defined by Edwards (1996, p. 292) as "In essence, P–E fit embodies the premise that attitudes, behaviour and other individual-level outcomes result not from the person or environment separately, but from the relationship between the two". Pervin (1989) elaborated that a "match" or "best-fit" of the individual to the environment will manifest itself in high performance, satisfaction and little stress, whereas lack of fit has opposite consequences.

Parsons' (1909) seminal work stressed the importance of both person and environment variables at the workplace. Today, both variables are regarded as crucial. However, somewhere between the two periods, academics became divided into two extreme views – one where a person's behaviour was caused entirely by the environment and, at the other extreme, the idea that the person (or personality) was solely responsible for their behaviour. Mischel (1968) criticised the traditional trait theories and proposed that it is the environment that causes behaviour and that this behaviour is situation-specific. However, trait theorists such as Cattell and Eysenck emphasise the interplay between multiple traits and environmental conditions in determining specific behaviours (Pervin, 1989). Merahbian (1968) explained that the instinct–need–habit–trait–factor theories assume that similar situations are likely to cause the same interpersonal behaviours from a particular individual but not necessarily from others. This sentiment was echoed by Bowers (1973) and Endler and Edwards (1978). Sarason et al. (1975)

concluded that neither personality nor the situation was better able to predict behaviour than the other. Pervin (1989) declared that most personality psychologists now are interactionists because they emphasise both person and situation variables in predicting behaviour.

PE fit is of practical significance to managers as it underlies most personnel selection models (Schneider, 1978). PE fit research is abundant (Buboltz et al., 1995) until today (Choi et al., 2020). Fit is measured at different levels, and when viewing fit at the organisation level, culture often becomes a relevant component in measurement (Kristof, 1996). In particular, the fit between the individual and the organisational culture (hereinafter known as PO fit) has become the focus of many studies (Kristof et al., 2005). However, before describing PO fit in more detail, we will mention briefly the measurement of fit at the different levels.

4.3   FIT LEVELS

According to Kristof (1996), and Kristof et al. (2005), fit exists at the following levels:

- Person–vocation (PV)
- Person–organisation (PO) – relationship with organisational culture and values
- Person–group (PG)
- Person–job (PJ), consisting of supply–value (S–V) fit and demand–abilities (D–A) fit
- Person–supervisor (PS), initially called "leader–subordinate congruence" by Ahmad (2008)

The person–vocation fit or PV fit involves looking at how the person may fit into his/her occupation. It looks at the broadest level of the work environment. "The fit of a person with a vocation, or person–vocation (P–V) fit, is important for workers and is a central concept in vocational psychology" (Glosenberg et al., 2019, p. 92). Using 81,445 responses from 74 countries to a vocational inventory, they found partial support for the generalisability of this theory. The researchers included the circular model of vocational interests and social cognitive career theory (SCCT) in their investigation. They found that the circular model was more valid in locales of high economic development. Also, people with more education had a better fit, especially in individualist countries, and people who had higher levels of education had a better fit, especially in higher-income countries. Many other studies have employed Holland's (1985) model in their analyses. The attraction–selection–attrition (ASA) model introduced by Schneider (1978) is a psychological theory positing that individuals are attracted to, selected by, and retained in organisations whose members are similar to themselves.

Next is the person–organisation fit or PO fit, which is the fit between the person and the organisation. When doing so, the organisational culture is often used as a proxy for the work environment. PO fit will then be assessed according to how well an individual fits with the organisational culture. More will be described in the next section.

Next is person–group fit, or PG fit, defined as the compatibility between individuals and their workgroup members. Personality homogeneity may influence behavioural and attitudinal outcomes for groups and their members (Driskell et al., 1987; Hackman & Morris, 1975). Most recently, Pudjiarti and Hutomo (2020) found that PG fit is positively related to innovative work behaviour and job performance.

The person–job fit is defined by Edwards (1991) as the fit between the abilities of a person and the demands of a job (i.e., D–A fit) and the desires of the person and the attributes of a job

(S–V fit). Work environment, in this context, is the job itself, i.e., the characteristics of the tasks a person is expected to accomplish in the course of employment.

Finally, the person–supervisor fit is the degree of congruence between the subordinate and the supervisor. Supervisor–subordinate personality similarity has been shown to be positively related to satisfaction with supervision (Ahmad, 2008).

4.4   PO FIT OR CONGRUENCE WITH ORGANISATIONAL CULTURE – DEFINITIONS AND MEASUREMENT

Of all the different types of fit, PO fit is arguably the most relevant when one of the variables examined is organisational culture. Kristof et al. (2005) cited Tom (1971) who introduced the concept of the organisation having a personality. The extent to which it matches the individual's personality creates a fit or congruence. So, an organisation's culture can be viewed as its "personality". Some researchers adapted the concept and focused on climate instead and the extent to which it matches the individual (Christiansen et al., 1997; Ryan et al., 1996). Chatman (1989) instead focused on the values shared by the person and the organisation. If a person has similar values as the organisation, then he/she has a high PO fit. Tepeci and Bartlett (2002) developed the Hospitality Industry Culture Profile, which assesses the fit between organisational culture and individual values. An eight-factor structure of hospitality culture is identified. They conceptualised PO fit as the fit between organisational culture and individual values and found that the PO fit could predict employees' job satisfaction and behavioural intentions. Kirsh (2000) explored organisational culture, climate and PE fit and their relationship to employment outcomes for mental health consumers using the Workplace Climate Questionnaire (WCQ) and the Organisational Culture Profile (OCP). The findings suggest the importance of assessing the organisational culture/climate and its congruence with individuals' value systems.

The Organisational Culture Profile or OCP (O'Reilly et al., 1991) is a values-based profile, and value congruence has become a widely accepted measure when examining PO fit (Kristof, 1996). The OCP uses 54 items that form eight factors in exploratory factor analysis. The instrument contains a set of value statements to assess the extent to which certain values characterise an organisation, and compares them with an individual's preference for these values. Borg et al. (2011) found that OCP can be embedded into Schwartz's Theory of Universals in Values (TUV), meaning that PO fit can be assessed more simply by the congruence of the person's and the organisation's positions on two value dimensions: risk versus rules, and results versus relations.

4.5   FIT CATEGORIES: COMPLEMENTARY AND SUPPLEMENTARY FIT

Before 1987, most studies did not distinguish between the different forms of fit and did not expressly state which category of fit they were investigating. Muchinsky and Monahan (1987) were among the first to categorise the different forms of fit, and they identified two types of fit: supplementary fit and complementary fit. Supplementary fit exists when "a person fits into some environmental context because he or she supplements or embellishes or possesses characteristics which are similar to other individuals in this environment" (p. 268). In supplementary fit, the work environment can comprise the people in the immediate workgroup (Meir et al., 1997) or the entire workforce (Schuerger et al., 1994). The supplementary fit approach is often used when analysing PO fit or the fit between the individual and the organisational culture. The premise of supplementary fit is that the more similar an individual's values are with the organisation's, the greater the fit.

On the other hand, complementary fit occurs when there is a "match between an individual's talents and the corresponding needs of the environment" (Muchinsky & Monahan, 1987, p. 268). In other words, the "characteristics of an individual serve to make whole or complement an environment's characteristics. The environment is seen as either deficient in, or requiring a certain type of person in order to be effective" (p. 271). Regarding complementary fit, Kristof (1996) pointed out that there are two components – supply–value fit (S–V fit) and demand–abilities fit (D–A fit). From the S–V fit perspective, organisations supply physical, financial, and psychological resources and the interpersonal and growth opportunities valued by employees (French et al., 1982; Livingstone et al., 1997). Fit occurs when an organisation satisfies individuals' needs, desires or values (Kristof, 1996). From the D–A fit perspective, organisations demand from their employees their effort, time, commitment, knowledge, skills and abilities (French et al., 1982; Livingstone et al., 1997). According to Kristof (1996), fit occurs when an individual has the abilities required to meet organisation demands. Essentially, D–A fit focuses primarily on meeting others' needs, while S–V fit focuses mainly on fulfilling one's own needs (Caplan, 1987; Livingstone et al., 1997). To encapsulate the different aspects of fit, we devised Figure 4.1.

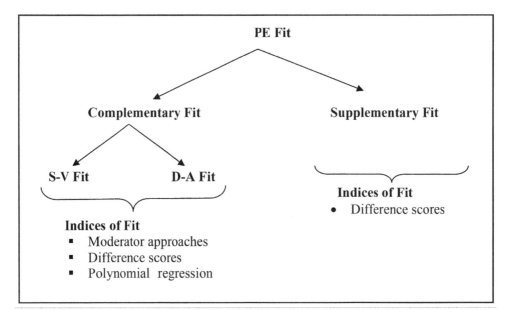

Figure 4.1   PE fit classification

S–V and D–A fit are usually examined from the person–job (PJ) fit perspective rather than PO fit. It is evident from Figure 4.1 that S–V and D–A fit are entirely different constructs, but, in the past, researchers were previously confused between the two (Edwards & Cooper, 1990; Livingstone et al., 1997). It is essential to distinguish between them because they are related to different outcomes (Livingstone et al., 1997). S–V fit is related to dissatisfaction, presumably because of unmet values about the job (Livingstone et al., 1997; Locke, 1969, 1976), whereas D–A fit is related to performance, simply because the job incumbent does not have the abilities demanded by the job (Livingstone et al., 1997; Hackman & Oldham, 1980; Naylor et al., 1980; Porter & Lawler, 1968).

Although research on fit involving organisational culture usually uses the supplementary fit model and not the complementary fit model, it is not wrong to argue that this approach can be taken when fit is framed as the extent to which the organisational culture supplies what a person values (i.e., S–V fit). This is the author's opinion, although previous studies have opted not to use this approach.

4.6   SUPPLEMENTARY AND COMPLEMENTARY FIT, AT THE VARIOUS FIT LEVELS

Supplementary fit can exist at each level of fit. At the PV fit level, a person would be coun-selled to pursue a particular vocation because his/her interests are most similar to some norm group (Holland, 1985; Muchinsky & Monahan, 1987). It assumes that people should be similar to be mutually compatible. The same premise applies to PO fit, and many of the studies on PO fit mentioned earlier have the supplementary model as their basis, i.e., that if a person's values are similar to those of the organisation, then a state of congruence is said to exist, and this leads to favourable job outcomes (Chatman, 1989).

Similarly, supplementary fit can exist at the group level (PG fit). Support has been found for the supplementary fit model, when Bass (1982) suggested that where task accomplishment depends on smooth, cooperative, conflict-free, coordinated efforts among the members, a homogeneous membership should be more productive than a heterogeneous one. Just as in PO fit, the interaction processes are better in teams where members are alike in opinions, interests and abilities (Byrne, 1971). Members can communicate easily with each other, and there will be less conflict, fewer differences in opinions, standards and ways of doing things (Bass, 1965; Hoffman, 1959). Similarly, Van Zelst (1952) found that workers liked it a lot better when their mates worked with them and that the work also became more attractive as a result. "Friends can work faster than strangers" (Bass, 1982, p. 205).

However, this contradicts Belbin's (1981) theory. Belbin (1981) advocated heterogeneity in groups and specified that each person within the group should have a unique role[1] (and presumably the personalities and behaviours that go along with it), therefore supporting the complementary fit model and the D–A fit. Yet both theories have empirical support. Meir et al. (1997), although cautious in drawing any rash conclusions, offered the following explana-tion as a possibility: heterogeneous groups may perform better in complex jobs that require brain-storming, whereas homogeneity is preferred in specialised jobs.

So, which is better? Supplementary or complementary fit? Schneider (1987) argued that the work environment must be measured in terms of the person, thereby supporting the sup-plementary fit model. Medcof and Hausdorf (1995), on the other hand, criticised Holland not for his use of typologies but rather for measuring the environment by measuring the people in them. They proposed that one should measure the environment itself and not the people in them. Apparently, Medcof and Hausdorf (1995) did not believe that there could be, in simultaneous existence, two legitimate ways of measuring the environment.

Subsequently, many studies have investigated both supplementary and complementary fit simultaneously. It seems that measuring more than one form of congruence can improve the validity of the congruence-outcome relationship. For instance, Meir and Melamed (1986) found that combinations of three different congruence aspects had an enhancing effect, that is, the higher the number of congruence aspects, the higher the well-being. The final words can be taken from Kristof's (1996) article:

> Although the model … distinguishes between the various perspectives of fit, it is not meant to suggest that they are contradictory. In fact, quite the opposite is true … the optimum P–O fit may be achieved when each entity's needs are fulfilled by the other and they share similar fundamental characteristics. (p. 6)

So, rather than comparing to see which is better, Shen et al. (2016) found that the combination of complementary and supplementary fit can significantly predict consumers' satisfaction and commitment to the community, leading to a willingness to contribute to value co-creation.

4.7   OTHER MEASUREMENT ISSUES: PERCEIVED, SUBJECTIVE AND OBJECTIVE FIT

Kristof et al. (2005) identified three ways to assess fit – perceived, subjective and objective. Perceived fit is when the individual makes a direct assessment of fit. Subjective fit is indirectly evaluated by comparing the P and E variables reported by the same person. Objective fit is calculated indirectly through the comparison of P and E reported from different sources.

Concerning perceived fit, this involves asking people directly whether they believe a good fit exists (Kristof 1996). This method is often used in PO fit studies involving organisational culture. For example, Posner et al. (1985) asked managers to rate how compatible their values were with their organisations. Cable and DeRue (2002) used three items to measure perceived fit: "The things that I value in life are very similar to the things that my organisation values", "My personal values match my organisation's values and culture", and "My organisation's values and culture provide a good fit with the things that I value in life". Cable and DeRue's (2002) questionnaire is one of the most popular methods of measuring fit with organisational culture, or PO fit.

However, Kristof (1996) advocated that the respondent should rate the individual separately from the environment and not assess the degree of fit. This is true with subjective fit. Edwards (1996) measured S–V fit by asking respondents how much each task is required in their jobs and how much of each task they prefer. Similarly, D–A fit was measured by asking about the level of skill required for each job and then by asking the respondent to assess his or her skill regarding that job. All responses are recorded on commensurate scales ranging from 1 to 10. By doing so, a direct assessment of fit is avoided, and arguably a more accurate assessment is achieved. However, respondents are still being asked, indirectly, to make implicit judgements of fit. A similar commensurate measure of S–V fit and D–A fit was used by Livingstone et al. (1997).

Another method (from now on called "the moderator approach") does not insist on commensurate measures. This focus on the interaction between the person and organisation is used in various studies (e.g., Chesney & Rosenman, 1980; Mateson & Ivancevich, 1982; Pritchard & Karasick, 1973). The person and the environment should be measured separately using entirely different instruments, and the types and ranges of both scales can be different altogether. The respondent is not required to assess fit either directly or indirectly – in fact, it makes it almost impossible for the respondent to attempt to assess fit. This makes the moderator approach superior in that the consistency bias inherent in the direct measurement of fit approach can be eliminated. However, it can be argued that the most significant advantage of this method is that objective measures of the environment can be used. Payne and Pugh (1983) defined objective measurement as a direct assessment without any conceptual transformation. One such example is the number of persons in a team, as used by Ahmad (2011), which are independent of the person being assessed. A person's values or personality can taint perceptions, and different individuals can perceive the same environment differently (Ahmad, 2011). Similarly, Hershberger et al. (1994, p. 24) said, "Managers within an organisation differ in their perceptions of autonomy, task structure, recognition and organisational support". Similarly, individuals in the same organisation may differ in their perceptions of the organisational culture (Ravlin & Meglino, 1987). Arguably the most crucial advantage of using objective measures of the work environment is that it enables the researcher to define it in absolute quantities instead of relative amounts. Caplan (1987) admitted that where response scales deal with relative amounts (e.g., "1 = none", "5 = a lot"), "a lot" may be viewed as "a lot compared to my ability to handle the work", or "a lot compared to what others have". A "moderate amount of responsibility for others, in an absolute sense, may be perceived as quite high by a person with little ability to assume such responsibility" (Kulik et al., 1987, p. 284).

Unfortunately, many studies (including those involving organisational culture) used perceptual measures of the work environment. For example, Barrick and Mount (1993) used a subjective measure of autonomy, assessed by the respondent himself/herself. Similarly, Lee et al. (1990) used perceived control as the environmental measure. They found that among Type A people, those who also have high perceived control have greater job satisfaction and perform better than those low in perceived control. Another study by Roberts and Foti (1998) initially attempted to use objective measures of work structure using company records but found it impossible because the documents were incomplete. Instead, the work structure was measured subjectively or perceptually. Blau (1987) also used a subjective measure of the work environment – perceived job scope – which was measured using a combination of four scales from the Job Characteristics Inventory (JCI; Sims et al., 1976): skill variety, task identity, autonomy, and feedback. Blau (1987) found that perceived job scope significantly moderated the relationship between the Protestant work ethic and job involvement. The problem with using the respondent to assess their work environment subjectively is that their abilities or personality may taint his/her assessment – a person who has high anxiety may perceive their work environment to be riskier than a person who has low anxiety. There is an obvious problem of single-source bias. The use of objective measures of the environment avoids this problem.

So, it would seem that from a methodological viewpoint, objective measures are superior to subjective measures. However, are there any drawbacks to using objective measures? Kristof et al. (2005) revealed that correlations involving objective measures have relatively lower levels of correlation (−0.18) compared to perceived fit (−0.49) and subjective fit (−0.44).

4.8   FINDINGS FROM SOME META-ANALYTIC STUDIES ON PE FIT

In a meta-analytic study by Tranberg et al. (1993), 27 studies were examined concerning the relationship between interest congruence and job or academic satisfaction. It was found that the methodologically weakest studies yielded the strongest satisfaction-congruence relations (the use of a one-item measure specifically designed for the study in question is considered the methodologically weakest one, whereas standardised measures with adequately reported reliability are considered the methodologically strongest).

Kristof et al. (2005) conducted a thorough meta-analysis of 172 PE fit studies. Results showed that PJ fit has the strongest correlations: 0.56 with job satisfaction, 0.47 with organisational commitment, −0.46 with the intention to quit, and a modest correlation with performance (0.20). When examining intention to quit, perceived fit and subjective fit have high correlations (−0.49 and 0.44 respectively), objective fit had the weakest correlation (−0.18). PO fit had strong correlations with organisational commitment (0.51), job satisfaction (0.44), organisational satisfaction (0.65) and intention to quit (−0.35). PO has a moderate correlation with contextual performance (0.27) and a low correlation with overall performance (0.07). Correlations between PO fit and other job attitudes were moderate (0.39 with co-worker satisfaction and 0.33 with supervisor satisfaction). PG fit was correlated with job satisfaction (0.31), organisational commitment (0.19) and intention to quit (−0.22). Person–supervisor (PS) fit has a strong correlation with job satisfaction (0.44), supervisor satisfaction (0.46) and LMX (0.43) but weakly related to organisational commitment (0.09).

Summary:

- Job satisfaction was strongly related to PJ (0.56), PO (0.44), PG (0.31) and PS fit (0.44).
- Organisational commitment was strongly related to PO (0.51) and PJ fit (0.47), but weakly related to PG (0.19) and PS fit (0.09).
- Co-worker satisfaction was strongly related to PG (0.42) and PO fit (0.39).
- Supervisor satisfaction was strongly related to PS fit (0.46) and less with PO (0.33), PJ (0.33), and PG fit (0.28).
- Organisational attraction was related to PO fit (0.46) and PJ fit (0.48).
- Turnover intentions were negatively related to PJ (−0.46), PO (−0.35) and PG fit (0.22).

4.9   MOST RECENT RESEARCH ON PE FIT

PE fit is still a popular topic of research today. This section describes some of the latest research on the subject. Until today, PE fit dimensions such as PO, PJ, PG and PS fit are related to satisfaction and turnover (Andela & Van der Doef, 2019). PE fit has many dimensions, and the lack of fit in one dimension can be compensated by another. The association between newcomer PJ misfit and turnover and performance can be buffered by multi-dimensional PE fit (Chi et al., 2020). In the context of polychronicity or multi-tasking, PE fit has also been shown to be a multidimensional concept, and the fit in all the dimensions combined can lead to well-being and performance (Wu et al., 2020). Choi et al. (2020) found that PE fit moderated the relationship between psychological capital (self-efficacy, optimism, hope, and resilience) and job performance, mediated by informal learning. Their study showed that the indirect effect of psychological capital on job performance through informal learning became stronger with low levels of PO fit and became significant. On the contrary, when the PO fit was high, the indirect effect was not significant.

Managers can take many steps to improve fit. For instance, organisational support has been shown to improve fit as formal mentoring support was positively related to newcomers' PO fit (Cai et al., 2020). PE fit was also a mediator of the relationship between perceived social support and perceived employability and career decision self-efficacy (Jiang, 2017). Improving PE fit is essential not only for managers but also for employees. PE fit has also been shown to have far-reaching implications as it has been linked with the realisation of the meaning of work and subsequently to the meaning of life (Zhang et al., 2019). The concept of PE fit has even been extended to person–family fit, that is, the extent to which the individual fits with the rest of the family members (akin to PG fit) (Padmasiri et al., 2019).

PE fit is a relatively stable construct in that the occasional dip in affect or performance is unlikely to have long-lasting consequences for employee PE fit perceptions. In contrast, people who regularly feel unhappy or unproductive at work will likely perceive low PE fit (Vleugels et al., 2018). Misfit has been linked to conflict, which in turn increases the likelihood of one becoming a victim of bullying (Vandevelde et al., 2020). The ability to manage the display of one's emotions or emotional labour (surface and deep acting) has been linked to perceived fit, impacting job involvement (Hsu & Lin, 2019).

Recent research has also tried to test whether an excess of ability is better than just a satisfactory amount. For example, if a person has more capabilities than is required for the job, would this lead to a better situation than if a person's abilities merely matched the job requirements? Bohndick et al. (2018) researched to test this specifically. They found that a match or fit between abilities and demands is better than where abilities exceeded the job demands. This is plausible because where a person has more capabilities than is required for a job, they will find the job not challenging and become bored. Such a situation exists with dead-end jobs where there is no route to further progression and improvement.

4.10 FINAL THOUGHTS: IS FIT ALWAYS A GOOD THING? EXPLORING THE DARK SIDE OF FIT

So far, only the benefits of a high degree of fit are described. Is it possible to have situations where the fit between a person and their work environment gives rise to negative outcomes?

Kulik et al. (1987) answered this question by distinguishing between the two forms of fit: high-growth needs and challenging jobs on the one hand, and low-growth needs and non-challenging work on the other. Although fit exists in both situations, they pointed out that the outcomes may be entirely different for each. Whereas high performance is expected from the first form of fit, it is not anticipated from the second form. However, increased job satisfaction may be an outcome of the second form of fit. Ahmad (2010) also found that less intelligent people are more satisfied with their pay if made to work in larger groups than small groups or work alone. In this study, those with lower intelligence were more comfortable when other group members compensated for their lack of ability. Similarly, if an organisation's culture did not value hard work and productivity, potentially less-motivated employees would more likely fit in that organisation.

4.11   CONCLUSION

This chapter defined PE fit as the congruence between the person and the work environment, of which culture is one aspect. PE fit can be viewed at many levels such as person–vocation, person–organisation, person–job, person–group and person–supervisor fit. A person–organisation fit is the most relevant when examining a person's congruence with the organisation's culture. If the person's values and beliefs are similar to that of the organisation, then a state of congruence or fit is said to exist. This will lead to positive work outcomes such as job performance, satisfaction, organisational commitment, organisational citizenship behaviour and intention to stay (Kristof et al., 2005).

Fit can be categorised as either supplementary and complementary. In the context of organisational culture, the supplementary fit approach is often adopted, i.e., the similarity between the person's values and the organisational values are to be preferred, as opposed to differences. The complimentary fit approach is usually not used here. However, in the author's view, it is not wrong to view fit as the extent to which the organisational culture supplies what a person values (i.e., S–V fit). We also discussed how fit could be measured in terms of perceived, subjective and objective fit. Of the three, perceived fit (which is the direct assessment of fit by the respondent) is the methodologically weakest (because of single-source bias), and objective fit (which has measurement from a source independent of the respondent) is the strongest methodologically. However, in terms of association and predictability, the perceived fit has the strongest associations with job outcomes, and objective fit has the weakest. From this perspective, research on perceived fit with organisational culture will probably have stronger relationships with job outcomes than research that used subjective or objective fit. The chapter finally concludes with a caution that fit is only beneficial if the organisational culture promotes positive work values and not laziness. The latter will only attract less-motivated individuals.

NOTE

1.   Belbin (1981) stated that there are eight roles – Chairperson, Shaper, Plant, Monitor/Evaluator Company Worker, Team Worker, Resource Investigator and Completer. According to Belbin, all the roles must be filled.

REFERENCES

Ahmad, K. Z. (2008). Relationship between leader–subordinate personality congruence and performance and satisfaction in the UK. *Leadership and Organization Development Journal, 29*(5/6), 396–411.
Ahmad, K. Z. (2010). An investigation of objective person–environment fit: The dark side of intelligence. *International Journal of Psychological Studies, 2*(2), 81–89.
Ahmad, K. Z. (2011). Warmth in groups and satisfaction with supervision. *International Journal of Business and Management, 6*(5), 129–136.
Andela, M. & Van der Doef, M. (2019). A comprehensive assessment of the person–environment fit dimensions and their relationships with work-related outcomes. *Journal of Career Development, 46*(5), 567–582.
Barrick, M. R. & Mount, M. K. (1993). Autonomy as a moderator of the relationships between the Big Five personality dimensions and job performance. *Journal of Applied Psychology, 78*, 1, 111–118.
Bass, B. (1965). *Organizational Psychology*. Boston: Allyn & Bacon.

Bass, B. (1982). Individual capability, team performance and team productivity. In M. D. Dunnette & E. A. Fleishman (Eds), *Human Performance and Productivity Volume 1: Human Capability Assessment*. New Jersey: Lawrence Erlbaum Associates.

Belbin, R. M. (1981). *Management Teams, Why They Succeed or Fail*. London: Heinemann.

Blau, G. J. (1987). Using a person–environment fit model to predict job involvement and organisational commitment. *Journal of Vocational Behavior*, *30*, 240–257.

Bohndick, C., Rosman, T., Kohlmeyer, S. & Buhl, H. (2018). The interplay between subjective abilities and subjective demands and its relationship with academic success: An application of the person–environment fit theory. *Higher Education*, *75*(5), 839–854.

Borg, I., Groenen, P. J. F., Jehn, K. A., Bilsky & W. Schwartz, S. H. (2011). Embedding the Organizational Culture Profile into Schwartz's Theory of Universals in Values. *Journal of Personnel Psychology*, *10*(1), 1–12.

Bowers, K. (1973). Situationism in psychology: An analysis and critique. *Psychological Review*, *80*, 307–336.

Buboltz, W. C., Ebberwein, C., Watkins, C. E. & Savickas, M. L. (1995). A comparison of the content, authors and institutions represented in the Career Development Quarterly and the Journal of Vocational Behavior. *Journal of Vocational Behavior*, *46*, 216–226.

Byrne, D. (1971). *The Attraction Paradigm*. New York: Academic Press.

Cai, Z., Wu, D., Xin, Y., Chen, Y. & Wu, H. (2020). Formal mentoring support, person–environment fit and newcomer's intention to leave. Does newcomer's uncertainty avoidance orientation matter? *Personnel Review*, *49*(8), 1749–1767.

Cable, D. M. & DeRue, D. S. (2002). The convergent and discriminant validity of subjective fit. *Journal of Applied Psychology*, *87*, 875–884.

Caplan, R. D. (1987). Person–environment fit theory and organizations: Commensurate dimensions, time perspectives, and mechanisms. *Journal of Vocational Behavior*, *31*, 248–267.

Chatman, J. A. (1989). Improving interactional organizational research: A model of person–organization fit. *Academy of Management Review*, *14*(3), 333–349.

Chesney, M. A. & Rosenman, R. H. (1980). Type A behavior in the work setting. In C. L. Cooper & R. Payne (Eds), *Current Concerns in Occupational Stress*. New York: John Wiley & Sons.

Chi, N. W., Fang, L. C., Shen, C. T. & Fan, H. L. (2020). Detrimental effects of newcomer person–job misfit on actual turnover and performance: The buffering role of multidimensional person–environment fit. *Applied Psychology: An International Review*, *69*(4), 1361–1395.

Choi, W., Noe, R. & Cho, Y. (2020). What is responsible for the psychological capital–job performance relationship? An examination of the role of informal learning and person–environment fit. *Journal of Managerial Psychology*, *35*(1), 28–41.

Christiansen, N., Villanova, P. & Mikulay, S. (1997). Political influence compatibility: Fitting the person to the climate. *Journal of Organizational Behavior*, *18*(6), 709–730.

Driskell, J. E., Hogan, R. & Salas, E. (1987). Personality and group performance. In C. Hendrick (Ed.), *Review of Personality and Social Psychology, Vol. 9. Group Processes and Intergroup Relations* (pp. 91–112). Sage Publications, Inc.

Edwards, J. R. (1991). Person–job fit: A conceptual integration, literature review and methodological critique. *International Review of Industrial/ Organizational Psychology*, *6*, 283–357.

Edwards, J. R. (1996). An examination of competing versions of the person–environment fit approach to stress. *Academy of Management Journal*, *39*(2), 292–339.

Edwards, J. R. & Cooper, C. L. (1990). The person–environment fit approach to stress: Recurring problems and some suggested solutions. *Journal of Organizational Behavior*, *11*, 293–307.

Endler, N. S. & Edwards, J. (1978). Person by treatment interactions in personality research. In L. A. Pervin & M. Lewis (Eds), *Perspectives in Interactional Psychology*. New York: Plenum.

French J. R. P., Caplan, R. D. & Harrison. R. V. (1982). *The Mechanisms of Job Stress and Strain*. London: John Wiley & Sons.

Glosenberg, A., Terence, T., Tara, B. David, B. & Lori, F. (2019). Person–vocation fit across the world of work: Evaluating the generalizability of the circular model of vocational interests and social cognitive career theory across 74 countries. *Journal of Vocational Behavior*, *112*, 92–108.

Hackman, J. R. & Morris, C. G. (1975). Group tasks, group interaction process and group performance effectiveness: a review and proposed integration. In L. Berkowitz (Ed.), *Advances in Experimental Social Psychology*. New York: Academic Press.

Hackman, J. R. & Oldham, G. R. (1980). *Work Redesign*. Reading, MA: Addison-Wesley.

Hershberger, S. L., Lichtenstein, P. & Knox. S. S. (1994). Genetic and environmental influences on perceptions of organizational climate. *Journal of Applied Psychology*, *1*, 24–33.

Hoffman, L. R. (1959). Homogeneity of member personality and its effect on group problem solving. *Journal of Abnormal and Social Psychology*, *58*, 27–32.

Holland, J. L. (1985). *Making Vocational Choices*. Florida: Psychological Assessment Resources.

Hsu, C. L., & Lin, J. C. (2020). Understanding continuance intention to use online to offline (O2O) apps. *Electron Markets*, *30*, 883–897.

Jiang, Z. (2017). Social support and career psychological states: An integrative model of person–environment fit. *Journal of Career Assessment*, *25*(2), 219–237.

Kirsh, B. (2000). Organizational culture, climate and person–environment fit: Relationships with employment outcomes for mental health consumers. *Work*, *14*, 109–122

Kristof, A. (1996). Person–organisation fit: An integrative review of its conceptualisations, measurement, and implications. *Personnel Psychology*, *49*, 1–49.

Kristof, A., Zimmerman, R. D. & Johnson, E. C. (2005). Consequences of individuals' fit at work: A meta-analysis of person–job, person–organization, person–group and person–superior fit. *Personnel Psychology*, *58*, 281–342.

Kulik, C. T., Oldham, G. R. & Hackman, J. R. (1987). Work design as an approach to person–environment fit. *Journal of Vocational Behavior*, *31*, 278–296.

Lee, C., Ashford, S. J. & Bobko, P. (1990). Interactive effects of "Type A" behavior and perceived control on worker performance, job satisfaction and somatic complaints. *Academy of Management Journal*, *33*(4), 870–881.

Livingstone, L. P., Nelson, D. L. & Barr, S. H. (1997). Person–environment fit and creativity: An examination of supply–value and demand–ability versions of fit. *Journal of Management*, *23*(2), 119–146.

Locke, E. A. (1969). What is job satisfaction? *Organizational Behavior and Human Performance*, *4*, 309–336.

Locke, E. A. (1976). The nature and causes of job satisfaction. In M. D. Dunnette (Ed.), *Handbook of Industrial and Organizational Psychology* (pp. 1297–1349). Skokie, IL: Rand McNally.

Mateson, M. T. & Ivacevich, J. M. (1982). Type A and B behavior patterns and health symptoms: Examining individual and organizational fit. *Journal of Occupational Medicine*, *24*, 585–589.

Medcof, J. W. & Hausdorf, P. A. (1995). Instruments to measure opportunities to satisfy needs and degree of satisfaction of needs, in the workplace. *Journal of Occupational and Organizational Psychology*, *68*, 193–208.

Meir, E. I. & Melamed, S. (1986). The accumulation of person–environment congruences and well-being. *Journal of Occupational Behaviour*, *7*(4), 315–323.

Meir, E. I., Hadas, C. & Noyfeld, M. (1997). Person–environment fit in small army units. *Journal of Career Assessment*, *5*, 21–29.

Merahbian, A. (1968). *An Analysis of Personality Theories*. New Jersey: Prentice Hall.

Mischel, W. (1968). *Personality and Assessment*. New York: John Wiley & Sons.

Muchinsky, P. M. & Monahan, C. J. (1987). What is person–environment congruence? Supplementary versus complementary models of fit. *Journal of Vocational Behavior*, *31*, 268–277.

Naylor, J. C., Pritchard, R. D. & Ilgen, D. R. (1980). *A Theory of Behavior in Organizations*. New York: Academic Press.

O'Reilly, C. A., Chatman, J. & Caldwell, D. F. (1991). People and organizational culture: A profile comparison approach to assessing person–organization fit. *Academy of Management Journal*, *34*(3), 487–516.

Padmasiri, M. K., Kailasapathy, P. & Jayawardana, A. K. (2019). Development of the person–family fit construct: An extension of person–environment fit into the family domain. *South Asian Journal of Human Resources Management*, *6*(2), 156–176.

Parsons, F. (1909). *Choosing a Vocation*. Boston, MA: Houghton Mifflin.

Payne, R. & Pugh, D. S. (1983). Organizational structure and climate. In M. D. Dunnette (Ed.), *Handbook of Industrial and Organizational Psychology*. New York: John Wiley & Sons.

Pervin, L. A. (1989). Persons, situations, interactions: The history and a discussion of theoretical models. *Academy of Management Review, 14*(3), 350–360.

Porter, L. W. & Lawler, E. E. (1968). *Managerial Attitudes and Performance*. Homewood, IL: Dorsey Press.

Posner, B. Z., Kouzes, J. M. & Schmidt, W. H. (1985). Shared values make a difference – an empirical test of corporate culture. *Human Resources Management, 24*(3), 293–309.

Pritchard, R. D. & Karasick, B. W. (1973). The effects of organizational climate on managerial job performance and job satisfaction. *Organizational Behavior and Human Performance, 9*, 126–146.

Pudjiarti, E. & Hutomo, P. (2020). Innovative work behaviour: An integrative investigation of person–job fit, person–organization fit, and person–group fit. *Verslas: teorija ir praktika, 21*(1), 39–47.

Ravlin, E. C. & Meglino, B. M. (1987). Effect of values on perception and decision-making – a study of alternative work values measures. *Journal of Applied Psychology, 72*, 4, 666–673.

Roberts, H. E. & Foti, R. J. (1998). Evaluating the interaction between self-leadership and work structure in predicting job satisfaction. *Journal of Business and Psychology, 12*(3), 257–267.

Ryan, A. M., Schmitt, M. J. & Johnson, R. (1996). Attitudes and effectiveness: Examining relations at an organizational level. *Personnel Psychology, 49*(4), 853–882.

Sarason, I. G., Smith, R. E. & Diener, E. (1975). Personality research: Components of variance attributable to the person and the situation. *Journal of Personality and Social Psychology, 32*, 199–204.

Schneider, B. (1978). Person–situation selection: A review of some ability–situation interaction research. *Personnel Psychology, 31*, 281–297.

Schneider, B. (1987). E = f(P,B): The road to a radical approach to person–environment fit. *Journal of Vocational Behavior, 31*, 353–361.

Schuerger, J. M., Ekeberg, S. E. & Kustis, G. A. (1994). 16 PF scores and machine operators' performance. *Perceptual and Motor Skills, 79*(3, Pt 2), 1426.

Shen, X. L., Li, Y. J. & Sun, Y. (2016) The roles of complementary and supplementary fit in predicting online brand community users' willingness to contribute. In D. Vogel, X. Guo, H. Linger, C. Barry, M. Lang & C. Schneider (Eds), *Transforming Healthcare Through Information Systems: Lecture Notes in Information Systems and Organisation*, vol 17. Cham: Springer.

Sims, H., Szilagyi, A. & Keller, R. (1976). The measurement of job characteristics. *Academy of Management Journal, 19*, 195–212.

Tepeci, M. & Bartlett, A. B. (2002). The Hospitality Industry Culture Profile: A measure of individual values, organizational culture, and person–organization fit as predictors of job satisfaction and behavioral intentions. *Hospitality Management, 21*, 151–170.

Tom, V. R. (1971). The role of personality and organizational images in the recruiting process. *Organizational Behavior and Human Performance, 6*, 573–592.

Tranberg, M., Slane, S. & Ekeberg, S. E. (1993). The relationship between interest congruence and satisfaction: a metaanalysis. *Journal of Vocational Behavior, 42*, 253–264.

Van Zelst, R. H. (1952). Sociometrically selected work teams increase production. *Personnel Psychology, 5*, 175–185.

Vandevelde, K., Baillien, E. & Notelaers, G. (2020). Person–environment fit as a parsimonious framework to explain workplace bullying. *Journal of Managerial Psychology, 35*(5), 317–322.

Vleugels, W., Cooman, R. D., Verbruggen, M. & Solinger, O. (2018). Understanding dynamic change in perceptions of person–environment fit: An exploration of competing theoretical perspectives. *Journal of Organizational Behavior, 39*, 1066–1080.

Wu, T. J., Gao, J. Y., Wang, L. Y. & Yuan, K. S. (2020). Exploring links between polychronicity and job performance from the person–environment fit perspective: The mediating role of well-being. *International Journal of Environmental Research and Public Health, 17*(3711), 1–12.

Zhang, H., Chen, K., Chen, C. & Schlegel, R. (2019). Personal aspirations, person–environment fit, meaning in work, and meaning in life: A moderated mediation model. *Journal of Happiness Studies, 20*, 1481–1497.

5. Multilevel issues in organizations and culture: a review of theoretical and methodological innovations for the study of national and organizational culture

Ronald Fischer, Johannes Karl, Gerard Janse van Rensburg and Maria Cristina Ferreira

Organizations are by definition multilevel structures: they involve individuals working in teams and departments as well as across different branches. Different organizations and sometimes even teams and departments within the same organization will develop their own cultural orientations. In turn, organizations are situated in different societies, which in turn have national cultural characteristics. In this chapter, we discuss some of the theoretical and methodological challenges when examining cultural questions for organizations.

DEFINING AND MEASURING CULTURES

Defining culture has been a fundamental challenge since the beginning of anthropology. The founding father of modern anthropology, Edward Tylor (1832–1917), had a rather encompassing definition of culture, stating that it is the "complex whole which includes knowledge, belief, art, morals, law, custom, and any other capabilities acquired by man as a member of society" (Tylor, 2010). Kroeber and Kluckhohn (1952) listed more than 150 definitions common in anthropology and the social sciences in the middle of the last century. Faulkner et al. (2006) updated this earlier list and identified six major clusters of definitions. The first cluster focuses on structural or pattern definitions, typically referring to culture as a system or framework of elements (ideas, behaviors, or symbols). In line with this cluster, within psychology culture is often defined as the "totality of equivalent and complementary learned meanings" (Rohner, 1984, pp. 119–120). These definitions are also central for much research in management and business research. A second cluster focuses on functions, that is origins of culture and cultural differences; a line which has attracted more research with development of cultural evolution as a separate area of academic research. A third cluster focuses on process: the social construction of culture and how culture influences social and psychological processes. Again, work in psychology that focuses on the social transmission of culture, including learning and socialization (e.g. Rohner, 1984) are good examples. A fourth cluster considers culture in terms of products and the artefacts produced by cultural processes. This is close to the original definitions by Tylor and such material approaches have had some influence on the international marketing literature. A fifth cluster defines culture in terms of refinement or "cultivation", drawing upon a more French civilization approach to culture (Kuper, 2000). A final cluster defines culture in terms of power and ideologies, which has been fundamental for critical and postmodern definitions of dominance and fragmentation. These definitions have influenced some of the critiques of Hofstede's work and we will outline some applications of this thinking within an international management research (see Peterson et al., 2018). There is no consensus in the literature, and we need to pay attention to the specific definitions of cultures that authors are using when reviewing the multilevel structure of culture. Nevertheless, we will be more strongly influenced by research that has drawn on the first three clusters (structure/pattern, process, function), but will draw on other approaches where necessary (see Fischer, 2017 for a more detailed discussion).

The most common approach within management research has been to focus on shared values (Taras et al., 2016). Members of a given group (society, culture, team, etc.) are socialized into the system and by doing so internalize group-specific values, which are therefore shared within groups and can be used to differentiate between groups. The downstream effects of such shared values are then reflected in the behaviors of that group, which can be characteristic of a given society (Leung & Morris, 2015) or may lead to or be associated with the artefacts created by members of that cultural community. The most central and important study in this regard is Hofstede's (1980, 2001) seminal value study of IBM. Here, he used an HR value survey distributed to employees in 53 countries and regions and identified four major dimensions. First, individualism versus collectivism is the degree to which people in a given country act as individuals and are giving priority to their own interest, vs an orientation to act as members of the group and giving priority to the interests of the group over those of the individual (for recent updates on this dimension, see Minkov et al., 2017). Second, power distance was closely aligned with individualism vs collectivism and deals with the levels of authority, the degree to which power is unequally distributed within a specific group and members of the group accept any unequal distribution of power and status. Third, the dimension of uncertainty avoidance captures differences in the degree to which members of different groups feel threatened by unknown or ambiguous situations and opt for more structured situations. Finally, masculinity and femininity capture the degree to which groups value assertiveness, competitiveness and achievement of goals over interpersonal relationships and care for others. This dimension also includes references to the genderedness of occupational roles according to traditional gender stereotypes. Hofstede (2001) later updated this framework by adding a fifth dimension, which emerged through work on Chinese cultural values (Hofstede & Bond, 1988), that differentiated the emphasis on the past and/or the present compared to an orientation to the future. Using broader datasets beyond a single corporation, Hofstede et al. (2010) added a sixth dimension, differentiating an emphasis on indulgence (valuing free gratification of desires and following impulses to enjoy life and have fun) versus restraint (valuing the suppression of needs and regulation behavior through social prohibitions) (Minkov, 2018; for a validation with independent data see Minkov et al., 2019).

This study has inspired a large number of additional multicultural collaborations that have sought to identify salient value dimensions. Schwartz (1992) developed structural theories of values, separating individual level (Schwartz, 1992; Schwartz et al., 2012) and culture level theories (Schwartz, 1994). At the individual level, Schwartz identified between ten and 19 value types that can be organized into four higher-order value orientations which vary along two major motivational axes: Conservation vs. Openness and Self-Transcendence vs Self-Enhancement. At the nation level, Schwartz differentiated these values using slightly different terminology (e.g., Conservation becomes Embeddedness; Openness becomes Autonomy) and splits these major dimensions slightly differently (e.g., separating self-enhancement into a hierarchy and mastery component). Although conceptually distinct, empirically these value structures tend to be highly similar and lead to similar empirical relationships (Fischer, 2013; Fischer & Poortinga, 2012).

A project that more directly followed Hofstede's dimensions, the GLOBE (Global Leadership and Organizational Behavior Effectiveness) project led by House et al. (2004) collected data with managers from 62 nations and differentiated values into nine dimensions, instead of the four (or later five) originally described by Hofstede. For example, individualism–collectivism was split into institutional collectivism characterized by the adoption of values and practices that emphasize collective action and distribution of resources, and in-group collectivism which captures the expression of loyalty and cohesion among individuals of specific smaller groups, such as, for example, the family or the organization. Power distance, future orientation (Hofstede's long-term orientation) and uncertainty avoidance remained as distinct dimensions, but new dimensions such as performance orientation (degree to which society encourages excellence in performance) and humane orientation (extent to which society reinforces altruism and care for others) were also added. Although the studies by Hofstede (1980, 2001), Schwartz and Boehnke (2004) and House et al. (2004) have used different items and terms to identify possible cultural dimensions, the overall pattern suggests relatively close resemblance of a number of core value dimensions that can be repeatedly identified in large-scale survey studies.

The Globe project is important for another aspect. House and colleagues differentiated between what is important for individuals (values, measured as "how things should be") and practices (conceptually similar to the concept of norms; measured as "how things are"). They found that values and practices do not necessarily converge, which reinvigorated work on cultural norms as an alternative conceptual framework for the study of national culture (Chiu et al., 2010; Leung & Morris, 2015; Morris et al., 2015).

Organizational culture is set between these two extremes at the individual vs nation level. The term culture was incorporated into the organizational literature in the 1970s by Pettigrew (1979) who focused on expressions such as "cooperative culture" or "organizational culture". Inspired by anthropological work, the early research was qualitative in nature, and quantitative approaches suffered from methodological and statistical ambiguities (see below). A separate line of research started focusing on properties of work groups under the umbrella term of organizational climate (see Ashkanasy et al., 2010). Organizational culture and climate overlap substantially at a conceptual level (Verbeke et al., 1998). Like definitions of culture reviewed above, both climate and culture include attitudes, beliefs, values and behaviors that characterize organizations and teams within organizations and differentiate them from other organizations and teams. In the last two decades, climate researchers returned to focus more on perceptions within teams (Anderson & West, 1998), whereas culture researchers focus on perceptions of the larger organization. Here, we focus more on this latter organizational culture work, specifically studies that have used a quantitative measurement perspective to capture visible characteristics of the organization that respondents can reflect and report on (see Ashkanasy et al., 2000, 2010; Fischer et al., 2005). A key distinction has been between values and practices, similar to the distinctions that have been drawn recently between values and norms at the nation level. Organizational practices are influenced by the organization's internal and external environment (Verbeke, 2000), and therefore thought to be more flexible and be changed with more ease compared to values that are more difficult to modify.

Among the various organizational culture measures developed over the years, two have been used more frequently in international research. What is notable in this respect is that organizational culture measures are often empirically driven and any factor structures described in one study often do not replicate, especially when examined in different cultural contexts (Sarros et al., 2016). Cameron and Quinn (2011) developed the Competing Values Framework differentiating (a) flexibility versus stability and (b) internal versus external focus that has been implemented in various instruments such as the FOCUS questionnaire (Muijen and et al., 1999). This framework in combination with an open systems approach (Katz & Kahn, 1978) inspired our group to develop an organizational practices survey that captures major conflicts that organizations have to navigate and resolve (focused around the amount of support to provide for employees, the regulation of norms and hierarchies and the extent to which innovation is important or not). This systems-based framework has been shown to be empirically valid and useful for measuring organizational culture in organizations from all inhabited continents (Fischer et al., 2014, 2019). The second major project is the afore-mentioned GLOBE project which measured organizational culture perceptions across 65 societies (House et al., 2004), using both values and practices at the organizational level that are matched to dimensions of national culture (therefore, it is different in its conceptualization and ontological nature to most other organizational culture measures). The converging lines of research on values and norms indicate that cultural variables can predict individual level work outcomes, but these relationships are dependent on interactions with variables at multiple levels. When taking this approach, one is immediately confronted with a range of conceptual as well as operational issues. We focus on these in the next section.

CONCEPTUAL AND METHODOLOGICAL CHALLENGES

Researchers need to work through a series of conceptual and methodological questions, when trying to explore cultural dynamics in organizations. The three basic issues of multilevel modeling are: (a) What is the appropriate level of a theory (and data) – do we want to draw conclusions about the behavior of individuals, teams, organizations or nations?; (b) what is the meaning of a construct at a given level and do meanings change as we move from one level to the next? (for example, do values of an individual capture the same motivational content as the values of a team?); and (c) how are constructs linked across levels – do organizational structures influence and constrain actions of individuals or do the actions of individuals constitute and construct the culture of an organization?

IDENTIFYING THE APPROPRIATE LEVEL OF THEORY AND DATA

The first step is the identification of whether generalizations are to be made about individuals, teams, organizations or nations, that is, defining the appropriate level of the study (Fischer et al., 2005; Klein et al., 1994). This question seems rather straightforward, yet there can be great ambiguities about the appropriate level of a theory and study. Constructs such as justice perceptions, self-efficacy or affect were developed at the individual level, but researchers have demonstrated these constructs can also be used at higher levels; for example by focusing on justice climate (Colquitt et al., 2002), group efficacy (Bandura, 1997), or group affect (George, 1990). Klein et al. (1994) described three alternative assumptions underlying any theoretical model: *homogeneity, independence*, and *heterogeneity*.

Homogeneity assumes that "group members are sufficiently similar with respect to the construct in question that they may be characterized as a whole" (Klein et al., 1994, p. 199), hence, variability within units is seen as error. This is one of the central assumptions of many of the culture definitions that we examined above. The second assumption is *independence*, in which individuals within work groups are seen as independent or free of group influence. This assumption underlies many statistical tests (e.g., individual scores are independent from each other). Here, the only true variation is between individuals (e.g., individual differences). The third assumption is called *heterogeneity, "frog-pond", within-group* or *parts effect* (e.g. Dansereau et al., 1984), capturing social comparison processes. The context is important here, with any observation being dependent on the respective score of the surrounding unit: the same frog appears small in a big pond, but large if the pond was small. In an organizational perspective, many phenomena related to working relationships or motivation follow this assumption, with individuals varying within a group which provides the contextual anchor, but variations between groups not being a key focus.

These assumptions feed directly into the measurement process. Chan (1998) described composition models which "specify the functional relationship among phenomena or constructs at different levels of analysis ... that reference essentially the same content but that are qualitatively different at different levels" (p. 234). These composition models help to distinguish whether a construct is supposed to capture differences between individuals or whether the construct is referencing collective constructs, that emerge through the interactions between multiple individuals (Morgeson & Hofmann, 1999). The properties and origins of the model are more fully described elsewhere (Chen & Bliese, 2005, Fischer, 2008; Hofmann & Jones, 2005). Here we only describe one individual and collective composition model, to demonstrate how they differ. One individual level composition model is the *summary index model* which describes groups through the simple aggregation of individual level data. For example, we could ask individuals about their personal values and then compute the average value score for all individuals in a specific unit. This is the classic approach that was used by Hofstede and Schwartz. Hofmann and Jones (2005) argue that the summary index model provides information on the mean or sum of a construct for a collection of *individuals*, but does not provide any meaningful information about the collective (work group in our example) and are best interpreted as the central tendency of individuals.

Collective constructs can be measured at the individual level, but it is important to rephrase the wording to capture collective phenomena. One classic example is the *Referent-shift model* which was developed in climate research (Chan, 1998) to avoid conceptual confusions between individual (psychological) and organizational (collective) climate. Individuals are asked to answer items focusing on the higher-level unit of investigation (work group or organization) and the referent for questions is changed from "I" to "we" or "this group". Hence, a value item would look like "In this work group, people value power". If there is agreement between individuals about each statement, it is possible to deduce collective level properties. Therefore, the distinction is that (a) researchers ask individuals about their perceptions of the higher unit (instead of self-reports) and (b) then the agreement of respondents is evaluated. As should be apparent, referent-shift models are similar to summary-index models in that both require reports of individuals, but differ in that summary-index models measure self-reports of individuals about their own characteristics, attitudes, abilities or values instead of perceptions of the larger unit and agreement between members of a unit is not evaluated.

Assessment of agreement is central for evaluating collective constructs such as culture, be it organization or national culture. Much of the debate has centered on what indices are best to use for assessing agreement and what empirical cut-offs are sufficient for indicating agreement. The most widely used index of agreement is r_{wg}, developed by James et al. (1984, 1993), which provides a single 0 to 1 score for each unit which is based on the variance of responses within units. Brown and Hauenstein (2005) summarized a number of shortcomings of this classic indicator and proposed an alternative measure a_{wg}, which varies between −1 and 1. A value of 1 means perfect agreement, a value of −1 indicates perfect disagreement and a value of 0 indicates that the variability is 50 percent of the possible variance at the mean. There have been heuristics about possible interpretations of cut-off values, but there has been relatively little empirical work to evaluate these cut-offs.

A second class of indicators are variations of intra-class correlations (ICC) (Shrout & Fleiss, 1979). The two most commonly used types are ICC(1) and ICC(2). ICC(1) is conceptually similar to a random one-way analysis of variance and provides an estimate of the proportion of the total variance of a measure that is explained by unit membership and can be (Bliese, 2000) interpreted as the extent of rater interchangeability (James, 1982). In contrast, ICC(2) is interpreted as the reliability of group means within a sample. ICC(2) is a variant of ICC(1) by adjusting ICC(1) for group size (Bliese, 2000). It shares similar shortcomings to other measures of reliability (e.g., Cronbach's alpha) in that it is dependent on the group size.

One important difference between agreement statistics such as r_{wg} or a_{wg} from ICC indices is that the former provide estimates of agreement within each group separately (yielding one unique estimate for each group), whereas ICC statistics compare the variability within groups to the variability between groups (yielding one estimate across all groups). ICC estimates do not provide estimates of whether interrater agreement varies substantially between groups. The extent to which individuals agree with each other is one important conceptual variable in organizational culture, as it captures culture strength (Lindell & Brandt, 2000; Schneider et al., 2002).

One important question for identifying the relevant level of theory is to consider whether units are important and meaningful. While organizations present clearly outlined units of measurement such as companies or departments, the measurement of national culture is less straightforward. Commonly, researchers have equated culture with nationality or ethnicity, based on the assumptions that geographic boundaries of nation states reflect cultural boundaries, and in line with definitions of culture, that cultural characteristics are equally shared amongst members of a nation state (Leung & Morris, 2015; Steel & Taras, 2010; Taras et al., 2009). The assumption that national culture is homogenous is increasingly challenged. For example, Fischer and Schwartz (2011) used agreement statistics that we reviewed above for various value data sets and found that up to 80 percent of variance in values might be due to individual differences rather than county differences. Similarly, Taras et al. (2016) found in a meta-analysis of 558 studies that while nation-state differences explained only 21 percent in variance of values, occupational differences explained up to 50 percent. This is not to say that nation states do not have value as units of investigation. Minkov and Hofstede (2011, 2014) reported that nation states are better empirical boundaries for classifying cultural orientations of individuals compared to ethnic or religious affiliation in modern Europe.

The extent to which nation states are meaningful units for cultural analysis has been extensively debated. Trying to provide a framework to this discussion, Peterson and colleagues (Peterson et al., 2018; Peterson & Søndergaard, 2014) proposed the FICE framework, which stands for functionalist, institutional, and critical events. Functional explanations for cultural differences align strongly with classic evolutionary theories (for a review see Lench et al., 2015), proposing that communities are facing a range of challenges that threaten their survival and that dominant solutions aimed at resolving these challenges can be captured in the dominant values or norms expressed by individuals within nation states (both via summary and referent shift models). Institutional explanations centre around the role of governing institutions and their physical (roads, urban planning), and non-physical influences (shared language, and educational policies) on social behavior. Finally, critical event theories focus on the lasting effects of singular events such as wars, plagues, or substantial economic changes and how they change psychological and social attributes of populations within the boundaries of nation states. In summary, the FICE framework integrates a range of possible processes that provide a theoretical foundation for the use of nation states as units of investigation as well as explanations of how cultural differences occur and are maintained (Figure 5.1).

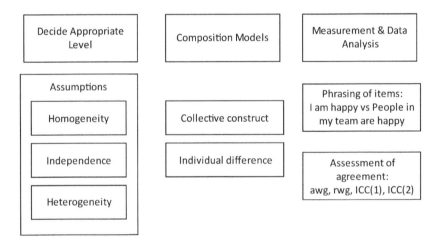

Figure 5.1   *Major questions for identifying and measuring constructs at the appropriate level*

ASSESSING MEANING CHANGES ACROSS LEVELS

One of the most perplexing questions has been how to interpret constructs that exist at more than one level. The common approach to empirically examine this question has been to conduct factor analysis (or other reduction techniques) with data at each level. Hofstede (1980) first clearly demonstrated the possibility to a larger audience that the factor structures at the individual and national level can be different, which has led to strong interest by cross-cultural researchers (for a more detailed description see Boer et al., 2018; Fischer, 2012, 2013; Fontaine and Fischer, 2011). The development of sophisticated multivariate statistics has simplified a previously complex analytical procedure and it is now possible to simultaneously estimate individual and group level structures and obtain overall indices of similarity and model fit (Fischer & Karl, 2019; Fontaine & Fischer, 2011; Huang, 2017). In summary, the question of changes in meaning of constructs across levels is contentious, but can readily be addressed through modern multivariate statistics.

RELATIONSHIP BETWEEN DIFFERENT CONSTRUCTS ACROSS LEVELS

Researchers are most interested in this last question, namely the relationship between constructs at different levels. We can distinguish three broad types of models: single-level models, cross-level models and homologous multi-level models (Kozlowski & Klein, 2000; Figure 5.2). Single-level models are the most common models because they describe relationships between variables at the same level of theory. Psychologists, for example, typically are interested in how individual difference variables relate to each other. Cross-level models are considerably more complex since they conceptualize relationships between variables across different levels. Organizational researchers are most familiar with top-down approaches that model effects of higher-level variables on lower-level variables (e.g., organizational culture influencing employee job satisfaction or performance). These models can be estimated with standard multilevel analytical techniques and are increasingly common. The alternative process of emergent or bottom-up processes is equally plausible, but empirically more challenging because they are methodologically more complex (Kozlowski & Klein, 2000). Some interesting recent applications have been published in management (Heyden et al., 2017) and medicine (Wigman et al., 2015). Heyden et al. (2017) examined 'top-down' and 'bottom-up' traditions in organizational change research to understand employees' varying dispositions to support change. Wigman and colleagues focused on psychopathology and investigated top-down and bottom-up to understand how individuals and diagnostic groups dynamically affect each other.

CONVERGENCE AND CONFLICT: PROCESSES ALIGNING AND OPPOSING INDIVIDUALS, ORGANIZATIONS AND CULTURES

Individuals are nested in organizations and organizations operate within societies and nation states. Hence, the respective relationships between processes at these three levels are of considerable interest for management researchers. A classic line of research highlights the contingency of the effectiveness of management strategies on the environmental and cultural context of an organization (Adler & Gundersen, 2008). The general assumption is that organizations show higher performance if the organizational practices match the cultural preferences of the local workforce (Hofstede, 1980, 2001). Understanding and acting on the fit between different levels (for example between the individual and the organization) is clearly important (Gelfand et al., 2007).

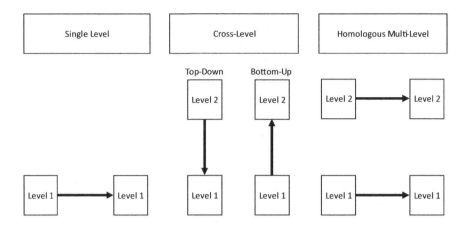

Figure 5.2   *Three classes of multi-level theories*

Individual actors are thought to coordinate their actions which give raise to larger-scale units which are more than the sum of their parts (Gao et al., 2015), a classic emergence phenomenon that we discussed above. The current general recommendation is for global managers to fit their management strategies to the local context (e.g. Berry, 2014). A considerable body of research highlights the contingency of the effectiveness of management strategies on the environmental and cultural context of an organization (Adler & Gundersen, 2008; Gelfand et al., 2007; Tsui et al., 2016). Organizations are thought to elicit higher performance if the organizational practices match the cultural preferences of the local workforce (Adler & Gundersen, 2008; Hofstede, 1980, 2001) and the technological environment (Ellis et al., 2002). These assumptions are shared by diverse meta-theories such as the structural contingency approach (Burns & Stalker, 1994) and culture fit theory (Aycan, 2005; Aycan et al., 2000). These broad contingency approaches have become a dominant management strategy that underlies much of strategic management and international business (Hoskisson et al., 1999).

Basic evolutionary processes can help to explain how organizational multi-level processes operate over time and lead to the emergence of shared cultures aligned with contingency approaches. Individuals aim to learn about relevant group norms and try to adopt successful behavior. For effective learning, they need to identify a variety of reliable sources to inform their behaviors. Yet, individuals focus on easily available information, which leads to commonly described *frequency biases* and *prestige biases*. Frequency bias is the tendency of individuals to preferentially copy the most common behavior variants in an environment (Boyd & Richerson, 1985; Henrich & Boyd, 1998). This tendency to utilize already widespread cultural information (such as norms and behaviors) within a group can help to facilitate knowledge transfer between members and typically leads to culturally shared knowledge to be more likely to be reproduced during interactions with other group members. Conversely, culturally novel knowledge is less likely to be passed on (possibly because utilizing new knowledge is less cognitively effective: Clark & Kashima, 2007). Over time this bias towards widespread knowledge leads to the stabilization of cultural knowledge within a group. A strong body of knowledge and shared norms might increase group cohesion, but this also reduces the probability that group members hold novel information that could benefit the group. In cases where novel information is needed, for example in a rapidly changing environment, the likelihood increases that new knowledge will be incorporated in the communal knowledge pool, potentially at the cost of cohesion (Stahl et al., 2010). In addition to this social learning strategy, individuals can also orient their behavior and values on successful individuals with high prestige. This mode of social information transmissions is called prestige bias and has been found to be associated with power positions of the person being copied rather than with domain knowledge (Reyes-Garcia et al., 2008). These learning processes can happen at all levels of the organizational hierarchy. Highly visible individuals such as organizational leaders are core and can be assumed to work as a selection pressure towards individuals that fail to utilize these learning strategies, resulting in person–culture mismatch.

EVOLUTIONARY AND DYNAMIC APPROACHES TO CULTURE AND ORGANIZATIONS

However, a core assumption that individuals and organizations are naturally aligned clashes with the reality of cultures as open systems (Bertalanffy, 1969). In an organizational context, individuals are neither permanently tied to an organization, nor are organizations constants, as they experience rapid large-scale shifts such as mergers or restructuring approaches. Social learning and reinforcement of norms within organizations is also not perfect and leads to considerable deviations within groups (which requires the assessment of agreement, as discussed above). Recently this complex systems dynamic has been examined from evolutionary perspectives to identify drivers that either align different levels of an organizational structure or set them up for competition (Kashima et al., 2019).

BEYOND CULTURE FIT

Examining cultural processes across multiple levels (individual to organization to country) simultaneously has started to provide new insights that confirm that broad contingency and culture fit approaches may be too simplistic to capture some of the dynamics that modern organizations are facing. Our team conducted a 17-country study involving 267 organizations (Fischer et al., 2019). Our focus was on certainty because certainty is an epistemic need of humans and dealing with uncertainty will take up crucial cognitive resources. Our human ancestors have evolved in specific evolutionary environments that shaped our cognitive systems in specific ways, prioritizing safety and security in our immediate environments and focusing our attention to immediate threats of survival and uncertainty. Because of these cognitive limitations, when faced with contexts of increased uncertainty, employees use available cognitive resources to cope with the perceived uncertainty to regain a sense of control, and therefore, they are unlikely to engage in discretionary or high-performance behaviors that would require additional cognitive demands. As a consequence, desirable behavior such as organizational citizenship behavior (Kenrick et al., 2010) is likely to be reduced.

Contingency and culture fit theory predict that organizations in high uncertainty contexts are better off to adopt practices and change their organizational culture to match this high level of uncertainty. From an evolutionary perspective, a different hypothesis could be proposed. In highly uncertain environments, organizational formalization can compensate and buffer any negative effects of uncertainty by providing structure and clarity and as a result reduce the needs of employees to expend cognitive resources on coping with uncertainty. Bringing in ideas from norm psychology, clear rules and procedures allow employees to use their perceptions of these clear rules as a form of "social autopilot" (in the form of "I know what is expected of me because I see what others are doing and how the organization runs") (Morris et al., 2015). In contrast to culture-fit arguments, organizations can actively counter contextual effects by increasing formalization which in turn facilitates higher levels of OCB in countries with high uncertainty. These hypotheses were supported in a three-level analysis involving perceptions of national culture practices and organizational culture perceptions across samples from all inhabited continents. Discretionary extra-role behavior focusing on making suggestions and improving work conditions increased with organizational formalization, but this effect was only observed in contexts with high uncertainty (Fischer et al., 2019). Hence, culture-fit arguments might be too simplistic when accounting for the complex realities that organizations are facing. Evolutionary models can help identify which behaviors and cognitive processes are most likely to be affected. Greater nuance and attention to cognitive capacities and constraints within specific contexts and organizations may help employees achieve their full potential. Hence, a greater integration of evolutionary, biological and philosophical discussions of group dynamics can help us sharpen our understanding how organizational culture processes are operating in modern organizations.

REFERENCES

Adler, N. J., & Gundersen, A. (2008). *International Dimensions of Organizational Behavior*. Thomson/ South-Western.

Anderson, N. R., & West, M. A. (1998). Measuring climate for work group innovation: Development and validation of the team climate inventory. *Journal of Organizational Behavior, 19*(3), 235–258.

Ashkanasy, N. M., Broadfoot, L. E., & Falkus, S. (2000). Questionnaire measures of organizational culture. In N. M. Ashkanasy, C. Wilderom, & M. F. Peterson (Eds.), *The Handbook of Organizational Culture and Climate* (pp. 131–146). Newbury Park, CA: SAGE Publications, Inc.

Ashkanasy, N. M., Wilderom, C. P. M., & Peterson, M. F. (Eds.) (2010). *The Handbook of Organizational Culture and Climate* (Second Edition). Newbury Park, CA: SAGE Publications, Inc.

Aycan, Z. (2005). The interplay between cultural and institutional/structural contingencies in human resource management practices. *International Journal of Human Resource Management, 16*(7), 1083–1119. https://doi.org/10.1080/09585190500143956

Aycan, Z., Kanungo, R. N., Mendonca, M., Yu, K., Deller, J., Stahl, G., & Kurshid, A. (2000). Impact of culture on human resource management practices: A 10-country comparison. *Applied Psychology: An International Review, 49*(1), 192–221. https://doi.org/10.1111/1464-0597.00010

Bandura, A. (1997). *Self-efficacy: The Exercise of Control*. W. H. Freeman/Times Books/ Henry Holt & Co.

Berry, H. (2014). Global integration and innovation: Multicountry knowledge generation within MNCs. *Strategic Management Journal, 35*(6), 869–890. https://doi.org/10.1002/smj.2140

Bertalanffy, L. V. (1969). *General System Theory: Foundations, Development, Applications* (Revised Edition). George Braziller Inc.

Bliese, P. D. (2000). Within-group agreement, non-independence, and reliability: Implications for data aggregation and analysis. In K. J. Klein, & S. W. J. Kozlowski (Eds.), *Multilevel Theory, Research, and Methods in Organizations: Foundations, Extensions, and New Directions* (pp. 349–381). Jossey-Bass.

Boer, D., Hanke, K., & He, J. (2018). On detecting systematic measurement error in cross-cultural research: A review and critical reflection on equivalence and invariance tests. *Journal of Cross-Cultural Psychology, 49*, 713–734. doi:10.1177/0022022117749042

Boyd, R., & Richerson, P. J. (1985). *Culture and the Evolutionary Process*. University of Chicago Press.

Brown, R. D., & Hauenstein, N. M. A. (2005). Interrater agreement reconsidered: An alternative to the rwg indices: *Organizational Research Methods, 8*(2), 165–184. https://doi.org/10.1177/1094428105275376

Burns, T., & Stalker, G. M. (1994). *The Management of Innovation* (Revised Edition). New York: Oxford University Press.

Cameron, K. S., & Quinn, R. E. (2011). *Diagnosing and Changing Organizational Culture: Based on the Competing Values Framework* (Third Edition). Jossey-Bass.

Chan, D. (1998). Functional relations among constructs in the same content domain at different levels of analysis: A typology of composition models. *Journal of Applied Psychology, 83*(2), 234–246. https://doi.org/10.1037/0021-9010.83.2.234

Chen, G., & Bliese, P. D. (2005). Conceptual framework and statistical procedures for delineating and testing multilevel theories of homology. *Academy of Management Proceedings, 2005*(1), A1–A6. https://doi.org/10.5465/ambpp.2005.18783405

Chiu, C.-Y., Gelfand, M. J., Yamagishi, T., Shteynberg, G., & Wan, C. (2010). Intersubjective culture: The role of intersubjective perceptions in cross-cultural research. *Perspectives on Psychological Science, 5*(4), 482–493. https://doi.org/10.1177/1745691610375562

Clark, A. E., & Kashima, Y. (2007). Stereotypes help people connect with others in the community: A situated functional analysis of the stereotype consistency bias in communication. *Journal of Personality and Social Psychology, 93*(6), 1028–1039. https://doi.org/10.1037/0022-3514.93.6.1028

Colquitt, J. A., Noe, R. A., & Jackson, C. L. (2002). Justice in teams: Antecedents and consequences of procedural justice climate. *Personnel Psychology, 55*(1), 83–109. https://doi.org/10.1111/j.1744-6570.2002.tb00104.x

Dansereau, F., Alutto, J. A., & Yammarino, F. J. (1984). *Theory Testing in Organizational Behaviour: The Varient Approach* (First Edition). Prentice Hall.

Ellis, S., Almor, T., & Shenkar, O. (2002). Structural contingency revisited: Toward a dynamic system model. *Emergence, 4*(4), 51–85. https://doi.org/10.1207/S15327000EM0404_6

Faulkner, S. L., Baldwin, J. R., Lindsley, S. L., & Hecht, M. L. (2006). Layers of meaning: An analysis of definitions of culture. In J. R. Baldwin, S. L. Faulkner, M. L. Hecht, & S. L. Lindsley (Eds.), *Redefining Culture: Perspectives Across the Disciplines* (pp. 27–52). Mahwah, NJ: Lawrence Erlbaum Associates Publishers.

Fischer, R. (2008). Multilevel approaches in organizational settings: Opportunities, challenges and implications for cross-cultural research. In F. van de Vijver, D. van Hemert, & Y. Poortinga (Eds.), *Individuals and Cultures in Multi-level Analysis* (pp. 173–196). Mahwah, NJ: Lawrence Erlbaum Associates.

Fischer, R. (2012). Value isomorphism in the European Social Survey: Exploration of meaning shifts in values across levels. *Journal of Cross-Cultural Psychology, 43*, 883–898. https://doi.org/10.1177/0022022111413276

Fischer, R. (2013). What values can (and cannot) tell us about individuals, society and culture. *Advances in Culture and Psychology, 4*, 218–272.

Fischer, R. (2017). *Personality, Values, Culture: An Evolutionary Perspective*. Cambridge University Press.

Fischer, R., & Karl, J. A. (2019). A primer to (cross-cultural) multi-group invariance testing possibilities in R. *Frontiers in Psychology, 10*. https://doi.org/10.3389/fpsyg.2019.01507

Fischer, R., & Poortinga, Y. H. (2012). Are cultural values the same as the values of individuals? An examination of similarities in personal, social and cultural value structures. *International Journal of Cross Cultural Management, 12*(2), 157–170. https://doi.org/10.1177/1470595812439867

Fischer, R., & Schwartz, S. (2011). Whence differences in value priorities? Individual, cultural, or artifactual sources. *Journal of Cross-Cultural Psychology, 42*(7), 1127–1144. https://doi.org/10.1177/0022022110381429

Fischer, R., Ferreira, M. C., Assmar, E., Baris, G., Berboroglu, G., Dalyan, F., Wong, C.C., Hassan, A., Hanke, K., Boer, D. (2014). Organizational practices across cultures: An exploration in six cultural contexts. *International Journal of Cross-Cultural Management, 14*, 105-125. https://doi.org/10.1177/1470595813510644

Fischer, R., Ferreira, M. C., Maria, E., Assmar, L., Redford, P., & Harb, C. (2005). Organizational behaviour across cultures: Theoretical and methodological issues for developing multi-level frameworks involving culture. *CCM International Journal of Cross Cultural Management, 5*(1), 27–48. https://doi.org/10.1177/1470595805050823

Fischer, R., Ferreira, M. C., Van Meurs, N., Gok, K., Jiang, D.-Y., Fontaine, J. R. J., Harb, C., Cieciuch, J., Achoui, M., Mendoza, M. S. D., Hassan, A., Achmadi, D., Mogaji, A. A., & Abubakar, A. (2019). Does organizational formalization facilitate voice and helping organizational citizenship behaviors? It depends on (national) uncertainty norms. *Journal of International Business Studies, 50*(1), 125–134. https://doi.org/10.1057/s41267-017-0132-6

Fontaine, J. R. J., & Fischer, R. (2011). Data analytic approaches for investigating isomorphism between the individual-level and the cultural-level internal structure. In D. Matsumoto (Ed.), *Cross-Cultural Research Methods in Psychology* (pp. 273–298). Cambridge University Press.

Gao, W., Qiu, L., Chiu, C., & Yang, Y. (2015). Diffusion of opinions in a complex culture system: Implications for emergence of descriptive norms. *Journal of Cross-Cultural Psychology, 46*(10), 1252–1259. https://doi.org/10.1177/0022022115610212

Gelfand, M. J., Erez, M., & Aycan, Z. (2007). Cross-cultural organizational behavior. *Annual Review of Psychology, 58*(1), 479–514. https://doi.org/10.1146/annurev.psych.58.110405.085559

George, J. M. (1990). Personality, affect, and behavior in groups. *Journal of Applied Psychology, 75*(2), 107–116. https://doi.org/10.1037/0021-9010.75.2.107

Henrich, J., & Boyd, R. (1998). The evolution of conformist transmission and the emergence of between-group differences. *Evolution and Human Behavior, 19*(4), 215–241. https://doi.org/10.1016/S1090-5138(98)00018-X

Heyden, M. L. M., Fourné, S. P. L., Koene, B. A. S., Werkman, R., & Ansari, S. (Shaz) (2017). Rethinking "top-down" and "bottom-up" roles of top and middle managers in organizational change: implications for employee support. *Journal of Management Studies, 54*(7), 961–985. https://doi.org/10.1111/joms.12258

Hofmann, D. A., & Jones, L. M. (2005). Leadership, collective personality, and performance. *Journal of Applied Psychology, 90*(3), 509–522. https://doi.org/10.1037/0021-9010.90.3.509

Hofstede, G. (1980). *Culture's Consequences: International Differences in Work-Related Values*. SAGE Publications.

Hofstede, G. (2001). *Culture's Consequences: Comparing Values, Behaviors, Institutions and Organizations Across Nations*. SAGE Publications.

Hofstede, G., & Bond, M. H. (1988). The Confucius connection: From cultural roots to economic growth. *Organizational Dynamics, 16*(4), 5–21. https://doi.org/10.1016/0090-2616(88)90009-5

Hofstede, G., Hofstede, G. J., & Minkov, M. (2010). *Cultures and Organizations: Software of the Mind, Third Edition*. McGraw Hill Professional.

Hoskisson, R. E., Wan, W. P., Yiu, D., & Hitt, M. A. (1999). Theory and research in strategic management: Swings of a pendulum. *Journal of Management, 25*(3), 417–456. https://doi.org/10.1016/S0149-2063(99)00008-2

House, R. J., Hanges, P. J., Javidan, M., Dorfman, P. W., & Gupta, V. (Eds.) (2004). *Culture, Leadership, and Organizations: The GLOBE Study of 62 Societies* (First Edition). SAGE Publications, Inc.

Huang, F. L. (2017). Conducting multilevel confirmatory factor analysis using R. Unpublished. https://doi.org/10.13140/rg.2.2.12391.34724

James, L. R. (1982). Aggregation bias in estimates of perceptual agreement. *Journal of Applied Psychology, 67*(2), 219–229. https://doi.org/10.1037/0021-9010.67.2.219

James, L. R., Demaree, R. G., & Wolf, G. (1984). Estimating within-group interrater reliability with and without response bias. *Journal of Applied Psychology, 69*(1), 85–98. https://doi.org/10.1037/0021-9010.69.1.85

James, L. R., Demaree, R. G., & Wolf, G. (1993). rwg: An assessment of within-group interrater agreement. *Journal of Applied Psychology, 78*(2), 306–309. https://doi.org/10.1037/0021-9010.78.2.306

Kashima, Y., Bain, P. G., & Perfors, A. (2019). The psychology of cultural dynamics: What is it, what do we know, and what is yet to be known? *Annual Review of Psychology, 70*(1), 499–529. https://doi .org/10.1146/annurev-psych-010418-103112

Katz, D., & Kahn, R. L. (1978). *The Social Psychology of Organizations* (Second Edition). Wiley.

Kenrick, D. T., Griskevicius, V., Neuberg, S. L., & Schaller, M. (2010). Renovating the pyramid of needs: Contemporary extensions built upon ancient foundations. *Perspectives on Psychological Science : A Journal of the Association for Psychological Science, 5*(3), 292–314. https://doi.org/10 .1177/1745691610369469

Klein, K. J., Dansereau, F., & Hall, R. J. (1994). Levels issues in theory development, data collection, and analysis. *Academy of Management Review, 19*(2), 195–229. JSTOR. https://doi.org/10.2307/258703

Kozlowski, S. W. J., & Klein, K. J. (2000). A multilevel approach to theory and research in organizations: Contextual, temporal, and emergent processes. In K. Klein, & S. W. J. Kozlowski (Eds.), *Multilevel Theory, Research, and Methods in Organizations: Foundations, Extensions, and New Directions* (pp. 3–90). Jossey-Bass.

Kroeber, A. L., & Kluckhohn, C. (1952). Culture: A critical review of concepts and definitions. *Papers. Peabody Museum of Archaeology & Ethnology, Harvard University, 47*(1), viii, 223.

Kuper, A. (2000). *Culture: The Anthropologists' Account.* Harvard University Press.

Lench, H. C., Bench, S. W., Darbor, K. E., & Moore, M. (2015). A functionalist manifesto: Goal-related emotions from an evolutionary perspective. *Emotion Review, 7*(1), 90–98. https://doi.org/10.1177/ 1754073914553001

Leung, K., & Morris, M. W. (2015). Values, schemas, and norms in the culture–behavior nexus: A situated dynamics framework. *Journal of International Business Studies, 46*(9), 1028–1050. https://doi .org/10.1057/jibs.2014.66

Lindell, M. K., & Brandt, C. J. (2000). Climate quality and climate consensus as mediators of the relationship between organizational antecedents and outcomes. *Journal of Applied Psychology, 85*(3), 331–348. https://doi.org/10.1037/0021-9010.85.3.331

Minkov, M. (2018). A revision of Hofstede's model of national culture: Old evidence and new data from 56 countries. *Cross Cultural & Strategic Management, 25*(2), 231–256. https://doi.org/10.1108/ CCSM-03-2017-0033

Minkov, M., & Hofstede, G. (2011). Is national culture a meaningful concept? Cultural values delineate homogeneous national clusters of in-country regions. *Cross-Cultural Research, 46*(2). https://doi.org/ 10.1177/1069397111427262

Minkov, M., & Hofstede, G. (2014). Nations versus religions: Which has a stronger effect on societal values? *Management International Review, 54*(6), 801–824. https://doi.org/10.1007/s11575-014 -0205-8

Minkov, M., Dutt, P., Schachner, M., Jandosova, J., Khassenbekov, Y., Morales, O., & Blagoev, V. (2019). What would people do with their money if they were rich? A search for Hofstede dimensions across 52 countries. *Cross Cultural & Strategic Management, 26*(1), 93–116. https://doi.org/10.1108/ CCSM-11-2018-0193

Minkov, M., Dutt, P., Schachner, M., Morales, O., Sanchez, C., Jandosova, J., Khassenbekov, Y., & Mudd, B. (2017). A revision of Hofstede's individualism–collectivism dimension: A new national index from a 56-country study. *Cross Cultural & Strategic Management, 24*(3), 386–404. https://doi .org/10.1108/CCSM-11-2016-0197

Morgeson, F. P., & Hofmann, D. A. (1999). The structure and function of collective constructs: Implications for multilevel research and theory development. *Academy of Management Review, 24*(2), 249–265. JSTOR. https://doi.org/10.2307/259081

Morris, M. W., Hong, Y., Chiu, C., & Liu, Z. (2015). Normology: Integrating insights about social norms to understand cultural dynamics. *Organizational Behavior and Human Decision Processes, 129*, 1–13. https://doi.org/10.1016/j.obhdp.2015.03.001

Muijen, J. J. van, et al. (1999). Organizational culture: The Focus Questionnaire. *European Journal of Work and Organizational Psychology, 8*(4), 551–568. https://doi.org/10.1080/135943299398168

Peterson, M. F., & Søndergaard, M. (2014). Countries, within-country regions, and multiple-country regions in international management: A functional, institutional, and critical event (FICE) perspective. *Management International Review, 54*(6), 781–800. https://doi.org/10.1007/s11575-014-0228-1

Peterson, M. F., Søndergaard, M., & Kara, A. (2018). Traversing cultural boundaries in IB: The complex relationships between explicit country and implicit cultural group boundaries at multiple levels. *Journal of International Business Studies, 49*(8), 1081–1099. https://doi.org/10.1057/s41267-017 -0082-z

Pettigrew, A. M. (1979). On studying organizational cultures. *Administrative Science Quarterly, 24*(4), 570–581. JSTOR. https://doi.org/10.2307/2392363

Reyes-Garcia, V., Molina, J. L., Broesch, J., Calvet, L., Huanca, T., Saus, J., Tanner, S., Leonard, W. R., & McDade, T. W. (2008). Do the aged and knowledgeable men enjoy more prestige? A test of predictions from the prestige-bias model of cultural transmission. *Evolution and Human Behavior, 29*(4), 275–281. https://doi.org/10.1016/j.evolhumbehav.2008.02.002

Rohner, R. P. (1984). Toward a conception of culture for cross-cultural psychology. *Journal of Cross-Cultural Psychology, 15*(2). https://doi.org/10.1177/0022002184015002002

Sarros, J. C., Gray, J., Densten, I. L., & Cooper, B. (2016). The organizational culture profile revisited and revised: An Australian perspective. *Australian Journal of Management, 30*(1), 159–182. https:// doi.org/10.1177/031289620503000109

Schneider, B., Salvaggio, A. N., & Subirats, M. (2002). Climate strength: A new direction for climate research. *Journal of Applied Psychology, 87*(2), 220–229. https://doi.org/10.1037/0021-9010.87.2 .220

Schwartz, S. H. (1992). Universals in the content and structure of values: Theoretical advances and empirical tests in 20 countries. In M. P. Zanna (Ed.), *Advances in Experimental Social Psychology* (Vol. 25, pp. 1–65). Academic Press. https://doi.org/10.1016/S0065-2601(08)60281-6

Schwartz, S. H. (1994). Beyond individualism/collectivism: New cultural dimensions of values. In U. Kim, H. C. Triandis, Ç. Kâğitçibaşi, S.-C. Choi, & G. Yoon (Eds.), *Individualism and Collectivism: Theory, Method, and Applications* (pp. 85–119). SAGE Publications, Inc.

Schwartz, S. H., & Boehnke, K. (2004). Evaluating the structure of human values with confirmatory factor analysis. *Journal of Research in Personality, 38*(3), 230–255. https://doi.org/10.1016/S0092 -6566(03)00069-2

Schwartz, S. H., Cieciuch, J., Vecchione, M., Davidov, E., Fischer, R., Beierlein, C., Ramos, A., Verkasalo, M., Lönnqvist, J.-E., Demirutku, K., Dirilen-Gumus, O., & Konty, M. (2012). Refining the theory of basic individual values. *Journal of Personality and Social Psychology, 103*(4), 663–688. https://doi.org/10.1037/a0029393

Shrout, P. E., & Fleiss, J. L. (1979). Intraclass correlations: Uses in assessing rater reliability. *Psychological Bulletin, 86*(2), 420–428. https://doi.org/10.1037/0033-2909.86.2.420

Stahl, G. K., Maznevski, M. L., Voigt, A., & Jonsen, K. (2010). Unraveling the effects of cultural diversity in teams: A meta-analysis of research on multicultural work groups. *Journal of International Business Studies, 41*(4), 690–709. https://doi.org/10.1057/jibs.2009.85

Steel, P., & Taras, V. (2010). Culture as a consequence: A multi-level multivariate meta-analysis of the effects of individual and country characteristics on work-related cultural values. *Journal of International Management, 16*(3), 211–233. https://doi.org/10.1016/j.intman.2010.06.002

Taras, V., Rowney, J., & Steel, P. (2009). Half a century of measuring culture: Review of approaches, challenges, and limitations based on the analysis of 121 instruments for quantifying culture. *Journal of International Management, 15*(4), 357–373.

Taras, V., Steel, P., & Kirkman, B. L. (2016). Does country equate with culture? Beyond geography in the search for cultural boundaries. *Management International Review, 56*(4), 455–487. https://doi.org/ 10.1007/s11575-016-0283-x

Tsui, A. S., Nifadkar, S. S., & Ou, A. Y. (2016). Cross-national, cross-cultural organizational behavior research: Advances, gaps, and recommendations. *Journal of Management, 33*(3). https://doi.org/10 .1177/0149206307300818

Tylor, E. B. (2010). *Primitive Culture: Researches into the Development of Mythology, Philosophy, Religion, Art, and Custom* (Vol. 2). Cambridge University Press. https://doi.org/10.1017/ CBO9780511705960

Verbeke, W. (2000). A revision of Hofstede et al.'s (1990) organizational practices scale. *Journal of Organizational Behavior, 21*(5), 587–602. https://doi.org/10.1002/1099-1379(200008)21:53.0.CO;2 -5

Verbeke, W., Volgering, M., & Hessels, M. (1998). Exploring the conceptual expansion within the field of organizational behaviour: Organizational climate and organizational culture. *Journal of Management Studies*, *35*(3), 303–329. https://doi.org/10.1111/1467-6486.00095

Wigman, J. T. W., van Os, J., Borsboom, D., Wardenaar, K. J., Epskamp, S., Klippel, A., MERGE, Viechtbauer, W., Myin-Germeys, I., & Wichers, M. (2015). Exploring the underlying structure of mental disorders: Cross-diagnostic differences and similarities from a network perspective using both a top-down and a bottom-up approach. *Psychological Medicine*, *45*(11), 2375–2387. https://doi.org/10.1017/S0033291715000331

PART II

QUANTITATIVE AND QUALITATIVE APPROACHES

6. Values-based methods for measuring organizational culture: logic, evidence and critique

Stefano Calciolari and Anna Prenestini

INTRODUCTION

The performance of an organization depends on several objective factors. Notably, a well-known model of firms' competitive advantage highlights six relevant external factors influencing business profitability – barriers to entry, substitutability of products, buyers' and suppliers' bargaining power, market share, and rivalry among competitors (Porter, 1980). As far as internal factors are concerned, another well-cited model emphasizes the role of five primary activities – inbound logistics, operations, outbound logistics, marketing and sales, and service – linked to four support activities – procurement, technology development, human resource management, and infrastructure (Porter, 1985).

However, there are several highly successful firms (e.g. Walmart, Comcast, Netflix) that started a business in unlikely market segments (discount retailing, media distribution), based on the competitive advantage prescriptions about external factors. In addition, the extant literature increasingly supports the idea that organizational culture, an intangible though powerful internal factor, drives a firm's performance and its success (Cameron & Quinn, 2011). A very diffuse definition of the concept is: 'It's the way things are done around here' (Deal & Kennedy, 2000). Organizational culture regards the 'tacit' rules of how tasks are accomplished at the workplace and indicates how employees view their organizations – the essential meaning they associate with what basically are their workplaces, and sometimes, their essence (Schneider & Barbera, 2014: 3).

The aforementioned definition reflects the concept's broadness, rendering the attempts to assess or measure it a challenging task. Perhaps this feature relates to the origins of the concept, as it emerged from anthropology and sociology, disciplines that have long been studying culture (without the organizational specification) as a way to describe differences, especially in fundamental values, that characterize social groups (Schneider & Barbera, 2014: 4).

Organizational culture can be often defined/interpreted as the fundamental beliefs, assumptions, values, norms, myths, and symbols underlying the observable patterns of behaviours in organizations. Such patterns of behaviours and ways of interacting may change because of exogenous factors (e.g. a new incentive structure), although they are likely to be restored if such stressors are not strong or long-lasting. This is because organizational culture, despite not being easily evident, is typically stable in organizations, contrary to the partially overlapping construct of the organizational climate (Schneider & Barbera, 2014). This is a relevant managerial aspect if one considers that change management often fails because organizations are unable to modify their culture (Cameron & Quinn, 2011).

Consequently, mastering methods that help diagnose organizational culture is important as the resulting knowledge supports strategic initiatives that require changing this 'soft' factor if it is not healthy or well aligned with the organization's strategy. The diagnostic findings can support the organization to tailor and fine-tune its transition from the current patterns of behaviours to those that will underpin the defined strategic goals.

A wide range of diagnostic methods is available in the literature and no specific approach can be considered the best – a method that works well for one investigation may not be suitable for another study. Any appropriate approach depends on: (a) the specific definitions of the key elements of the assessment, that is, 'culture' and 'organization'; (b) the intended use of the results; and (c) the availability of resources. Considering these aspects might lead to unambiguously identifying a coherent 'measurement' approach.

In this chapter, we assume the notion of culture previously reported and re-elaborate the visual depiction from Schein (2017): 'learned patterns of beliefs, values, assumptions, and behavioural norms that manifest themselves at different levels of observability'. Figure 6.1 illustrates a conceptual view of the notion in terms of manifestation layers: the degree of observability decreases from the outer layers inward, and the cultural meaning of external layers lies in how they are perceived by insiders through the interpretation lenses of the (deeper) inner layers.

For the notion of organization, we consider the group of all the people included within the institutional boundaries of the legal entity, acting as juridical subject in the market. Therefore, we refer to the 'accumulated shared learning of that group' as a whole (Schein, 2017: 21).

However, the culture of an organization is not uniform across the entity – although some attributes may be found consistent throughout, other characteristics may be prevalent only in some sections of the organization. Different types of cultures (so-called 'sub-cultures') tend to emerge from sub-groups that may decide to differentiate themselves from each other using, for instance, distinct artefacts, and may be associated with different levels of power and influence. Rivalry and competition between the different cultural sub-groups are quite typical phenomena and these dynamics are also likely to change over time. Sub-cultures may be malleable, that is, easily subject to changes in their artefacts and values, or may exhibit high resistance to change, developing as 'counter cultures' (Scott et al., 2003). In this respect, Martin (2002) examined organizational cultures according to three different perspectives and classified them into:

- Integrated cultures, where a broad consensus exists on the basic values and behaviours deemed acceptable within the whole organization (a situation that seems ideal rather than actually diffused in practice).
- Differentiated cultures, where multiple groups of people within the organization have different, and at times incompatible, beliefs and values. In such circumstances, the development of sub-cultures, misunderstandings, and even conflicts are expected over time.
- Fragmented cultures, where many cultures emerge and diverge completely. The differences between sub-cultures can be more marked than the commonalities. Therefore, agreements between the groups are possible only temporarily, when all the different parties aim for specific goals. In the case of fragmented cultures, the organization is characterized by changing alliances and considerable uncertainty and ambiguity.

Finally, resource availability is an aspect to be considered in the research design. The important factors in this respect are the eventual fees associated with the use of specific artefacts (e.g. standardized questionnaire), the number of data sources involved (e.g. minimum sample size for a survey), and the human resource intensity characterizing the application of the selected method to each data source.

In the following sections, we first provide an overview of the different categories of approaches and methods that scholars employ to analyse organizational culture, an intangible asset. Second, we focus the attention on the Competing Values Framework (CVF) and the Organizational Culture Inventory® (OCI®) – two methods with rather different methodological characteristics and worth comparison. Finally, we draw some concluding reflections on the quantitative instruments and suggestions for future research on organizational culture.

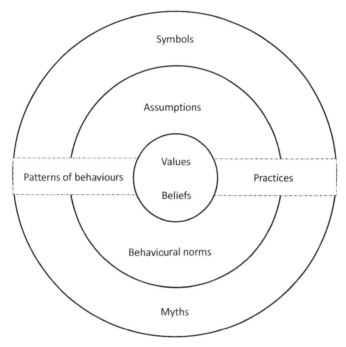

Source: Adapted from Hofstede et al. (1990: 291).

Figure 6.1   *Manifestations of culture: from observable/shallow to abstract/deep*

OVERVIEW OF THE DIFFERENT APPROACHES

The first important methodological distinction is between qualitative and quantitative approaches. Scholars choosing methods falling in the former category embrace the complexity of the phenomenon more directly and reject any attempt to measure culture. They may want to explore, for instance, underlying collective assumptions through in-depth interviews or projective metaphors, or describe in detail the organizational life and the underlying values affecting its 'modus operandi' utilizing ethnographic research (Ouchi & Wilkins, 1985). We do not further discuss this methodological alternative in this chapter, although it has relevant complementary traits with the methods that we focus on.

As far as quantitative methods are concerned, they rely on structured instruments administered through surveys to the personnel or selected (key) members of an organization. Typically, they ask questions on individuals' perceptions about observable (e.g. practices, symbols) or unobservable (e.g. values, norms) collective patterns within their organizations. Each instrument is based on an underlying theoretical framework or conceptual logic organizing values and associating them with specific meanings, sometimes allowing to triangulate complex aspects such as collective assumptions. Quantitative methods, generally based on self-reported questionnaires, have several strengths compared with qualitative methods (Jung et al., 2009; Tucker et al., 1990; Yauch & Steudel, 2003): (a) they can be administered more quickly and cost-effectively; (b) they allow to manage larger samples; (c) the collected data can be used for comparisons between groups, organizations, and across industries; (d) they allow repeatability, and consequently, longitudinal studies. The use of quantitative methods among academics working in the management field seems to have increased since the late 1980s, when scholars started testing them in several industries, although their use peaked in the 1990s (Jung et al., 2009).

Following Scott and colleagues (2003), two technically different approaches exist: dimensional and typological. Dimensional approaches aim to explore the presence and relative strength of specific cultural dimensions in an organization and can cover different features that the literature associates with the multifaceted concept of culture (Jung et al., 2009). Therefore, the approaches falling in this category produce a numerical summary of predefined dimensions of organizational culture. They may suggest the direction toward which a culture improves along each dimension, thereby guiding practical interventions toward intended organizational development. The typological approaches are more coherent with a constructivist approach and interpret culture less linearly, thus allowing for representing contrasting dynamics as well. This category of approaches allows categorizing each organization into predefined archetypes (Cooke & Szumal, 2000). Each category of approaches has instruments designed for specific types of organizations or professional groups.

We decided on an in-depth investigation of one instrument from each of the two mentioned approaches. The selection of the two instruments was based on the following criteria:

- The instrument used in organizations operating in different sectors (thus excluding instruments developed for a specific type of organization).
- Presence of a comprehensive range of dimensions enabling the evaluation of the culture of a whole organization – thereby excluding instruments aimed at assessing single groups – and capacity of examining abstract/deep aspects of the culture (such as values and beliefs).
- Strong theoretical underpinning (Scott et al., 2003).

For the typological approach, we selected the CVF, while for the dimensional approach, we chose the OCI®.

Table 6.1   *Examples of tools included in the two categories of quantitative methods*

Typological approaches	Competing Values Framework (CVF)
	Harrison's Organizational Ideology Questionnaire
	Quality Improvement Implementation Survey*
Dimensional approaches	Organizational Culture Inventory® (OCI®)
	MacKenzie's Culture Questionnaire
	Survey of Organizational Culture (SOC)
	Corporate Culture Questionnaire
	Core Employee Opinion Questionnaire
	Hofstede's Organizational Culture Questionnaire
	Denison Organizational Culture Survey (DOCS)
	Organizational Culture Survey
	Hospital Culture Questionnaire*
	Nursing Unit Culture Assessment Tool*
	Practice Culture Questionnaire*

Note: * Sector-specific instruments
Source: Elaborated from Scott and colleagues (2003).

A RELEVANT TYPOLOGICAL APPROACH: THE COMPETING VALUES FRAMEWORK

The CVF is one of the most used instruments aimed to assess the culture of organizations according to a typological approach. The roots of the instrument date back to the 1980s, starting from the construct and the criteria of organizational effectiveness. Quinn and Rohbaugh (1981, 1983) were among the first to introduce the idea of a framework for organizational analysis based on competing values. They identified three value dimensions that are the foundations of the modern CVF framework: the first value dimension relates to organizational focus (from an internal focus to an external one); the second value dimension to organizational structure (from an emphasis on stability to an emphasis on flexibility); the third value dimension relates to organizational means and ends, from an emphasis on important processes (e.g. planning and goal setting) to an emphasis on outcomes. The latter two are now embedded in a single dimension. The four basic models in their framework were the open system, rational goal, internal processes, and human relations. Cameron (1985) developed a CVF questionnaire to analyse the organizational cultures and their relationship with effectiveness in institutions of higher education. Brief scenarios were constructed describing the dominant characteristics of each of the four cultural types, namely: clan, hierarchy, adhocracy, and market. The structure and data collection method of the instrument are used even now.

The CVF distinguishes organizational cultures based on two main dimensions: the first concerns the 'internal focus', which describes how processes are carried out within an organization; the second dimension regards the 'external focus', identifying the orientation of the organization to the external environment. As far as the internal focus is concerned, operating processes can be based alternatively on: (i) personal relationships between the people inside the organization, characterized by flexibility, individuality, and spontaneity; or (ii) mechanistic processes, focused on control, order, and stability.

For the second dimension, the orientation can be focused on: (i) the internal environment, with an emphasis on organizational integration and smoothing; or (ii) the external environment, with an emphasis on competition and differentiation.

Based on these two dimensions, the CVF defines four culture (arche)types: clan, developmental, hierarchical, and rational (Figure 6.2).

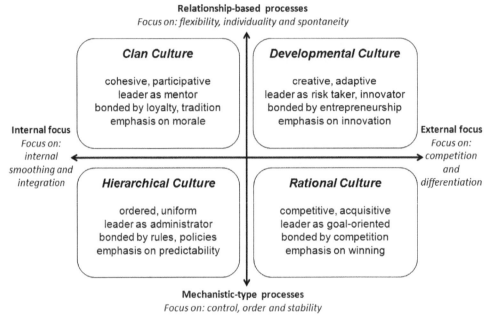

Source: Davies et al. (2007).

Figure 6.2   *CVF dimensions and organization culture (arche)types*

Clan cultures are internally focused and their operating processes are relationship-based. They are cohesive and participative; therefore, the organization is seen as a second family. Leaders are viewed as mentors, so their actions support and facilitate teamwork and group interaction. Members are bonded to organizations by loyalty and tradition. A *developmental* culture (also called adhocracy) is focused on satisfying external stakeholders and adapting its organization to push for innovations. Its leaders are risk-takers and visionaries who expect these characteristics from their organizational members. The structure of an organization changes concerning the objectives and activities they define to meet the dynamic external demand. The *hierarchical* culture type emphasizes the internal focus and enforcement of rules and regulations that influence how an organization works. Organizational effectiveness is defined in terms of predictability, control, and stability, while leaders tend to be administrators and conservative people. A *rational* culture is focused on achieving goals and facing external competition; as such, the leaders are viewed as being goal-oriented. This organizational culture type focuses more on realizing better relative market position and access to external resources.

The CVF model assumes that culture is not absolute: organizations do not reflect only one of the four types of culture but have competing values within them. Consequently, organizations display a combination of each culture type with one of the archetypes dominating the others.

In this section, we describe Mannion and colleagues' (2010) version of the CVF question-naire (see Appendix), based on five questions, for the characteristics of brevity and validation in several studies. However, other authors have developed different variants of the instrument.[1]

The CVF questionnaire offers respondents a set of four possible descriptions (items) of an organization, corresponding to the different types of culture. The questions cover five selected organizational aspects: (i) general characteristics, (ii) leadership, (iii) cohesion, (iv) emphasis, and (v) rewards. Within each of the five questions, the respondents must allot 100 points among the four items, according to the extent they think each description fits their current organization. The cultural type receiving the largest score across the five aspects identifies the dominant cultural archetype for the individual. The dominant cultural type for an organization is calculated by aggregating the individual scores of all the respondents.

In assessing organizational culture, the CVF questionnaire can be used at different levels of the organizations and/or can target different respondents, aiming to obtain robust estimates of the organizational dominant culture and respond to specific research questions. One of the advantages is that the CVF questionnaire is an instrument that does not need an adaptation to the different target populations.

Most of the studies administered the questionnaire to the senior management teams (SMTs) of the sampled organizations. This approach is due to two main motivations: (a) the strong influence of the SMT on the strategic orientation and the attitudes and behaviours of the personnel (Chaganti & Sambharya, 1987); (b) the SMT's comprehensive perspective on the organization (Cameron, 1985) and the organizational culture in terms of values, behaviours, and artefacts (Lee et al., 2021). Some studies have considered three or four responses from senior management as sufficient to robustly define the dominant culture type of an organ-ization (Calciolari et al., 2018; Davies et al., 2007; Gerowitz, 1998; Gerowitz et al., 1996; Prenestini et al., 2015).

Other studies administered the instrument – only or in addition to Chief Executive Officers and SMTs – to middle managers (Pasricha et al., 2018; Ralston et al., 2006), sometimes focalizing on specific functions such as human resource and quality managers (Knapp, 2015). Finally, several studies defined professionals or the employees of an organization as the target population (Cash et al., 2019; Debski et al., 2020; Sasaki et al., 2017). From this perspective, when used on sub-levels of the organizations (e.g. specific business/organization units) results can be useful for benchmarking specific sub-cultures.

Further contributions of Cameron and colleagues (Cameron, 1985; Cameron & Freeman, 1991) investigated two interesting aspects: (a) the congruence of the culture, ranging from complete incongruence (when a different culture was evaluated as dominant in each organiza-tional aspect/question) to complete congruence (in case the same culture was dominant in each aspect/question); (b) the strength of the culture based on the number of points ascribed to the specific attribute of the culture in each question (the higher the number of points, the stronger or more dominant the specific culture). However, the studies found that cultural strength and cultural congruence were not as powerful in predicting organizational effectiveness as culture type (Cameron & Quinn, 2011).

The instrument has four important points of strength. First, it is characterized by a solid theoretical basis (Scott et al., 2003). Second, it was validated in several studies in public and private organizations of different sectors: higher education (Calciolari et al., 2018; Cameron, 1985; Cameron & Freeman, 1991; Debski et al., 2020; Kwan & Walker, 2004), healthcare (Argote, 1989; Davies et al., 2007; Gerowitz, 1998; Gerowitz et al., 1996; Jackson, 1997; Lee et al., 2021; Prenestini et al., 2015; Shortell et al., 2000), and many other fields (Al-Khalifa & Aspinwall, 2001; Howard, 1998; Valmohammadi & Roshanzamir, 2015; Zeb et al., 2021). Third, although originally developed in the United States, it was successfully applied in many countries/regions, including Canada and the United Kingdom (Davies et al., 2007; Gerowitz et al., 1996), Europe (Calciolari et al., 2018; Prenestini et al., 2015), Middle East (Al-Khalifa & Aspinwall 2001; Zeb et al., 2021), Asia (Lau and Ngo, 2004; Lau et al., 2002; Ralston et al., 2006; Pasricha et al., 2018; Sasaki et al., 2017), and Australia (Lamond, 2003). Last, but not least, the instrument has largely been used to test the relationship between performance and cultural characteristics of the organization (Calciolari, et al., 2018; Cameron & Freeman, 1991; Davies et al., 2007; Gerowitz, 1998; Gerowitz et al., 1996).

When scholars used the CVF questionnaire to test the relationship between culture and performance, they adopted a theoretical perspective assuming that organizational cultures can be empirically measured, manipulated, or changed to improve organizational effectiveness and performance. Hence, according to this perspective, the traits and characteristics of the different cultural types can be linked to specific expected performance. In the past two decades, the healthcare sector has been one of the most examined for the relationship between culture and performance (Calciolari et al., 2018; Jacobs et al., 2013; Mannion et al., 2005; Prenestini & Lega, 2013; Scott et al., 2003). The literature review by Lee and colleagues (2021) reported 24 empirical healthcare studies that linked the assessment of the organizational culture with performance through the CVF questionnaire.

Several limitations of the CVF framework have been discussed in the extant literature. Many of them are related to the very nature of quantitative instruments that we discuss later in the chapter. For more specific limitations, Hartnell and colleagues (2011) conducted a meta-analytical investigation on 84 studies with 94 independent samples and found that the CVF's culture types are significantly associated with organizational effectiveness but not always with the same relationship defined by the theoretical model. Their findings might affect the nomological validity of the CVF, suggesting that the idea of the dominant culture does not consider the different synergistic interaction among the values that define an organization's culture. However, the CVF might not support the theoretical relationships between the single dominant culture and the performance perfectly, but the specific limit does not affect the validity of the instruments for at least two reasons: first, it is rooted in the idea that the values are competing and the beliefs are expressed differently in an organization; second, it can still be considered a good instrument for assessing organizational culture even if the theoretical characteristics and the achievement of specific performance do not completely overlap.

A RELEVANT DIMENSIONAL APPROACH: THE ORGANIZATIONAL CULTURE INVENTORY®

One of the most interesting and successful dimensional approaches for measuring the organizational culture is the OCI®, which was developed during the early 1980s by Cooke and Lafferty (1983) for intra-organizational as well as inter-organizational comparisons in research, and from a managerial perspective, for promoting survey-guided programmes for organizational development and cultural change. The OCI® assesses selected sets of norms specifying how the members of an organization (or an organizational unit, at least those in similar positions) are expected to approach their work and interact with each other. These norms aim to describe the mental attitude (ways of thinking and believing) and behavioural styles (ways of behaving) implicitly or explicitly required for people to 'fit in' and 'meet expectations' in a social group (Cooke & Lafferty 1986; Cooke & Rousseau 1988).

The OCI® evaluates the following 12 sets of norms or 'styles' (Cooke & Szumal, 2000):

1. *Achievement norms*: these concern the expectations for attitudes/orientations to set challenging (though realistic) goals, establish plans to reach defined goals, and enthusiastically pursue them.
2. *Self-actualizing norms*: these relate to the expectations about organization members enjoying their work, developing themselves, and taking on new and interesting tasks.
3. *Humanistic-encouraging[2] norms*: these encourage individuals to be supportive, constructive, and open to influence in their mutual interactions.
4. *Affiliative norms*: these contribute to building an environment where people are expected to be friendly, cooperative, and sensitive to their group's satisfaction.
5. *Approval norms*: these tend to create a context where people are expected to agree with, gain the approval of, and be liked by others.
6. *Conventional norms*: these pertain to the expectations of conformance, following the rules, and making a good impression.
7. *Dependent norms*: these relate to the expectations for individuals to do what they are told and clear all decisions with superiors.
8. *Avoidance norms*: these concern the practice of shifting responsibilities to others and avoiding any likelihood of being blamed for a problem.
9. *Oppositional norms*: these contribute to building an environment where people are expected to be critical, oppose the ideas of others, and make safe (though ineffective) decisions.
10. *Power norms*: these pertain to the expectations that each person take charge, control subordinates, and comply with the demands of superiors.
11. *Competitive norms*: these push people to operate in a 'win–lose' framework, outperform others, and compete (rather than collaborate) with their peers.
12. *Perfectionistic[3] norms*: these tend to create a context where people are expected to appear competent, keep track of everything, and work long hours to attain objectives with a narrow scope.

The 12 sets of norms are defined by two underlying dimensions: (a) the first distinguishes between concern for people – or interpersonal style – and a concern for duties – or task-related style; (b) the second distinguishes between expectations for behaviours directed toward fulfilling higher-order satisfaction needs and those directed toward protecting lower-order security needs. Based on these dimensions, the 12 sets of norms are grouped into three types of organizational cultures: Constructive, Passive/Defensive, and Aggressive/Defensive.

In any culture type, specific norms tend to play a dominant role (see also Table 6.2):

• The set of norms #1–4 prevail in the Constructive culture type and overall foster people interaction and approaching tasks in ways that help to meet higher-order satisfaction needs.
• The Passive/Defensive culture type is mainly characterised by set #5–8, which encourage or implicitly require members to interact with people in ways that are unlikely to threaten their security.

- The last four sets of norms are dominant in Aggressive/Defensive culture type and drive members to approach tasks in cogent ways to protect their security.

The OCI® measures the mentioned sets of norms through 120 items, and the instrument can be administered with a hand-scored version, a computer-scored version, or a web-based version.[4] Sample items include, 'To what extent are people expected to cooperate with others' and 'To what extent are people expected to turn the job into a contest', with responses based on a 5-point Likert scale (anchored to: 'Not at all', 'To a slight extent', 'To a moderate extent', 'To a great extent', 'To a very great extent'). Respondents are asked to provide their perceptions/opinion about both the current and the ideal situation (e.g. Ideally, to what extent should people be expected to …?) regarding any norm, thereby enabling measure gaps and orienting the direction of change. Empirical studies support the construct validity and reliability of the instrument (Cooke & Rousseau, 1988; Cooke & Szumal, 1993; Glisson & James, 2002; Xenikou & Furnham, 1996).

The OCI® scores of items are summed within each set of norms, with the scale of each set ranging from 10 to 50, and plotted on a Circumplex (see Figure 6.3), a circular diagram around which the sets of norms are positioned according to their degree of similarity. The sets of norms on the right-hand side of the Circumplex reflect expectations for behaviours that are people-oriented; those on the left-hand side reflect expectations for behaviours that are task-oriented. The set of norms toward the top of the Circumplex foster behaviours directed toward the fulfilment of higher-order satisfaction needs; those near the bottom promote behaviours aimed to fulfil lower-order security needs.

The radials (or concentric circles from the centre of the diagram outward) represent the 10th, 25th, 50th, 75th, 90th, and 99th percentiles. The score associated with each set of norms can be placed on each radial: the higher the value (within the mentioned 10–50 range), the progressively stronger are the norms characterizing the specific style. Frequently, a bold line or a coloured area is indicated in each set, indicating the average score, which helps to easily visualize the intensity of each set of norms.

The OCI® framework relies on the idea that culture has three fundamental features, namely, the direction (or content) of culture – synthetically indicated by the sets of norms – the strength of the norm – represented by the percentile associated with the summated score of each set of norms – and the intensity of culture – indicated by the standard deviation of the summated score – and refers to the extent of agreement among respondents. The model assumes that the shared cognitions of culture are acquired through the social learning and socialization processes, exposing individuals to activities and interactions, communicated information, and observable artefacts. Naturally, the acquired mentioned cognitions also influence operating activities, interpersonal interactions, and information flows. This is a typical bidirectional fashion of the relationship between unobservable and observable traits of the organizational culture.

The widespread use and extensive psychometric testing of the OCI® render it an attractive instrument at both the academic and professional level. However, it also has certain limitations. First, the number of items is relatively high, thus making its administration demanding. In addition, it embeds both a diagnostic and prescriptive function (Bellot, 2011) and may introduce preference bias for certain norms (e.g. minorities are likely to report higher scores for defensive norms). Finally, it is subject to proprietary analysis, eliminating the possibility of internal organizational evaluation.

Table 6.2　　*Descriptions of the 12 styles measured by the OCI® (and sample items)*

Culture Type	Dominant sets of norms
Constructive Norms	**Achievement**
(Cultural styles promoting satisfaction behaviours)	An achievement culture characterizes organizations that do things well and value members who set and accomplish their own goals. Members are expected to set challenging but realistic goals, establish plans to reach these goals, and pursue them with enthusiasm. *(Pursue a standard of excellence; Openly show enthusiasm)*
	Self-actualizing
	A self-actualizing culture characterizes organizations that value creativity, quality over quantity, and both task accomplishment and individual growth. Members are encouraged to gain enjoyment from their work, develop themselves, and take on new and interesting activities. *(Think in unique and independent ways; Do even simple tasks well)*
	Humanistic/Encouraging
	A humanistic/encouraging culture characterizes organizations that are managed in a participative and person-centred way. Members are expected to be supportive, constructive, and open to influence in their dealings with one another. *(Help others to grow and develop; Take time with people)*
	Affiliative
	An affiliative culture characterizes organizations that place a high priority on constructive interpersonal relationships. Members are expected to be friendly, open, and sensitive to the satisfaction of their work group. *(Deal with others in a friendly, pleasant way; Share feelings and thoughts)*

Culture Type	Dominant sets of norms
Passive/Defensive Norms (Cultural styles promoting people/security behaviours)	**Approval** An approval culture describes organizations in which conflicts are avoided and interpersonal relationships are pleasant–at least superficially. Members feel that they should agree with, gain the approval of, and be liked by others. (*'Go along' with others; Be liked by everyone*) **Conventional** A conventional culture is descriptive of organizations that are conservative, traditional, and bureaucratically controlled. Members are expected to conform, follow the rules, and make a good impression. (*Always follow policies and practices; Fit into the 'mould'*) **Dependent** A dependent culture is descriptive of organizations that are hierarchically controlled and do not empower their members. Centralized decision making in such organizations leads members to do only what they are told and to clear all decisions with superiors. (*Please those in positions of authority; Do what is expected*) **Avoidance** An avoidance culture characterizes organizations that fail to reward success but nevertheless punish mistakes. This negative reward system leads members to shift responsibilities to others and avoid any possibility of being blamed for a mistake. (*Wait for others to act first; Take few chances*)
Aggressive/Defensive Norms (Cultural styles promoting task/security behaviours)	**Oppositional** An oppositional culture describes organizations in which confrontation and negativism are rewarded. Members gain status and influence by being critical and thus are reinforced to oppose the ideas of others. (*Point out flaws; Be hard to impress*) **Power** A power culture is descriptive of nonparticipative organizations structured on the basis of the authority inherent in members' positions. Members believe they will be rewarded for taking charge, controlling subordinates and, at the same time, being responsive to the demands of superiors. (*Build up one's power base; Demand loyalty*) **Competitive** A competitive culture is one in which winning is valued and members are rewarded for outperforming one another. Members operate in a 'win–lose' framework and believe they must work against (rather than with) their peers to be noticed. (*Turn the job into a contest; Never appear to lose*) **Perfectionistic** A perfectionistic culture characterizes organizations in which perfectionism, persistence, and hard work are valued. Members feel they must avoid any mistakes, keep track of everything, and work long hours to attain narrowly defined objectives. (*Do things perfectly; Keep on top of everything*)

Source: Copyright © 1987, 2021 by Human Synergistics, Inc. Reproduced by permission.

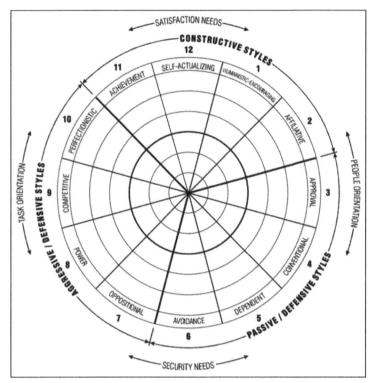

Figure 6.3   *OCI® circumplex*

DISCUSSION AND CONCLUSIONS

Organizational culture is a complex and ambiguous concept, objectively hard to be comprehensively captured using value-based instruments. The first limitation stems from the conceptualization of organizational culture itself because it leads to several alternative theoretical formulations in the literature (Tucker et al., 1990). From a methodological perspective, some scholars and practitioners may argue that a quantitative instrument can hardly capture a concept that is 'ambiguous, often slippery, and difficult to pin down' (Scott et al., 2003). One may also consider the 'coverage' offered by an instrument for the different though intertwined levels or aspects any culture exhibits. Schein (2017) argues that at the most basic level, culture is represented by the underlying and implicit assumptions ('beliefs') that define human thinking and behaviour, characterizing the relationships with the environment. The rules and practices that govern interactions and the organizational 'values', operating at a more conscious level and shaping the goals and standards of individuals' worth, emerge from such assumptions (Davies et al., 2000). The more observable part of the culture is composed of artefacts (from mission statements to credos to formal recognitions to the layout of the offices and the dress code). This might complicate the choice, because cultural manifestations at a deep level may require to be triangulated based on traits at the other levels.

The second limitation is linked to the first and concerns the comparability of analyses based on different instruments. It may be inconsistent to compare the findings of different quantitative methods because they are likely to assess rather different cultural constructs.

Even if the previous limitations were overcome, some scholars (Schein, 2017) have argued that only in-depth interviews or long-term ethnographic research can uncover the real traits of the organizational culture. However, rigorous empirical research can perhaps identify particular aspects of an organization's culture. For instance, a robust and validated quantitative questionnaire can effectively enable a scholar to address empirical questions of broader scope and requiring systematic or longitudinal comparisons in a large number of organizations. Tucker and colleagues (1990) conducted ten empirical studies using a quantitative method, as well as several in-depth interviews with leaders/managers and ethnographic investigations. Their findings suggest that organizational culture is quite scrutable and correspondence exists among the various assessment methods. Moreover, surveys have the advantage of being efficient and unobtrusive compared to qualitative methods.

A fourth limitation relates to the data management underlying the quantitative assessment of organizational culture. The premise is that, by definition, culture is a collective phenomenon; therefore, results are rational only at a group level, even when the data collection source is the individual. However, methods of aggregating individual data to represent collective responses are typically crude and their validity not infrequently uncertain (Scott et al., 2003).

Finally, an implementation risk of the quantitative instruments concerns the existence of sub-cultures within an organization. Such sub-groups are characterized by different values and power. Therefore, selecting representative samples of respondents to allow subgroup analysis alongside the whole organizational analysis may be useful (Scott et al., 2003).

Culture is but one metaphor for organization, stemming from an anthropological paradigm of research (Williams, 1983). It is the trigger engaging organization members on the level of meaning. From such a perspective dimensional versus typological approaches have specific limits. According to Jung and colleagues (2009), dimensional approaches are rooted in anthropological studies on national cultures and offer the advantage of focusing on specific cultural variables. However, national cultures create values that are acquired in early youth, while organizations provide members with the opportunity to create a culture in the form of practices that can be judged, taught, and generally communicated to others at the workplace (Hofstede, 2001). Dimensional tools concentrating on values rather than practices may be of limited utility in the assessment of organizational culture (Jung et al., 2009).

By contrast, Jung and colleagues (2009) contend that the descriptive language and labels frequently adopted by typological approaches risk not only stereotyping different cultural domains but also investing them with a moral valence. Such categorization may interfere with the anthropological perspective that the organizational culture is a value-neutral concept. However, the dimensional approaches are not exempt from this very critique when it considers the systematic preference showed for certain dimensions (as we mentioned when analysing OCI®).

In conclusion, from an academic viewpoint, the development of value-based quantitative instruments represented a leap in the study of organizational cultures because of their main advantages: repeatability, comparability, cost-effectiveness and limited time-consuming burden, more unobtrusiveness, and larger samples. Naturally, any of these strengths is gratuitous and can be vitiated by a weak implementation (Tucker et al., 1990).

From a managerial perspective, the importance of assessing the receptiveness to, and impact of, organizational change and development are increasingly being acknowledged. The reviewed value-based questionnaires and other quantitative instruments represent versatile and reasonably efficient toolkits for monitoring the organizational culture before and after a process of change and eventually analyse elements of resilience to better manage them. Similar to other dimensional approaches, the OCI® was designed as part of a self-scoring, multilevel diagnostic system for promoting individual change and organizational development (Cooke et al., 1987). In this respect, the dimensional frameworks and questionnaires seem to be more useful for measuring specific cultural traits that represent interesting signals for planning organizational development or assessing the outcomes of organizational change initiatives. Consequently, the dimensional approaches are often part of consulting projects and their questionnaires are commercial products.

Depending on the main investigation goals, it is possible to employ more than one instrument, or even adopt both qualitative and quantitative methods in a single study. For instance, different methods may examine different layers of culture, thereby providing a more comprehensive picture of the organization (including eventual contradictions or discrepancies between layers) or inform testable hypotheses or uncover the meaning of quantitative findings (Scott et al., 2003). However, when conducting multimethod evaluations, minimizing the risk of contamination or priming effects between methods is critical. The investigators must reconcile results to the nature of what is studied, without relying exclusively on a single instrument or even a set of instruments.

ACKNOWLEDGEMENTS

The authors checked the accuracy of the OCI® proprietary concepts and methods, explained in the dedicated section, directly with Human Synergistics, Inc., and they fully acknowledge their original source. Research and Development by: Robert A. Cooke, Ph.D. Style names, descriptions and items are copyrighted © and used by permission. From Organizational Culture Inventory by Robert A. Cooke and J. Clayton Lafferty, 1987, Plymouth, MI: Human Synergistics International. Copyright © 1987, 2021 by Human Synergistics, Inc. Reproduced by permission. The OCI style descriptions and items may not be reproduced without the express and written permission of Human Synergistics.

NOTES

1. In Cameron and Quinn (2011), the instrument based on CVF is labelled Organisational Culture Assessment Instrument – or OCAI – and contains one additional aspect (corresponding to a further question) compared with the Mannion and colleagues' survey: the management style (or management of employees) characterizing each of the cultures.
2. This style was previously labelled 'humanistic–helpful' in some sources such as Cooke and Rousseau (1988).
3. This style was previously labelled 'competence–perfectionistic' in some sources – such as Cooke and Rousseau (1988).
4. Paige (2004) refers to a computer-scored version of the instrument consisting of 96 items, but Human Synergistics informed us that such version was discontinued and that currently all versions of the questionnaire comprise 120 items (which is the version retaining high psychometric integrity). Reduced forms of the instrument were available, though we do not have information about their validity and reliability, and Human Synergistics confirmed that they no longer exist.

REFERENCES

Al-Khalifa, K. N., & Aspinwall, E. M. (2001). Using the Competing Values Framework to investigate the culture of Qatar industries. *Total Quality Management, 12*(4), 417–428.

Argote, L. (1989). Agreement about norms and work-unit effectiveness: Evidence from the field. *Basic and Applied Social Psychology, 10*(2), 131–140.

Bellot, J. (2011). Defining and assessing organizational culture. *Nursing Forum, 46*(1), 29–37.

Calciolari, S., Prenestini, A., & Lega, F. (2018). An organizational culture for all seasons? How cultural type dominance and strength influence different performance goals. *Public Management Review, 20*(9), 1400–1422.

Cameron, K. S. (1985), Cultural congruence, strength, and type: Relationships to effectiveness. Working Paper n. 401b, Graduate School of Business Administration, University of Michigan.

Cameron, K. S., & Freeman, S. J. (1991). Cultural congruence, strength, and type: Relationships to effectiveness. *Research in Organizational Change and Development, 5*, 23–58.

Cameron, K. S., & Quinn, R. E. (2011). *Diagnosing and Changing Organizational Culture Based on the Competing Values Framework*. San Francisco: Jossey-Bass.

Cash, R. E., White-Mills, K., Crowe, R. P., Rivard, M. K. & Panchal, A. R. (2019). Workplace incivility among nationally certified EMS professionals and associations with workforce-reducing factors and organizational culture, *Prehospital Emergency Care, 23*(3), 346–355.

Chaganti, R., & Sambharya, R. (1987). Strategic orientation and characteristics of upper management. *Strategic Management Journal, 8*(4), 393–401.

Cooke, R. A., & Lafferty, J. C. (1983). *Level V: Organizational Cultural Inventory (Form I)*. Plymouth, MI: Human Synergistics.

Cooke, R. A., & Rousseau, D. M. (1988). Behavioural norms and expectations: A quantitative approach to the assessment of organizational culture. *Group & Organization Studies, 13*(3), 245–273.

Cooke, R. A., & Szumal, J. L. (1993). Measuring normative beliefs and shared behavioural expectations in organizations: The reliability and validity of the Organizational Culture Inventory. *Psychological Reports, 72*(3, Pt 2), 1299–1330.

Cooke, R. A., & Szumal, J. L. (2000). Using the organizational culture inventory to understand the operating cultures of organizations. In Ashkanasy, N. M., Wilderom, C. P. M., & Peterson, M. F. (Eds.), *Handbook of Organizational Culture and Climate* (Vol. 4), pp. 147–162, Thousand Oaks: Sage.

Cooke, R. A., Rousseau, D. M., & Lafferty, J. C. (1987). Thinking and behavioural styles: Consistency between self-descriptions and descriptions by others. *Educational and Psychological Measurement, 47*, 815–823.

Davies, H. T. O., Nutley, S. M., & Mannion, R. (2000). Organisational culture and quality of health care. *Quality in Health Care, 9*, 111–119.

Davies, H. T. O., Mannion, R., Jacobs, A., Powell, A. E., & Marshall, M. N. (2007). Exploring the relationship between senior management team culture and hospital performance. *Medical Care Research and Review, 1*(64), 46–65.

Deal, T. E., & Kennedy, A. A. (2000). *Corporate Cultures: The Rites and Rituals of Corporate Life*. Cambridge: Perseus.

Debski, M., Cieciora, M., Pietrzak, P., & Bołkunow, W. (2020). Organizational culture in public and non-public higher education institutions in Poland: A study based on Cameron and Quinn's model. *Human Systems Management, 39*, 345–355.

Gerowitz, M. B. (1998). Do TQM interventions change management culture? Findings and implications. *Quality Management in Health Care*, 6(3), 1–11.

Gerowitz, M. B., Lemieux-Charles, L., Heginbothan, C., & Johnson, B. (1996). Top management culture and performance in Canadian, UK and US hospitals. *Health Services Management Research*, 9, 69–78.

Glisson, C., & James, L.R. (2002). The cross-level effects of culture and climate in human service teams. *Journal of Organizational Behaviour*, 23, 767–794.

Hartnell, C. A., Ou, A. Y., & Kinicki, A. (2011). Organizational culture and organizational effectiveness: A meta-analytic investigation of the Competing Values Framework's theoretical suppositions. *Journal of Applied Psychology*, 96(4), 677–686.

Hofstede, G. (2001). *Culture's Consequences: Comparing Values, Behaviours, Institutions, and Organizations Across Nations* (2nd ed.). Thousand Oaks: Sage.

Hofstede, G., Neuijen, B., Ohayv, D. D., & Sanders G. (1990). Measuring organizational cultures: A qualitative and quantitative study across twenty cases. *Administrative Science Quarterly*, 35(2), 286–316.

Howard, L. W. (1998). Validating the competing values model as a representation of organizational cultures. *International Journal of Organizational Analysis*, 6(3), 231–250.

Jackson, S. (1997). Does organizational culture affect out-patient DNA rates? *Health Manpower Management*, 23, 233–236.

Jacobs, R., Mannion, R., Davies, H. T. O., Harrison, S., Konteh, F., & Walshe, K. (2013). The relationship between organizational culture and performance in acute hospitals. *Social Science and Medicine*, 76(1), 115–125.

Jung, T., Scott, T., Davies, H. T. O., Bower, P., Whalley, D., McNally, R., & Mannion, R. (2009). Instruments for exploring organizational culture: A review of the literature. *Public Administration Review*, 69(6), 1087–1096.

Knapp, S. (2015). Lean Six Sigma implementation and organizational culture. *International Journal of Health Care Quality Assurance*, 28(8), 855–863.

Kwan, P., & Walker, A. (2004). Validating the Competing Values Model as a representation of organizational culture through inter-institutional comparisons. *Organizational Analysis*, 12(1), 21–39.

Lamond, D. (2003). The value of Quinn's Competing Values Model in an Australian context. *Journal of Managerial Psychology*, 18(1/2), 46–59.

Lau, C.-M., & Ngo, H.-Y. (2004). The HR system, organizational culture and product innovation. *International Business Review*, 13, 685–703.

Lau, C.-M., Tse, D. K., & Zhou N. (2002). Institutional forces and organizational culture in China: Effects on change schemas, firm commitment and job satisfaction. *Journal of International Business Studies*, 33(3), 533–550.

Lee, J. Y., McFadden, K. L., Lee, M. K., & Gowen C. R. III (2021). U.S. hospital culture profiles for better performance in patient safety, patient satisfaction, Six Sigma, and lean implementation, *International Journal of Production Economics*, 234.

Mannion, R., Davies, H. T. O., Harrison, S., Konteh, F., Greener, I., McDonald, R., Dowswell, G., Walshe, K., Fulop, N., Walters, R., Jacobs, R., & Hyde, P. (2010). Changing management cultures and organisational performance in the NHS (OC2). National Co-ordinating Centre for the National Institute for Health Research Service Delivery and Organisation Programme (NCCSDO).

Mannion, R., Davies, H. T. O., & Marshall, M.N. (2005). *Cultures for Performance in Health Care*. Maidenhead: Open University Press.

Martin, J. (2002). *Organizational Culture: Mapping the Terrain*. Thousand Oaks, CA: Sage.

Ouchi, W. G., & Wilkins, A.L. (1985). Organizational culture. *Annual Review of Sociology*, *11*, 457–483.

Paige, R. M. (2004). Instrumentation in intercultural training. In Landis, D., Bennett, J. M., & Bennett, M. J. (Eds.), *Handbook of Intercultural Training*, pp. 85–128, Thousand Oaks: Sage.

Pasricha, P., Singh, B., & Verma, P. (2018). Ethical leadership, organic organizational cultures and corporate social responsibility: An empirical study in social enterprises. *Journal of Business Ethics*, *151*(4), 941–958.

Porter, M. E. (1980). *Competitive Strategy: Techniques for Analyzing Industries and Competitors*. New York: The Free Press.

Porter, M. E. (1985). *Competitive Advantage: Creating and Sustaining Superior Performance*. New York: The Free Press.

Prenestini, A., & Lega, F. (2013). Do senior management cultures affect performance? Evidence from Italian public healthcare organizations. *Journal of Healthcare Management*, *58*(5), 336–352.

Prenestini, A., Calciolari, S., Lega, F., & Grilli, R. (2015). The relationship between senior management team culture and clinical governance: Empirical investigation and managerial implications. *Health Care Management Review*, *40*(4), 313–323.

Quinn, R. E., & Rohrbaugh, J. (1981). A competing value approach: Measuring performance in the employment service. *Public Productivity Review*, *5*, 122–140.

Quinn, R. E., & Rohrbaugh, J. (1983). A spatial model of effectiveness criteria: Toward a competing values approach to organizational analysis. *Management Science*, *3*, 363–377.

Ralston, D.A., Terpstra-Tong, J., Terpstra, R. H., Wang X., & Egri C. (2006). Today's state owned enterprises of China: Are they dying dinosaurs or dynamic dynamos? *Strategic Management Journal*, *27*, 825–843.

Sasaki, H., Yonemoto, N., Mori, R., Nishida, T., Kusuda, S., & Nakayama T. (2017). Assessing archetypes of organizational culture based on the Competing Values Framework: The experimental use of the framework in Japanese neonatal intensive care units. *International Journal of Quality in Health Care*, *29*(3), 384–391.

Schein, E. H. (2017). *Organizational Culture and Leadership*. New Jersey: Wiley.

Schneider, B., & Barbera, K. M. (2014). *The Oxford Handbook of Organizational Climate and Culture*. Oxford: Oxford University Press.

Scott, T., Mannion, R., Davies, H. & Marshall, M. (2003). The quantitative measurement of organizational culture in health care: A review of the available instruments. *Health Services Research*, *38*(3), 923–945.

Shortell, S., Jones, R., Rademaker, A., Gillies, R., Dranove, D., Hughes, E., Budetti P. P., Reynolds K. S., & Huang C. F. (2000). Assessing the impact of total quality management and organizational culture on multiple outcomes of care for coronary artery bypass graft surgery patients. *Medical Care*, *38*(2), 201–217.

Tucker, R. W., McCoy, W. J., & Evans, L. C. (1990). Can questionnaires objectively assess organizational culture? *Journal of Managerial Psychology*, *5*(4), 4–11.

Valmohammadi, C., & Roshanzamir, S. (2015). The guidelines of improvement: Relations among organizational culture, TQM and performance. *International Journal of Production Economy*, *164*, 167–178.

Williams, R. (1983). *Keywords: A Vocabulary of Cultures and Society*. New York: Oxford University Press.

Xenikou, A., & Furnham, A. (1996). A correlational and factor analytic study of four questionnaire measures of organizational culture. *Human Relations*, *49*, 349–371.

Yauch, C. A., & Steudel, H. J. (2003). Complementary use of qualitative and quantitative cultural assessment methods. *Organizational Research Methods*, *6*(4), 465–481.

Zeb, A., Akbar, F., Hussain, K., Safi, A., Rabnawaz, M., & Zeb, F. (2021). The competing value framework model of organizational culture, innovation and performance. *Business Process Management Journal*, *27*(2), 658–683.

APPENDIX – CVF INSTRUMENT

The version of the CVF instrument discussed in this chapter is based on the questionnaire included in the research report 'Changing Management Cultures and Organizational Performance in the NHS (OC2)' (Mannion et al., April 2010) and used with NHS Hospital Trusts.

Evaluating the culture of your ORGANIZATION

There are **5 questions** below. Each question is about a different aspect of your ORGANIZATION: for example, its leadership or its reward system.

Please, distribute **100 points** among the four descriptions depending on how similar the description is to your ORGANIZATION. For each question, please, use **all 100 points**. Please, answer according to what you think, not what others in your ORGANIZATION think and don't think too hard – we want your gut reactions.

For example, in Question 1 if ORGANIZATION A seems very similar to yours, B seems somewhat similar and C and D do not seem similar at all, you might give 70 points to A, 30 to B and none to C and D. Question 1 and other examples might look as follows:

Question 1		Question 2		Question 3		Question 4	
A	70	A	25	A	80	A	0
B	30	B	25	B	10	B	0
C	0	C	25	C	0	C	100
D	0	D	25	D	10	D	0
Total	100	Total	100	Total	100	Total	100

Please answer according to what you think that your ORGANIZATION is like now. There are no **right** or **wrong** answers! None of the descriptions are any better than the others – they are just different. Don't think too hard – we want your gut reactions.

Table 6A.1   Organization characteristics

QUESTION 1: ORGANIZATION characteristics	
(please distribute all 100 points)	
points	
A	ORGANIZATION A is a very personal place.
	It's like an extended family.
B	ORGANIZATION B is a very dynamic and entrepreneurial place.
	People are willing to take risks.
C	ORGANIZATION C is a very formalised and structured place.
	Bureaucratic procedures influence how things are done.
D	ORGANIZATION D is very task orientated.
	The main concern is getting the job done and people aren't very personally involved.
total	

Table 6A.2   Organization leadership

QUESTION 2: ORGANIZATION leadership	
(please distribute all 100 points)	
points	
A	The leaders in ORGANIZATION A are warm and caring.
	They seek to develop their staff members' full potential.
B	The leaders in ORGANIZATION B are risk takers.
	They encourage risk taking and innovation from their staff.
C	The leaders in ORGANIZATION C are rule enforcers.
	They expect staff to follow rules, policies and procedures.
D	The leaders in ORGANIZATION D are co-ordinators and facilitators.
	They encourage staff to meet the organization's objectives.
total	

Table 6A.3   Organization cohesion

QUESTION 3: ORGANIZATION cohesion	
(please distribute all 100 points)	
points	
A	The glue that holds ORGANIZATION A together is loyalty and tradition.
	Staff commitment to the organization is high.
B	The glue that holds ORGANIZATION B together is a commitment to innovation and development.
	Organization B likes to lead the way.
C	The glue that holds ORGANIZATION C together is formal rules and policies.
	Maintaining a smooth running operation is important.
D	The glue that holds ORGANIZATION D together is an emphasis on accomplishing tasks and goals.
	People want to get jobs done.
total	

Table 6A.4   Organization emphasis

QUESTION 4: ORGANIZATION emphasis	
(please distribute all 100 points)	
points	
A	ORGANIZATION A puts a strong emphasis on *cohesion and staff morale.*
B	ORGANIZATION B puts a strong emphasis on *growth and readiness to meet new challenges.*
C	ORGANIZATION C puts a strong emphasis on *permanence and stability.*
D	ORGANIZATION D puts a strong emphasis on *competitiveness and achievement.*
total	

Table 6A.5   Organization 'rewards'

QUESTION 5: ORGANIZATION 'rewards'	
(By 'rewards' we mean praise, acknowledgement of success etc., as well as resources and financial incentives)	
(please distribute all 100 points)	
points	
A	ORGANIZATION A distributes its rewards fairly among staff members.
	Everyone is treated equally.
B	ORGANIZATION B distributes its rewards based on individual initiative.
	Those who are most productive are most rewarded.
C	ORGANIZATION C distributes its rewards based on rank.
	The higher you are the more you get.
D	ORGANIZATION D distributes its rewards based on the achievement of objectives.
	Those who achieve their objectives are rewarded.
total	

THAT'S ALL! Thank you for taking the time to complete this questionnaire.

We very much appreciate your help with this research. Please do not hesitate to contact us with any queries or questions. If you would like to see the results of our analysis, please, give your contact details below:

*You should be reassured that all information that we receive will be **anonymized**, with no comments or responses attributed to any individual or organization. [...]*

7. Measuring organizational culture: converging on definitions and approaches to advance the paradigm[1]

Jennifer A. Chatman and Andrew Choi

In writing a chapter about how to measure organizational culture, a necessary starting point is to ask what we mean by organizational culture. This question identifies an inherent challenge, which is that ever since Pettigrew (1979) published his pioneering paper bringing the study of culture into the domain of organizational research, scholars have disagreed about how to define culture, how it should be studied, and, not surprisingly, how to measure it (e.g., Giorgi et al., 2015). One aspect of culture that makes a unified definition elusive is that it is a truly multi-disciplinary construct. In 1963, leading anthropologists Kroeber and Kluckhohn (1963) reported that there were 164 different meanings for the term "culture" in the anthropology literature alone. And, focusing specifically on the term "organizational culture," scholars reported 54 different definitions (Verbeke et al., 1998). With fields such as anthropology, economics, finance, organizational behavior, sociology, and strategy focusing on culture, the various perspectives inevitably use different lenses in defining what it means.

Scholars have been calling for unifying the culture paradigm in organizational research for some time but that call has recently intensified. In 2014, Denison et al. highlighted this persistent challenge, noting the lack of a widely shared and agreed upon definition for the term. In 2015, Giorgi and colleagues (p. 3) said that, "in spite of this renewed interest in culture – or perhaps because of it – research in organization theory has become increasingly fragmented, and with it, a proliferation of definitions and conceptualizations has emerged." In 2016, Chatman and O'Reilly tracked the fragmented history of culture research and noted the challenge of advancing the domain of culture and accumulating knowledge on a comparable construct without first developing a unified definition and systematic methods that allow comparisons across studies of culture. And in 2019, during the first academic conference devoted entirely to organizational culture (https://haas.berkeley.edu/berkeley-haas-culture-conference/2019-conference-highlights/), scholars across the disciplines of organizational behavior, economics, political science, sociology, and psychology voiced a desire for a unified approach to studying culture since it was not even clear if the different approaches were studying the same phenomenon. As a result, despite the scholarly attention that has been devoted to understanding and measuring organizational culture, the domain is at risk of stagnating and failing to advance without a unified theoretical paradigm.

In this chapter, we briefly trace the progress – and sources of the lack of progress, including fragmentation and inherent challenges – of the organizational culture domain and offer support for a unified definition of organizational culture, which is a prerequisite for developing valid and reliable methods. We then identify the most promising empirical methods to assess culture that emphasize construct validity (ensuring that they are measuring culture and not something else), reduce bias (by addressing the challenges of small sample sizes, demand effects, and socially desirable responding), increase accessibility, and enable the accumulation of knowledge so that a comprehensive and unified theory of culture can emerge.

HISTORICAL CONSTRAINTS ON THE LACK OF PROGRESS IN THE ORGANIZATIONAL CULTURE DOMAIN

Theoretical Challenges

Though there were a number of reasons why theory development in the culture domain stalled (Chatman & O'Reilly, 2016), one of the most significant was a set of divisive debates that, while advancing the field in some ways, eventually impeded paradigm development. Many of these debates have been resolved and researchers have called for others to be retired. For example, the culture versus climate debate has been largely resolved, with researchers acknowledging that both constructs are important and distinctive (e.g., Ostroff et al., 2012). As compared to culture, climate is defined in terms of aggregated individual attitudes about specific domains such as safety or customer service (e.g., Schneider et al., 2013), with researchers focusing on only one climate dimension at a time, rather than profiles of dimensions (e.g., Tucker et al., 2016). This contrasts with organizational culture, which is typically identified as patterns of expectations and behaviors that members share and that are related to one another as a more coherent whole (e.g., Schein, 2010).

The status of the debate about whether culture is better defined as something organizations *are* (an *emic* approach) versus something organizations *have* (an *etic* approach) is more complex. This debate spawned decades of controversy about whether culture could be measured systematically or whether it had to be experienced through deep immersion (Martin, 2002). Advocates of the qualitative approach believe that cultures are unique and only by fully revealing the deep meaning of rituals and symbols can unconscious or implicit beliefs and assumptions be accessed (e.g., Alvesson & Berg, 1992; Martin, 2002). They argue that assuming commonality among organizations may cause researchers to miss key features that are unique to each organization. One critique of the ethno-methodological approach is that focusing on what is unique about each organization precludes the ability to aggregate knowledge and build generalizable theories about organizational culture (e.g., Chatman & O'Reilly, 2016).

Defining organizational culture

A potential resolution to the *etic* versus *emic* debate resides in Schein's (2010) foundational and widely accepted conception of organizational culture as consisting of three interrelated layers: (1) underlying assumptions and beliefs (that may be conscious or unconscious), (2) norms and values about appropriate attitudes and behaviors (that may be espoused or real), and (3) artifacts that may reflect these (e.g., symbols and language). Specifically, researchers interested in understanding underlying assumptions and beliefs may need to immerse themselves in a culture to fully grasp such conscious and unconscious assumptions. In contrast, the other two layers are more accessible through systematic research methods that enable comparisons across organizational cultures. We focus on *norms* that can act as a social control system in organizations because "norms translate into observable behaviors and attitudes which are relevant, and because informants can report on and articulate them, in contrast to the difficulty of surfacing underlying assumptions and beliefs and the ambiguity of cultural artifacts" (Chatman & O'Reilly, 2016: 216).

Researchers have coalesced around the idea that, while many approaches to measuring culture are valuable, such measures must be systematic, replicable, and typically derive from many examples within a sample (e.g., Lu et al., 2019). With these resolutions emerging, debates that previously divided researchers have receded, paving the way for culture research to advance (Chatman & O'Reilly, 2016). The domain is now poised to develop a robust and unified framework for understanding culture, though even with a shared definition, a number of empirical challenges unique to studying organizational culture must still be addressed.

Empirical Challenges to Advancing the Organizational Culture Research Domain

There are a number of empirical challenges that have stalled research on organizational culture. Some arise from the nature of the construct itself, while others are derived from weaknesses in popular approaches to assessing culture.

Empirical challenges arising from the nature of the construct

Four distinctive features of organizational culture make it challenging to measure. First, organizational culture, identified in terms of patterns of norms that are shared, represents a large set of interrelated attributes (Chatman, 1991; O'Reilly et al., 1991). The resulting measurement challenges include creating an approach that informants can use to reliably profile their organization's culture – one that enables an evaluation of the full set of relevant norms and how each relates to the other in relative importance, since culture influences how members of organizations react to competing priorities (Chatman, 1989). Second, assessing culture via shared norms requires parsing these norms into both the content that characterizes the organization but also the structural properties of culture – the extent to which members agree on the relative importance of each norm, and the level of intensity with which each norm is collectively held (Chatman et al., 2014). Third, culture exists on many levels – at the national level (Gelfand et al., 2011), the industry level (Chatman & Jehn, 1994), and the group level (e.g., Chatman & Flynn, 2001), but organizational culture requires assessment at the organizational level. Collecting culture data one organization at a time is extremely time consuming and this challenge has surely stifled culture data collection efforts to date.

Finally, assessing culture can be subject to a set of biases. A primary concern are biases (e.g., social desirability, retrospective rationality) that arise from members of an organization being motivated to make their organization look good to outsiders and themselves when asked to assess their own culture (Chatman et al., 1986). A second challenge is selection bias since those who choose to respond to culture assessments or comment on their organization's culture may be different from those who choose not to respond. And, finally, beyond attempts to intentionally bias culture assessments, organizational members or outside informants (e.g., Kotter & Heskett, 1992), may have biases that they are unaware of as they assess an organization's culture, such as a lack of information based on their vantage point – by function, tenure, geographic location, or level.

Empirical challenges derived from weaknesses in approaches to assessing culture

The primary weakness of existing scales measuring culture is a lack of construct validity. Chatman and O'Reilly (2016) offer a detailed analysis of the most popular culture assessments and show how many were not originally designed to assess culture specifically and are more likely assessing the murkier construct of organizational effectiveness. This is a problem because the scales may still generate predictive validity (e.g., organizational effectiveness predicts organizational effectiveness), without construct validity (e.g., that culture is causing observed levels of effectiveness).

As one example, the Organizational Culture Assessment Instrument (OCAI), based on the Competing Values Framework (CVF, e.g., Cameron et al., 2006), consists of a survey with six categories (Dominant Organizational Characteristics, Leadership Style, Management of Employees, Organizational Glue, Strategic Emphasis, Criteria for Success) in which respondents distribute 100 points among four items for each category representing the four competing values. The CVF theory suggests that the four core values represent opposite or competing assumptions, with each value being the opposite of the value at the other end of the continuum. However, it is not clear what about the Competing Values Framework is actually competing. Hartnell et al. (2011) conclude that, "Results suggest that the CVF's culture types in opposite quadrants are not competing" (p. 687). Of greater concern, however, is the difficulty of ascertaining the construct validity of the OCAI. While culture in the form of norms and values may be part of the CVF model, it also includes the assessment of other constructs such as organizational structure, leadership, organizational practices, agreement, and strategy. This breadth and ambiguity in the construct and its measurement is visible in a meta-analysis of 89 studies using the CVF (Hartnell, et al., 2011). Although the results show some predictive validity in that different types of cultures are sometimes related to subjective measures of organizational outcomes, the authors conclude that there is only modest support for the nomological validity of the framework and that, "The results suggest that identifying 'dominant culture' types may be of limited utility because they do not account for culture's bandwidth" (Hartnell et al., 2011: 687). Ostroff and Schulte (2014) also note that although there is an assumption that an internally consistent set of values underlies each of the four culture types, no evidence exists confirming this.

Absent convergent and discriminant validity, it is difficult to distinguish the CVF, and other approaches to culture that are similarly lacking in construct validity, from other related organizational constructs like organizational climate and structure. Culture becomes, at once, many aspects of organizations – everything – and ultimately an indistinct construct – nothing. And, even if organizations can be viewed as inhabiting these cultural types by displaying certain attributes and practices, it is unclear whether an organization inhabits them because they value them *per se*. Thus, though an instrument claiming to measure culture correlating with, say, organizational performance may be useful for confirming to managers that culture is important, insights regarding organizational culture itself are constrained by the lack of construct validity of many prevailing approaches to measuring organizational culture (Chatman & O'Reilly, 2016).

APPROACHES TO MEASURING ORGANIZATIONAL CULTURE

Measures of organizational culture need to unequivocally and specifically measure organizational culture, and developing a unified theory of culture is essential to establishing the construct validity of culture measures. Building upon Schein's (2010) theoretical framework of culture which focuses on assumptions, norms and values, and cultural artifacts, another requirement is that each measure of culture specifies the layer it assesses. In evaluating culture measures below, we focus both on the empirical strengths and weaknesses of each approach, using our list of empirical challenges above as criteria, and on the layer of culture that each purports to measure.

An Illustration of Survey Methods Leveraging Informants – the Organizational Culture Profile (OCP)

One of the most valid ways to assess culture is to directly ask informants, typically those immersed in the culture, to respond to questions that clearly ask for judgments regarding patterns of norms and behavior within their culture. As an illustrative survey approach, we discuss the Organizational Culture Profile (OCP – Chatman, 1991; Chatman et al., 2014; O'Reilly et al., 1991), one of the most heavily used survey methods for assessing culture (for a comprehensive review of the other popular survey methods, please see Chatman and O'Reilly, 2016).

The OCP, and its focus on soliciting input from knowledgeable informants, was designed explicitly to assess organizational culture. The theory underlying the OCP is that organizational culture is a form of social control and the associated normative social influence that results from the behavioral norms arising within organizations. More specifically, culture is a system of shared values that define what is important and norms – socially created standards that help members interpret and evaluate events and actions – that define appropriate attitudes and behaviors for organizational members (O'Reilly & Chatman, 1996). Chatman and O'Reilly (2016) emphasize the intentional lack of an a priori framework utilized in the construction of the OCP. Instead, they began by identifying a universe of descriptors for culture and then narrowing them down with regards to the categories of generalizability, comprehension, readability, redundancy, and the relative variance expected for a given descriptor across various organizations (Caldwell et al., 2008; Chatman, 1991; O'Reilly et al., 1991).

The OCP measures three aspects of cultural norms: norm content, norm consensus, and norm intensity (Chatman et al., 2014). Previous discussions acknowledged the uneven emphasis placed upon culture content over culture strength (Harrison & Carroll, 2006) or strength over content as seen through the "culture strength index" (Kotter & Heskett, 1992; Sørenson, 2002). Either way, there had not been a conscious effort to separate these distinct attributes, leading some to conclude that many studies of culture confounded content and strength (Chatman et al., 2014). This raised questions about whether, for example, an innovative culture is the same as a culture in which members do not agree about the relative importance of a comprehensive set of norms within their organization. Parsing culture solves this problem by defining *norm content* as the substance of the cultural norm, or the appropriate behaviors and attitudes described through the norm. In contrast, *norm intensity* is the force with which cultural norms are held, or the degree of salience and the degree to which a norm may be identity defining. And *norm consensus* is the extent to which members agree broadly about an organization's system of cultural norms (Chatman et al., 2014).

The OCP uses the Q-sort methodology (Block, 1978) in which informants must consider 54 norm statements and allocate them into nine categories ranging from "most characteristic" to "least characteristic" of their organization's culture. This approach requires informants to implicitly compare each norm statement to every other norm statement to determine which norms are held most and least intensively, providing information about both norm substance and norm intensity (O'Reilly et al., 1991). In this way, the OCP avoids social desirability bias, particularly as compared to a Likert-type scale in which informants could mark the highest anchor for an unlimited number of items, and has been found to be free of such biases (Chatman, 1991). It also makes it possible for informants to essentially rank order the comprehensive set of norm statements reliably (Chatman, 1991). Agreement in how similarly members prioritize the 54 items is also assessed, and provides a metric for the level of consensus across the comprehensive set of cultural norms (Chatman et al., 2014). Though the range is not infinite, the number of possible configurations of the 54 items is extremely high (Chatman, 1991).

Empirical evidence of the OCP shows that the 54 items cluster into six to eight independent dimensions (e.g., Marchand et al., 2013; Sarros et al., 2005). In particular, Chatman and O'Reilly report six dimensions – (1) adaptiveness or innovation, (2) results-orientation, (3) detail-orientation, (4) collaboration or teamwork, (5) customer-orientation, and (6) integrity (Chatman et al., 2014; O'Reilly et al., 2014) – and the six dimensions appear consistent with the dimensions other researchers have identified (Berson et al., 2008; Borg et al., 2011; Detert et al., 2000; Tsui et al., 2006). The OCP has demonstrated predictive validity in person–organization fit research and organizational performance research (e.g., Adkins & Caldwell, 2004; Chatman et al., 2014; Elfenbein & O'Reilly, 2007; Judge & Cable, 1997; Kristof-Brown et al., 2005; Sheridan, 1992; Vandenberghe, 1999).

Critique of informant-generated survey methods for assessing culture

Even though the OCP offers significant face validity in assessing culture, it still suffers from many of the same shortcomings of any self-reported survey measure. These shortcomings must be addressed, including minimizing the effect of social desirability bias on responses, and accumulating adequate data across an organization and across time periods to ensure that the findings are representative and reliable. Any survey method has the potential to suffer from selection bias if the entire population does not respond – which is typically a challenging goal. And, though informants are typically in a good position to assess the culture of the organizations of which they are members, they may be unaware of aspects of the culture or subject to other biases, such as self-justifying behavioral accounts, or retrospective rationality (Staw, 1981) that make their observations less objective and potentially less accurate. Finally, these methods tend to be labor-intensive and typically generate smaller samples of organizations at a slower pace, though researchers have often sampled a large sample of essential firms within targeted industries to control for industry and environment effects and isolate the effects of organizational culture (e.g., Chatman & Jehn, 1994; Chatman et al., 2014; Sheridan, 1992). That said, a variety of other methods can be used to overcome these shortcomings, which we review below.

Computational Linguistics as a Measure of Organizational Culture

One of the fastest-growing methods of assessing culture is the computational linguistics approach. It has been enabled by major increases in computing capacity and the existence of huge amounts of potentially relevant digital data, which can be used to measure cultural variables such as norms, cultural fit, and enculturation trajectories (e.g., Popadak, 2013; Srivastava et al., 2017). The computational approach enables analyses that have eluded prior researchers by being, at once, granular, rich, and dynamic. The approach analyzes language use which, unlike surveys, is unobtrusive and more behaviorally-oriented (e.g., Lu et al.,

2019), and makes it feasible to track the micro-dynamics of person–culture fit and culture change. Though such tracking was possible using survey methods, it has been significantly more cumbersome because of the frequency with which informants would have to be asked to report on the culture.

Researchers using computational linguistics make a credible claim that language is a useful signal of cultural alignment. Indeed, economists have long viewed language accommodation as a key indicator of cultural assimilation (e.g., Crémer, 1993). Language represents conventions and brings meaning to the surface, at the behavioral level. Organizations develop idiosyncratic conventions that are inevitably embedded in language use among members. Further, language convergence can reflect social distance. These arguments, presented in a variety of papers (e.g., Goldberg et al., 2016; Lu et al., 2019; Srivastava et al., 2017) are helping to build theory that differentiates between cognition and behavior mostly pertaining to person–culture fit (enculturation).

Analytical approaches to using computational linguistics to assess culture
A number of data sources and categorization techniques have been used to assess culture. We briefly review studies relying on email data, Glassdoor data, and other publicly available third-party websites that serve as a venue for reviews about various work organizations, and we discuss the methodological approach researchers have used to construct the culture data, both of which are important for judging construct validity.

Linguistic inquiry and word count (LIWC)
In one study, Lu and colleagues (2019) operationalize behavioral cultural fit as the similarity between an individual's language and her reference groups' using the Interactional Language Use Model (ILUM) (Goldberg et al., 2016; Srivastava et al., 2017). They argue that linguistic similarity can sometimes reflect alignment for non-cultural reasons – for example, two people coordinating on a shared task might use similar language even when they are culturally incompatible. As such, the researchers focus on the similarity of linguistic style between an individual and her reference group. Drawing on previous sociological work on culture (e.g., Doyle et al., 2017), ILUM uses the well-established and widely used Linguistic Inquiry and Word Count (LIWC) lexicon (Pennebaker et al., 2007) to measure linguistic style. LIWC is a semantic dictionary that maps words into 64 high-level distinct emotional, cognitive, and structural categories. A comprehensive body of work demonstrates that the linguistic units identified by LIWC relate to a wide and universal array of meaningful psychological categories (Tausczik & Pennebaker, 2010). Using LIWC, the researchers claim to focus on expressions that are inherently cultural, while downplaying linguistic exchanges that are organization- or context-specific or primarily related to functional coordination between organizational members. In offering an example, Lu et al. (2019: 14) suggest that:

> [A]n organization with an aggressive and competitive culture … might manifest linguistically in expressions of certainty, negation, and the use of swear words and other forms of non-deferential language. Contrast such a normative environment with one characterized by politeness and the use of tentative and inclusive language, indicating a collaborative and non-confrontational culture. LIWC is specifically designed to capture such culturally meaningful dimensions.

Substantively, Lu et al. (2019) distinguish between person–culture fit based on value congruence (between an individual and their organization) and perceptual accuracy, or a person's ability to accurately identify the organizational. Lu and his colleagues (2019) find that value congruence predicts voluntary departure while perceptual accuracy predicts behavioral fit, or closer language use alignment between the focal individual and her reference group. Even more novel, they show that perceptual accuracy is informed by a focal individual's network. Further, the paper uses multiple methods – both computational linguistics to analyze emails over the course of a year in a mid-sized company, but also OCP data collected from a large representative sample of organizational members. The study shows that the email data and the OCP data align, offering the first evidence of convergent validity between the linguistic approach and more traditional, validated informant-based survey methods. Finally, as with many of the digital trace data approaches, the authors use machine learning methods to extend the findings longitudinally.

In another study drawing on the same approach, Srivastava and colleagues (2017) define an enculturation trajectory as an individual's temporal pattern of person–culture fit, which they argue can change over time and can precede more significant behavioral changes such as voluntary departure. Srivastava and his colleagues (2017) analyzed 10.24 million internal emails collected over five years in a 650-person organization. The analysis, at its most fundamental level, compares each focal actor's language use to those of her colleagues within the organization. Greater similarity equates to greater fit while less language accommodation signals lower fit. This study confirms what we know from prior research – that those who do not fit with the culture of their organization typically leave (e.g., Chatman, 1991; O'Reilly et al., 1991) – and the temporal frequency of the data enables the researchers to detect precisely when people begin to show signs of disengaging from the organization and ultimately, when they are likely to leave. The approach avoids a host of response biases and is also more substantively rich than typical network analyses, which only detect and analyze ties to others (e.g., frequency of contact).

The logistics involved in creating data sets typically involves collecting emails on a server. The data are cleaned, examined, typically in monthly increments, and each focal individual's language use is compared to a relevant group within the organization (e.g., members of their work group, network ties). These language accommodation scores can then be used to track behavioral manifestations of culture and cultural fit over time (Srivastava et al., 2017), or they can be connected to attainment measures (Goldberg et al., 2016). In either case, the data are granular and open up the possibility of answering questions such as, when is fit typically established for an organizational newcomer? How does early enculturation influence subsequent performance and longevity in a firm? And what are the markers of voluntary and involuntary departure? Some of these are new questions, while others have been considered before but could not be easily or convincingly answered. Importantly, the consequences of person–culture fit that the computational work to date reveals correspond to past research using existing methods, primarily survey based, for assessing culture fit. The advantage of this alignment is that it establishes convergence and the construct validity of this approach as well as prior approaches, which sets the stage to ask and answer questions that will advance theory development.

Latent Dirichlet Allocation (LDA)

The LDA approach is another way of unobtrusively deriving culture-relevant data without imposing research-driven categories on the data (e.g., Puranam et al., 2017). LDA is a model of the probabilistic generation of a text corpus, and is able to identify "topics" most commonly present in a set of sentences such as a data set of emails. Each topic is basically a weighted set of words that tend to co-occur. The model is trained on a set of sentences, identifying the most common topics in the training set. Then, the LDA model can be fit to another set of sentences, such as those derived from Glassdoor reviews, to extract information regarding fit or alignment. Corritore et al. (2019) use this method to examine the causes and consequences of cultural fragmentation. They examined Glassdoor reviews of 492 publicly traded organizations and found support for their hypotheses that only interpersonal cultural heterogeneity undermined coordination and predicted volatility in firm performance, while intrapersonal cultural heterogeneity was associated with increased creativity and patents at the firm level.

In a quest to improve researchers' ability to "show versus tell," that is, to minimize the need to justify the interpretations of findings, Marchetti and Puranam (2019) offer a refined approach to LDA topic modeling, prototypical-text based interpretation (PTBI). Marchetti and Puranam (2019: 3) claim that this approach provides comprehensive rules by which prototypical text sections and topic structure are identified from data extracted from an algorithm. They further identify three advantages to PTBI: (1) it reduces researchers' need to exert judgment in interpreting topics, (2) it offers a guide and framework for "transparently recording the inevitable choices that researchers must make in the process of prototypical text extraction," and (3) it enhances the transparency and replicability of the interpretation process by revealing the selections of prototypical text from the corpus that form the basis for topic interpretation by the researcher. Using Netflix, an organization with a sophisticated and transparent culture, Marchetti and Puranam were able to map the algorithmically induced topics derived from the PTBI method on to the cultural values that Netflix has articulated in publicly available sources, finding high correspondence between the two (42 of 57 unique concepts map onto the seven cultural dimensions they identified for Netflix).

Other analytical methods
Other researchers have used a combination of methods to derive cultural data from unobtrusive digital sources. In one of the most interesting examples, Popadak (2013) used automated text analysis and data from three websites collecting comments on organizations. The data represented 4,600 firms over a 10-year period, including reviews by more than 1.8 million employees. Popadak's (2013) analysis used 400 million words to construct culture dimensions consistent with those identified by O'Reilly and colleagues (2014): adaptability, collaboration, customer-orientation, detail-orientation, integrity, results-orientation, and transparency. She calculated the normalized dot product between two vectors, which is weighted so that it captures the unique concept in each two set of texts. In short, she created a master text (set of all potential words and phrases for culture) and an aggregate text (aggregated reviews for a firm). The pool of potential words and phrases (the master texts) is from WordNet, a lexical database of semantic relations, and it is created by considering relatedness (Jiang & Conrath, 1997). The aggregate text is compared to the master text to measure a firm on each of the seven dimensions. Popadak (2013) then used textual similarity to compare the actual words in the online employee reviews ("aggregate text") with the words in the master list that describe each of seven cultural dimensions.

Popadak's (2013) analysis relies on regression discontinuity, dividing firms at the closest limit in terms of whether they were supported or not by shareholder votes (51 percent versus 49 percent). She found that variations in corporate governance affected the culture of the firm and that culture, in turn, was associated with performance. In particular, firms that closely lost governance elections were more likely to subsequently emphasize being results-oriented and less likely to emphasize being customer-oriented compared to those who closely won their governance elections. And, cultures that emphasized results more intensely and customers less intensely experienced a 1.4 percent decline in firm value over time.

Similarly, Moniz (2017) collected data from 417,000 employee reviews of 2,300 firms from 2008 to 2015 on Glassdoor. He found that firm value increased among organizations whose culture was aligned to their strategic goals. Using data from the Great Place to Work survey, Guiso, Sapienza and Zingales (2015) have shown that a firm's stated values are not related to firm performance, but a culture that emphasizes integrity is associated with subsequent performance. And, in a unique sample of 683,052 organizations across 57 countries, Polzer et al. (2018) are focusing on digitized calendars to examine variations in how many meetings people attend from one organization to the next. This is a truly unobtrusive measure of culture that is not subject to biases inherent in language use; however, the validity of meetings as representing cultural norms or artifacts must still be developed.

Critiques of the computational linguistic approaches
These approaches demonstrate an exciting and vital step forward for the organizational culture paradigm. This use of email and Glassdoor data and similar sources to analyze language accommodation is also a useful complement to self-reported culture data. Researchers have argued that language use is a dominant medium through which cultural information is exchanged. On the other hand, the case needs to be made for the validity of language use, particularly email communication or anonymous company reviews collected by third-party organizations, such as Glassdoor, as measures of culture. And, as with all methodological approaches, there are significant weaknesses inherent in these methods that warrant mentioning.

One critique of the linguistic approach is that language use is not the only indicator of culture and culture fit and represents only a narrow slice of behavior. Email is a stylized communication form that likely predetermines how people interact regardless of their organizational culture. People have varying beliefs about the extent to which emails are public or private, and there are multi-level norms (e.g., at the group, organization, professional, and societal levels) governing how people write and comprehend emails. An overreliance on email data may lead to a stilted view of culture. For example, we know that people can feel both more and less restrained as they communicate digitally. Further, these comments are more likely associated with individual attitudes – or the organization's climate – than with employees who are serving as informants of the culture and reporting on broad patterns of norms. And, email studies to date have only examined email correspondence within a single firm so their level of analysis is necessarily the individual (or possibly the work unit), which doesn't optimize for computational approaches which should have the promise of large samples of organizations.

Comments on sites such as Glassdoor and Great Place to Work are subject to significant selection bias, with employees or former employees who have especially strong positive or negative views about the organization being more likely to comment. Indeed, organizations often coach employees to review their organization favorably on such websites and published surveys given the reputational benefits of being reviewed positively.

Qualitative culture researchers would argue that written language is not a particularly rich form of communication and that culture resides in deep assumptions, shared values, and observable behavior (e.g., Martin, 2002). And even quantitative culture researchers might argue that organizational informants are pretty reliable and valid sources for explicit reports on an organization's culture, and that email is, at best, an indirect source of cultural information.

Meeting schedules, as a manifestation of culture, may also be limited in that some organizations may have compliance requirements imposed by regulators or other structural constraints that could lead researchers to draw conclusions about culture that actually arise from other organizational or contextual forces. And, though researchers claim that these approaches to understanding the meaning in emails, reviews of organizations, and meeting schedules are unobtrusive measures of culture, they are still imposing assumptions about the connection between such behaviors and an organization's culture as do researchers who design surveys.

Thus, there is some risk in investing exclusively in language-based data to represent culture and culture fit. Researchers need to both validate and understand how digital trace data fit into the construct of organizational culture and its other manifestations (e.g., dress, beliefs, informants' stated perspective, celebrations, senior leader communications). Finally, the exact theoretical gains that have been derived from these new methodologies are a little harder to judge. The work has not really challenged existing theories of culture, and it hasn't necessarily brought more clarity to the definition of it, nor identified particularly novel outcomes. What it has done is allow for more fine-grained tests – when does someone start to show signs of departing an organization? How long might it take for merging firms to become productive and integrated? These are valuable and substantial contributions, and the hope is that theoretical advancement will soon occur.

Computer Simulations and Laboratory Experiments Manipulating Aspects of Organizational Culture

Another influential approach to studying organizational culture is computer simulations and computational modeling (Carroll & Harrison, 1998; Harrison & Carroll, 1991; Srivastava et al., 2017). This method has been less focused on norm content, and more on norm agreement and intensity. For example, researchers have investigated simulated organizations experiencing demographic changes to examine how norm agreement and intensity, and specifically the transmission of culture, is influenced by member churn (employee entry and departure) (e.g., Harrison & Carroll, 1991). Harrison and Carroll (2006) proposed that research relying on surveys to assess culture could be complemented by the use of a formal model that theorizes the link between observable factors such as rates of employee entry and turnover. Through the use of a formal model, it becomes possible to better understand the underlying theoretical processes without being constrained by selection bias or identification issues. Through a model consisting of a hiring function, socialization function, and a turnover function, a computer simulation is able to show several characteristics about cultural systems, such as its equilibrium, robustness, and strength during various stages (Harrison & Carroll, 1991).

However, there are challenges in using this approach to draw conclusions about how organizational culture operates. First, there are no real data involved in the simulations. Second, the computational models rely on realistic assumptions in identifying relevant variables, their likely levels or range, and their relationships to one another. As such, researchers must have some sense, mostly gleaned from empirical investigations of actual organizational cultures, about the relevant variables to specify, their typical levels and range, and their likely relationship to one another. For example, regarding hiring, researchers can examine various levels of under-, optimal, and over-recruiting of new employees or new-recruit diversity, and the varying enculturation levels associated with new recruits relative to existing members and how they affect cultural transmission (Harrison & Carroll, 1991). One of the strengths of the simulation method is in identifying the links between a simulated norm of behavior, various levels of demographic movement within an organization, and the resulting cultural characteristics such as robustness and culture strength.

Experimental Approaches to Measuring Culture

Researchers have examined organizational culture by experimentally manipulating its content (e.g., Chatman et al., 1998, 2019) or focusing on agreement levels about various norms (e.g., Weber & Camerer, 2003). For example, Chatman and colleagues (1998) simulated cultures that either emphasized individualism or collectivism and found that members of collectivistic cultures were more productive and creative when they also represented diverse demographic attributes. And Chatman and colleagues (2019) showed that experimentally manipulated collectivistic cultures caused members to blur demographic differences among them, affecting the quality of group decisions. Weber and Camerer (2003) considered norm consensus to be observed through higher efficiency among newly merged groups.

And, in what can be considered a quasi-field experiment, Martinez et al. (2015) observed an organizational intervention in which both a technical and a culture change solution were used to solve a significant safety issue in a hospital; central line-associated blood stream (CLABS) infections, which are a very serious threat to patients. Martinez and her colleagues (2015) suggested how to conduct analyses that would isolate the effects of culture on measured reductions in CLABS, such as whether a reduction of CLABS was associated with changes in survey-based self-reported norms among employees. By manipulating culture and using random assignment, such experiments (and interventions) can generate enormous causal insight into how culture influences behavior and organizational performance. These designs need not be complex, but empirical analyses must be able to control for alternative explanations of any behavioral change.

CONCLUSIONS AND FUTURE DIRECTIONS FOR MEASURING ORGANIZATIONAL CULTURE

Advancing the organizational culture paradigm requires that researchers coalesce around a definition of organizational culture. Organizational culture researchers have increasingly adopted definitions focused on culture as norms (Chatman & O'Reilly, 2016) and have studied norms and artifacts (Schein, 2010). A second requirement is that researchers hold each other accountable for theoretical precision in defining, empirically validating, and articulating a theory of culture including where it comes from, how it operates, and what it produces. Third, paradigm development would benefit by identifying a set of commonly agreed upon problems, and then working systematically to solve those problems. Some examples include understanding the links between culture and other key organizational constructs such as strategy, structure, leadership, and employee composition. A second may focus on how culture is established, transmitted and changes over time, including identifying the leading indicators of change as well as the most significant enablers and obstacles. And a third might examine unusual combinations of norm content (e.g., high integrity and low transparency, high cooperation and high competition) or of norm content and norm agreement, such as whether strong cultures can also emphasize innovation and avoid inertial thinking. A fourth question might focus on subcultures within organizational cultures, addressing the fragmentation question, and a fifth might focus on the dynamics of person–culture fit.

If researchers could derive this list of big problems, they could then work together to address them, each from their own methodological vantage point. Though it may be difficult to imagine individual research teams conducting full cycle research (Chatman & Flynn, 2005), given the challenges of mastering multiple methodologies, full cycle research could occur at the paradigm level. This is essential because, as we have illustrated above, each of the primary approaches to assessing culture has unique strengths – informant-reported surveys are face and construct valid, digital trace data enables large samples, dynamic tracking, and unobtrusive measures, simulations can enable unconstrained tests of relationships among large numbers of variables simultaneously, and experiments allow causal inferences. Each also has distinct weaknesses – informant-reported surveys are subject to informant biases and accumulating samples from a large numbers of organizations is effortful, digital trace data are not necessarily indicators of culture and can lack construct validity (and so far, email data has only been used within a single firm), simulations are only as good as the assumptions that they are based on and lack external validity, and experiments can lack external validity and are limited in their generalizability to organizations.

As we hope we have made clear, the *only* way of addressing the inherent weaknesses of each method is to cross-validate them with the other methods. Organizational culture is a central topic in organizational research and it is viewed as immensely important to managers (Graham et al., 2017). Our goal has been to lay out a set of methodological options for assessing culture and to urge researchers to accumulate comparable, conceptually valid knowledge and advance our understanding of organizational culture as a paradigm. The path to this goal is obvious; culture must be defined clearly and assessed using multiple measures.

NOTE

1.   We thank Megan Gorges for her valuable comments on earlier drafts of this chapter.

REFERENCES

Adkins, B., & Caldwell, D. (2004). Firm or subgroup culture: Where does fitting in matter most? *Journal of Organizational Behavior: The International Journal of Industrial, Occupational and Organizational Psychology and Behavior, 25*(8), 969–978.

Alvesson, M., & Berg, P. (1992). *Corporate Culture and Organizational Symbolism*. Berlin: Walter de Gruyter.

Berson, Y., Oreg, S., & Dvir, T. (2008). CEO values, organizational culture and firm outcomes. *Journal of Organizational Behavior: The International Journal of Industrial, Occupational and Organizational Psychology and Behavior, 29*(5), 615–633.

Block, J. (1978). *The Q-sort Method*. Palo Alto: Consulting Psychologists Press.

Borg, I., Groenen, P. J., Jehn, K. A., Bilsky, W., & Schwartz, S. H. (2011). Embedding the organizational culture profile into Schwartz's theory of universals in values. *Journal of Personnel Psychology, 10*(1), 1–12.

Caldwell, D. F., Chatman, J. A., & O'Reilly, C. A. (2008). Profile comparison methods for assessing person–situation fit. In C. Ostroff, & T. Judge (Eds.), *Perspectives on Organizational Fit* (pp. 356–360). Mahwah, NJ: Lawrence Erlbaum Associates.

Cameron, K. S., Quinn, R. E., DeGraff, J., & Thakor, A. V. (2006). *Competing Values Leadership: Creating Value in Organizations.* Cheltenham, UK and Northampton, MA, USA: Edward Elgar Publishing.

Carroll, G. R., & Harrison, J. R. (1998). Organizational demography and culture: Insights from a formal model and simulation. *Administrative Science Quarterly, 43*(3), 637–667.

Chatman, J. A. (1989). Improving interactional organizational research: A model of person–organization fit. *Academy of Management Review, 14*(3), 333–349.

Chatman, J. (1991). Matching people and organizations: Selection and socialization in public accounting firms. *Administrative Science Quarterly, 36*, 459–484.

Chatman, J., & Flynn, F. (2001). The influence of demographic composition on the emergence and consequences of cooperative norms in groups. *Academy of Management Journal, 44*(5), 956–974.

Chatman, J., & Flynn, F. (2005). Full-cycle micro organizational behavior research. *Organization Science, 16*(4), 434–447.

Chatman, J., & Jehn, K. (1994). Assessing the relationship between industry characteristics and organizational culture: How different can you be? *Academy of Management Journal, 37*, 522–553.

Chatman, J. A., & O'Reilly, C. A. (2016). Paradigm lost: Reinvigorating the study of organizational culture. *Research in Organizational Behavior, 36*, 199–224.

Chatman, J., Bell, N., & Staw, B. (1986). The managed thought: The role of self-justification and impression management in organizational settings. In D. Gioia, & H. Sims (Eds.), *The Thinking Organization: Dynamics of Social Cognition.* San Francisco, CA: Jossey-Bass (pp. 191–214).

Chatman, J. A., Caldwell, D. F., O'Reilly, C. A., & Doerr, B. (2014). Parsing organizational culture: How the norm for adaptability influences the relationship between culture consensus and financial performance in high-technology firms. *Journal of Organizational Behavior, 35*(6), 785–808.

Chatman, J., Greer, L., Sherman, E., & Doerr, B. (2019). Blurred lines: How collectivism mutes the disruptive and elaborating effects of demographic heterogeneity in Himalayan expeditions. *Organization Science, 30*(2): 235–259.

Chatman, J., Polzer, J., Barsade, S., & Neale, M. (1998). Being different yet feeling similar: The influence of demographic composition and organizational culture on work processes and outcomes. *Administrative Science Quarterly, 43*(4): 749–780.

Crémer, J. (1993). Corporate culture and shared knowledge. *Industrial and Corporate Change, 2*(3), 351–386.

Corritore, M., Goldberg, A., & Srivastava, S. B. (2019). Duality in diversity: How intrapersonal and interpersonal cultural heterogeneity relate to firm performance. *Administrative Science Quarterly, 65*(2).

Denison, D., Nieminen, L., & Kotrba, L. (2014). Diagnosing organizational cultures: A conceptual and empirical review of culture effectiveness surveys. *European Journal of Work and Organizational Psychology, 23*(1), 145–161.

Detert, J. R., Schroeder, R. G., & Mauriel, J. J. (2000). A framework for linking culture and improvement initiatives in organizations. *Academy of Management Review, 25*(4), 850–863.

Doyle, G., Goldberg, A., Srivastava, S., & Frank, M. (2017, July). Alignment at work: Using language to distinguish the internalization and self-regulation components of cultural fit in organizations. In *Proceedings of the 55th Annual Meeting of the Association for Computational Linguistics (Volume 1: Long Papers)* (pp. 603–612).

Elfenbein, H. A., & O'Reilly III, C. A. (2007). Fitting in: The effects of relational demography and person–culture fit on group process and performance. *Group & Organization Management, 32*(1), 109–142.

Gelfand, M. J., Raver, J. L., Nishii, L., Leslie, L. M., Lun, J., Lim, B. C., ... & Aycan, Z. (2011). Differences between tight and loose cultures: A 33-nation study. *Science, 332*(6033), 1100–1104.

Giorgi, S., Lockwood, C., & Glynn, M. A. (2015). The many faces of culture: Making sense of 30 years of research on culture in organization studies. *Academy of Management Annals, 9*(1), 1–54.

Goldberg, A., Srivastava, S. B., Manian, V. G., Monroe, W., & Potts, C. (2016). Fitting in or standing out? The tradeoffs of structural and cultural embeddedness. *American Sociological Review*, *81*(6), 1190–1222.

Graham, J. R., Harvey, C. R., Popadak, J. A., & Rajgopal, S. (2017). *Corporate Culture: Evidence from the Field* (No. w23255). SSRN. National Bureau of Economic Research.

Guiso, L., Sapienza, P., & Zingales, L. (2015). The value of corporate culture. *Journal of Financial Economics*, *117*(1), 60–76.

Harrison, J., & Carroll, G. (1991). Keeping the faith: A model of cultural transmission in formal organizations. *Administrative Science Quarterly*, *36*(4), 552.

Harrison, J. R., & Carroll, G. (2006). *Culture and Demography in Organizations*. Princeton, NJ: Princeton University Press.

Hartnell, C. A., Ou, A. Y., & Kinicki, A. (2011). Organizational culture and organizational effectiveness: A meta-analytic investigation of the competing values framework's theoretical suppositions. *Journal of Applied Psychology*, *96*(4), 677–694.

Jiang, J. J., & Conrath, D. W. (1997). Semantic similarity based on corpus statistics and lexical taxonomy. *Proceedings of the International Conference on Research in Computational Linguistics (ROCLING), Taiwan (1997)*. arXiv preprint cmp-lg/9709008.

Judge, T. A., & Cable, D. M. (1997). Applicant personality, organizational culture, and organization attraction. *Personnel Psychology*, *50*(2), 359–394.

Kotter, J. P., & Heskett, J. L. (1992). *Corporate Culture and Performance*. New York, NY: Free Press.

Kristof-Brown, A. L., Zimmerman, R. D., & Johnson, E. C. (2005). Consequences of individuals' fit at work: A meta-analysis of person–job, person–organization, person–group, and person–supervisor fit. *Personnel Psychology*, *58*, 281–342.

Kroeber, A. L., & Kluckhohn, C. (1963). *Culture: A Critical Review of Concepts and Definitions*. Vintage: New York.

Lu, R., Chatman, J. A., Goldberg, A., & Srivastava, S. B. (2019). Deciphering the cultural code: Cognition, behavior, and the interpersonal transmission of culture. University of California, Berkeley, Working Paper.

Marchand, A., Haines, V. Y., & Dextras-Gauthier, J. (2013). Quantitative analysis of organizational culture in occupational health research: A theory-based validation in 30 workplaces of the organizational culture profile instrument. *BMC Public Health*, *13*(1), 443.

Marchetti, A., & Puranam, P. (2019). Interpreting topic models using prototypical text: From "telling" to "showing." Working paper, INSEAD.

Martin, J. (2002). *Organizational Culture: Mapping the Terrain*. Thousand Oaks, CA: Sage Publications.

Martinez, E., Beaulieu, N., Gibbons, R., Pronovost, P., & Wang, T. (2015). Organizational culture and performance. *American Economic Review*, *105*(5), 331–335.

Moniz, A. (2017). Inferring employees' social media perceptions of corporate culture and the link to firm value. Available at SSRN 2768091.

O'Reilly, C. A., & Chatman, J. A. (1996). Culture as social control: Corporations, cults, and commitment. *Research in Organizational Behavior*, *18*, 157–200.

O'Reilly, C. A., Caldwell, D. F., Chatman, J. A., & Doerr, B. (2014). The promise and problems of organizational culture: CEO personality, culture, and firm performance. *Group & Organization Management*, *39*(6), 595–625.

O'Reilly, C. A., Chatman, J., & Caldwell, D. F. (1991). People and organizational culture: A profile comparison approach to assessing person–organization fit. *Academy of Management Journal*, *34*(3), 487–516.

Ostroff, C., & Schulte, M. (2014). A configural approach to the study of organizational culture and climate. In B. Schneider, & K. M. Barbera (Eds.), *The Handbook of Organizational Climate and Culture*. Oxford: Oxford University Press.

Ostroff, C., Kinicki, A. J., & Muhammad, R. S. (2012). Organizational culture and climate. In N. W. Schmitt, & S. Highhouse (Eds.), *Handbook of Psychology*, New York: John Wiley and Sons.

Pennebaker, J., Booth, R., & Francis, M. (2007). LIWC2007: Linguistic inquiry and word count. Austin, Texas: liwc.net.

Pettigrew, A. M. (1979). On studying organizational cultures. *Administrative Science Quarterly*, *24*(4), 570–581.

Popadak, J. (2013). A corporate culture channel: How increased shareholder governance reduces firm value. SSRN, 2345384.

Polzer, J., DeFilippis, E., & Tobio, K. (2018). Countries, culture, and collaboration. Presented at the Academy of Management Meetings, Chicago, IL.

Puranam, D., Narayan, V., & Kadiyali, V. (2017). The effect of calorie posting regulation on consumer opinion: A flexible Latent Dirichlet Allocation model with informative priors. *Marketing Science*, *36*(5), 726–746.

Sarros, J. C., Gray, J., Densten, I. L., & Cooper, B. (2005). The Organizational Culture Profile revisited and revised: An Australian perspective. *Australian Journal of Management*, *30*, 159–182.

Schein, E. H. (2010). *Organizational Culture and Leadership*, 4th ed. San Francisco, CA: Jossey-Bass.

Schneider, B., Ehrhart, M. G., & Macey, W. H. (2013). Organizational climate and culture. *Annual Review of Psychology*, *64*, 361–388.

Sheridan, J. E. (1992). Organizational culture and employee retention. *Academy of Management Journal*, *35*(5), 1036–1056.

Sørensen, J. B. (2002). The strength of corporate culture and the reliability of firm performance. *Administrative Science Quarterly*, *47*(1), 70–91.

Srivastava, S. B., Goldberg, A., Manian, V. G., & Potts, C. (2017). Enculturation trajectories: Language, cultural adaptation, and individual outcomes in organizations. *Management Science*, *64*(3), 1348–1364.

Staw, B. M. (1981). The escalation of commitment to a course of action. *Academy of Management Review*, *6*(4), 577–587.

Tausczik, Y. R., & Pennebaker, J. W. (2010). The psychological meaning of words: LIWC and computerized text analysis methods. *Journal of Language and Social Psychology*, *29*(1), 24–54.

Tsui, A. S., Wang, H., & Xin, K. R. (2006). Organizational culture in China: An analysis of culture dimensions and culture types. *Management and Organization Review*, *2*, 345–376.

Tucker, S., Ogunfowora, B., & Ehr, D. (2016). Safety in the C-suite: How chief executive officers influence organizational safety climate and employee injuries. *Journal of Applied Psychology*, *101*(9), 1288–1299.

Vandenberghe, C. (1999). Organizational culture, person–culture fit, and turnover: A replication in the healthcare industry. *Journal of Organizational Behavior*, *20*, 175–184.

Verbeke, W., Volgering, M., & Hessels, M. (1998). Exploring the conceptual expansion within the field of organizational behaviour: Organizational climate and organizational culture. *Journal of Management Studies*, *35*(3), 303–329.

Weber, R. A., & Camerer, C. F. (2003). Cultural conflict and merger failure: An experimental approach. *Management Science*, *49*(4), 400–415.

8. Methodological alignment in qualitative research of organisational culture

Alireza Javanmardi Kashan and Anna Wiewiora

Research has long established that organisational culture is an important aspect of organisational life (Kieser, 1997), and organisational culture has evolved as a strong paradigm in organisational studies. However, the existing literature has accommodated different views about fundamentals such as defining organisational culture and how we think it works (Martin, 2002). While some scholars consider culture as an independent variable, others believe that organisational culture is not a variable, which can be easily captured, but is the organisation itself including its identity, which is constantly created and recreated (Smircich, 1983). In addition, some scholars believe that organisational culture can be captured as 'us' (our values, beliefs, assumptions) and 'them' (the values of others) (Anthony, 1994). Presence of subcultures means that it is difficult to define organisational culture as an organisation-wide phenomenon, which is clear and known and can establish harmony and coherence in the organisation. The divergent views on organisational culture and the way the knowledge about culture has been structured have led to 'ambiguity' and 'fragmentation' of the organisational culture phenomena (Martin, 2002).

Qualitative research on the relationships between organisational culture and management systems have used different lenses based on different conceptualisations of such relationships. This has created distinct pockets of studies with different ontological and epistemological assumptions. Therefore, qualitative research on organisational culture can be characterised as diverse, disparate, and controversial (Alvesson, 2012). These diverse approaches to conceptualise organisational culture mean that there is a need to systematically capture methodological approaches used for studying organisational culture including ontological and epistemological assumptions, data collection and analysis methods. In this chapter, we are presenting different approaches and the methods used to study organisational culture, which may assist organisational culture researchers to select appropriate design and methods for the purpose of their unique studies of organisational culture.

ASSUMPTIONS IN QUALITATIVE RESEARCH ON ORGANISATIONAL CULTURE

Organisational culture scholars have followed different or even opposing assumptions about organisational culture. Culture has been viewed as a variable, as a metaphor or as symbolic.

Culture as a Variable

Culture as a variable refers to culture as a construct among other constructs, which work as mechanisms for manipulating an organisation, its people, and its systems. This view is often adopted by scholars who are objectivists and assume that organisational culture is a discrete object that can be identified and measured (Eriksson & Kovalainen, 2015; Martin, 2002). The organisational culture is represented in the measurement instruments, such as the competing values framework (Cameron and Quinn, 2011). Czarniawska-Joerges (1992) questioned such an instrumental approach as she believed that the organisational culture cannot be explained satisfactorily through distinct concepts and measures and can only be understood through the interpretations of the organisational complexities. The researchers who use culture-as-variable assumptions take a neutral position in their studies and are mindful of keeping their distance from the cultural reality. These researchers consider that multiple local realities exists and recognise that the organisational culture is based on subcultures. Based on this view, culture can be viewed as the commonalities across organisational members (Aguinis & Henle, 2003).

Culture as a Metaphor

Culture as a metaphor sees organisations as cultures. As such, the culture is not independent of the organisation but is the organisation itself. Smircich (1983, p. 348) clarifies that 'culture as a metaphor promotes a view of organisations as expressive forms and manifestations of human consciousness. Organisations are understood and analysed not through the economic or material terms, but in terms of their expressive, ideational, and behavioural aspects.' Based on this view, organisational culture is not just another piece of the puzzle, it is the puzzle (Pacanowsky & O'Donnell-Trujillo, 1983, p. 146). Therefore, the research agenda of the culture as a metaphor view is to explore an organisation as a socially shared – intersubjective – experience. This view is typically adopted by interpretivists who assume that organisational culture reality should be understood through interpretations. The organisational culture is not measured using instruments and proxies. Because the culture is believed to reside in the minds of people in the organisation, the researcher cannot discover them from a distance, but needs to engage with people and observe their behaviours and the decisions they make to truly understand the culture. According to the interpretivist view, we can find organisational beliefs and values implicitly embedded in the management approaches as they are enacted during the life of the organisation (Weick, 1995). As a result, in order to explore the organisational culture embedded in the practices, we need to discover the members' interpretations of the practices associated with management systems (like control, leadership, structure, etc).

Symbolic View

Some scholars believe that culture is neither an independent variable affecting management systems nor a socially constructed reality. Instead, the symbolic view considers culture as a local and contextual reality. A symbol can be defined as an object – a word or statement, a kind of action or a material phenomenon (Cohen, 1974). The symbolic nature of organisational culture can be described as words, movements, or things which reflect and carry a meaning greater and wider than the one that those words, movements, or things originally have (Janićijević, 2011). The symbolic view of culture introduces a two-level conceptualisation of organisational culture where the local behaviour may be the symbol representing the higher-level shared value which is embedded in the meaning behind those behaviours. Hofstede and Peterson (2000) stress the importance of contextuality and remind us that human actions and interactions which build the culture reality take place in different contexts. Aligned with this view, the advances in the research on management systems have not led to standard-isation of management systems, but to acknowledging the context specificity of the design of the management systems and the balance between general conception and local differentiation (Van Muijen, 1999). The exemplar of this could be the broad diffusion of the adoption of the balanced scorecard system (Kaplan & Norton, 2001) which has not resulted in the standardi-sation of its application despite appearing to be a value-free system of 'calculative practices' (Miller, 1994). In fact, investigation of the obstacles to the implementation of the balanced scorecard system reveals the context specificity and cultural roots of this system (Harrison & McKinnon, 1999).

Based on the symbolic view, organisational culture is one reality which can be manifested differently and in different behaviours based on the local contexts underpinning these behav-iours. In this sense, organisational culture is less rational and instrumental and more an expres-sive social tissue around us that gives meaning to the organisational practices. The meaning behind different behaviours could reflect that shared organisational culture which guides local activities. 'Meanings' uncover the value embedded in things and is the message and inter-pretation we associate with an object or an utterance. Organisational culture is the system of such publicly and collectively accepted meanings operating for a given group at a given time. Meaning is a way of linking to things and adding a subjective belief to organisational prac-tices and making them symbols and representations of cultural reality. Critical research will compare and contrast the competing interpretations of the culture and consider how the local structure drives behaviours of local people. The critical research helps discover the shared organisational culture reality through analysis of the symbols and behaviour.

DATA COLLECTION METHODS

In this chapter, we present six most common qualitative research methods: observation, inter-views, focus groups, Q methodology, secondary data, and case studies.

Observation

Observation includes observing behaviours as well as the identification of symbols and arte-facts that reveal information about culture. Observing behaviours and symbols can include watching and recording companies' celebrations and other organisational events and rituals. As much as possible, researchers should try to accurately capture and record the details of a ritual or practice, while not influencing them. Identifying and recognising symbols involve observation of practices and behaviours that employees carry in the organisation. For example, experimentations with new technologies indicates cultural values like risk taking or openness to experience. Cross-functional brainstorming sessions where everyone has a fair go to express their opinions indicates cultural values of diversity and openness to different views. Symbols often have meanings in the eyes of members but may not be easily identified or understood by the external observer (Martin, 2002). This concern adds a dimension to observation in relation to the level of researchers' objectiveness or distance from the research context, which is reflected in difference between types of observation methods used in research.

These are three types of observational research. The first type involves social interaction with subjects in the field and direct observation of relevant events (McCall & Simmons,

1969, p. 1). The researcher, as an active observer, uses subjective experiences as critical data for understanding cultural symbols. For example, Howard-Grenville (2006) in a case study in high-tech manufacturing, used participant observation to understand the influence of organisational culture on how an organisation's members define, or 'set' problems and the strategies they draw on to solve such problems. A second type of the observational research is ethnography (Hammersley & Atkinson, 1995), which includes the generation of descriptions of culture gained by immersion in the culture studied. This may contribute to studies following the interpretivist approach. The third type is objective observation (Silverman, 2002) where the researcher keeps their distance and remains objective and is mindful of potential biases in the process of observation.

Interviews

A useful method for gaining a rich data on culture is through conducting interviews. Interviews involve a conversation guided by a series of questions asked by the researcher (interviewer) from the informant (interviewee). Interviews are particularly beneficial for collecting data about cognitive elements of organisational culture (presumptions, values, norms, and attitudes). Researchers can also use interviews to collect data on the more observable symbols and outcomes of the hidden cultural values captured in expressions, stories, myths, anecdotes, and jargon.

There are different types of interviews related to different theory-building approaches. Structured interviews may be used with more targeted questions about predetermined categories. Studies adopting critical views tend to do ethnographic interviews (Spradley, 1979) which are used to understand informants' conceptions of culture based on the role of their specific context in formation of their conception. Interpretivist research tend to use semi-structured or unstructured longer interviews that involve open discussions to make connections between categories and participants' cultural meanings. For example, Baumgartner (2009) used open discussions to identify the embedding of sustainability aspects in the organisational culture of a company. Carter (1995) used open discussions to access research participants' values and beliefs and allow them to elaborate and reflect on their experiences (Gartner et al., 1992). Insights from such discussions allow the researcher to discover the causal relationships between events and the cultural values behind them (Black & Bern, 1981). As the researcher listens to the stories, they should consider the values and beliefs of the research participants.

The semi-structured interview is the most frequent type of interview method used to investigate culture. It allows potentially deeper insights into the understanding of culture and its complexities. For example, semi-structured interviews help unpack aspects of cultural values and underlying assumptions. Participants can further elaborate on their personal beliefs and perceptions about the ways of doing, such as what is permitted and what is not, in their respective work units. These insights allow researchers to gain a deeper understanding of practices that guide and inform the actions of organisational members and how these practices impact various outcomes (such as performance, learning, wellbeing, and burnout). This in turn can lead to potentially novel findings and research contributions. For example, Wiewiora et al. (2013) used semi-structured interviews to investigate the role of organisational culture regarding the project managers' willingness to share knowledge beyond their projects, in a project-based organisational context. Semi-structured interviews follow a certain set of questions, guided by the interview protocol, but also allow conversational, two-way communication (Yin, 2009).

Conducting semi-structured interviews helps to clarify the responses and offer participants the opportunity to provide valuable comments and feedback. In addition, using semi-structured interviews allows the investigator to pick up non-verbal cues from the participants, which can assist in deeper understanding of the culture and its facets.

Preparing an interview protocol is a good practice to ensure a more systematic data collection process and to keep the researcher focused on the topic. The interview protocol should include brief information about the study, data collection procedures, and interview questions. Interview questions should include demographic questions about the participants, and semi-structured questions about the focus of the research. The questions should be framed in a way to provide flexibility for the researcher to ask follow-up questions and further inquire about the phenomena and explore new insights which emerged during the interview. Entering the field includes preparation work such as negotiating and obtaining access to the interview participants and gaining their consent (Fernández, 2004). Before conducting the interviews, participants should be informed about any possible risks and benefits relevant to the data collection and research and, if relevant, reassured about the confidentiality of the interview.

Focus Groups

Focus groups refers to group interviews with participants who share some common characteristics (for example, work in the same location, under the same management, or represent similar demographic). Focus groups can collect qualitative data which reveal the social realities of a cultural group (Morgan, 1993). The investigator then has the chance of better understanding the terminology and language used by the participants in structuring and organising their social reality. The researcher also has the opportunity to identify different viewpoints within the group as well as the shared cultural meanings among the group members (Morgan, 1993). Unlike interviews, focus groups allow the investigator to observe the dynamics of the groups and the counter influences between the participants (Neuendorf, 2002). In contrast to using observation, researchers can moderate and manipulate the structure of these dynamics and interactions. These features of the focus group are critical to explore specific issues in a given context. The focus group is a useful method to identify the cultural assumptions 'because the group provides the stimulus to bring out what is ordinarily hidden' (Schein, 1985, p.127). Group members' viewpoints may spark experiences as well as ideas from others (Mertens, 1998). This also opens up pathways to new topics during the discussion, where the researcher can probe and further explore hidden aspects of culture that emerged during the focus group discussion. The active role of the researcher is critical in leading the discussions to probe and elaborate on the emerging ideas.

Depending on the nature of the study, the researcher may prefer to explore diverse ideas rather than identify the consensus among the participants, or vice versa. The researcher can also decide if the configuration of the participants should be homogeneous or heterogeneous (Oetzel, 2001). Chang and Lu (2007) used focus groups in the context of Taiwanese organisations to explore relationships between the organisational culture, and stressors and wellbeing of employees. They used eight focus groups to explore stressors, characteristics of organisation culture, and stressors related to organisation culture. Fox et al. (2005) employed three rounds of focus groups to explore and examine the factors that contribute to successful transition of new staff to the workplace. Montgomery et al. (2013) explored the impact of highly contextualised organisational cultures in hospitals on health professionals' burnout and the quality of medical care in eight European countries. In this large-scale use of focus groups, researchers used a systematic approach to recruit participants across different countries, totalling 153 physicians, 133 nurses, and 46 patients.

In most cases, focus groups are combined with other methods in organisational culture research. In this way, focus groups can be used to interpret the results of an earlier study, or for exploratory purposes to set the foundation for the follow-up investigation to gain more in-depth understanding of the issues that emerged during the focus groups. For example, Best et al. (2013) used three focus groups as complementary methods to surveys and interviews, in their investigation of the organisational culture interventions required at different stages of project management to increase effectiveness. They examined the relationship between the interventions and effectiveness in a survey which was followed up by interviews to elaborate the nature of those interventions. Focus groups were then used for the purpose of brainstorming and interpreting the data gained in the survey and interviews. In another example, Doran (2002) used three focus groups to identify the product categories used in different cultures in her study of cultural differences in information search and use. Once the product categories were identified in the focus groups, she developed interview questions related to each of the emerging categories. Dougherty and Smythe (2004) used a case study to explore the relationship between organisation culture and sexual harassment using sense-making theory. Within this case study, they integrated focus groups with interviews for the purpose of triangulation. Dickson et al. (2000) also integrated focus groups with interviews for triangulation and identification of cultural dimensions in their cross-cultural study to explore the differentiating factors among different organisations' cultures. In the same vein, Alkhoraif and McLaughlin (2018) integrated focus groups with interviews to explore the type of organisational culture supportive of successful implementation of lean management.

Q Methodology

There has been increasing interest in the use of Q methodology in qualitative research. Chatman and her fellow researchers (Chatman, 1989; Chatman & Jehn, 1994; O'Reilly et al., 1991) are pioneers in using Q methodology in organisational culture studies. They adopted the method to better understand cultures by exploring factors underlying individuals' behaviours and shared elements among subjective meanings (Howard, 1995).

To apply Q methodology, the Q sort technique is used where participants receive a pile of cards with a statement on each of them. Each statement include combinations of variables and participants are asked to sort the cards from left to right and from 'Most Uncharacteristic' to 'Least Characteristic' (Brown, 1996). Once all participants finalise sorting their cards, factor analysis is then conducted on the results. Contrary to the standard factor analysis based on the R method where correlation among variables is attained, in the Q sort technique correlations among participants are obtained (Brown, 1996). This factor analysis reveals the latent factors which explain differences in the behaviour of individuals, and groups individuals into clusters based on shared beliefs (McKevitt et al., 2012). Q methodology can be used by studies with the assumption of culture as a metaphor to identify the cultural values specific to the organisation under study. Participants sort cards with value statements, which reportedly reflect several common factors or value dimensions. The way they sort the cards would be reflective of their underlying values and beliefs and the differences between their priorities in ranking cards is based on their different levels of latent values and beliefs.

In contrast to more generalisable global organisational culture frameworks, such as the competitive values framework, Q methodology helps researchers explore the context-specific values and recognise the culture types relevant to the local context of the study (which could be the same or different from the global theories). In other words, while conventional culture surveys assess the relative position of each individual/organisation against predetermined variables and benchmarks, using Q methodology we can focus on the salient configuration of variables within a person or an organisation. This approach is used in cultural studies for different purposes. For example, O'Reilly et al. (1991) used Q methodology to develop an Organisational Culture Profile (OCP) and investigated person–organisation fit. Jacobson and Aaltio-Marjosola (2001) used Q methodology to understand the experience of women managers in a cross-cultural research, while Howard (1998) used Q methodology to validate a competitive value model.

Q methodology can be used in combination with other methods discussed above and secondary data (see below). Barry and Proops (1999) and Brown (1996) argued that Q methodology provides insights into individuals' subjective views about phenomena (Robbins & Krueger, 2000) and can help researchers interpret data collected using other methods by revealing the latent factors behind the behaviour of individuals. The advantage of using Q methodology in research is its ability to generate results based on individuals' perspectives, meanings, and opinions instead of researchers' perceptions (Previte et al., 2007). Using an inductive approach, the method aims to generate person-types instead of generalisable variables.

Secondary Data

Secondary data includes the data, publications, reports, white papers, or other documents which are prepared primarily for other purposes, but which the researcher can use to interpret and understand organisational culture. Secondary data can be used to search for cultural artefacts and symbols. For example, company websites often include information about the company's vision and values, which reveal insights about organisational culture and what it stands for.

Case Studies

Qualitative study of organisational culture can use any one of the above-mentioned data collection methods; however, most often the qualitative researcher uses a mix of them particularly in the case study approach, which is commonly used to examine organisational culture. The case study approach to research offers a comprehensive, real, and accurate picture of organisational culture with all its complexities. Particularly, in-depth single case studies explore more layers of the organisational culture in one organisation including the history and the context of the organisational culture. Longitudinal case studies examine a phenomenon or 'case' as it changes over time. Leidner et al. (2006) used semi-structured interviews and analysis of publications by the organisation and its members to explore how organisational culture influences knowledge management practices. Similarly, Lucas and Kline (2008) used multiple methods: observations, semi-structured interviews with groups and individuals, and field notes and documents to study the relationship between organisational culture, group dynamics, and organisational learning in the context of organisational change. Foster-Fishman and Keys (1997) used interviews, observation, and archival data review to understand the interaction between empowerment and organisational culture. Using a case study approach allows researchers to dive deeper into the organisational context and understand facets of its culture through access to various data sources and use of multiple data collection methods.

DATA ANALYSIS METHODS IN QUALITATIVE RESEARCH ON CULTURE

Data analysis in organisational culture research generally consists of interpretations of the insights of the researchers and the participants' experience of the organisational culture, which allows the reader to understand the culture and 'get it' (Shotter, 1993). Data from interviews, focus groups, observations and secondary data on culture captures practices, stories, and insights about what is important in the organisation, what is valued, what is discouraged, and how things are done. There are several analytical methods that can be used to capture the multi-faceted reality of organisational culture based on the interaction between meanings, symbols, artefacts, and the actions.

Content Analysis

Qualitative content analysis is a descriptive analysis method consisting of techniques for analysing data and elucidating themes. It is a disciplined process of coding, developing and examining interpretations with the aim of explaining or describing organisational culture or some of its aspects via themes emerging from the content analysis of the data. Studies based on content analysis focus on the characteristics of language as communication with attention to the content or contextual meaning of the text (Tesch, 1990). Text data may be in verbal, print, or electronic form and may have been collected from narrative responses, open-ended survey questions, interviews, focus groups, observations, or print media such as articles, books, or manuals (Kondracki et al., 2002).

One approach in content analysis is focusing on a lower level of inferences and interpretations, rather than an abstract level of interpretation. This approach provides the explicit depiction of the text, not emphasising the implicit meaning behind it. This analytical method is usually applied in a research design with the goal of describing an organisational culture rather than explaining it based on existing theories or frameworks. This approach is normally suitable when the researcher supposes that the existing theory or constructs are not able to explain the cultural reality. To analyse the data, the researcher identifies common passages from the text and categorises these passages into themes (Kondracki et al., 2002). Researchers immerse themselves in the data to allow new insights to emerge. This approach is usually referred to as inductive category development (Mayring, 2000).

A second approach to content analysis first uses existing theories and frameworks to identify themes or categories (Potter & Levine-Donnerstein, 1999). Potter and Levine-Donnerstein (1999) believe that the pre-existing constructs and theory if elaborated can explain the textual data and cultural reality. The goal of this type of content analysis is to extend existing theories and to provide knowledge and understanding of the particular organisational culture in the context of an existing theory (Downe-Wamboldt, 1992). This approach to data analysis can be considered as a deductive use of theory (Potter & Levine-Donnerstein, 1999). In this approach, the data about the artefacts and behaviours are analysed to identify the organisation's basic cultural assumptions. This type of research mainly uses established organisational culture frameworks such as Schein's (1990) to guide the analysis.

Discourse Analysis

Discourse analysis examines sets of texts that describe and constitute organisational realities, as well as the complex relationships among texts (Phillips & Hardy, 2002). Discourse analysis can be seen as a theoretical framework based on social constructionist epistemology that considers texts and talk as carrying and constructing the social reality not merely reflecting or representing it (Gergen, 1999). Discourse analysis provides a set of techniques for examining how the socially constructed ideas and objects that comprise the social world are formed and retained. While content analysis is typically used to identify social reality, discourse analysis attempts to uncover the way in which the social reality was produced and is held in place.

According to Fairclough (1992) discourses have three main dimensions: pieces of talk or text, the collection of texts that gives them meaning, and the social context in which they occur. As such, in the discourse analysis, the researcher decodes the talks, texts and behaviours to find the meanings implanted within them, based on the context in which they interplay. Discourse analysis can therefore accommodate the complex and multifaceted reality of organisational culture by elaborating the context-specific aspects of the culture. While some researchers have used discourse analysis with a narrow focus on its technical aspects to draw 'surface meanings' out of conversations, other scholars have applied the broader capacities of discourse analysis to understand the culture of respondents (Silverman, 2002). During discourse analysis, the researcher focuses on talks, texts, and behaviours (as evidence of the discourses) and works backward to uncover the culture reality. For example, Pettigrew (1979) analysed documentary sources, including private papers, speeches, administrative documents, and other archival material to investigate some of the constructs and processes related to the formation of organisational cultures. Discourse analysis therefore adds a useful focus on the processes of social construction (Munir & Phillips, 2005), and the understanding of organisational culture as a socially constructed phenomenon.

Narratives

Narratives are defined as 'spoken or written text giving an account of an event/action or series of events/actions, chronologically connected' (Czarniawska, 2004, p. 17). Similar to discourse analysis, analysis of narratives follows the social constructionist approach that emphasises the relationship between people and their context (Fletcher, 2006). However, narratives focus on the role of organisational members' sense of organisational culture reality and how the values inside them shape the events and meanings (Mumby, 1987).

Values are embedded in events and stories about events can uncover how values could be the guiding principles for the decisions. Research participants provide insights by generating a 'plot' (White, 1981) that integrates the individual events or series of actions to a 'meaningful whole' (Czarniawska, 2004). As Gergen (2005, p. 110) described:

> in establishing a given endpoint and endowing it with value, and in populating the narrative with certain actors and certain facts as opposed to others, the narrator enters the world of moral and political evaluation. Value is placed on certain goals (e.g., winning, as opposed to non-competition) certain

individuals (heroes and villains as opposed to communities) and particular modes of description …
the culture's ontology and sense of values is affirmed and sustained.

A deeper understanding of organisational culture can be constructed from narratives. For
example, organisational culture studies have applied narratives to learn how organisational
decision-makers act to change and institutionalise the organisational culture (Armenakis et al.,
2011; Diochon & Anderson, 2010). Organisations are seen as a web of stories (Boje, 2011)
which are included within the objective cultural structures. The researcher can play an active
role in analysis and use narratives not only to find how organisational members make sense
of organisational life, but also to link those sense-makings to the organisation-wide value
structure through researchers' 'sense-giving' (Weick, 1995). When organisational members
(cultural actors) attach emotional and symbolic attributions to their stories, researchers can
'give sense' to them by referring to the values and beliefs informed by the cultural structure.
Researchers can listen to how respondents 'make sense' of organisational practices and then
try to give sense to the emergent meanings by interpreting them against theories.

DIFFERENT THEORY-BUILDING APPROACHES

Based on the view of the culture reality and the epistemological assumptions taken by the
researcher, different theory-building approaches are used to evaluate the data. Here we present
three theory-building approaches.

Realism

Realism assumes objective reality external to the mind of the researcher that is reflected onto
the scientific data and theories. Realists wish to reveal the true reality of this objective world.
Research based on assumptions of realism adopts static views on the relationships between
cognitive and behavioural components of culture (for example Schein's (1990) dominant
model of culture).These are based on linear and predefined relationships among artefacts,
espoused values and norms, and core assumptions, and these behavioural elements captured in
data should represent the predefined higher-order themes. The static view assumes the culture
as a predefined structure, which can be manifested in different contexts differently. Less
emphasis is given to the process behind the emergence and cultural change throughout the
organisation. This view recognises the commonality of some beliefs or rules (Smircich, 1983)
and tries to identify them by following the value structure and through a top-down approach to
explain the organisational culture.

Interpretivism

Interpretivism seeks to describe how different meanings held by different persons or groups
generate and maintain a reflection of truth, especially against competing definitions of reality.
The research uncovers and describes the meanings that employees apply in real settings. It
examines how particular versions of reality become shared, dominant, and/or contested in
comparison with other meanings and understandings (Gephart, 2004). The aim of this research
is to improve understanding of the process of generating meanings and concepts used by

employees in organisational settings. An interpretivism position is taken such that multiple realities co-exist which affect how people understand and react to the objective world. These diverse meanings are present among different groups forming their behaviour in their particular context. Studying organisational culture from the interpretivism perspective focuses on 'how individuals interpret and understand their experience and how these interpretations and understandings relate to action' (Smircich, 1983, p. 351). As a result, this view focuses on both ideas (beliefs, meanings) as well as the organisational practices that members of an organisation carry out that respond to and recreate these meanings and values (Riley, 1983).

While realists see social structures as independent of the human actions which inform organisational practices, interpretivists believe that 'social structures' and 'real causes' are socially constructed. The interpretivism research considers the dynamic and bidirectional relationships between artefacts, symbols, assumptions, and values (Hatch, 1993). This is referred to as a 'dynamic view' that concentrates on the behavioural content of the culture and how research participants communicate the culture and the context. Following the dynamic view, researchers uncover the beliefs or rules through a bottom-up approach and from the organisational practices and artefacts (Sackmann, 1992).

Critical View

The critical view focuses on the dialogic and dialectical processes (Lincoln & Guba, 2000) of how the taken-for-granted truths unfold. Critical research is based on the view that reality is constructed based on the crystallisation of social, political, and economic values over time. Similarly to interpretivism, critical research believes that conflicting views of reality exist, and it uses interpretive methods to discover different meanings held by groups in power-laden relationships. However, in the critical view, one version of truth exists, and one reality will thrive among the competing ones. Based on this view, organisational culture operates aligned with Bhaskar's (1989) idea which suggested that social structures, which control relationships among people and organisations, are full of meanings and are informed and changed by people's interaction. A point of difference between the critical view and interpretivism is that critical research also acknowledges that the social structure is the base for a range of interactions among people. The process of study helps discover the shared organisational culture reality through analysis of the symbols and behaviour. Some studies focus on employees' behaviours and the meaning they carry and the role of individuals in the development or transformation of a dominant perspective (Jermier et al., 1991). Other research emphasises the symbols (incidents, texts, contradictions, and signs) rather than the individuals' behaviours (Gephart, 2004). Meanings conveyed by symbols represent strategies of action, which control how people define problems and identify solutions. Researchers can analyse the symbols to identify and explain the culture and behaviours of individuals operating in that culture.

QUALITATIVE DATA CODING METHODS

In the qualitative analysis of organisational culture, choosing the analytical method and coding strategy depends on the researcher's approach to theory building (Van Maanen, 2011) including realism, interpretivism, or critical view:

Deduction

Studies based on the realism tradition tend to rely on content or thematic analysis to find manifestations of the predefined concepts. Researchers following realism tend to apply data analysis methods based on deductive reasoning and using the process of subsumption. Subsumption comes from set of pre-known features, aligned with a theoretical framework, and provides evidence for generalisation and knowledge development. Based on the logic of deduction the research subject embodies application of an existing theory in a new setting. Such logic of deduction reasoning is applied for data analysis in 'etic' research (Martin, 2002), based on which the organisational culture is analysed according to predefined themes, which the researcher will investigate on the basis of findings of prior studies. The major cultural variables and factors are predetermined and are studied based on the existing theoretical models. The purpose of data analysis is elaboration of existing concepts and exploration within the boundaries of them. Data analysis following deduction can be attributed more closely to latent content analysis or thematic analysis referring to the process of interpretation of content, or deductive coding application (Mayring, 2000).

   In the process of data analysis, the coding that the researcher uses is based on abstract and general interpretations which are called 'thin descriptions' (Geertz, 1973). Using thin descriptions based on short and brief statements is empirically inadequate, in that it provides linkages to theoretical themes and portrays the actions in a way that omits most of the references to the context. The use of thin description operationalises the assumptions of objectivity through which text is turned into a tool for gathering quantifiable data. This is mostly the case where qualitative research is conducted to link the organisational culture to management systems. In such studies, the culture reality tends to be seen as a variable (or a function of the organisation) which has associations with other functional variables in management systems. To generate qualitatively testable models, 'objective' expressions are used with stable, context-free meanings words and statements as opposed to 'indexical' expressions which include words and statements whose meanings change based on the context of use.

Induction

Data analysis based on interpretivism applies the logic of induction. In inductive research, the qualitative features discovered by the researcher are used as evidence for existence of similar (or associated) features in a similar real setting even though the researcher has no direct evidence for them. Each case under study can represent a new insight to be uncovered during the study. While deductive logic makes inferences from a sample to a large population, the inductive logic makes inferences from certain characteristics observed to other and complementary characteristics of population, which are not perceived in the data. Both these approaches admit that abstract cultural values and observable behaviours are building blocks of organisational culture reality, but the interplay between them is assumed differently, which is then reflected in different analysis and interpretation strategies. Realists emphasise the objective values and beliefs in determining and shaping the behaviour, while interpretivists emphasise the role of behaviour and human interaction in producing and changing values and beliefs. Such a difference in epistemological assumptions and the associated reasoning is reflected in the coding approach undertaken in the qualitative research.

Different coding strategies are taken in etic or emic research of organisational culture reality. The logic of inductive reasoning is used for data analysis in emic research (Martin, 2002). Emic research does not use predefined themes; rather they are established during the research itself and based on the organisation or culture members' different views. The interpretations will be based on thick description. Thick description is a deep and context specific description, which includes all the information informed by cultural contexts and makes emergence of the categories from the data explicit and visible. In the process of data analysis, as expected, researchers avoid using preconceived themes (Kondracki et al., 2002), instead allowing the categories and names for categories to flow from the data. Researchers immerse themselves in the data to allow new insights to emerge (Kondracki et al., 2002).

Abduction

Abductive reasoning involves travelling back and forth between lower level and concrete aspects of empirical data and more abstract interpretations of them. It is a third way between inductive reasoning and deductive logic (Atkinson et al., 2003). Such an approach to data analysis works through theory-making based on interpretations made to the collected data. In the studies of this type, the theories which already developed in the literature cannot integrate different interpretations and meanings obtained from empirical data. Therefore, it is required to theorise or extend an existing theory (Burawoy, 1991) to accommodate the data and explain the new variations observed in the phenomena.

Abduction is to move from a conception of something to a different, possibly more developed or deeper conception of it (Richardson & Kramer, 2006). Rather it represents a general way of generating theory (or, even more generically, a way of having ideas on the basis of empirical research. This approach falls between the etic and emic research where data analysis is not focusing on descriptive categories or abstract themes, but focuses on interpretations. The major point of departure which differentiates this data analysis approach from realism and interpretivism approach is the travelling back and forth between data collection, analysis, and literature. Based on this approach, once a researcher comes across an interpretation, she will go back to field to collect more evidence around the interpretation developed and compare the findings with the literature, and then decide to stay with the interpretation or change it as the analysis progresses. Through rounds of iteration between data collection, data analysis and comparing with literature, the researcher will end up with a set of interpretations and the associated themes which are well supported with empirical evidences.

The data analysis approach matching with this type of research follows Gioia and his colleagues' approach (Gioia et al., 2012) based on the formation of first-order and second-order codes. Based on their approach, the researcher can manage connecting the subjective experiences to theories, as they gain both 'first-order' descriptive categories and 'second-order' abstract interpretations from the stated experiences of research participants. The second-order interpretations communicate the research participant's experiences in a common language in the relevant literature which is familiar to the academic reader. The studies using this method operationalise the interpretation strategy based on a data structure which presents a hierarchical approach for coding data in two separate phases with different coding strategies (see, e.g., Corley & Gioia, 2004, p. 184). In the first round of coding, researchers use 'open coding' which applies research participants' words in their contextual meanings to shape first-order categories based on constant comparison (Strauss & Corbin, 1990) among a variety of extracts. Building upon the first-order categories, the researcher should use axial coding to form second-order interpretations at the abstract level of the hierarchical data structure which serves particular theoretical themes.

FINAL REMARKS

Organisational culture is recognised as an important field of research, particularly in relation to studies on management systems in organisations. However, different views and definitions of culture have created a field of research which is diverse, disparate, and controversial (Alvesson, 2012; Martin, 2002). Different views of culture are based on different ontological and epistemological assumptions, which require different research methods. Qualitative researchers need to recognise the differences between these views and the methods available for the study of organisational culture. To respond to this need, we present different views of organisational cultures and the different philosophical assumptions that underpin these views. We cannot draw clear boundaries for the use of methods in association with certain assumptions and theory-building approaches, and different data collection methods can be used for different purposes. Observation, interviews, focus groups, Q methodology and secondary data have been used in studies with different assumptions and theory-building approaches. Similarly, each of the analytic methods discussed above can potentially serve to enable different theory-building approaches. For example, we know that interpretivism explores contexts through comprehensive descriptions while the critical approach looks for evidences of the roles of individuals or symbols in constructing organisational culture reality.

For analysis, we can therefore use narratives for exploring individuals' values, based on interpretivism research. Analysis of the narratives can also adopt a critical view, based on which the researcher examines the role of individuals in the emergence of organisational culture. Studies using discourse analysis have mostly adopted a critical view in which the researcher's intention is to examine how symbols can be interpreted to uncover the culture. Discourse analysis can also follow the interpretivism approach and be used to explore the meaning behind symbols in accordance with their context of occurrence, for example by exploring local meanings.

In this chapter we presented the most commonly used methods for data collection, data analysis, and data processing in qualitative research in the field of organisational culture. The features of these methods were explained and discussed in terms of their application to study organisational culture. The information and discussions provided in this chapter may help qualitative researchers develop a more integrated view of a qualitative research design to study organisational culture using aligned methods and assumptions.

REFERENCES

Aguinis, H., & Henle, C. A. (2003). The search for universals in cross-cultural organizational behavior. *Organizational Behavior: A Management Challenge, 355*.

Alkhoraif, A., & McLaughlin, P. (2018). Lean implementation within manufacturing SMEs in Saudi Arabia: Organizational culture aspects. *Journal of King Saud University – Engineering Sciences, 30*(3), 232–242.

Alvesson, M. (2012). *Understanding organizational culture*. Sage.

Anthony, P. (1994). *Managing culture*. Buckingham, UK: Open University Press.

Armenakis, A., Brown, S., & Mehta, A. (2011). Organizational culture: Assessment and transformation. *Journal of Change Management, 11*(3), 305–328.

Atkinson, P., Coffey, A., & Delamont, S. (2003). *Key themes in qualitative research: Continuities and changes*. Oxford, UK: Altamira Press.

Barry, J., & Proops, J. (1999). Seeking sustainability discourses with Q methodology. *Ecological Economics, 28*(3), 337–345.

Baumgartner, R. J. (2009). Organizational culture and leadership: Preconditions for the development of a sustainable corporation. *Sustainable Development, 17*(2), 102–113.

Best, A., Smit, J., & de Faber, L. (2013). Interventions and their relation to organizational culture and project management. *Procedia-Social and Behavioral Sciences, 74*, 329–338.

Bhaskar, R. (1989). *Reclaiming reality: A critical introduction to contemporary philosophy*. London: Verso.

Black, J. B., & Bern, H. (1981). Causal coherence and memory for events in narratives. *Journal of Verbal Learning and Verbal Behavior, 20*(3), 267–275

Boje, D. M. (Ed.). (2011). *Storytelling and the future of organizations: An antenarrative handbook* (Vol. 11). Routledge.

Brown, S. R. (1996). Q methodology and qualitative research. *Qualitative Health Research, 6*(4), 561–567.

Burawoy, M. (1991). *Ethnography unbound*. Berkeley, CA: University of California Press

Cameron, K. S., & Quinn, R.E. (2011). *Diagnosing and changing organizational culture: Based on the competing values framework*. San Francisco, CA: John Wiley & Sons.

Carter, R. T. (1995). *The influence of race and racial identity in psychotherapy: Toward a racially inclusive model* (Vol. 183). John Wiley & Sons.

Chang, K., & Lu, L. (2007). Characteristics of organizational culture, stressors and wellbeing: The case of Taiwanese organizations. *Journal of Managerial Psychology, 22*(6), 549–568.

Chatman, J. A. (1989). Improving interactional organizational research: A model of person–organization fit. *Academy of Management Review, 14*(3), 333–349.

Chatman, J. A., & Jehn, K. A. (1994). Assessing the relationship between industry characteristics and organizational culture: How different can you be? *Academy of Management Journal, 37*(3), 522–553.

Cohen, Y. A. (1974). *Man in adaptation: The cultural present, Volume 2* (2nd ed.). Transaction Publishers.

Corley, K. G., & Gioia, D. A. (2004). Identity ambiguity and change in the wake of a corporate spin-off. *Administrative Science Quarterly, 49*(2), 173–208.

Czarniawska, B. (2004). *Narratives in social science research*. London, UK: Sage Publications.

Czarniawska-Joerges, B. (1992). *Exploring complex organizations: A cultural perspective*. Beverly Hills, CA: Sage Publications Inc.

Dickson, M. W., Aditya, R. N., & Chhokar, J. S. (2000). Definition and interpretation in cross-cultural organizational culture research: Some pointers from the GLOBE research program. In M. Ashkanasy, C. Wilderom & M. Peterson (Eds), *Handbook of organizational culture and climate* (pp. 447–464). Sage.

Diochon, M., & Anderson, A. R. (2010). Ambivalence and ambiguity in social enterprise: Narratives about values in reconciling purpose and practices. *International Entrepreneurship and Management Journal, 7*(1), 93–107.

Doran, K. (2002). Lessons learned in cross-cultural research of Chinese and North American consumers. *Journal of Business Research, 55*(10), 823–829.

Dougherty, D., & Smythe, M.J. (2004). Sensemaking, organizational culture, and sexual harassment. *Journal of Applied Communication Research, 32*(4), 293–317.

Downe-Wamboldt, B. (1992). Content analysis: Method, applications, and issues. *Health Care for Women International, 13*(3), 313–321.

Eriksson, P., & Kovalainen, A. (2015). *Qualitative methods in business research: A practical guide to social research*. Sage Publications Inc.

Fairclough, N. (1992). *Critical language awareness*. New York, NY: Longman

Fernández, W. D. (2004). Using the Glaserian approach in grounded studies of emerging business practices. *Electronic Journal of Business Research Methods, 2*(2), 83–94.

Fletcher, R. (2006). The impact of culture on web site content, design, and structure. *Journal of Communication Management.* 10(3), 259–273.

Foster-Fishman, P. G., & Keys, C. B. (1997). The person/environment dynamics of employee empowerment: An organizational culture analysis. *American Journal of Community Psychology, 25*(3), 345–369.

Fox, R., Henderson, A., & Malko-Nyhan, K. (2005). 'They survive despite the organizational culture, not because of it': A longitudinal study of new staff perceptions of what constitutes support during the transition to an acute tertiary facility. *International Journal of Nursing Practice, 11*(5), 193–199.

Gartner, W. B., Bird, B. J., & Starr, J. A. (1992). Acting as if: Differentiating entrepreneurial from organizational behavior. *Entrepreneurship Theory and Practice, 16*(3), 13–32.

Geertz, C. (1973). *The interpretations of cultures.* New York, NY: Basic Books.

Gephart, R. P. (2004). Qualitative research and the Academy of Management Journal. *Academy of Management Journal, 47*(4), 454–460.

Gergen, K. J. (1999). *An invitation to social construction.* London, UK: Sage Publications Inc.

Gergen, K. J. (2001). Psychological science in a postmodern context. *American Psychologist, 56*(10), 803–813.

Gergen, K. J. (2005). Narrative, moral identity, and historical consciousness. *Narration, Identity, and Historical Consciousness, 3,* 99.

Gioia, D. A., Corley, K. G., & Hamilton, A. L. (2012). Seeking qualitative rigor in inductive research: Notes on the Gioia methodology. *Organizational Research Methods, 16*(1), 15–31.

Hammersley, M., & Atkinson, P. (1995). *Ethnography: Practices and Principles* (2nd ed.). New York, NY: Routledge.

Hatch, M. J. (1993). The dynamics of organizational culture. *Academy of Management Review, 18*(4), 657–693.

Harrison, G. L., & McKinnon, J. L. (1999). Cross-cultural research in management control systems design: A review of the current state. *Accounting, Organizations and Society, 24*(5–6), 483–506.

Hofstede, G., & Peterson, M. F. (2000). Culture: National values and organizational practices. *Handbook of Organizational Culture and Climate, 3,* 401–416.

Howard, A. E. (1995). *The changing nature of work.* Jossey-Bass.

Howard, L. W. (1998). Validating the competing values model as a representation of organizational cultures. *International Journal of Organizational Analysis, 6*(3), 231–250.

Howard-Grenville, J. A. (2006). Inside the 'black box': How organizational culture and subcultures inform interpretations and actions on environmental issues. *Organization & Environment, 19*(1), 46–73.

Jacobson, S. W., & Aaltio-Marjosola, I. (2001). 'Strong' objectivity and the use of Q-methodology in cross-cultural research: Contextualizing the experience of women managers and their scripts of career. *Journal of Management Inquiry, 10*(3), 228–248.

Janićijević, N. (2011). Methodological approaches in the research of organizational culture. *Economic Annals, 56*(189), 69–99.

Jermier, J. M., Slocum Jr, J. W., Fry, L. W., & Gaines, J. (1991). Organizational subcultures in a soft bureaucracy: Resistance behind the myth and facade of an official culture. *Organization Science, 2*(2), 170–194.

Kaplan R. S., & Norton D. P. (2001). *The strategy-focused organisation: How balanced scorecard companies thrive in the new business environment.* Boston: Harvard Business School Press.

Kieser, A. (1997). Rhetoric and myth in management fashion. *Organization, 4*(1), 49–74.

Kondracki, N. L., Wellman, N. S., & Amundson, D. R. (2002). Content analysis: Review of methods and their applications in nutrition education. *Journal of Nutrition Education and Behavior, 34*(4), 224–230.

Leidner, D., Alavi, M., & Kayworth, T. (2006). The role of culture in knowledge management: A case study of two global firms. *International Journal of e-Collaboration (IJeC), 2*(1), 17–40.

Lincoln, Y. S., & Guba, E. G. (2000). The only generalization is: There is no generalization. *Case Study Method,* 27–44.

Lucas, C., & Kline, T. (2008). Understanding the influence of organizational culture and group dynamics on organizational change and learning. *The Learning Organization, 15*(3), 277–287.

Martin, J. (2002). *Organizational culture: Mapping the terrain, foundations for organizational science.* Thousand Oaks, CA: Sage.

Mayring, P. (2000, June). Qualitative content analysis. *Forum Qualitative Sozialforschung, 1*(2), 20.

McCall, G. J., & Simmons, J. L. (Eds.). (1969). *Issues in participant observation: A text and reader* (Vol. 7027). Addison-Wesley Pub. Co.

McKevitt, D., Davis, P., Woldring, R., Smith, K., Flynn, A., & McEvoy, E. (2012). An exploration of management competencies in public sector procurement. *Journal of Public Procurement, 12*(3), 333–355.

Mertens, D. (1998). *Research methods in education and psychology.* Thousand Oaks, CA: Sage Publications.

Miller, D. (1994). *Modernity, an ethnographic approach: Dualism and mass consumption in Trinidad.* Oxford: Berg.

Montgomery, A., Todorova, I., Baban, A., & Panagopoulou, E. (2013). Improving quality and safety in the hospital: The link between organizational culture, burnout, and quality of care. *British Journal of Health Psychology, 18*(3), 656–662.

Morgan, D. L. (1993). Qualitative content analysis: A guide to paths not taken. *Qualitative Health Research, 3*(1), 112–121.

Mumby, D. K. (1987). The political function of narrative in organizations. *Communications Monographs, 54*(2), 113–127.

Munir, K. A., & Phillips, N. (2005). The birth of the 'Kodak Moment': Institutional entrepreneurship and the adoption of new technologies. *Organization Studies, 26*(11), 1665–1687.

Neuendorf, K. A. (2002). *Defining content analysis: Content analysis guidebook.* Thousand Oaks, CA: Sage.

Oetzel, J. G. (2001). Self-construals, communication processes, and group outcomes in homogeneous and heterogeneous groups. *Small Group Research, 32*(1), 19–54.

O'Reilly III, C. A., Chatman, J., & Caldwell, D. F. (1991). People and organizational culture: A profile comparison approach to assessing person–organization fit. *Academy of Management Journal, 34*(3), 487–516.

Pacanowsky, M. E., & O'Donnell-Trujillo, N. (1983). Organizational communication as cultural performance. *Communications Monographs, 50*(2), 126–147.

Pettigrew, A. M. (1979). On studying organizational cultures. *Administrative Science Quarterly, 24*(4), 570–581.

Phillips, N., & Hardy, C. (2002). *Discourse analysis: Investigating processes of social construction* (Vol. 50). Sage Publications.

Potter, W. J., & Levine-Donnerstein, D. (1999). Rethinking validity and reliability in content analysis. *Journal of Applied Communication Research, 27*(3), 258–284.

Previte, J., Pini, B., & Haslam-McKenzie, F. (2007). Q methodology and rural research. *Sociologia Ruralis, 47*(2), 135–147.

Richardson, R., & Kramer, E. H. (2006). Abduction as the type of inference that characterizes the development of a grounded theory. *Qualitative Research, 6*(4), 497–513.

Riley, D. (1983). *War in the nursery: Theories of the child and mother.* London: Virago.

Robbins, P., & Krueger, R. (2000). Beyond bias? The promise and limits of Q method in human geography. *Professional Geographer, 52*(4), 636–648.

Sackmann, S. A. (1992). Culture and subcultures: An analysis of organizational knowledge. *Administrative Science Quarterly, 37*(1), 140–161.

Schein, E. H. (1985). Defining organizational culture. *Classics of Organization Theory, 3*(1), 490–502.

Schein, E. (1990). Organizational culture. *American Psychologist, 45*(2), 109–119

Silverman, D. (2002). Interpreting qualitative data. *Organization Studies, 23*(1), 161.

Shotter, J. (1993). *Conversational realities: Constructing life through language.* London, UK: Sage.

Smircich, L. (1983). Concepts of culture and organizational analysis. *Administrative Science Quarterly, 28*(3), 339–358.

Spradley, J. P. (1979). *The ethnographic interview.* New York, NY: Holt, Rinehart & Winston.

Strauss, A., & Corbin, J. (1990). *Basics of qualitative research.* Sage publications.

Tesch, R. (1990). *Qualitative research: Analysis types and software tools.* New York, NY: Farmer

Van Maanen, J. (2011). *Tales of the field: On writing ethnography.* University of Chicago Press.

Van Muijen, J.J. (1999). Organizational culture: The focus questionnaire. *European Journal of Work and Organizational Psychology*, *8*(4), 551–568.

Weick, K. E. (1995). *Sensemaking in organizations* (Vol. 3). Sage.

Wiewiora, A., Trigunarsyah, B., Murphy, G., & Coffey, V. (2013). Organizational culture and willingness to share knowledge: A competing values perspective in Australian context. *International Journal of Project Management*, *31*(8), 1163–1174.

White, H. (1981). The value of narrativity in the representation of reality. In W. J. T. Mitchell (Ed.), *On narrative* (pp. 1–24). Chicago: The University of Chicago Press.

Yin, R. K. (2009). *Case study research: Design and methods* (4th ed.). Thousand Oaks, CA: Sage Publications Inc.

9. Mixed methods research approaches to measuring organisational culture

Roslyn Cameron and Leesa Taylor

INTRODUCTION

Mixed methods is referred to as the third methodological movement and has become a legitimate methodological approach which has been buoyed by the growth of the mixed methods research (MMR) scholarly community. This community has developed solid methodological foundations since the early 2000s. Certain disciplines and sub-disciplines have been at the forefront of the current MMR movement and include education, evaluation, nursing and health and the social sciences generally. Nonetheless, the utility and coverage of MMR has also spread more broadly and includes the growing acceptance of MMR across an array of business and management disciplines (Cameron & Molina-Azorin, 2011). Reference will be made to Molina-Azorin and Cameron (2015) who documented the history and emergent utility of multi-methods and MMR across business disciplines.

A significant contribution of this chapter lies in applying dimensions of a set of quality criteria to the good reporting of MMR studies to a selection of published articles which utilise MMR approaches to the study of organisational culture. A sample of six studies were chosen across a variety of disciplines and these were then analysed using key aspects of the quality framework for the good reporting of MMR studies. We conclude with some recommendations for organisational culture scholars in relation to the advantages of using MMR but also cautionary warnings to encourage these scholars to become diligent in researching the MMR scholarly foundations, MMR designs, MMR nomenclature and visual display systems.

DEFINITIONS OF MMR

There is an abundant number of definitions for MMR. In fact, this led Johnson et al. (2007), in an article published in the *Journal of Mixed Methods Research* (JMMR) to seek and publish a definition based on the analysis of 19 different definitions provided by 21 well-recognised and published mixed methods researchers. Incorporating all their diverse perspectives they landed on the following definition:

> Mixed methods research is the type of research in which a researcher or team of researchers combines elements of qualitative and quantitative research approaches (e.g., use of qualitative and quantitative viewpoints, data collection, analysis, inference techniques) for the broad purposes of breadth and depth of understanding and corroboration. (Johnson et al., 2007, p. 123)

This definition reflects the approach that when a researcher combines quantitative data with the qualitative data, or described in another way, the statistical trends with lived experiences, they obtain a better understanding than by using one method alone.

Creswell and Plano Clark (2017) feel that a definition for mixed methods should incorporate many different viewpoints and therefore suggest that they rely on the definitions of the core characteristics of mixed methods as defined by Creswell (2014, p. 3):

1. Collection and analysis of quantitative and qualitative data in response to research questions.
2. Use of rigorous qualitative and quantitative methods.
3. Combination or integration of quantitative and qualitative data using a specific type of mixed methods design, and interpretation of this integration.
4. Sometimes, framing of the design within a philosophy or theory.

This description provides a combination of methods, research design and philosophy, and highlights key components of design and conducting a study (Creswell & Plano Clark, 2017).

Not only is it important to understand what a mixed method study is, it is also important to understand what it is not. Mixed method is not simply the gathering of both quantitative and qualitative data, as a key element of mixed methods is the integration of the data. It is not just using the MMR label in the study and it should not be confused with a mixed model approach, multi-method research or an evaluation technique. It is not simply the addition of qualitative data to a quantitative design, or vice versa. Not only is data integration required but also there needs to be a methodological rational for applying MMR (Creswell, 2014).

METHODOLOGICAL CONTINUUM

While definitions of mixed methods research are contested, so are the classifications of MMR designs and associated typologies. It can also be very confusing for those novice researchers when they first start exploring MMR designs as there are a vast array of these. This caused Leech and Onwuegbuzie (2007, p. 265) to state:

> Over the last several years, a plethora of research designs have been developed. However, the number of designs that currently prevail leaves the doctoral student, the beginning researcher, and even the experienced researcher who is new to the field of mixed methods research with the challenge of selecting optimal mixed methods designs.

Since then much has been written on MMR designs and the *Journal of Mixed Methods Research* is a prime source for accessing high quality MMR studies which follow MMR conventions and designs. There is also a growing number of MMR texts available from reputable publishing houses.

Saunders et al. (2019) refer to a continuum of designs from simple to complex in their classification system as depicted in Figure 9.1.

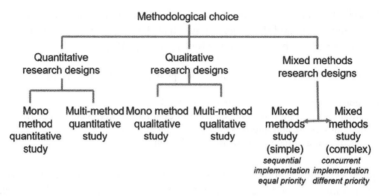

Source: Saunders et al. (2019).

Figure 9.1　　Methodological choice continuum

PURPOSES FOR USING MMR

Several members of the MMR scholarly community have developed a set of purposes for undertaking MMR. The earliest and oft noted is that developed by evaluation researchers, Greene et al. (1989). They posited five main purposes for utilising MMR: triangulation, complementarity for elaboration or clarification, development, initiation and expansion. These are summarised in Table 9.1.

Table 9.1　　Purposes for utilising MMR

Purpose	Purpose descriptor
Triangulation	seeks convergence, corroboration, correspondence of results from the different methods.
Complementarity	seeks elaboration, enhancement, illustration, clarification of the results from one method with the results from the other method.
Development	seeks to use the results from one method to help develop or inform the other method, where development is broadly construed to include sampling and implementation, as well as measurement decisions.
Initiation	seeks the discovery of paradox and contradiction, new perspectives of frameworks, the recasting of questions or results from one method with questions or results from the other method.
Expansion	seeks to extend the breadth and range of inquiry by using different methods for different inquiry components.

Source: Adapted from Greene et al. (1989, p. 259).

These purposes showcase the different forms of utility that MMR has across research inquiry and complement the need to have a variety of MMR designs best suited to the purposes for utilising MMR studies. The next section overviews the use of MMR across a arrange of management disciplines and sub-disciplines.

MMR ACROSS BUSINESS AND MANAGEMENT DISCIPLINES

In the first *SAGE Handbook of Mixed Methods in Social and Behavioral Research*, Currall and Towler (2003) examined the use of MMR in management and organisational research. They conclude that there needs to be a broadening of research training for business and management research students which exposes them to both quantitative and qualitative methods and to encourage more innovative, interesting and applied and practical methods.

The emergence of MMR prevalence studies began soon after and are studies which investigate the utility of MMR across a discipline or field of inquiry. MMR prevalence studies are described as:

> A new line of research has emerged in mixed methods (MM) over the past 5 years: one that examines the prevalence rates of methodological approaches within the social/behavioral sciences. In this line of research, investigators determine the proportion of qualitative (QUAL), quantitative (QUAN), and MM research studies that occur within journals in the social/behavioural sciences over a specified time period. (Alise and Teddlie, 2010, p. 103)

Molina-Azorin and Cameron (2015) examined the use of mixed methods in business and management research in their chapter in the *Oxford Handbook of Multimethod and Mixed Methods Research Inquiry*. In this chapter they summarised 15 MMR prevalence studies across approximately 12 business and management disciplines including: international business, entrepreneurship, strategic management, marketing, HRM, organisational behaviour and project management. The fields with the highest percentage of MMR studies published included international business and strategic management (17 percent and 14–17 percent respectively). The fields with the least MMR studies published were in project management and marketing (1.5 percent and 2 percent respectively). These MMR prevalence studies themselves were published from 2006 to 2013 and the time periods of the prevalence studies varied greatly. For example, a study on MMR in strategy (Molina-Azorin, 2012) used a 27-year publication period (1980–2006) and the newest was undertaken for publications in project management published in 2010 (Sankaran et al., 2012).

Other prevalence studies not captured by Molina-Azorin and Cameron (2015) include MMR prevalence studies in management sub-disciplines for example, leadership (Stentz et al., 2012) and sports management (van der Roest et al., 2015). Bazeley (2015) also examined the use of MMR in management research by looking at MMR papers published in the *Academy of Management Journal* and *Administrative Science Quarterly* in two periods: 2006 and 2014. This produced a total of 83 MMR studies. The review of these led Bazeley to conclude that "organizational and management researchers have been slow to adopt mixed methods approaches to research. Articles for both periods and in both journals were clearly dominated by studies that employed statistical analyses of archival, database, experimental or survey data, with little change over the period" (Bazeley, 2015, p. 27).

WHY MMR IS SUITABLE FOR OC STUDIES

Molina-Azorin and Cameron (2015) indicated that mixed methods research can add value in management research as it offers insight into both individual level (qualitative) and firm-level (quantitative) domains. There is a clear history of mixed methods being used in management research as far back as the 20th century when the Hawthorne study was conducted. The Hawthorne studies investigated employee behaviour using experiment and interviewing as well as observational data (Harrison et al., 2020).

The complex nature of understanding human behaviour often requires both breadth and depth, something mixed methods provides (Harrison et al., 2020). Organisational culture by nature is complex as it is based on human behaviour within a group while learning to cope, it has been defined by Hayes (2010) as "the pattern of basic assumptions that are invented, discovered or developed by a group as it learns to cope with its problems of external adaptation and internal integration" (p.110). Poth (2018) speaks about how integrative thinking with complexity can bring innovation to research design. Organisations and organisational culture are complex and multi-layered phenomenon and this defies organisational culture researchers to step up to this challenge. Adopting mixed methods research designs to study organisational culture is a good fit. It provides data collection and analysis opportunities across an array of methods, data sources and time frames and provides designs that have data integration as central to the analytical process. Poth (2018, p. 8) asserts that "in the light of complexity researchers often reduce, control, or simply ignore the effects of complexity, and these responses have become the basis for our traditional research practice tendencies over time". Mixed methods research allows us to better capture the complexity.

Examples of studies undertaken using an MMR design in this domain have highlighted some of the benefits of both the depth and breadth they achieved and how it enhanced their outcomes.

Listyowardojo et al. (2017) reported in their study the importance of using an MMR design when assessing safety culture, especially when the results are to be used for improvement. They found that where a survey provided a positive response to the safety culture, the interview findings were contrary as they were able to pinpoint challengers. Listyowardojo et al. (2017) related that they felt that if they had only relied on one of the data sources, they may have misinformed management. They also highlight the other advantage of using an MMR design as compensating for weaknesses of quantitative and qualitative methods, using the example of the survey findings which identified a strong and significant association between hours of work and working conditions, where the interviews had revealed the high workloads to be an issue across all departments. Other organisational cultural MMR studies have also stated that they gained a more in-depth understanding and achieved a richness of the quantitative findings by using an MMR design (White et al., 2016; Zeitlin et al., 2014).

These are examples of where the research teams have found the design to have added value to the findings, but it would also be fair to say that not all research goals require this level of breadth and depth, therefore it is important to also understand some of the common criticism of the MMR design.

Common Criticisms

Common criticisms tend to be targeted at those claiming to utilise MMR and then not referring to the growing body of MMR scholarly foundations, designs and nomenclature. The second common criticism is the lack of data integration between the qualitative and quantitative data. In addition to this, not justifying the rationale for adopting an MMR design and therefore justifying methodological choices is also a common criticism.

A recent review of the rigour in MMR studies published in four highly ranked management journals for a six-year period by Harrison et al. (2020) identified articles which collected both qualitative and quantitative data. They undertook a scan of the following journals over the period 2009–2014: *Academy of Management Journal*, *Administrative Science Quarterly*, *Strategic Management Journal*, and the *Journal of Management*. The content analysis identified 195 articles which used both qualitative and quantitative data. In addition to the content analysis which identified these published articles the researchers applied a rigour in MMR framework to these published studies.

Harrison et al. (2020) made the distinction between rigour and quality to develop what they refer to as the Rigorous Mixed Methods framework. The framework focuses on four primary elements and two advanced elements. The primary elements are "rigorous data collection", "rigorous data analysis", "integration" and the fourth is "use of specific mixed methods design types".

A total of 195 articles were identified as combining both qualitative and quantitative data. These were then coded as either: low level rigour, medium level rigour or high level rigour. The large majority of the identified 195 articles were coded as low level rigour (n = 128 or 65.6 percent). The most common reason for this low level ranking was: "complete lack of emphasis on the mixed portion of the methodology, despite reporting some component of both qualitative and quantitative data collection as part of the research study" (Harrison et al., 2020, p. 7). The second round of coding including two extra categories: low–medium and medium–high. These have been combined in Table 9.2.

Table 9.2   Summary of rigour review of four ranked management journals

Journal 2009–2014	MMR percent	SMIGO rank	# articles combined both QUAL /QUAN data	Low level rigour + low–medium	Medium level rigour + medium–high	High level rigour
Academy of Management Journal	20.1	Q1	72	39 + 8	13 + 8	4
Administrative Science Quarterly	16.3	Q1	15	5 + 1	7 + 1	1
Strategic Management Journal	20.0	Q1	73	58 + 6	4 + 4	1
Journal of Management	10.0	Q1	35	26 + 5	4 + 0	0
				128 + 20	28 +13	
Total	16.75 (n=1164)		**195**	**148**	**41**	**6**

Source: Adapted from Harrison et al. (2020, p. 8).

Harrison et al. concluded that the majority of articles (65.6 percent) were categorised as low levels of MMR rigour.

This suggests significant room for improvement in the utilization of mixed methods in the management discipline. Of the 195 articles, only 9.7% were deemed to have medium to high methodological rigor. This shows that while highly Rigorous Mixed Methods work is being done, it has yet to become the norm. (Harrison et al., 2020, p. 20)

The following section describes the sample of MMR studies which investigated aspects of organisational culture and the results of the analysis of these studies applying dimensions of a MMR quality framework for reported MMR studies.

MMR UTILITY IN MEASURING ORGANISATIONAL CULTURE: EXAMPLES OF MMR IN OC STUDIES

A databased search for "mixed methods research and organisational culture" resulted in identifying six published studies that have utilised a mix of qualitative and quantitative data collection methods to study and measure aspects of organisational culture. There is no claim as to the systematic rigour of this sample selection other than seeking a diversity of articles for the purpose of investigating a range of cross-disciplinary applications and research of mixed methods in measuring OC. These articles have been published from 2014 to 2017 and therefore are relatively recent. The journals that have published these are spread across a range of disciplinary areas of inquiry and are not all corralled around business and management disciplines. This reflects the cross-disciplinary nature of the study of organisational culture and includes the following topic areas: management, quality and safety, healthcare and services (health services, multidisciplinary healthcare, healthcare leadership) and children and services.

Below is a list of the studies and the journal they are published in and Table 9.3 provides a summary of these studies in terms of what aspect of organisational culture they were measuring.

Study 1: Curry et al. (2015) Organizational culture change in U.S hospitals: a mixed methods longitudinal intervention study. *Implementation Science*

Study 2: Listyowardojo et al. (2017) A safety culture assessment at a public maternity and infant hospital in China. *Journal of Multidisciplinary Healthcare*

Study 3: van Dun et al. (2017) Values and behaviors of effective lean managers. *European Management Journal*

Study 4: Ward et al. (2017) Imbuing medical professionalism in relation to safety. *BMJ Open*

Study 5: White et al. (2016) Barriers and facilitators of Canadian quality and safety teams. *Journal of Healthcare Leadership*

Study 6: Zietlin et al. (2014) A mixed-methods study of the impact of organizational culture on workforce retention in child welfare. *Children and Youth Services Review*

Table 9.3   *Summary of identified articles and organisational culture measures*

No.	Citation	Organisational culture: measures
1	Curry et al. (2015) Organizational culture change in U.S. hospitals: A **mixed methods** longitudinal intervention study	Leadership: models, leadership concepts and capacities Open systems theory and AIDED model of diffusion The five components are: assess, innovate, develop, engage, and devolve (AIDED) Measures of mortality
2	Listyowardojo et al. (2017) A safety culture assessment by **mixed methods** at a public maternity and infant hospital in China.	Safety culture: dimensions of safety culture Survey used a validated safety attitude questionnaire (short form) assessing six safety culture dimensions: teamwork climate, safety climate, job satisfaction, stress recognition, perception of unit and hospital management and working conditions The interview guide focused on four main themes: working conditions, teamwork climate, safety climate and perception of hospital management
3	van Dun et al. (2017) Values and behaviors of effective lean managers: **Mixed-methods** exploratory research.	Lean management: effective lean middle management (ELMM). Four out of the five values resemble Schwartz et al.'s (2012) self-transcending values. These top five values were ranked the highest by the effective lean middle managers and their associates: "honesty", "participation and teamwork", "responsibility", "candour" and "continuous improvement" (p. 8) Work behaviours of the lean leader and the underlying work values on which those behaviours are believed to depend (p. 2)
4	Ward et al. (2017) Imbuing medical professionalism in relation to safety: A study protocol for a **mixed-methods** interventionfocused on trialling an embedded learning approach that centres on the use of a custom designed board game.	Workplace culture: Supportive culture in raising issues of concern regarding patient safety. Open disclosure. Shaping a culture of responsiveness and learning Leadership inclusiveness survey (adapted) (Nembhard & Edmondson, 2006) and psychological safety surveys (Edmondson, 1999) The development of a serious game as a form of education using the PlayDecide Framework (Michael & Chen, 2006) The two surveys (listed above) and semi-structured interviews will be used to measure: leadership inclusiveness, psychological safety and incidents of safety concerns
5	White et al. (2016) Barriers and facilitators of Canadian quality and safety teams: A **mixed-methods study** exploring the views of health care leaders.	Barriers to effectiveness of quality and safety teams Barriers/themes identified in both data sources were: resources, time and capacity; data and information technology availability; leadership, organisational plan and culture; and team composition and processes Measures to investigate the impact of the Canadian acute care quality and safety teams were established using an online survey and semi-structured interviews, the instruments were generated through a scoping and expert review by health service researchers and decision makers.
6	Zietlin et al. (2014) A **mixed-methods study** of the impact of organizational culture on workforce retention in child welfare.	Perceived organisational culture: workers intention to remain employed Theoretical understanding of organisational culture includes relationships and values Measures to investigate the factors that lead to job turnover were established by using a modified version of a survey instrument developed to examine job satisfaction and potential turnover among public child welfare workers (Strolin-Goltzman et al., 2007) with an open-ended question at the end and focus groups to gain greater understanding

O'Cathain et al. (2008) developed a set of criteria for judging the quality of mixed methods research which they referred to as GRAMMS, the good reporting of a mixed methods study. The GRAMMS included the following six criteria:

1. Describe the *justification* for using a mixed methods approach to the research question
2. Describe the *design* in terms of the *purpose, priority and sequence of methods*
3. Describe *each method* in terms of *sampling, data collection* and *analysis*
4. Describe where *integration* has occurred, how it has occurred and who has participated in it
5. Describe any *limitation* of one method associated with the presence of the other method
6. Describe any *insights* gained from mixing or integrating methods.

We have utilised the first four criteria of the GRAMMs to further analyse the six chosen studies and specifically looked for the provision of a rationale (justification) for utilising mixed methods, use of a mixed methods research design, flow chart or visual depiction of the MMR design demonstrating sequencing/timing and stages or phases of the research design and evidence of data integration. All six studies explicitly referred to a mixed methods study in their titles and upon further investigation only three of the six studies explicitly stated and used an MMR design.

Table 9.4   *Summary of GRAMMS analysis*

Study	Title	Justification or rationale for MMR	MMR design	Data integration	Visual: data methods, sequence and dominance
Curry et al. (2015)	Explicit	Explicit	Explicit: Longitudinal convergent design	Explicit	*Partial:* Gannt chart only
Listowardojo et al. (2017)	Explicit	Explicit	*Partial:* Sequential mixed methods approach	*Not Explicit*	*Not Explicit*
van Dun et al. (2017)	Explicit	*Not Explicit*	Explicit: Convergent parallel design	*Not Explicit*	*Partial:* Flow chart provided however no MMR notation system applied
Ward et al. (2017)	Explicit	*Not Explicit*	*Partial:* Mixed-methods intervention	*Not Explicit*	*Not Explicit*
White et al. (2016)	Explicit	Explicit	Explicit: Multiphased mixed methods sequential explanatory design	*Not Explicit*	*Not Explicit*
Zietlan et al. (2014)	Explicit	Explicit	*Partial:* Two-phased mixed-methods design	Explicit	*Partial:* Flow chart provided however no MMR notation system applied

The other three referred to using mixed methods but did not supply an actual MMR design. Curry et al. (2015) utilised a *longitudinal convergent design*, van Dun et al. (2017) used a *convergent parallel design* and White et al. (2016) used a *multiphased mixed methods sequential explanatory design*. Four of the studies explicitly provided a rationale for using an MMR approach and only two studies explicitly discussed and described data integration. Two of the studies used a visual flow chart to depict the data collection and sequence and a third produced a data collection Gantt chart. However, none of the studies associated with MMR and none utilised the MMR notation system. A summary of the analysis results is provided in Table 9.4.

Based on the analysis we conclude that the studies which have met the most of the GRAMMS framework were Curry et al. (2015) and Zietlan et al. (2014). Curry et al. (2015) explicitly stated a rationale for using MMR and utilised an MMR design, integrated the data and partially provided a visual (Gantt chart) for the data collection. Zietlan et al. (2014) explicitly stated a rationale for using MMR and integrated the data; however, they only partially provided a visual for the data collection and did not use a specific MMR design. Van Dun et al. (2017) was by far the more complex of the designs utilising a convergent parallel design; however, not presenting a rationale for using MMR nor detailing the integration of the data. A flow diagram for the research design was provided; however, it did not utilise the MMR notation system common used in MMR. Unfortunately, none of the studies meet all four of the chosen criteria of the GRAMMS quality framework.

CONCLUSION

This chapter has provided an overview of mixed methods research and its application to organisational culture studies. Six published studies which have utilised an MMR approach to organisational culture studies were analysed using four criteria from the GRAMMS, a quality framework for the quality reporting of MMR studies. The analysis and findings demonstrates that the full gamut of MMR research designs, MMR nomenclature, and notation systems and reporting procedures is still not near mature application in this field of inquiry. We conclude with some recommendations for organisational culture scholars in relation to the advantages of using MMR but also cautionary warnings to encourage these scholars to become diligent in researching the MMR scholarly foundations, MMR designs, MMR nomenclature, visual display systems and MMR notation systems.

Cameron (2011, p. 264) made a call to the first generation of business and management scholars to "begin to take opportunities for instigating change and innovation in relation to the building of mixed methods research capacity within their respective schools/faculties". She went onto make four recommendations in respect to this: the introduction of MMR training activities; proactive fostering of multimethod and multi-disciplinary research teams; changes to academic reward structures that include the positive impacts of combining quantitative and qualitative data in research through MMR designs; and more inclusive editorial policies that encourage not only quantitative and qualitative studies but also MMR studies. Harrison et al. (2020) also support encouraging journal editors in business and management disciplines to become more open towards MMR studies for publication. Molina-Azorin (2016) also supports such initiatives and views this as an opportunity for business and management researchers to expand their methodological skills and increase rigour in their conceptualisation of research projects. Cameron (2018) went on to insist that researchers and scholars who plan to utilise

MMR approaches to postgraduate business and management studies need to be not only well versed in qualitative and quantitative methods but also MMR approaches, subsequently arguing for the need for methodological trilingualism. So not only do they need to be versed in both qualitative and quantitative data collection methods and analysis (methodological bilingualism), but also versed in mixed methods research designs, nomenclature and notation systems (methodological trilingualism). Harrison et al. (2020) in their study of MMR in top management journals also support the use of academic panels, workshops and conferences to encourage dialogue and exposure to mixed methods research and its extant literature and designs. Overwhelmingly, their study found no reference to the extant mixed methods literature which in itself is a concern given the strong establishment of MMR across multiple academic disciplines.

Referencing mixed methods literature and labelling articles as mixed methods give a study more sophistication and signal an understanding of the distinct methodological approach. Tapping into the existing body of mixed methods literature could lead to more rigorous articles, as authors become aware of the challenges and benefits of established approaches (Harrison et al., 2020, p. 20).

REFERENCES

Alise, M.A. , & Teddlie, C. (2010). A continuation of the paradigm wars? Prevalence rates of methodological approaches across the social/behavioral sciences. *Journal of Mixed Methods Research*, 4(2), 103–126.

Bazeley, P. (2015). Mixed methods in management research: Implications for the field. *Electronic Journal of Business Research Methods*, 13(1), 27–35.

Cameron, R. (2011). Mixed methods in business and management: A call to the "first generation". *Journal of Management & Organization*, 17(2), 245–267. https://doi.org/10.5172/jmo.2011.17.2.245

Cameron, R. (2018). Developing mixed methods research skill: Becoming methodologically trilingual. In R. Erwee, P. Danahar, M. Harmes, H. Marcus, & F. Padró (Eds.), *University Development and Administration: Post-graduate Education in Higher Education*. Cham: Springer.

Cameron, R., & Molina-Azorin, J. F. (2011). The acceptance of mixed methods in business and management research. *International Journal of Organizational Analysis*, 19(3), 256–270.

Creamer, E (2018). *An Introduction to Fully Integrated Mixed Methods Research*. Thousand Oaks, CA: Sage.

Creswell, J. W. (2014). *A Concise Introduction to Mixed Methods Research*. Thousand Oaks, CA: SAGE Publications Inc.

Creswell, J. W., & Plano Clark, V. L. (2017). *Designing and Conducting Mixed Methods Research* (Third edition). Thousand Oaks, CA: SAGE Publications Inc.

Currall S.C., & Towler A.J. (2003). Research methods in management and organizational research: toward integration of qualitative and quantitative techniques. In A. Tashakkori, & C. Teddlie (Eds.), *Handbook of Mixed Methods in Social and Behavioral Research*, pp 513–526. Thousand Oaks, CA: Sage.

Curry, L. A., Linnander, E. L., Brewster, A. L., Ting, H., Krumholz, H. M., & Bradley, E. H. (2015). Organizational culture change in U.S. hospitals: A mixed methods longitudinal intervention study. *Implementation Science*, 10(1), 1–11. https://doi.org/10.1186/s13012-015-0218-0

Edmonson, E. (1999). Psychological safety and learning behavior in work teams. *Administrative Science Quarterly*, 44(2), 350–383. http://www.jstor.org/stable/2666999

Greene, J., Caracelli, V., & Graham, W.F. (1989). Toward a conceptual framework for mixed-method evaluation designs. *Educational Evaluation and Policy Analysis*, 11, 255–274.

Harrison, R. L., Reilly, T. M., and Creswell, J. W. (2020). Methodological rigor in mixed methods: An application in management studies. *Journal of Mixed Methods Research*, 14(4), 1–23. doi:10.1177/1558689819900585

Hayes, J. (2010). *The Theory and Practice of Change Management*. UK: Palgrave Macmillan.

Johnson, R. B., Onwuegbuzie, A. J., & Turner, L. A. (2007). Toward a definition of mixed methods research. *Journal of Mixed Methods Research*, 1(2), 112–133. https://doi.org/10.1177/1558689806298224

Leech, N.L., & Onwuegbuzie, A.J. (2009) A typology of mixed methods research designs. *Quality and Quantity*, 43, 265–275. https://doi.org/10.1007/s11135-007-9105-3

Listyowardojo, T. A., Yan, X., Leyshon, S., Ray-Sannerud, B., Yu, X. Y., Zheng, K., & Duan, T. (2017). A safety culture assessment by mixed methods at a public maternity and infant hospital in China. *Journal of Multidisciplinary Healthcare*, 10, 253–262. https://doi.org/10.2147/JMDH.S136943

Michael, D., & Chen, S. (2006). *Serious Games: Games that Educate, Train and Inform*. Boston: Thomson.

Molina-Azorin, J. F. (2012). Mixed methods research in strategic management: Impact and applications. *Organizational Research Methods*, 15, 33–56.

Molina-Azorin, J. F. (2016). Mixed methods research: An opportunity to improve our studies and our research skills. *European Journal of Management and Business Economics*, 25, 37–58.

Molina-Azorin, J. F., & Cameron, R. (2015). History and emergent practices of multimethods and mixed methods in business research. In S. Hesse-Biber & B. Johnson (Eds.), *Oxford Handbook of Multimethod and Mixed Methods Research Inquiry* (pp. 466–485). Oxford University Press.

Nembhard, I. M., & Edmondson, A. C. (2006). Making it safe: The effects of leader inclusiveness and professional status on psychological safety and improvement efforts in health care teams. *Journal of Organizational Behavior*, 27, 941–966.

O'Cathain, A., Murphy, E., & Nicholl, J. (2008). The quality of mixed methods studies in health services research. *Journal of Health Services Research & Policy*, 13(2), 92–98. https://doi.org/10.1258/jhsrp.2007.007074

Poth, C. (2018) *Innovation in Mixed Methods Research: A Practical Guide to Integrative Thinking with Complexity*. London: SAGE.

Sankaran, S., Cameron, R., & Scales, J. (2012). The utility of mixed methods in project management research, 12th EURAM Conference Proceedings, *Social Innovation for Competitiveness: Organisational Performance and Human Excellence*, 6–8 June 2012, Rotterdam.

Saunders, M., Lewis, P., Thornhill, A., & Bristow, A. (2019). *Research Methods for Business Students* (8th ed.). Essex: Pitman Publishing.

Schwartz, S. H., Cieciuch, J., Vecchione, M., Davidov, E., Fischer, R., Beierlein, C., Ramos, A., Verkasalo, M., Lönnqvist, J.-E., Demirutku, K., Dirilen-Gumus, O., & Konty, M. (2012). Refining the theory of basic individual values. *Journal of Personality and Social Psychology*, 103(4), 663–688. https://doi.org/10.1037/a0029393

Stentz, J., Clark, V., & Matkin, G. (2012). Applying mixed methods to leadership research: A review of current practices. *Leadership Quarterly*, 23. 10.1016/j.leaqua.2012.10.001

Strolin-Goltzman, J., Auerbach, C., McGowan, B. G., & McCarthy, M. L. (2007). The relationship between organizational characteristics and workforce turnover among rural, urban, and suburban public child welfare systems. *Administration in Social Work*, 32(1), 77–91. https://doi.org10.1300/J147v32n01_06

van Dun, D. H., Hicks, J. N., & Wilderom, C. P. M. (2017). Values and behaviors of effective lean managers: Mixed-methods exploratory research. *European Management Journal*, 35(2), 174–186. https://doi.org/10.1016/j.emj.2016.05.001

van der Roest, J.-W., Spaaij, R., & van Bottenburg, M. (2015). Mixed methods in emerging academic subdisciplines: The case of sport management. *Journal of Mixed Methods Research*, 9(1), 70–90.

Ward, M., McAuliffe, E., Ní Shé, É., Duffy, A., Geary, U., Cunningham, U., & Korpos, C. (2017). Imbuing medical professionalism in relation to safety: A study protocol for a mixed-methods intervention focused on trialling an embedded learning approach that centres on the use of a custom designed board game. *BMJ Open*, 7(7), 1–7. https://doi.org/10.1136/bmjopen-2016-014122

White, D. E., Norris, J. M., Jackson, K., & Khandwala, F. (2016). Barriers and facilitators of Canadian quality and safety teams: A mixed-methods study exploring the views of health care leaders. *Journal of Healthcare Leadership*, 8, 127–137. https://doi.org/10.2147/JHL.S116477

Zeitlin, W., Augsberger, A., Auerbach, C., & McGowan, B. (2014). A mixed-methods study of the impact of organizational culture on workforce retention in child welfare. *Children and Youth Services Review*, 38, 36–43. https://doi.org/10.1016/j.childyouth.2014.01.004

PART III

SPECIAL TOPICS OF ORGANISATIONAL CULTURE MEASUREMENT

10. Culture change: measurement approaches and challenges

Julian Randall

CULTURE AND THE IMPACT OF CHANGE

Uncertainty, it seems, is part of the change experience for most people at work. Whether we look at dissonance theory (Festinger, 1957) or expectancy theory (Vroom, 1964), we can see that change usually challenges what individuals expect from their job, work and career, and that uncertainty about future direction can lead to resistance. Challenge to 'the way we do things round here' (Deal and Kennedy, 1982) will often lead to surprise, and that surprise usually requires sensemaking by those who experience it (Weick, 1995). Lazarus and Folkman (1984) suggest that this is an appraisal based on two questions: what am I threatened with?, and what can I do about it? Surprise can also arise due to situations of ambiguity during change – often presented with apparently contradictory objectives which are difficult to reconcile, sometimes leading to ambivalence. Piderit (2000) suggests this operates at three levels:

- Cognitive (what I think about the change)
- Emotional (what I feel about the change)
- Intentional (what I intend to do about it)

If such contradictions remain unresolved then change may trigger resistance rather than acceptance (Randall and Procter, 2008).

For the individual undergoing change there can be varying outcomes. Gabriel et al. (2010), for example, investigated the experience of managers being laid off at around 50 years of age. These managers were divided between those who portrayed the loss of their job as merely a temporary disruption to their career, those who saw it as the end of their career, and those who portrayed it as the start of a 'moratorium' or opportunity to open a new chapter in their working lives. Other authors have looked at retirement from work, with Robertson (2000) referring to those who see the 'handwriting on the wall' in this respect, and Vough et al. (2015) focusing on how imposed change is interpreted and responded to differently by different managers, some interpreting the experience as being 'discarded', while others viewed it as an 'epiphany' – perhaps a chance to embark on something they had always wanted to achieve.

Schein and Van Maanen (2013) have shown how individuals look for sources of stability during career changes. These they refer to as 'career anchors', which are made up of 'that combination of perceived areas of competence, motives, and values that you discover you would not give up if you faced a career decision that might not allow you to fulfil it' (Schein and Van Maanen, 2013: 1). Fraher and Gabriel (2014) looked at furloughed pilots in this theoretical context and suggested that such career anchors serve to stabilize occupational rather than organizational identity. Their study focused on the trauma of job furlough and identified pilots who were 'stuck' in their job, desperate to get back into flying, and compared them with those who moved on successfully to alternative careers.

For individuals who move on successfully through change events there can be a sense of emancipation. Having experienced an 'arresting moment' (Greig, 2012) they find a 'fork-in-the-road' (Obodaru, 2017) which leads on perhaps to an unexpected opportunity. Archer (2012: 43) describes these subjects as 'meta-reflexives' whose vocation/ideals now coincide with a work project that engages with the work practices they had come to know and find fulfilling, perhaps based on the career anchors they relied upon in their earlier working life (Archer, 2003).

PENETRATING AND CHANGING ORGANIZATIONAL CULTURE

So far, we have touched on individuals and their responses to change events, particularly when that change is imposed. But this raises the question of the extent that individual responses can be used to gauge group or corporate culture. In that context, what is it that can be assessed as being organizational culture?

Firstly, a definition: 'Culture is the way we do things round here' (Deal and Kennedy, 1982). Most of us can probably relate to that from experience of any new work situation which we have entered. We may experience differences in the way people work and interact with one another, even if they are doing the same type of work that we have been used to elsewhere. In Deal and Kennedy's definition we could say that if culture is a just a set of observable behaviours, it offers the manager the chance of altering the way we do things round here through training people to do things differently and then reinforcing processual change to ensure that the change endures (Burnes, 2004; Dawson, 2003). However, there is a deeper aspect of culture that remains to be uncovered: our values and attitudes. In this respect Schein (1985) suggests that there are three levels to culture:

1. First, there are *visible artefacts* – what we see when we walk into an organization. Uniforms, colour schemes, emblems and branding are examples of this often immediately apparent to us. Such artefacts are easy to change and are often associated with rebranding following a merger or amalgamation of companies.
2. Secondly, there are *values* which underwrite what people do. If we look more closely at the way people behave at work, we may notice that there is a priority to what they do. Working groups often have views about the value of what they do and will focus their efforts on what they regard as being important.
3. The deepest level, however, is what Schein calls *basic assumptions*. These, he says, are the often unconscious but deeply held norms and beliefs that underwrite what we do and govern how we behave. Schein suggests that these assumptions are often only surfaced when they are challenged by outside agencies – as in imposed change by external change agents or new managers. If this change runs counter to current strongly-held basic assumptions, there may well be resistance to the change programme.

In this chapter we will look at how we can use different approaches to assess what values and basic assumptions lie behind the culture in a workplace, how we as researchers can try to surface those assumptions, and finally, how that can assist us to manage change more effectively, achieving positive outcomes, rather than encountering resistance generated from the staff involved. Smircich (1983) makes this distinction clear when she says that culture is something that an organization *is* (the traits of its people) and also something that an organization *has* (the perceptions of its people – their attitudes to their job, their work, their career, their managers and the organization itself and its clients). These basic assumptions are often used as criteria to interpret events in the world, and working groups then derive meaning and ascribe value to those events, especially during imposed change.

There is a commonly stated belief among academics that 70 percent of change events fail to achieve their stated objectives (Wilcocks and Grint, 1997). This seems an unacceptably high failure rate and raises the question why this is so. Of course, it may be that the change programme was poorly designed, poorly presented and implemented, and not reinforced. But it may also be because the expectancy of those commissioning the change was unrealistic to begin with, or that they were attempting to do something that was unlikely to be achieved within a formal programme of change.

One cultural context that has become more apparent over time is change that impinges on the expectancy of professional groups. Nicolini and his colleagues (2008) referred to such groups as embedded or bounded communities. So, for example, medical professionals may well resist what they see as challenging their professional boundaries or eroding their traditional status. Reay and Hinings (2005, 2009) illustrate the resistance that doctors put up to government-led changes to the health service, which they viewed as threatening their professional position. The researchers described this competing between medical professionals and government as 'institutional logics'. Under budgetary pressure the doctors appeared to give way and accept the imposed change, which led to the institutional logics collaborating. However, the researchers noted that once the change initiative was completed, the institutional logics resumed their competition with each other.

In this chapter we will look at how we can use the different approaches to assess what is the culture in a workplace, how we as outsiders can uncover basic assumptions, and finally, how that can assist us to avoid resistance, achieve collaborative change outcomes, and set up long-term evaluation and integration of change initiatives.

SURFACING BASIC ASSUMPTIONS: THE QUALITATIVE APPROACH

Hinings et al. (2004) note that organizational studies have long privileged a quantitative approach to research. What is measurable and testable commends itself as more reliable and therefore generalizable. Clegg et al. (1996: 7) put it more directly: 'protectionism is not atypical of the broader intellectual establishment in the US, where the rationalist, quantitative, normative approaches associated with functionalism and normal science have gained their strongest foothold'.

Social scientists using a positivist approach want to measure accurately and compare their results and draw valid conclusions from their data. In comparison, the qualitative approach of talking to people and recording what they say has often been deemed a less reliable means of supporting research hypotheses, sometimes referred to as 'anecdotal evidence'.

Glaser and Strauss (1967) gave qualitative researchers a qualitative methodology, which has been accepted and developed ever since for researching individuals and groups to uncover what they think and feel about their lives at work and place its emerging empirical data in the context of underpinning theory. They refer to substantive theory, which underlies the researchers' beliefs about the research context in which they are working. This allows us to frame our research and explore the replies we receive from our research subjects. Glaser and Strauss accepted that our emerging empirical data can then provide support for emerging formal theory (1967: 79). For the researcher that means linking the findings to current academic debates, which resonate with the empirical data. In their own case they researched nurses' care of perceived higher status patients which they then recast as 'how professional services are distributed according to the social value of clients' (Glaser and Strauss, 1967: 80).

For many researchers this will mean embarking on interviews, a topic explored by Silverman (2013: 83), revealing three contexts for interviewing participants. Firstly, positivistic analysis – 'data gives us access to facts about the world', secondly, the work of interpretivists – the emotional responses that accompany subjects' experience, and thirdly a constructionist approach, with the focus on the way in which subjects express themselves, sometimes referred to as 'focused interaction' (Silverman, 2013: 86).

Individuals describe their experience not only with factual accounts but also with stories and narratives, which illustrate how they interpret and evaluate their experiences (Gabriel, 2000). Geertz (1973) referred to such deeper accounts as containing 'rich description in which words are chosen that convey deeply held beliefs and feelings about the experiences recounted'. Such accounts are sometimes referred to as sense-giving, as the research participant answers the researcher's questions, and sensemaking, as the researcher is engaged in interpreting the replies heard (Gioia and Chittipeddi, 1991). Qualitative research is not intended to replace quantitative research, but to complement it. Quantitative research tells us what has happened; qualitative research tells us why people think it happened and how they interpret its value and importance.

APPROACHES TO CHANGE: STEP APPROACHES AND PHASES OF CHANGE

How does qualitative research help us to support positive responses from those involved in change programmes? Change agents often use a step approach and there have been many different step approaches to managing change programmes. Among the earliest is Lewin's (1947) three-step approach:

1. Unfreeze the current situation
2. Implement change
3. Refreeze behaviours around the desirable performance

This is sometimes referred to as the ice model. It depends on surfacing the beliefs and assumptions within the group – Lewin employed T-groups or sensitivity groups as his first step, after which change to these emergent values is introduced, and finally there is a reinforcement of the new behaviours around newly defined values or standards of performance.

Since Lewin's three-step approach there have been many other step approaches, many of them following what is sometimes referred to as a problem-solving approach to change. The steps can be summarized as follows:

1. Identify the need for change
2. Select an intervention technique
3. Gain top management support

4. Plan the change process
5. Overcome resistance to change
6. Evaluate the outcome

Bullock and Batten (1985) attempted to rationalize the many variations that practitioners and change agents have used in their different step approaches. They identified four phases into which the many different step approaches could be included and compared. Within each phase different elements were to be included. And the phases themselves could be run concurrently, unlike steps, which are usually seen as separate, distinct, and mostly sequential. Bullock and Batten outlined the phases and elements as shown in Table 10.1.

Table 10.1   Table of phases and elements

Change phases	Change elements
1. Exploration	a. Need awareness
	b. Search
	c. Contracting
2. Planning	a. Diagnosis
	b. Design
	c. Decision
3. Action	a. Implementation
	b. Evaluation
4. Integration	a. Stabilization
	b. Diffusion
	c. Renewal

Source: Adapted from Bullock and Batten (1985).

As part of their research they examined 31 different step approaches and identified which of the phases was frequently omitted from step approaches and they identified exploration and integration. This suggests that change agents frequently have a plan for change and seek to implement it without exploring its acceptance by the receiving culture. It also might suggest that once the change programme has been completed the change agent leaves and the final phase of integrating the change remained unaddressed in the long term.

The different agents involved in change programmes often come from different backgrounds. They can be managers, consultants or academics. Their basic assumptions about change are often quite distinctive and bringing them together prior to a change initiative can improve the opportunities for successful change outcomes (Burnes and Randall, 2015). Qualitative approaches facilitate this approach to change.

THE BACKGROUND OF HUMAN RESOURCE MANAGEMENT (HRM) THEORY

The exploration phase is important as it allows the researcher the opportunity to surface basic assumptions relating to everyday management and change. We will relate our approaches to change with the outcomes that are open to the change agent through involving staff and seeking participative change and will explore the methods and means which are available to us to achieve this (Randall et al., 2019). But, before we do that, we can familiarize ourselves with the underlying principles of HRM theory which first emerged in 1984. The summarizing belief of HRM theory was 'people are our most important resource' (Beer et al, 1984; Fombrun et al, 1984). This theory has been significant for human resource practitioners and staff alike and summarizes the links between managers' interventions with staff day-to-day, and the expectancies that staff have about their job, work, career, and the organization. The outline of HRM theory has been summarized by Guest (1987) who suggested that proper implementation of the management interventions that govern a working life usually include recruitment and selection, induction training, supervision, management, review, appraisal, reward, development, and communication. Properly implemented HRM theory suggests attention to these functions gives rise to such HR outcomes referred to by Guest as strategic integration, commitment, flexibility, and quality. From these HR outcomes *organizational outcomes* such as high-level problem solving/change, innovation, and cost effectiveness, and low turnover/absence/grievance should follow.

In their book *Reappraising HRM*, Blyton and Turnbull (1992) offer several chapters whose authors examine the evidence for these outcomes, as does Guest himself. They are useful indicators for change agents to assess whether change events have had the outcomes that were sought, and are the beginnings of measurement, assessment and comparison within a business. They are also useful comparators with other organizations in the same sector.

They alert us to *interference costs*, which most organizations are unaware of, but the cost of which can be considerable. These include error/wastage rate, staff turnover, sick absence, intermittent absence, customer complaints/returns, breakdowns/repairs, time/stock loss, and temporary staff cover.

All of these factors can be measured and therefore can be compared over any period of time and this will be the *quantitative aspect* of the change management context. After that, the change agent can move around the organization and explore whether the standards are in place and whether staff know what these are and what are the strategic outcomes for the company. A *qualitative* approach can probe the meaning and value that individuals and groups attribute to cultural change.

QUALITATIVE RESEARCH AND EXPLORATION: INTRODUCTORY STAFF MEETINGS

We have already referred to the work of Lewin and his sensitivity or T-groups. Such initial meetings with staff can be a significant opportunity for the researcher/change agent to find out more about the company and those working in it, before embarking on any change events. Small groups of staff (up to 15) can be convened, and they should ideally be mixed groups representing the main departments in the organization rather than single disciplines at the same time. The purpose is to open up the group to the need for change and previous experience of change management in the company. This is sometimes referred to as threshold knowledge.

The first step (question) to ask the group is: *What are the principal challenges that the company faces over the next two years?* The second step is to ask the group to *put the points raised in prioritized order*. This will often lead to a discussion, revealing different views between individuals and groups within the company on issues which might not have been expressed previously (Schein, 1985). These meetings can contribute to our knowledge of Steps 1 and also 2, allowing exploration of underlying beliefs about change. It may also lead into Step 3: exploring alternative solutions (at the very least, what people did not like about change events in the past may well surface). For the researcher this can provide an indication of what is sometimes referred to as threshold knowledge – what the group knows already and takes for granted but which now may seem to be challenged by the prospect of a programme of change.

QUALITATIVE INTERVIEWS ONE-TO-ONE

In this section we will review some of the organizations we worked with, how qualitative research was undertaken and how this linked to change initiatives that the organization was undergoing at the time or subsequently.

Case Study 1: Civil Service

Our first qualitative research began in 1996 during a change programme amalgamating two divisions in the Civil Service in Scotland. The people involved were senior civil servants, with mostly about 30 years' service. In the past they had gone through office closures and similar rationalizations, which were dealt with either by routine staff turnover rates, moving staff around the organization, or putting a temporary block on recruitment during which staff were reassigned elsewhere. On this occasion, however, some senior managers themselves were made redundant. The top level of the organization had never been targeted in this way before. So, with two smaller divisions amalgamated into a larger body, one senior post at the top was retained (and one made redundant), with one deputy (and three redundancies) and eight assistant deputies (and 12 redundancies). The response to this imposed change was reflected in the interviews that we conducted and alerted us to the basic assumptions that senior staff believed had been violated. Specifically, that the Civil Service had traditionally offered job security to its staff and that this imposed change was the beginnings of a political strategy to impose efficiency savings on the Civil Service, abandoning the principle of job security for its staff.

Link to phases

Exploration
Our research questions were divided into three sections of four questions in each section. Firstly, we asked individual managers to describe how they started in the organization, their training and development, their progression through the organization, and any mentors and development support they had. Secondly, we asked about their current work, people they were responsible for, scope of the work, demands of the job, and management support. Thirdly, we asked the about the future as they saw it now, their career, their prospects, and their hopes and fears for the future. Our final question was: 'If a young person (a friend or family member) came and asked your advice about joining the organization, what would you say?'

Many of the responses from the senior managers were direct and to the point. The emotional level of their responses was illustrated by the images they used to describe their feelings:

We were stabbed in the back.

We were betrayed.
Anyone can have a go at us.
My manager was a cold fish.

Two stories emerged that were particularly striking. One came from a senior manager who had gone down to London for a meeting and was given a lift to the airport by his boss on the Friday. On the Monday the boss rang him and said, 'You are leaving. But don't tell anyone yet.' So, he had to go into a meeting with his fellow managers without being able to tell them what was to happen to him. He subsequently set up his own business and became very successful as a financial advisor to big business. But the surprise remained with him.

The second account came from a training manager who was told he would have to compete with a colleague to win his job in the newly merged department. He and his colleague had come up through the organization together so were friends as well as colleagues. He asked his boss (head of HR) jokingly: 'Does this could mean I could be out of a job?', to be told simply, 'That's right'. He won his job but did not forget what he saw as the injustice done to his colleague and friend.

Exploring challenges during change to the organization gives rise to accounts which may resonate with theories and debates current among academics, managers and consultants (Burnes and Randall, 2015). One current theory at that time highlighted workers' *psychological contract* (Rousseau, 1995). Rousseau distinguished what she called *transactional* parts of the work contract (time, payment, terms and conditions), from what she called the *relational* part (loyalty and trust). Hence our final question identified the advice from these senior managers, which was 'do not even think about joining the organization'. It also resonated with the research findings of the job insecurity literature, which found that those who stayed in their jobs following compulsory redundancy were likely to be as disaffected as those that had been forced to leave (Hallier and Lyon, 1996). So, this was another academic debate to which our findings could contribute.

We also viewed the data in the theoretical context of *autonomy* which was again a topical academic discourse about people forced to leave work, taking the opportunity to set up in business on their own (Bandura, 1982; Ryan and Deci, 2000). We identified this as an emerging theme, too, and for most of the senior managers their response was, 'Who would want someone like me – an ex-Civil Servant in my fifties?'. Some managers, mostly in their thirties, found alternative careers similar to the epiphany moment (described by managers who enjoyed the opportunity of a different and new working life). However, for the majority there was a feeling of being discarded (Vough et al., 2015).

THE IMPACT OF CHANGE: SURFACING BASIC ASSUMPTIONS

As we remarked earlier, change will challenge basic assumptions in ways that cannot always be predicted by change agents or managers. What individuals believe governs the way they interpret events that take place in their world, and from this they derive meaning (right/ wrong) and ascribe value (good/bad). Schein (1967) observed that this is part of the process of consultation where individuals start to revise their own opinions about the value of their job, work, career and the organization. Listening to the impact of change can often surface basic assumptions and alert us to the challenges that lie ahead during change programmes. This can lead to the second phase of planning the change events to involve the work group thereby leading to acceptable approaches to change.

One way of surfacing basic assumptions was outlined by Louis (1980a, b). She suggested that asking about previous experiences of change can be a useful and indirect way of probing to find out how individuals interpreted change in the past. She suggested four questions that are useful in achieving this:

What happened that surprised you?
What happened that didn't surprise you?
What didn't happen that surprised you?
What didn't happen that didn't surprise you?

Louis said that when an individual is surprised it suggests that a basic assumption has been disconfirmed. So statements such as, 'A good manager would never have done that' indicates something about the expectancies that the individual has about how a good manager should behave – which the example presented does not have, apparently (Isabella, 1990).

This approach links with surprise and sensemaking which has been a significant topic in the organization studies discipline (Weick, 1995). It resonates with the work of Lazarus and Folkman (1984), who suggested that once exposed to a threat, two questions arise for individuals threatened: What am I facing? What can I do about it?

In our research interviews we included such evaluative questions and the responses frequently led to accounts and stories which illustrated the ambiguity and ambivalence that our research subjects experienced.

Link to phases

Planning
During our initial focus group and individual interviews, our research subjects identified *market testing* as an impending threat to their working teams. This was a government initiative to put public sector work out to compulsory competitive tender. The managers embarked on a programme of research into the best practice of privatized providers likely to bid for their work.

Action
They drew up and submitted their own in-house bids for the business based on their findings. Eighty percent of the business put out to competitive tender was won by the in-house groups. This phase relates well to Step 4 of our problem solving: select a solution – the delegates made it clear what they would prefer to happen and then undertook the bid procedure themselves.

Case Study 2: Civil Service

Our continuing research in the Civil Service led to two other research programmes that we embarked upon subsequently at the same level of management. In 2003 there was an invitation to conduct consultancy on the work of the Band 11s (previously Assistant Collectors) in the UK. There were 20 of them so they were a cohesive group, proudly assertive of their management role across the UK.

Link to phases

Exploration
As the interview data unfolded, reservations surfaced about the way in which they were being managed. Having conducted the interviews we then analysed the results separately before coming back and discussing what we considered were the significant indicators arising from the empirical data (Randall & Procter, 2008).

We chose the theoretical lens featured in the work of Piderit (2000) who identified three levels of ambivalence that can arise during change:

- Cognitional (what people think about the change)
- Emotional (what people feel about the change)
- Intentional (what people want to do about the change)

It alerted us to the fact that there can be conflicting levels in which individuals can see the need for change but don't like it, and can either sit it out, oppose it, or decide to leave anyway, suggesting that ambiguity needs to be resolved during successful change (sense and sensemaking again).

We also identified three informal groups within that body of 20 Band 11s. Those we referred to as the older group (managers with 30 years' experience), the younger group (managers on an accelerated promotion path with ten years' experience), and the new group of older and experienced managers recently recruited from the private sector for their financial expertise. Each group responded quite differently to the situation they found themselves in and their accounts featured very different responses to the challenges of reorganization which then faced them.

It is worth pointing out that empirical data emerging from qualitative research does not link to all the phases in every case. But what it does do is allow the researcher and change agent to the possible links to change phases which can emerge from research subjects' accounts.

Integration
We were able to summarise and feed back our findings to the Board, thereby contributing to Step 4 of the problem-solving steps: select a solution. The issues arising from qualitative interviews informed the Board in finding acceptable ways of embarking on change in the organization (Randall and Proctor, 2008).

Case Study 3: Civil Service

Later, two departments in the Civil Service were amalgamated with the present authors given the opportunity to further explore the merger.

Link to phases

Exploration
We interviewed 20 senior civil servants and were able to explore the issues that arose as a result of the merger and the way that it was handled. It would be fair to say that the larger of the two groups attained dominance and that led to imposed change on the smaller group in

which 74 offices went down to 11 and 20,000 (out of 100,000) people were made redundant from the organization over a period of three years.

Planning and action
We went on to conduct three research interventions, and subsequently explored the changes in managers' expectancies about the organization after several imposed change programmes over a period of over ten years (Procter and Randall, 2015). Our findings led to an informed discussion, which we had with the Board about the outcomes of change – but also the long-term changes of attitude, which we had experienced over that period in the people at the top of the organization, in particular a readier acceptance of change.

This linked to Step 6 of the problem-solving list: evaluate the outcome. Longitudinal study, dipping into the organization at different periods of its development, can be a significant contribution, allowing reflection on long-term changes in staff perception and expectancy following organizational change (Proctor and Randall, 2015).

DEALING WITH DIFFICULT PARTICIPANTS AND INACCESSIBLE GROUPS

Two further examples are provided in which qualitative interviews helped to drill down into organizations that can be defensive and protective towards outside researchers. In both cases the lead researcher either had access to the network already or had once been part of the network in a professional capacity. Both research programmes gave rise to unexpected findings.

Case Study: Doctors and Counsellors Supporting Adult Survivors of Childhood Sexual Abuse

Bounded communities, as we have seen, are often to be found in the medical sector (Nicolini et al., 2008). Even though working together, they are not always welcoming to working across professional boundaries and can be defensive of their discipline and its practices in the face of what they often view as outside interference. In the case of these practitioners we had a contact with an organizer of a voluntary organization who introduced us to a multi-disciplinary group of doctors and counsellors working together in Fife, North-east Scotland.

Link to phases

Exploration
We interviewed all of the members of the group and began to realize that there was innovative work going on to span the boundaries between the disciplines, given that patients are likely to depend on both medical practitioners' and counsellors' support. What emerged from the research interviews was an awareness of the constraints of working in the health service – for medical practitioners these included changing government guidelines and funding initiatives, and their frustration with inflexible working patterns. As one doctor said, 'They (the NHS) have a surgical model of practioning, where you get more support for seeing more patients for a shorter time, whereas my patients need longer, and I can therefore see fewer of them.'

Planning and action
On the positive side they were all enthusiastic about the benefits of collaboration with voluntary counsellors as an opportunity to exchange successes working with one another. Medical practitioners were supportive of the work of the voluntary agencies and in some ways envied them their freedom to respond more flexibly to patient need.

Integration
Once again qualitative data are likely to yield data and information arising in all four phases, and link to Step 6 of the problem-solving list: evaluate the outcome (Munro and Randall, 2007). Data were subsequently viewed under the Foucauldian lens of Care of the Self (Randall and Munro, 2010).

Case Study: Priests and Seminarians Who Left the Church Ministry

Following an invitation to attend a fortieth anniversary of ordination in 2012, we attended, aware that this was a one-off occasion which could offer significant data on vocation and change. We conducted interviews with a class of 27 who started at a Catholic seminary together. Nine were ordained and two of them had died, leaving two still in service whilst the others had since left and moved on to secular occupations. We invited them to reflect on how they saw their lives, looking back on their subsequent experiences. We entitled the research proposal, *Losing a vocation and finding a calling.* We looked particularly at the experience our subjects had in leaving the Church's ministry, their work experience since then, and their views about the significance of faith in their lives.

Link to phases

Action
What we found was that all except two priests out of the class of 27 had left to get married, but more significantly all had then undertaken work that involved looking after other people – including social work, childcare, ex-prisoner support, and higher education. It was as if having taken off the clerical collar, they just went on doing what they would have been doing had they stayed in the Church.

This resonated for us with the work of Archer (2003) on meta-reflexivity in which she identified the links between the ideal embodied in the original calling (service beyond self), the job or project chosen as its vehicle (the priesthood), and the practices involved in the work (pastoral work, caring, counselling). Archer suggested that if the project no longer offers a clear link between vocational ideal work project and job practice, then an alternative project is chosen which restores the links between them. In the case of our research subjects, all had chosen jobs in pastoral support or social work – caring professions – leaving to take up similar practices elsewhere outside the Church, and restoring the calling of service beyond self that they originally felt drawn and committed to.

The choice of social and similar work might well seem an obvious destination for such research subjects. However, it was clear from our accounts that our subjects had choices and they chose to devote themselves to others. One of them was offered a job in the City of London but said, 'I did not want to spend my life making rich people richer.' So, he spent his life finding homes for children in need of adoption (which he has continued to do in his retirement). Another subject who had a law degree set up giving advice in a housing charity to the homeless and those who could not afford the normal fees. He received the award of a Member of the British Empire for his lifetime's dedication to his work among the deprived and homeless.

Integration
So, what is the point of such interviews? We think that exit interviews are an important part of Step 6: evaluate the outcome. Organizations that fail to do this are liable to continue to lose large numbers of people on whose professional services they depend. Health services will face similar challenges with staff retention in the post-Covid world.

THE ROLE OF THE INTERNAL CHANGE AGENT

Our current research is focused on the internal change agent. In the last two years there has been a growing interest in the work of those within a company who help others to develop through training, support, mentoring, and evaluation of change programmes (Sturdy et al., 2016; Wright, 2009).

Link to phases

Exploration
We have chosen the context of boundary spanning, which is another current academic debate that looks at the interpersonal, technical, structural, and cultural boundaries that staff have to cross confidently in global businesses (Orlikowski, 2002; Wright, 2009). In the first stage, we undertook 18 interviews – some in the UK and some in Australia. We focused particularly on the organizational outputs and individual outcomes of the work of internal change agents and have been encouraged by the greater awareness that there is of the importance of being able to monitor increased effectiveness – this being a reduction in interference costs, and support for continuing professional development for individuals.

This brings us back to where we started this chapter – the quantitative work of measuring the outcomes of change and the qualitative work to probe the views and beliefs of those who have been involved. This, in our view, is an important and significant way in which we can link change to the cultural values which underpins an organization. Changing behaviours is easy. But changing attitudes is the significant change that affects how our values and basic assumptions about our work, career, and the organizations we work with have been influenced in the longer term to take account of change.

CONCLUDING COMMENTS

This chapter has been inspired by the question of how qualitative research has helped organizations change their culture. We believe that the qualitative perspective has enabled us to drill down into the values and basic assumptions that individuals have about their job, work, career, and the organization, and enabled us to evaluate the experience of past change and the prospect of future adoption of development opportunities. In this way, through narratives, 'occurrences are located in space and time and translated into meaningful events by organizational actors' (Patriotta, 2003: 352). These narratives are 'individuals' representations of the relationship between past, present, and future events' (McAdams, 1999). In this way, a narrative lens offers insight into how people frame, plot, manipulate, and understand the meaning of work and non-work events (Maitlis and Sonenshein, 2010). Grounded theory aims to make these patterns visible and understandable. As Eastman (2012: 89) asserts: 'Gathering data with broad and deep coverage of your emerging categories strengthens both the precision and the theoretical plausibility of your analysis.'

Our aim was to outline the importance of a qualitative perspective in engaging organizational culture change and the importance of responses of individuals and groups to change in their organizations. It has certainly done that for us and has been a significant means of surfacing the organization's culture by listening to the accounts of those who live it (Gabriel 2000; Watson, 2009) and learning from their experience.

REFERENCES

Archer, M. (2003). *Structure, Agency, and the Internal Conversation*. Cambridge: Cambridge University Press.
Archer, M.S. (2012). *The Reflexive Imperative in Late Modernity*. Cambridge: Cambridge University Press.
Bandura, A. (1982). Self-efficacy mechanism in human agency. *American Psychologist*, 37(2), 122–147.
Beer, M., Spector B., Lawrence, P.R., Mills, D.Q. and Walton, R.E. (1984). *Managing Human Assets*. New York: The Free Press.
Blyton, P. and Turnbull, P. (1992) *Reappraising HRM*. London: Sage.
Bullock, R.J. and Batten, D. (1985). It's just a phase we're going through: A review and synthesis of OD phase analysis. *Group and Organisation Studies*, 10(4), 383–412.
Burnes, B. (2004). Kurt Lewin and the planned approach to change: A reappraisal. *Journal of Management Studies*, 41(6), 977–1002.
Burnes, B. and Randall, J.A. (eds) (2015). *Perspectives on Change: What Academics, Consultants, and Change Managers Really Think about Change*. London: Routledge.
Clegg, S.R., Hardy, C. and Nord, W.R. (1996). *Handbook of Organization Studies*. Sage Publications, Inc.
Dawson, P. (2003). *Understanding Organizational Change: The Contemporary Experience of People at Work*. London: Sage.
Deal, T.E. and Kennedy, A.A. (1982). *Corporate Cultures: The Rights and Rituals of Corporate Life*. Reading, MA: Addison-Wesley.
Eastman, J. (2012). Rebel manhood. The hegemonic masculinity of the Southern rock music. Revival. *Journal of Contemporary Ethnography*, 35, 189–219.
Festinger, L. (1957). *A Theory of Cognitive Dissonance*. Stanford University Press.
Fombrun, C.J., Tichy, M.M. and Devanna, M. A. (1984). *Strategic Human Resource Management*. New York: John Wiley.
Fraher, A.L. and Gabriel, Y. (2014). Dreaming of flying when grounded: Occupational identity and occupational fantasies of furloughed airline pilots. *Journal of Management Studies*, 51(6), 921–951.
Gabriel, Y. (2000). *Storytelling in Organizations: Facts, Fictions, Fantasies*. Oxford: Oxford University Press.
Gabriel, Y., Gray, D. E. and Goregaokar, H. (2010). Temporary derailment or the end of the line? Managers coping with unemployment at 50. *Organization Studies*, 31(12), 1687–1712. https://doi.org/10.1177/0170840610387237
Geertz, C. (1973). *The Interpretation of Cultures*. Basic Books.
Gioia, D.A. and Chittipeddi, K. (1991). Sensemaking and sensegiving in strategic change initiation. *Strategic Management Journal*, 12(6), 433–448.

Glaser, B.G. and Strauss, A. (1967). *The Discovery of Grounded Theory: Strategies for Qualitative Research*. Chicago: Aldine.

Greig, G., Gilmore, C., Patrick, H. and Beech, N. (2012). Arresting moments in engaged management research. *Management Learning*, 44(3), 267–285.

Guest, D.E. (1987). Human resource management and industrial relations. *Journal of Management Studies*, 25(5), 503–521. doi.org/10.1111/j.1467-6486.1987.tb00460.x

Hallier, J. and Lyon, P. (1996). Job insecurity and employee commitment: Managers' reactions to the threat and outcomes of redundancy selection. *British Journal of Management,* 7(1), 107–123.

Hinings, C.R., Greenwood, R., Reay, T. and Suddaby, R. (2004). The dynamics of change in organizational fields. In M.S. Poole & A.H. Van de Ven (eds), *Handbook of Organizational Change and Innovation* (pp. 304–323). Oxford University Press.

Isabella, L.A. (1990). Evolving interpretations as a change unfolds: How managers construe key organizational events. *Academy of Management Journal*, 33(1), 7–41.

Lazarus, R.S. and Folkman, S. (1984). *Stress, Appraisal and Coping*. New York: Springer.

Lewin, K. (1947). *Field Theory in Social Science*. Harper & Row, New York.

Louis, M.R. (1980a). Surprise and sensemaking: What newcomers experience in entering unfamiliar organizational settings. *Administrative Science Quarterly*, 25, 226–251.

Louis, M.R. (1980b). Career transitions: Varieties and commonalities. *Academy of Management Review*, 5(3), 329–340.

Maitlis, S. and Sonenshein, S. (2010). 'Sensemaking in crisis and change: Inspiration and insight from Weick (1988)'. *Journal of Management Studies*, 47(3), 551–580.

McAdams, D.P. (1999). Personal narratives and the life story. In Pervin, L. and John, O. (eds), *Handbook of Personality: Theory and Research*, 2nd edition (pp. 478–500). New York: Guildford Press.

Munro, I. and Randall, J.A. (2007). I don't know what I'm doing, how about you? Discourse and identity in practitioners of the survivors of childhood sexual abuse. *Organization*, 14(6), 887–907.

Nicolini, D., Powell, J., Conville, P. and Martinez-Solano, L. (2008). Managing knowledge in the healthcare sector: A review. *International Journal of Management Reviews*, 10(3), 245–263.

Obodaru, O. (2017). Forgone, but not forgotten: Toward a theory of forgone professional identities. *Academy of Management Journal*, 60(2), 523–553.

Orlikowski, W.J. (2002). Knowing in practice: Enacting a collective capability in distributed organizing. *Organization Science*, 13(3), 249–273.

Patriotta, G. (2003). Sensemaking on the shopfloor: Narratives of knowledge in organizations. *Journal of Management Studies*, 40(2), 349–375.

Piderit, S. (2000). Rethinking resistance and recognizing ambivalence. *Academy of Management Review*, 25, 783–794.

Procter, S.J. and Randall, J.A. (2015). Understanding employee attitudes to change in longitudinal perspective: A study in UK public services 1996–2007. *Qualitative Research in Organizations and Management: An International Journal*, 10(1), 38–60.

Randall, J.A. and Munro, I. (2010). Foucault's care of the self: A case from mental health work. *Organization Studies,* 39(11), 1485–1504.

Randall, J.A. and Procter, S.J. (2008). Ambiguity and ambivalence: Senior managers' accounts of organizational change in a restructured government department. *Journal of Organizational Change Management*, 21(6) 686–700.

Randall, J.A., Burnes, B. and Sim, A.J. (2019). *Management Consultancy: The Role of the Change Agent*. London: Red Globe Press.

Reay, T. and Hinings, C.R. (2005). The recomposition of an organizational field: Healthcare in Alberta. *Organization Studies*, 25(3), 351–384.

Reay, T. and Hinings, C.R. (2009). Managing the rivalry of institutional logics. *Organization Studies*, 30(6), 629–652.

Robertson, A. (2000). I saw the handwriting on the wall: Shades of meaning in reasons for early retirement. *Journal of Aging Studies*, 14, 63–79.

Rousseau, D.M. (1995). *Psychological Contracts in Organizations: Understanding Written and Unwritten Agreements*. New York: Sage.

Ryan, R.M. and Deci, E.L. (2000). Self-determination theory and the facilitation of intrinsic motivation, social development, and well-being. *American Psychologist*, 55(1), 68–78.

Schein, E.H. (1967). *Process Consultation: Lessons for Managers and Consultants*. Reading, MA: Addison-Wesley.

Schein, E.H. (1985). *Organizational Culture and Leadership*. San Francisco, CA: Jossey Bass.

Schein, E.H. and Van Maanen, J. (2013). *Career Anchors: The Changing Nature of Careers Self-Assessment*. NY: Wiley.

Silverman, D. (2013). *Doing Qualitative Research: A Practical Handbook*. London: Sage.

Smircich, L. (1983). Concepts of culture and organizational analysis. *Administrative Science Quarterly*, 28(3), 339–358.

Sturdy, A., Wright, C. and Wylie, N. (2016). Managers as consultants: The hybridity and tensions of non-bureaucratic management. *Organization*, 23(2), 184–205.

Vough, B., Bataille, D.E., Sung, C.N. and Lee, M.D. (2015). Going off script: How managers make sense of the ending of their careers. *Journal of Management Studies*, 52, 414–441.

Vroom, V.H. (1964). *Work and Motivation*. New York: Wiley.

Watson, T.J. (2009). Narrative, life story and manager identity: A case study in autobiographical identity work. *Human Relations*, 30(4), 515–552.

Weick, K.E. (1995). *Sensemaking in Organizations*. Thousand Oaks, CA: Sage.

Wilcocks, L. and Grint, K. (1997). Reinventing the organization? Towards a critique of business process organization. In McGloughlin, I. and Harris, M. (eds), *Organizational Change and Technology*. London: ICP.

Wright, C. (2009). Reinventing human resource management: Business partner, internal consultants and the limits of professionalism. *Human Relations*, 61(8), 1063–1086.

11. High-performance cultures: a framework for navigating definition and measurement challenges

Adelle J. Bish

INTRODUCTION

Creating and sustaining high-performance organizations is an elusive goal for many organizational leaders. Scholars, working initially from a broader organizational culture perspective, continue to investigate the emergence and management of culture that perpetuates high performance in organizations. This leads to consideration of the concept of high-performance cultures: those that enable and sustain performance expectations and outcomes in order to achieve organizational objectives. However, despite decades of debate and investigations, questions remain about the definition and measurement approaches for the assessment of high-performance culture.

The aim of this chapter is to discuss the challenges involved with defining high-performance culture and measuring it. A two-phase review process was conducted to facilitate this objective. First, existing measures were reviewed to identify common performance-related dimensions, followed by the identification of specific instruments that, with adaptation, have utility for high-performance culture research. The review process revealed that a core issue is the lack of an agreed definition of high-performance culture. This then creates a situation where there are a wide variety of tools being used to measure different conceptualizations of high-performance culture. Researchers must design an approach given the purpose of the study and the context in which it takes place. To assist with this decision-making process, the review process reported in this chapter concludes with a proposed framework for designing the appropriate methodology based on the research purpose. The framework identifies a number of questions to consider as part of the research design phase when attempting to explore or assess high-performance cultures. This chapter is organized as follows: first an overview of high-performance cultures is presented, followed by the findings of the two-phase review process to determine shared performance dimensions across existing measures and identify specific instruments that may be useful for studying high performance cultures. A discussion of the use of mixed method design follows, and the chapter concludes with the presentation of a proposed decision-making framework for the design of high-performance cultures research.

HIGH-PERFORMANCE CULTURES

It is widely agreed that organizational culture is defined as a set of beliefs and values shared by members of the same organization that influences their behaviors (Schein, 1990, 1999; O'Reilly et al., 1991). As such, organizational culture reflects common ways of thinking and behaving. Researchers and practitioners try to understand, and conceptualize organizational culture, to define its nature and key determinants (Jung et al., 2009). For some time it has been argued that creating a strong organizational culture is a tool to influence employee behavior and improve performance (e.g., Deal & Kennedy, 1982). However, robust evidence of this culture–performance relationship has been harder to establish (Siehl & Martin, 1990; Wilderom et al., 2000). While Sackmann's (2011) review of empirical evidence provides support for the view that there are direct effects of culture on organizational performance, other work illustrates a more complicated relationship involving mediation, moderation and reciprocal effects (Denison et al., 2014). Thus, researchers continue to investigate direct effects as well as other mechanisms, and in many workplaces senior leaders and managers continue to pursue cultural change as one tool for creating and managing desired levels of performance (Sackmann, 2011).

High performance culture can be conceptualized as a type of organizational culture that is focused upon performance at the individual and organizational levels. From a management perspective, creating and sustaining a high-performance culture is often associated with the achievement of organizational objectives. Culture then is an important dimension of organizational strategy, as it implies that people within the organization share common ways of thinking about performance (e.g., what is expected, how to contribute) and adopt desired behaviors in order to perform to the required standards (Guest, 1997). These shared ideas and behaviors do not emerge by accident. Promoting a high-performance culture is a deliberate management strategy. Organizational systems, particularly those for human resource management (HRM), have been identified as potentially powerful levers for shaping and changing organizational culture (Schein, 1983, 2010; Ulrich, 1997). High-performance organizations and high-performance cultures are particularly relevant to the field of HRM, and talent management in particular (Guest, 2011; Stahl et al., 2012), as it is thought that this type of organizational culture can serve to create a focal point around performance. An explicit focus on performance, development and rewards helps to provide a compelling employee value proposition (Lawler, 2005), and when based on compatible values, serves as an important employer-branding tool for attracting talent (Bish et al., 2021). Indeed, Kontoghiorghes (2016, p. 1833) found that talent attraction and retention was related with the extent "to which the organization is perceived to have a change, quality, and technology-driven culture, and characterized by support for creativity, open communications, … and the core values of respect and integrity". In addition, to these effects, Kontoghiorghes's (2016, p. 1833) findings indicate that high-performance organizational cultures are "also highly conducive to the development of high commitment and motivating work systems".

High-Performance Work Systems and High-Performance Work Practices

HRM strategy and policy contributes to both the development and maintenance of shared patterns of "norms, values and informal rules within organizations" through selection, training, career development and reward structures (Guest, 1997). High-performance culture has been identified as an outcome of adopting a high-performance work systems (HPWS) approach to human resource management, where human resource management practices are bundled together such that they have mutually reinforcing impacts (Huselid, 1995). Typically these high-performance work practices (HPWP) are defined as "a group of separate but interconnected human resource (HR) practices designed to enhance employees' skills and efforts"

(Takeuchi et al., 2007 p. 1069). The intense interest and adoption of high-performance work practices stems from the belief that they are related to higher levels of performance as they directly influence employees' abilities, motivation and opportunity to contribute (Appelbaum et al., 2000; Messersmith et al., 2011; Takeuchi et al., 2007). Central to the concept of HPWS is the premise that these positive practices result in "mutual gains", with higher perceptions of organizational justice, less role conflict and overall positive employee outcomes (Salin & Notelaers, 2020).

There is no absolute agreement on what constitutes a definitive set of high-performance practices. However, there is general agreement that high-performance work practices include: "sophisticated" recruitment and selection, performance-based pay systems, employee development, high levels of employee involvement and participation, and formal performance management (Becker & Huselid, 1998; Messersmith et al., 2011). In organizations that adopt HPWPs you expect to find enriched job design and high involvement from management (Wood et al., 2012), development and training activities driven by the needs of the business (Becker & Huselid, 1998) to promote flexibility, empowerment, openness and information sharing, with an emphasis on tracking progress towards established performance goals (Batt, 2002; Den Hartog & Verburg, 2004).

Enabling High Performance Culture

Adopting HPWS is seen as a way of creating an enabling culture as this system may also act as a culture-embedding mechanism (Den Hartog & Verburg, 2004) where the system works to reinforce desired behaviors and plays an important role in shaping and maintaining the desired culture. High-performance culture is an extension of this conceptualization, reflecting the notion that organizations that adopt high-performance work practices create over time a culture that values performance and excellence (Kaliprasad, 2006). These expectations, facilitated by the use of HPWP, aim to shape behaviors and create a collective understanding of performance expectations, goals, participation, incentives and rewards. In this context, what is critical is that these performance expectations are shared and understood by employees, and employees have positive perceptions about the intent of these practices (as being directed towards their development and well-being as well as improved performance for example, see Nishii et al., 2008; Wang et al., 2020). Researchers have argued that HRM systems can influence employees by symbolically framing (Rousseau, 1990) and directly communicating (Bowen & Ostroff, 2004) key organizational values and behaviors (Mossholder et al., 2011). Indeed, one of the promoted benefits of adopting an HPWP approach is that these systems generate a "high level of collective human capital and encourage a high degree of social exchange within an organization, and that these are positively related to the organization's overall performance" (Takeuchi et al., 2007, p. 1069).

For example, Den Hartog & Verburg (2004) studied 175 organizations in the Netherlands and found support for the emergence of HPWSs consisting of a set of practices that placed an emphasis upon employee development, robust selection practices and the provision of goals and direction for employees. Results indicated significant impact from this system on organizational performance outcomes as well as positive relationships with three organizational culture orientations (goal, innovation and support), thus supporting the proposed link between high-performance work systems and firm performance and organizational culture. While organizational culture in this particular study was a dependent variable, the study highlights the complex relationships between HPWSs, culture and performance, that researchers are still trying to unpack.

Attempts have been made to distil the key elements of high performance culture. Illustrating this point, the qualitative case study conducted by Warrick et al. (2016) on the organizational culture of Zappos sought to identify key components of high-performance cultures and illustrate how these cultures are established and maintained. Their study identified five key elements of the workplace culture at Zappos that they argue are indicative of high-performance cultures: (a) committed leaders, (b) practiced core values, (c) customer-focused strategy, (d) HR practices aligned with core values, and (e) management practices aligned with core values. This study helps to explain what we are looking for in high-performance cultures, especially in terms of how all elements need to be integrated, and the importance of management behaviors in both creating culture but perhaps more importantly in sustaining high-performance cultures through the consistency of their actions.

Despite ongoing interest in high-performance work practices, there is no well-accepted definition of high-performance culture. Researchers may argue that an organization has a high-performance culture based on their use of HPWPs, assuming that the use of HPWPs as an organizational strategy influences the shared values and beliefs of those working within the business, building a culture that is focused upon performance (Den Hartog & Verburg, 2004). These assumptions and lack of agreed definition of high-performance culture puts greater priority on researchers to confirm how they intend to define high-performance culture, and whether it is conceptualized as being driven by HPWPs (and therefore study these practices in order to understand the nature of this culture).

MEASUREMENT APPROACHES

There are numerous approaches to measuring the broader concept of organizational culture. There are also measurement instruments available for measuring specific types of culture, and critical dimensions of an organization's culture; however, currently there is no standard instrument for assessing and exploring high performance cultures. Ultimately the decision about which measurement tool to use involves consideration of a range of factors, including how you define high-performance culture, the purpose of the investigation, how the results will be used, and the availability of resources (Scott et al., 2003).

Decisions about research design and methodology must first establish agreement upon how high-performance culture will be defined in the study. For those involved in participative research (with an organizational partner or client), this agreement about definitions is an important point of clarification that needs to occur in the early stages of the project. In this case the conversation is more directly impacted by how the business intends to use the results (e.g., for exploration, analysis, identification) (Scott et al., 2003). Whatever the end goal is, the study must be reported with clear explanation of how high-performance culture was defined and operationalized in the study. Next, the purpose of the study and the organizational context needs clarification. The literature provides compelling evidence for the need to consider context when studying culture. This may include leadership behaviors and human resource practices within the business as well as external industry factors that may shape cultural norms (Chaudhry et al., 2016). Finally, a fundamental measurement challenge for those investigating high performance cultures is that there is not one measurement instrument that has been designed specifically for this purpose. While there is no standard instrument, there are some common performance dimensions across studies of organizational culture, based in part on shared performance values.

Review of Performance Dimensions in Organizational Culture Instruments

To assess high-performance cultures using quantitative measures, researchers can select from a range of predefined dimensions of culture from existing measures. The choice of dimensions and survey items is guided in part by the organizational context (what constitutes high performance, outstanding performance), and the aspects of culture that relate most directly to this context. For example, with an organization that aims to be a leader in innovation, a culture assessment could focus on attitudes to, and beliefs about, innovation; the attitude towards mistakes; the attitude towards change (Mackenzie, 1995). As mentioned previously, without one instrument for the study of high-performance culture, careful consideration is required of existing measures to select the dimensions and items most relevant for the purpose of the study and the performance characteristics under investigation. To clarify options available, a two-phase review process was undertaken. The first phase was to identify performance-related dimensions that are common across existing measures of organizational culture. Based on these common dimensions, the second phase of the review identified specific organizational culture measures that appear most relevant for investigating high-performance culture – either in terms of profiling, evaluating, or assessing existing culture and/or desired culture.

Common Performance Dimensions Across Measures

The review across existing measures for dimensions that focus on performance and/or behaviors and values that support performance expectations revealed several key themes. To the extent that these measures can be used to assess high-performance culture, they share some common ground in three main areas: (a) there is a focus and high value placed on results/ objectives; (b) there is a focus and high value placed on innovation and adaptability, and (c) there is a focus and high value placed on how people are managed. The focus on people is both in terms of manager and employee behaviors and human resource practices adopted to facilitate performance. Table 11.1 illustrates the findings of phase one, presenting common performance-related dimensions from prominent dimensions of culture in existing measures. These dimensions can be considered both in terms of general dimensions that relate to what we expect to find in high-performance cultures, such as a focus on achievement, as well as context-specific dimensions. Depending on the organizational context, there may be specific dimensions (behaviors and attitudes) that warrant inclusion as well, such as a focus on innovation.

Table 11.1   *Common performance dimensions across organizational culture instruments*

Performance Themes	General Dimensions (Adapted from Jung et al., 2009, p. 1091)	Context-Specific Dimensions (Driven by needs of the business)
Results/Outcomes Orientation	Achievement/accomplishment	Customer focus
	Focus/long-term focus	Managing risks
	Results	Safety performance
	Goals/goal clarity/goal orientation	Efficiency
	Performance/performance facilitation/performance measures	Stability, dependability/reliability
	Values/core values/espoused values	
	Vision	
Innovation and Adaptability Orientation	Learning/individual learning/organizational learning	Innovation/innovativeness/risk taking Change/attitudes to change/creating change
People and HR Practices	Employee commitment/employee participation	Ethics/valuing ethics
	Development/development capability/employee development	Safety performance
		Recruitment
	Performance measures	Turnover
	Rewards	
	Task(s)/task structure	
	Relations/relationships	
	Workforce/work environment	

Adapting Existing Culture Measures

The identification of common performance dimensions leads to a more detailed analysis of appropriate existing measures with the aim of generating options for adapting these to suit high-performance culture research questions. Reviews by Scott et al. (2003) and Jung et al. (2009) provided a solid foundation. In their review of instruments for measuring organizational culture in the health care sector, Jung et al. (2009) identified 70 instruments and highlighted the frustrating task of selecting the most appropriate instrument given that similar instruments have the same name, and some that have been modified retained the original name. Jung et al. (2009, p. 1090) also observed that instruments varied widely in terms of what they aimed to achieve – ranging from "formative" to "diagnostic". An instrument can be used to explore organizational culture and/or as part of a cultural "renewal process" (formative), or to identify and assess culture with the aim of modifying them so that the culture is more closely aligned to "characteristics associated with high-performance" organizations (diagnostic). Furthermore, instruments typically are based on either a dimensional or typological approach. Dimensional approaches focus on assessing the presence and relative strength of cultural dimensions in a specific setting (Ashkanasy et al., 2000). There are a limited number of dimensional instruments that take an emergent approach, asking individuals to explain what culture is within their organizational context, developing themes and rating these in terms of importance (e.g. Cultural Assessment Survey, Cultural Consensus Analysis, and the Twenty Statements Test) (Jung et al., 2009) which could potentially be used to explore and analyze high-performance cultures. However, Jung et al. (2009, p. 1090) conclude that in most cases predefined sets of dimensions are used with an emphasis upon "tangible and intangible aspects that are assumed to correlate with individual and organizational performance" (including shared beliefs, emotions, goals, practices, structures, values and vision). A typological approach to measuring cultures investigates culture based on the dominant characteristics of the organization, with organizations being categorized into predefined types (Ashkanasy et al., 2000). Jung et al. (2009) highlights that these types can be descriptive in nature (Cultural Audit), or based on psychoanalytical concepts (Competing Values Framework, or the Organizational and Team Culture Indicator).

In summary, based on a review of quantitative instruments for measuring organizational culture, the following approaches are considered to be highly relevant for assessment of high performance culture: the Competing Values Framework (Quinn, 1988; Quinn & Rohrbaugh, 1983); Harrison's Organizational Ideology Questionnaire (Harrison, 1975); the Organizational Culture Inventory (Cooke and Lafferty 1989); Organizational Culture Assessment Instrument (OCAI) (Cameron & Quinn, 1999, 2011); Denison Organizational Culture Survey (Denison, 1990); and the Core Employee Opinion questionnaire (Buckingham & Coffman, 2014). Importantly, researchers must determine the performance dimensions most relevant to their conceptualization of high performance culture and adapt these existing measures to suit their particular research questions. As a starting point, Table 11.2 illustrates key dimensions in these instruments that are relevant for the purpose of studying high-performance culture.

Next, a brief discussion of the most relevant dimensions, or elements, shown in Table 11.2 for each measure is provided.

Competing Values Framework

One of the most widely used instruments for measuring organizational culture, including high-performance cultures, is the Competing Values Framework (CVF) (Quinn & Rohrbaugh (1983). In developing the CVF, Quinn and Rohrbaugh (1983) argued that in terms of the relationship between culture and organizational effectiveness, differences in effectiveness criteria could be better understood when they were organized along two axes. One axis indicates whether an organization is focused inward or outward, and the other axis indicates whether the organization prefers flexibility or control in terms of its organizational structures. The CVF therefore proposes four quadrants, where each quadrant represents a type of organizational culture, with each one having its own particular emphasis in terms of desired outcomes and preferred ways to achieve those outcomes (Goodman et al., 2001).

The Rational quadrant with its values on goals and performance stands out as being very relevant to high-performance culture. Here the focus is external with end goals of productivity and efficiency supported by organizational processes that value planning and goal setting (Goodman et al., 2001). However, this may conflict with other demands for flexibility as the organization grows by being adaptable and ready to respond as opportunities emerge, depicted in the 'Developmental' quadrant. Even more conflict may be experienced along the 'external vs. internal' axis, as the development of a high-performance culture and use of HPWS, focus on internal concerns such as employee development and individual growth (Den Hartog & Verburg, 2004). Theoretically, a high-performance culture also requires attention to the capabilities of employees and the ongoing development of talent for the level of cohesion and morale to sustain itself, consistent with the Group quadrant. This is somewhat at odds with the simultaneous need to be focused on the external environment to sustain performance and assess competitive advantage.

Table 11.2   *Overview of specific culture instruments for measuring high performance culture*

Culture instrument	Dimensions related to high-performance culture	Performance characteristics
Competing Values Framework (CVF) (Quinn & Rohrbaugh, 1983; Quinn, 1988)	Rational	Productivity, efficiency, competitiveness, aggressiveness, results orientation, planning and goal setting, action oriented, producing outputs. Values: Planning and goal setting
	Developmental	Flexibility, creativity, experimentation, risk, autonomy, adaptation, readiness, innovative
Organizational Culture Inventory (OCI) (Cooke & Lafferty, 1989) Organizational Culture Profile (OCP) (shorter version) (O'Reilly et al., 1991)	Constructive	OCI: Achievement, self-actualizing, humanistic-encouraging, and affiliative behaviors OCP: Being competitive, achievement orientation, having high expectations for performance, being results oriented, being analytical, action oriented, being aggressive
Organizational culture assessment instrument (OCAI) (Cameron & Quinn, 2011)	Adhocracy	Dynamic, entrepreneurial, and creative place to work; Employees are willing to take risks Leaders are innovators and risk takers Research and innovation Long-term emphasis on development and attaining new innovations Encourages individual initiative and freedom
	Market	Results-oriented organization People are competitive and goal-oriented Leaders are hard workers, creators, advanced, tough and demanding Winning is overall goal Long-term emphasis is on competitiveness and attainment of forecasted goals and targets Aggressive and ambitious style
Harrison's Organizational Ideology Questionnaire (Harrison, 1975)	Task accomplishment	Characteristics of achievers; how tasks are assigned; motivation; attitude to training; what motivates cooperative behaviors

Culture instrument	Dimensions related to high-performance culture	Performance characteristics
Denison Organizational Culture Survey (Denison & Mishra, 1995; Denison & Neale, 1996; Denison et al 2014)	Involvement	Personal engagement of individuals. Focus is internal dynamics of business and on flexibility.
	Consistency	Shared values; efficient systems and processes Focus is internal and stable
	Adaptability	Employee ability to understand customer needs, learn new skills and to change in response to demand Focus is external and on being flexible
	Mission	Clear purpose and direction, shared vision Focus is external and on stability
Core employee opinion questionnaire (Buckingham & Coffman, 2014)	Strong workplace	*Developmental focus:* Is there someone at work who encourages my development? This last year, have I had opportunities at work to learn and grow? *Progress towards goals:* In the last six months, have I talked to someone about my progress? *Shared commitment to quality:* Are my co-workers committed to doing quality work? *Mission and purpose:* Does the mission/purpose of my company make me feel my work is important?

While these conflicts may exist, Quinn (1988) argues for the need to embrace elements of each quadrant, working towards achieving the appropriate balance rather than developing a sole emphasis on one of the cultures. However, context is important. Depending on the organizational context, what the mission and objectives are, and industry, the Developmental quadrant, with its focus on flexibility, creativity, experimentation, risk, autonomy, adaptation, readiness, and innovative, may be more relevant.

Harrison's Organizational Ideology Questionnaire

Research interested in assessing the underlying ideology of an organization could utilize Harrison's Organizational Ideology Questionnaire (OIQ) (Harrison, 1972, 1975). The OIQ is based on four dimensions of organizational culture: power relationships, role definition, task accomplishment and self-development. Respondents rank statements in terms of how representative they are of the organization and the respondent's own attitudes and beliefs in relation to 15 organizational issues. Survey items most relevant to the study of high performance can be found in the task accomplishment dimension (the emphasis placed on the tasks that are done in the organization), such as, 'what characterizes achievers in the organization?' And 'what motivates work?' and in the self-development dimension (the regard given to individuals at the workforce), such as, 'What is the organization's attitude to training employees?' (Ashkanasy & Holmes, 1995; Harrison, 1975).

Organizational Culture Inventory and Organizational Culture Profile

The Organizational Culture Inventory (OCI) (Cooke & Lafferty 1989) is based on the assessment of thinking styles. This inventory "assesses 12 sets of norms that describe the thinking and behavioral styles that might be implicitly or explicitly required for people to 'fit in' and 'meet expectations' in an organization in terms of work and interaction with each other" (Cooke & Szumal 2000, p. 148). Two dimensions define the behavioral norms. The first dimension distinguishes between a concern for people and a concern for task. The second dimension distinguishes between expectations for behaviors that are either focused on fulfilling higher-order satisfaction needs or those focused on protecting and maintaining lower-order security needs. The 12 sets of norms are categorized into three general types of organizational cultures: Constructive, Passive/Defensive, and Aggressive/Defensive.

High-performance cultures can be seen to be most closely related to the 'Constructive' culture: "characterized by norms for Achievement, Self-Actualizing, Humanistic-Encouraging, and Affiliative behaviors, encourage members to interact with people and approach tasks in ways that will help them to meet their higher-order satisfaction needs" (Cooke & Szumal, 2000, p. 148). Evidence suggests that the norms associated with constructive culture are positively associated with group outcomes of quality of teamwork and unit level outcomes, and quality of working relationships and individual outcomes of high performance, motivation and job satisfaction (Cooke & Szumal, 2000).

The Organizational Culture Profile (OCP) (O'Reilly et al., 1991), a shortened version of the OCI, originally intended to explore person–organization fit, is also values based. Marchand et al. (2013) compared the OCP scale items with the CVF and found that for measuring high-performance culture there are similarities between the CVF's Rational culture type (productivity, efficiency, competitiveness, aggressiveness, results orientation, planning and goal setting, action oriented, producing outputs) and the OCP items of being competitive, having an achievement orientation, having high expectations for performance, being results oriented, being analytical, action oriented, and being aggressive. There are also similarities between the CVF Developmental culture type (flexibility, creativity, experimentation, risk, autonomy, adaptation, readiness, innovative), with OCP items including willingness to experiment, not being constrained by many rules, being quick to take advantage of opportunities, being innovative, and risk taking.

Organizational Culture Assessment Instrument

The Organizational Culture Assessment Instrument (OCAI) (Cameron & Quinn, 2011), based on the CVF, is a validated research method to examine organizational culture. The instrument consists of four competing values that correspond with four types of organizational culture (Clan, Adhocracy, Market and Hierarchy). Of these, the Adhocracy and Market culture types appear most relevant to the study of high-performance culture. The characteristics of Adhocracy culture include organizational commitment to research and innovation; leaders are innovators and risk takers; and the encouragement of individual initiative and entrepreneurial behaviors. These behaviors are driven by shared values around agility, transformation and innovative outputs (Cameron & Quinn, 2011). In Market culture, a results-oriented organization, with a long-term focus on competitiveness and attainment of goals, perceives leaders as being hard workers, with high expectations. Finally, depending on the organizational context, the overall mission and purpose of the organization, a Hierarchy culture might be more appropriate to sustain high performance. For example, with its focus on procedures, policies, and leaders' focus on efficiency and effective performance as they coordinate activities (Cameron & Quinn, 2011), this type of culture could support a focus on efficiency, if this is part of the overall purpose of the business (e.g. utility companies keeping the lights on).

Denison Organizational Culture Survey

The Denison Organizational Culture Survey (Denison, 1990; Denison & Neale, 1996; Denison et al., 2014) assesses cultural effectiveness and is explicitly designed to measure relatively visible and observable aspects of organizational culture, practices and behaviors, rather than invisible and not directly observable aspects of culture such as values and basic assumptions. The cultural effectiveness model at the heart of this instrument proposes four key traits as drivers of organizational performance: involvement, consistency, adaptability and mission (Denison & Mishra, 1995). The survey asks respondents to indicate agreement/disagreement with statements describing the way things are usually done where they currently work. These traits and overall framework were developed from mixed methods approaches studying the cultural characteristics of low- and high-performing organizations. The framework acknowledges that tensions exist within organizations, presenting challenges to achieve the most appropriate balance in terms of traits, and propose that the survey is a way to assess how and to what extent high-performing organizations achieve this balance (Denison et al., 2014). Denison et al. (2014, p. 156) concluded that these studies revealed that "the highest performing organizations find ways to empower and engage their people (involvement), facilitate coordinated actions and promote consistency of behaviors with core business values (consistency), translate the demands of the organizational environment into action (adaptability), and provide a clear sense of purpose and direction (mission)". As the development of this tool was driven by exploration of the characteristics of high-performing organizations, the survey can provide a useful profile approach for the study of high-performance cultures. Of particular value is the notion of balance that is central to the underlying theory, as this allows for consideration of organizational context when assessing the extent to which an organization is effectively balancing the competing demands of involvement (empowerment, team orientation, capability development), consistency (core values, agreement, coordination, integration), adaptability (creating change, customer focus, organizational learning), and mission (strategic direction and intent, goals and objectives, vision) (Denison & Mishra, 1995; Denison et al., 2014). Adaptability, being able to respond to shifts in the external environment and create change has been associated with employee commitment (Taylor et al., 2008) and, with its focus on risk taking and learning from mistakes (Fey & Denison, 2003), particularly resonates with high-performance culture. Together with a strong sense of mission, providing meaning and direction to organizational members (O'Reilly & Chatman, 1996), as well as serving as a point of reference, clarifying appropriate courses of action (Denison & Mishra, 1995), these two elements could prove useful in assessing high-performance culture.

Core Employee Opinion Questionnaire

The Core Employee Opinion questionnaire (Buckingham & Coffman, 2014), developed by Gallop, aims to support managers in assessing what they need to do in order to achieve higher performance outcomes. The questionnaire identifies 12 characteristics of a strong workplace from a high-performing employee's perspective. The premise being that if employees believe that these 12 characteristics are evident in their organization, this represents a strong workplace that therefore attracts and retains talent while enabling people to perform at their best (Buckingham & Coffman, 2014). So, the tool is looking at workplace "strength" in terms of its ability to motivate and retain employees and what managers can do to support employees in working towards their strengths. If we believe that "strong" workplaces are an example of high performance cultures, this assessment tool could provide useful data about employee perceptions. Indeed, Kontoghiorghes (2016) adapted some items from the Core Employee Opinion questionnaire to study high-performance organizational culture and talent management. To support high-performance cultures in particular, four questions focused on *developmental opportunities* (e.g., "This last year, have I had opportunities at work to learn and grow?" and, "Is there someone at work who encourages my development?"); *progress towards goals* (e.g., "In the last six months, have I talked to someone about my progress?"), and a *shared commitment to quality outcomes* (e.g., "Are my co-workers committed to doing quality work?") are particularly relevant. This instrument also focuses on employee voice, recognition, and the extent to which the supervisor, or someone in the workplace, cares about them as a person, and friendships at work. The inclusion of the supervisor is an asset, as the influence of this role in creating and sustaining desired culture has at times been overlooked (Lewis, 1996; Schein, 2010).

In conclusion, as shown previously in Table 11.2, these existing measures provide a starting point for the design of methods to study high-performance culture. This is by no means an exhaustive list of organizational culture inventories. There are many available, with varying empirical evidence to support their reliability and validity. The collections discussed here have been selected due to their potential utility in the study of high-performance cultures given their shared performance-related dimensions and some shared emphasis upon results/objectives, innovation and adaptability and people. Depending on the research purpose, these measures could be adapted to allow investigation of both the nature of the external focus of the organization, and its ability to adapt to changes, as well as the internal focus on developing employees, ensuring consistency of management behaviors to support performance goals, setting performance expectations and rewarding success.

In addition to reviewing existing measures of organizational culture, researchers investigating high-performance culture may also need to take a closer look at the HRM practices within the organization. This data serves to provide necessary context regarding the type of performance behaviors that are valued in the business and how these are supported through HRM practices. As mentioned earlier, this could involve evaluating the extent to which the organization has implemented HPWPs.

Exploring High-Performance Cultures through High-Performance Work Practices

In addition to the use of existing culture survey instruments, researchers can investigate the extent to which the organization utilizes HPWPs. As high-performance cultures conceptually should emerge within organizations that adopt HPWS or HPWP, researchers may focus initially on assessing these practices, and how these are perceived and interpreted by employees to assess the influence of these on the emergence of a high-performance culture. The dilemma here though is that you need to collect data about both the evidence of these practices being in use, and also that these practices have influenced employees as a group. Researchers need to be able to assess the extent to which the practices helped to create shared assumptions about how to adapt, perform and thrive in the organization (Schein, 2010) in order to draw conclusions about the effect on high-performance culture. We would need to see evidence of shared understanding in regards to performance expectations and organizational goals in order to propose that we are measuring culture as opposed to individual perceptions and attitudes. Table 11.3 provides examples of HPWPs that may facilitate the emergence of high-performance cultures based on the objective(s) of each practice and their implementation together. In addition to the practices identified here, we could also examine the extent to which management expects flexibility and involvement of employees, and whether there is empowerment of employees and a focus upon tracking progress towards performance targets, as these are all part of an HPWS approach (Den Hartog & Verburg, 2004). Measuring shared perceptions about these practices would help to identify and analyze the strongest dimensions of high performance culture in a particular organizational setting.

Table 11.3   *High-performance work practices relevant to the study of high-performance cultures*

Example HPWPs relevant to high-performance cultures
Selective recruitment practices
Performance feedback
Employee development
Goal setting
Expectation setting
Compensation related to performance
Incentives based on performance
Information sharing
Open communication
Employee participation
Employee development
Continuous improvement practices
Knowledge management systems

Source: Adapted from Den Hartog & Verburg (2004), Kaliprasad (2006).

Research conducted by Den Hartog and Verburg (2004) on the relationship between high-performance work systems and organizational performance indicates that the goal and innovative orientations are positively related to HPWPs (employee skills, pay-for-performance, job evaluation and task analysis to improve productivity). In their study Den Hartog and Verburg (2004, p. 60), used the FOCUS measure of organizational culture (Van Muijen, 1999), which is based upon the competing values model (Quinn, 1988). It utilizes the two dimensions of organizational focus (internal or external) and organizational structure (flexibility or control), to create four culture orientations: the "support", the "innovative", the "rules, and the "goal orientation" (Den Hartog & Verburg, 2004; Den Hartog et al., 1996). Den Hartog and Verburg (2004) proposed that each culture orientation would require certain types of high performance work practices – that specific practices would help to create and sustain a particular type of culture. For the two orientations most relevant to high-performance cultures (innovative and goal orientations), Den Hartog and Verburg (2004) argued that the innovative orientation, with its emphasis upon creativity, openness to change and experimentation, would relate to HPWPs that emphasize flexibility, empowerment and openness. The goal orientation, with its focus on objectives, productivity and functionality, would relate to (and require) HPWPs that focus on performance measurement, measuring achievement of goals, and performance-based pay systems.

In summary, performance dimensions shared across existing measures and several specific instruments, together with examination of the use of HPWPS, provide options for research methodology. It is also important to note at the design stage that existing organizational culture studies confirm that there is value in triangulating data (Hofstede et al., 1990). Given the inherent challenges involved with assessing culture, it makes sense to gather data with different methods from a range of sources where possible. The following section provides an overview of options to consider.

Mixed Methods

Based on the preceding discussion about issues in measuring high-performance cultures, there is benefit in adopting a mixed methods design, in part to accommodate the strengths and limitations of methodologies, including surveys (Hofstede et al., 1990; Ostroff et al., 2003). While survey methodology is widely used, these instruments do not allow for investigation of the "deeper" elements of culture (Schein, 2010). Denison et al. (2014) acknowledge the benefits of surveys (less expensive, establishes benchmarks for comparisons) (Ashkanasy et al., 2000; Tucker et al., 1990), as well as the notable limitations of not exploring the deeper levels of culture (symbolic meaning, values and assumptions) (Schein, 2010; Rousseau, 1990; Yauch & Steudel, 2003). Ashkanasy et al. (2000, p. 132) concludes that culture surveys are most appropriate when the focus of investigation is at the level of "observable and measurable manifestations of culture" and when the aim is to be able to compare culture across organizations using the same set of culture concepts. For high-performance culture research, these points highlight the utility of survey methods if a core objective of the study is to be able to assess and compare dimensions of performance culture across organizations, with a focus on observable elements of culture, such as values regarding performance, employee development, and behavioral norms. This approach may also be the best option when time constraints, human resources or organizational policy make more intensive methods less viable (Tucker et al., 1990).

The benefits of "triangulation" of methods (Jick, 1979; Patton, 1990) have been known for some time. This approach is particularly relevant to the study of high-performance cultures, as the data collected from a variety of methods may tap into different levels of culture, allowing us to compare different aspects of culture against each other, as well as investigating deeper elements of culture. This approach also allows for study of the influence of HRMPs. As Scott et al. (2003, p. 939) explain: "If an espoused value such as 'we believe in patient-centered care' emerges during an investigation, it should trigger a search for corroborating artifacts, such as evidence of meaningful patient participation and advocacy."

Qualitative methods such as observation, interviewing (Schein, 1999, 2010), and focus groups provide rich, contextual data, appropriate for the study of culture. Another approach for exploring characteristics of high-performance organizations and the extent to which these characteristics are recognized in a consistent, shared manner by organizational members is Q-methodology (Cross, 2005) (see Chapter 16 of this book for an example of the use of Q-methodology; Bish, et al., 2022). Typically, this approach involves providing participants with a predetermined set of value statements and asking them to arrange these into categories, usually to represent a continuum ranging from least to most of a particular characteristic (e.g., Organizational Culture Profile, O'Reilly et al., 1991). It is argued that this approach provides a greater degree of robustness when measuring attitudes and subjective opinions when compared to alternative methods (Cross, 2005). The value statements shown to participants can be customized, guided by high-performance organization theory, to adapt to organizational context as appropriate. This method provides rich insights into the extent that attitudes and behaviors in relation to performance are shared, and how these manifest themselves in the organizational culture. Content analysis of archival data (e.g., annual reports, performance appraisals) can also be employed if the aim is to examine the influence of high-performance cultures on individual and organizational performance outcomes. Action research methodology (see Ashkanasy & Holmes, 1995) is also an option. Overall, the optimal data collection strategy would be longitudinal – being able to capture culture, the shared patterns of norms, values and informal rules, as it emerges over time (Guest, 2011), and the influence of the external environment and internal management on performance over time (Denison et al., 2014).

In summary, research design involves trade-offs and a multi-method approach helps to "harness" the benefits of both paradigms (Yauch & Steudel, 2003). Blending quantitative and qualitative measures helps to provide a more nuanced understanding of culture within an organization (Rousseau, 1990; Scott et al., 2003). If possible, beginning cultural exploration with a period of qualitative assessment is ideal, as the insights gained from that assessment could then be used to select the most appropriate quantitative instrument and method of administration (Yauch & Steudel, 2003).

DECISION-MAKING FRAMEWORK

This chapter has explored challenges associated with studying high-performance cultures, specifically in terms of research purpose and context and approaches to measurement. The review and identification of performance dimensions shared across specific culture instruments informs the design of high performance culture research. The key decision points outlined in this chapter are reflected in the proposed framework presented in Figure 11.1. The questions answered at each step in the process, driven by the purpose and context of the research, assist in developing a robust and appropriate research design for the study of high performance cultures.

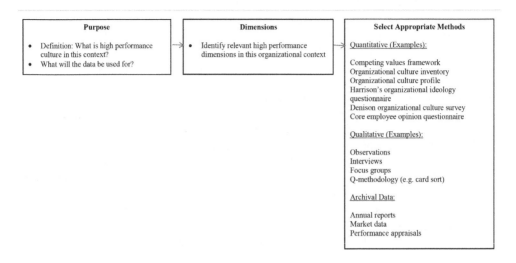

Figure 11.1   Decision-making framework for high-performance culture research design

CONCLUSION

This chapter explored multiple challenges involved with measuring high-performance culture. At the heart of these challenges is the lack of agreed definition of high-performance culture and lack of standard measures to evaluate high-performance culture. Findings from a two-phase review process were discussed to highlight shared performance dimensions across existing organizational measures and to identify specific options that could be adapted for the study of high-performance cultures. This review process generated a proposed framework to assist researchers in designing the appropriate methodology based on the purpose of the study. The framework identifies a number of questions to consider in the research design phase when attempting to assess or develop high performance cultures. Collectively, the review of existing measures and the proposed decision-making framework advance the rigor of high-performance culture research methodology and provide a guide for future research.

REFERENCES

Appelbaum, E., Bailey, T., Berg, P., Kalleberg, A. L., & Bailey, T. A. (2000). *Manufacturing Advantage: Why High-Performance Work Systems Pay Off*. Ithaca, NY: Cornell University Press.

Ashkanasy, N. M., & Holmes, S. (1995). Perceptions of organizational ideology following merger: A longitudinal study of merging accounting firms. *Accounting, Organizations and Society*, *20*(1), 19–34.

Ashkanasy, N. M., Broadfoot, L. E., & Falkus, S. (2000). Questionnaire measures of organizational culture. In N. M. Ashkanasy, C. P. M. Wilderom, & M. F. Peterson (Eds.), *Handbook of Organizational Culture and Climate* (pp. 131–146). Thousand Oaks, CA: Sage Publications.

Batt, R. (2002). Managing customer services: Human resource practices, quit rates, and sales growth. *Academy of Management Journal*, *45*(3), 587–597.

Becker, B. E., & Huselid, M. A. (1998). High performance work system and firm performance. *Personnel and Human Resources Management*, *16*, 53–101.

Bish, A. J. Shipton, H., & Jorgensen, F. (2021). Employee attributions of talent management. In K. Sanders, H. Yang, & C. Patel (Eds.), *Handbook on HR Process Research* (pp. 132–144). Cheltenham, UK and Northampton, MA, USA: Edward Elgar Publishing.

Bish, A.J., Becker, K., & Irmer, B. (2022). Leadership capabilities: the influence of organizational purpose and culture in the nonprofit sector. In C. Newton & R. Knight, (Eds.), *Handbook of Research Methods for Organisational Culture*. Edward Elgar Publishing.

Bowen, D. E., & Ostroff, C. (2004). Understanding HRM–firm performance linkages: The role of the "strength" of the HRM system. *Academy of Management Review, 29*(2), 203–221.

Buckingham, M., & Coffman, C. (2014). *First, Break All the Rules: What the World's Greatest Managers Do Differently*. New York: Simon and Schuster.

Cameron, K. S., & Quinn, R. (1999). *Diagnosing and Changing Organizational Culture*. Massachusetts: Addison-Wesley.

Cameron, K. S., & Quinn, R. E. (2011). *Diagnosing and Changing Organizational Culture: Based on the Competing Values Framework*. New York: John Wiley & Sons.

Chaudhry, A., Yuan, L., Hu, J., & Cooke, R. A. (2016). What matters more? The impact of industry and organizational factors on organizational culture. *Management Decision, 54*(3), 570–588.

Cooke, R. A., & Lafferty, J. C. (1989). *Organizational Culture Inventory*. Plymouth, MI: Human Synergistics.

Cooke, R. A., & Szumal, J. L. (2000). Using the organizational culture inventory to understand the operating cultures of organizations. In N. M. Ashkanasy, C. P. M. Wilderom, & M. F. Peterson, (Eds.), *Handbook of Organizational Culture and Climate* (pp. 147–162). Thousand Oaks, CA: Sage Publications.

Cross, R. M. (2005). Exploring attitudes: The case for Q methodology. *Health Education Research, 20*(2), 206–213.

Deal, T. E., & Kennedy, A. A. (1982). *Corporate Cultures: The Rites and Rituals of Organizational Life*. Reading, MA: Addison-Wesley.

Den Hartog, D. N., & Verburg, R. M. (2004). High performance work systems, organisational culture and firm effectiveness. *Human Resource Management Journal, 14*(1), 55–78.

Den Hartog, D. N., Van Muijen, J. J., & Koopman, P. L. (1996). Linking transformational leadership and organizational culture. *Journal of Leadership Studies, 3*(4), 68–83.

Denison, D. R. (1990). *Corporate Culture and Organizational Effectiveness*. New York: John Wiley & Sons.

Denison, D. R., & Mishra, A. K. (1995). Toward a theory of organizational culture and effectiveness. *Organization Science, 6*(2), 204–223.

Denison, D.R., & Neale, W. (1996). *Denison Organizational Culture Survey*. Ann Arbor, MI: Aviat.

Denison, D., Nieminen, L., & Kotrba, L. (2014). Diagnosing organizational cultures: A conceptual and empirical review of culture effectiveness surveys. *European Journal of Work and Organizational Psychology, 23*(1), 145–161.

Fey, C. F., & Denison, D. R. (2003). Organizational culture and effectiveness: Can American theory be applied in Russia? *Organization Science, 14*(6), 686–706.

Goodman, E. A., Zammuto, R. F., & Gifford, B. D. (2001). The competing values framework: Understanding the impact of organizational culture on the quality of work life. *Organization Development Journal, 19*(3), 58.

Guest, D. E. (1997). Human resource management and performance: A review and research agenda. *International Journal of Human Resource Management, 8*(3), 263–276.

Guest, D. E. (2011). Human resource management and performance: Still searching for some answers. *Human Resource Management Journal, 21*(1), 3–13.

Harrison, R. (1972). Understanding your organization's character. *Harvard Business Review, 5*(3), 119–128.

Harrison, R. (1975). Diagnosing organization ideology. In J. Jones, & J. Pfeiffer (Eds.), *The 1975 Annual Handbook for Group Facilitators* (pp. 101–107). La Jolla, CA: University Associates.

Hofstede, G., B. Neuijen, D. Ohayv, & G. Sanders. (1990). Measuring organizational cultures: A qualitative and quantitative study across twenty cases. *Administrative Science Quarterly, 35*, 286–316.

Huselid, M. A. (1995). The impact of human resource management practices on turnover, productivity, and corporate financial performance. *Academy of Management Journal, 38*(3), 635–672.

Jick, T. D. (1979). Mixing qualitative and quantitative methods: Triangulation in action. *Administrative Science Quarterly*, *24*(4), 602–611.

Jung, T., Scott, T., Davies, H. T., Bower, P., Whalley, D., McNally, R., & Mannion, R. (2009). Instruments for exploring organizational culture: A review of the literature. *Public Administration Review*, *69*, 1087–1096.

Kaliprasad, M. (2006). The human factor I: Attracting, retaining, and motivating capable people. *Cost Engineering*, *48*(6), 20–26.

Kontoghiorghes, C. (2016). Linking high performance organizational culture and talent management: Satisfaction/motivation and organizational commitment as mediators. *International Journal of Human Resource Management*, *27*(16), 1833–1853.

Lawler, E. E. (2005). Creating high performance organisations. *Asia Pacific Journal of Human Resources*, *43*(1), 10–17.

Lewis, D. (1996). The organizational culture saga – from OD to TQM: A critical review of the literature. Part 1 – concepts and early trends. *Leadership & Organization Development Journal*, *17*, 12–19.

Mackenzie, S. (1995). Surveying the organizational culture in an NHS trust. *Journal of Management in Medicine*, *9*(6), 69–77.

Marchand, A., Haines, V. Y., & Dextras-Gauthier, J. (2013). Quantitative analysis of organizational culture in occupational health research: A theory-based validation in 30 workplaces of the organizational culture profile instrument. *Public Health*, *13*(43), 1–11.

Messersmith, J. G., Patel, P. C., Lepak, D. P., & Gould-Williams, J. S. (2011). Unlocking the black box: Exploring the link between high-performance work systems and performance. *Journal of Applied Psychology*, *96*, 1105–1118.

Mossholder, K. W., Richardson, H. A., & Settoon, R. P. (2011). Human resource systems and helping in organizations: A relational perspective. *Academy of Management Review*, *36*(1), 33–52.

Nishii, L. H., Lepak, D. P., & Schneider, B. (2008). Employee attributions of the "why" of HR practices: Their effects on employee attitudes and behaviours, and customer satisfaction. *Personnel Psychology*, *61*(3), 503–545.

O'Reilly, C. A., & Chatman, J. A. (1996). Culture as social control: Corporations, cults, and commitment. *Research in Organizational Behavior*, *18*, 157–200.

O'Reilly, C.A., Chatman, J., & Caldwell, D.F. (1991). People and organizational culture: A profile comparison approach to assessing person–organization fit. *Academy of Management Journal*, *14*, 487–516.

Ostroff, C., Kinicki, A. J., & Tamkins, M. M. (2003). Organizational culture and climate. In W. C. Borman, D. R. Ilgen, & R. J. Klimoski (Eds.), *Handbook of Psychology: Industrial and Organizational Psychology* (*12*, pp. 565–593). Hoboken, NJ: John Wiley & Sons.

Patton, M. Q. (1990). *Qualitative Evaluation and Research Methods* (2nd ed.), Newbury Park, CA: Sage Publications.

Quinn, R. E. (1988). *Beyond Rational Management: Mastering the Paradoxes and Competing Demands of High Performance*. San Francisco, CA: Jossey-Bass.

Quinn, R. E., & Rohrbaugh, J. (1983). A spatial model of effectiveness criteria: Towards a competing values approach to organizational analysis. *Management Science*, *29*(3), 363–377.

Rousseau, D. M. (1990). Assessing organizational culture: The case for multiple methods. In B. Schneider (Ed.), *Organizational Culture and Climate* (pp. 153–192). San Francisco, CA: Jossey-Bass.

Sackmann, S. A. (2011). Culture and performance. In N. Ashkanasy, C. Wilderom & M. Peterson (Eds.), *The Handbook of Organizational Culture and Climate* (2nd ed., pp. 188–224). Thousand Oaks, CA: Sage Publications.

Salin, D., & Notelaers, G. (2020). Friend or foe? The impact of high-performance work practices on workplace bullying. *Human Resource Management Journal*, *30*(2), 312–326.

Schein, E. H. (1983). The role of the founder in creating organizational culture. *Organizational Dynamics*, *12*(1), 13–28.

Schein, E. H. (1990). Organizational culture. *American Psychologist*, *45*, 109–119.

Schein, E. H. (1999). *The Corporate Culture Survival Guide: Sense and Nonsense About Culture Change*. San Francisco, CA: Jossey-Bass.

Scott, T., Mannion, R., Davies, H., & Martin, M. (2003). The quantitative measurement of organizational culture in health care: A review of the available instruments. *Health Services Research*, *38*(3), 923–945.

Siehl, C. & Martin, J. (1990). Organizational culture: A key to financial performance? In B. Schneider (Ed.), *Organizational Climate and Culture* (pp. 241–281). San Francisco, CA: Jossey-Bass.

Stahl, G., Björkman, I., Farndale, E., Morris, S. S., Paauwe, J., Stiles, P., ... & Wright, P. (2012). Six principles of effective global talent management. *Sloan Management Review*, *53*(2), 25–42.

Takeuchi, R., Lepak, D. P., Wang, H., and Takeuchi, K. (2007). An empirical examination of the mechanisms mediating between high-performance work systems and the performance of Japanese organizations. *Journal of Applied Psychology*, *92*(4), 1069–1083.

Taylor, S., Levy, O., Boyacigiller, N. A., & Beechler, S. (2008). Employee commitment in MNCs: Impacts of organizational culture, HRM and top management orientations. *International Journal of Human Resource Management*, *19*(4), 501–527.

Tucker, R. W., McCoy, W. J. & Evans, L. C. (1990). Can questionnaires objectively assess organizational culture? *Journal of Managerial Psychology*, *5*(4), 4–11.

Ulrich, D. (1997). Measuring human resources: An overview of practice and a prescription for results. *Human Resource Management*, *36*(3), 303–320.

Van Muijen, J. J. (1999). Organizational culture: The focus questionnaire. *European Journal of Work and Organizational Psychology*, *8*(4), 551–568.

Wang, Y., Kim, S., Rafferty, A., & Sanders, K. (2020). Employee perceptions of HR practices: A critical review and future directions. *International Journal of Human Resource Management*, *31*(1), 128–173.

Warrick, D. D., Milliman, J. F., & Ferguson, J. M. (2016) Building high performance cultures. *Organizational Dynamics*, *1*(45), 64–70.

Wilderom, C. P., Glunk, U., & Maslowski, R. (2000). Organizational culture as a predictor of organizational performance. In N. M. Ashkanasy, C. P. M. Wilderom, & M. Peterson (Eds.), *The Handbook of Organizational Culture and Climate* (pp. 193–209). Thousand Oaks, CA: Sage.

Wood, S., Van Veldhoven, M., Croon, M., & de Menezes, L. M. (2012). Enriched job design, high involvement management and organizational performance: The mediating roles of job satisfaction and well-being. *Human Relations*, *65*(4), 419–445.

Yauch, C. A., & Steudel, H. J. (2003). Complementary use of qualitative and quantitative cultural assessment methods. *Organizational Research Methods*, *6*(4), 465–481.

12. Measuring culture of innovation: from assessment to action

Jay Rao and Shelby Danks

In an increasingly competitive landscape both domestically and internationally, organizational leaders from all sectors have identified innovation as one of the most important organizational competencies necessary to drive and sustain performance over time. An organization's dedication to ensuring a culture of innovation, in particular, has become increasingly more relevant within the last two decades. A 2008 McKinsey survey of nearly 1,400 executives from around the world (Barsh et. al., 2008) reported that 94 percent of respondents unanimously concluded that people and corporate culture were the most important drivers of innovation. The same study showed that applied resources and processes were either underutilized or not achieving scale to have a financial impact. Booz Allen also surveyed the innovation practices of Global 1,000 firms and reported on them since 2005. In their 2011 report (Jaruzelski et al., 2011), Booz Allen concluded:

> The elements that make up a truly innovative company are many: a focused innovation strategy, a winning overall business strategy, deep customer insight, great talent, and the right set of capabilities to achieve successful execution. More important than any of the individual elements, however, is the role played by corporate culture – the organization's self-sustaining patterns of behaving, feeling, thinking, and believing – in tying them all together. (p. 2)

Such reports from the voices from the field have encouraged a growing interest in academic research on the organizational enablers and inhibitors to the creation of a culture that is capable of both continuous and breakthrough innovation, as well as the need for practical tools for organizations to use to achieve these ends. The primary purpose of this chapter is to describe key developments in defining and assessing the organizational culture of innovation, present the InnoQuotient instrument as an example of a practitioner-oriented measurement model for such assessment, and present a case summary to illustrate how organizations can utilize results from its assessment to drive action and improvement.

Given the importance of this powerful organizational enabler, the number of instruments and tools aimed at the measurement and assessment of innovation culture have increased in the academic literature. Researchers studying enterprise innovation culture, as well as how to measure it, have drawn from the well-established findings from culture theorists such as O'Reilly (1989), Schein (1990), Hofstede (1991), Denison (1996) and Tellis et al. (2009), and have proposed multiple measurement models intended to tap the key enablers that facilitate innovation in organizations, and assess the extent to which these enablers are perceived by its employees and/or other stakeholders as present in their organizations. Table 12.1 illustrates many of these key instruments that have been developed to measure and/or assess innovation culture or a related construct.

Table 12.1   *Sample of instruments measuring culture of innovation or a related construct*

Reference	Purpose	Instrument	Subscales
Aiman-Smith et al., 2005	Summarize the development of a tool to measure Value Innovation Potential	Value Innovation Potential Assessment Tool (VIPAT)	Meaningful work, risk-taking culture, customer orientation, agile decision-making, business intelligence, open communication, empowerment, business planning, learning
Anderson & West, 1998	Measure and relate facets of climate for innovation and innovativeness	Team Climate Inventory	Vision, participative safety, task orientation, support for innovation
Dobni, 2008	Develop a comprehensive instrument for measuring innovation culture	Dobni (2008)	Innovation propensity, organizational constituency, organizational learning, creativity and empowerment, market orientation, value orientation, and implementation context
Hoe, 2011	Develop an instrument	Hoe (2011)	Shared vision, management support, community and individual creativity, implementation, and motivators
Humphreys et al., 2005	Apply instrument to evaluate an SME organization over time	Francis's (2000) Centrim G2 Innovation Audit	Direction, capability, culture, learning, structure and process, and decision making
Kuščer, 2013	Test elements of mountain destination innovativeness; develop measure	Kuščer (2013)	Sociocultural sustainability and stakeholder participation, environmental sustainability (natural environment), and proactiveness
Rao & Weintraub, 2013a	Propose and advocate for use of instrument	Innovation Quotient Survey	Values, behaviors, climate, resources, processes, and success
Remneland-Wikhamn & Wikhamn, 2011	Propose and validate instrument	Open Innovation Climate Measure	Innovation and flexibility, outward focus, and reflexivity
Sušanj, 2000	Examine differences in innovation culture and climate in different countries	FOCUS Questionnaire	Risk-taking, open to criticism, forefront of technology, flexibility, challenging old ideas, searching for new markets, pioneering
Tohidi et al., 2012	Propose and validate a measurement scale to capture learning capabilities	Organizational Learning Capabilities	Managerial commitment/empowerment, experimentation, risk taking, interaction with the external environment and openness and knowledge transfer and integration

Source: Adapted from Danks et al. (2017a).

In their literature review of instruments measuring culture of innovation, Danks et al. (2017a) evaluated each of these existing instruments against the criteria of alignment to rigorous models of innovation determinants from the literature (content validity), reliability, parsimony, and interpretation or user-friendliness (Kimberlin & Winterstein, 2008; Switzer et al., 1999). This analysis identified that, at the time, five instruments were aligned to the key factors and/or components of innovation culture that had been included in the groundbreaking theoretical models of Crossan and Apaydin (2010), Hurley and Hult (1998), and Sun et al. (2012). However, little evidence was found that any of them, save the InnoQuotient instrument developed by Rao and Weintraub (2013a), had been used in practical settings to support leaders in the measurement and assessment of innovation culture as a critical capability. While many of these instruments had been utilized in empirical investigations of culture of innovation and its relationship to other critical success factors, very few of them had been broadly applied in organizations, or found useful for practitioners seeking to understand how they can improve their organizational culture of innovation. In addition, Danks et al. (2017a), in their study, singled out the InnoQuotient instrument as the one that had the potential to most parsimoniously capture the key elements of innovation culture using fewer items than many of the other frequently used instruments.

We therefore propose the InnoQuotient instrument below as an example of a practitioner-oriented measurement model and tool that can support diagnosis, reflection, and the identification of action steps organizations can take to progress on their journey toward the development of a culture conducive to innovation.

THE INNOQUOTIENT MODEL – THE BUILDING BLOCKS OF A CULTURE OF INNOVATION

The InnoQuotient instrument, developed by Rao and Weintraub (2013a), assesses an individual's perception of the culture of innovation in the organization where the participant is employed. The aggregate results of the instrument measure the performance of an organization along each of the six building blocks that contribute to a culture of innovation – *values, behaviors, climate, resources, processes*, and *success*. Each of the six components were drawn from concepts that Rao and Weintraub (2013a) had identified as critical building blocks for building organizational innovative capability, which has been corroborated by other key researchers over the past decade (e.g., Bakovic et al., 2013; Brettel & Cleven, 2011; Chen, 2011; Herrmann et al., 2007; McAdam et al., 2007; O'Cass & Ngo, 2007; O'Connor et al., 2007; Saunila & Ukko, 2013). Each of these six building blocks are further described below:

- *Values*. An organization's values are composed of three factors – *entrepreneurial, creativity*, and *learning*. Organizations that value innovation, have an entrepreneurial spirit toward exploring opportunities to create new things, tolerate ambiguity, encourage diverse perspectives, provide the freedom to pursue new opportunities, constantly experiment, and are not afraid to take risks, predicts key behaviors that increase the likelihood of innovation (Rao & Weintraub, 2013a). Sarros et al. (2008) found that organizational vision significantly predicted the climate for organizational innovation. Clarity of vision toward attaining specific innovative objectives (Anderson & West, 1998; Slater et al., 2014) and shared vision as a means to avoiding specific innovation fads (Hoe, 2011) have been shown to serve as key factors that contribute to innovation performance. Chen (2011) also found the role of vision as a key factor of service innovation culture to predict innovation in organizations, mediated by charged behavior – which also included factors of challenging ideas and taking risks. Studies have also corroborated the supposition that an organization's willingness to take risks predict the presence of radical product innovations (Bakovic et al., 2013; Brettel & Cleven, 2011; Herrmann et al., 2007). Finally, O'Cass and Ngo (2007) identified that innovation culture predicted brand performance and market orientation.
- *Behaviors*. A leader's ability to *energize, engage*, and *enable* are the three key leadership behaviors (and factors) that Rao and Weintraub (2013a) demonstrated to be necessary for leading innovation in organizations. Leaders who provide additional support for innovation through personally modeling and taking initiative, coaching, feedback, influence strategies, challenge, and other methods impact innovation (Chen, 2011; O'Connor et al., 2007; Saunila & Ukko, 2013; Scott & Bruce, 1994; Sharifirad & Ataei, 2012; Slater et al.,

2014; Xerri & Brunetto, 2011). Steiber and Alänge's (2013) case study of Google identified the importance of leaders as facilitators of the innovation process. Velasco et al.'s
(2013) cross-company case study illustrated the importance of leadership in mobilizing
an organization toward innovation. Other investigations that sought to measure culture of
innovation identified leadership, management support, or empowerment as a key factor
that contributes to the success of innovation efforts (Aiman-Smith et al., 2005; Anderson
& West, 1998; Enzing et al., 2011; Hoe, 2011; Tohidi et al., 2012).

- *Climate.* The three factors of climate – *collaboration*, *safety*, and *simplicity* – involve the
focus on community, diversity, teamwork, trust, integrity, openness, a lack of bureaucracy,
accountability, and decision-making as key drivers of innovation (Rao & Weintraub,
2013a). Enzing et al. (2011) identified that company culture, as characterized by flexibility, openness, cooperation, human focus, and so on, predict short- and longer-term
market success of products in the food and beverage industry. Other studies reinforced
this effect in other industries (Anderson & West, 1998; Hoe, 2011; McAdam et al., 2007;
Panuwatwanich, Stewart, & Mohamed, 2009; Saunila & Ukko, 2013; Shahin & Zeinali,
2010; Velasco et al., 2013; Xerri & Brunetto, 2011). Of these constructs, the prevalence
of agility and flexibility in decision-making, along with localized autonomy in particular, has shown to be highly predictive of opportunities for innovation across industries
(Aiman-Smith et al., 2005; Humphreys et al., 2005; McAdam et al., 2007; O'Cass & Ngo,
2007; Panuwatwanich et al., 2009; Shahin & Zeinali, 2010).

- *Resources.* The building block that Rao and Weintraub (2013a) propose that appears to be
the least frequently studied in the literature is that of resources. Rao and Weintraub (2013a)
propose that without resources, which include *people*, *systems*, and *projects*, innovation is
less likely to occur, as often human resources in particular are those most likely to produce
innovation within an organization. Previous studies affirm the importance of human
resources as key to delivering innovative results (Saunila & Ukko, 2013; Scott & Bruce,
1994). O'Connor et al.'s (2007) case study particularly investigated the role of assets
(human, relational, physical, and monetary) and found that that sum of these assets produce
the capacity for an organization to innovate within its industry. Saunila and Ukko's
(2013) investigation of the factors that contribute to innovation capability found that "the
expertise of the employees play an important role for the development of the innovation
capability of the organization" (p. 1001); a finding corroborated by others who have evaluated the role of knowledge and expertise of individuals throughout an entire organization
(Enzing et al., 2011; Hoe, 2011; Scott & Bruce, 1994; Velasco et al., 2013). Some studies
have focused on the use of monetary and technological resources, although exclusively
focused on research and development expenditures and technologies, and their influence
on innovation outcomes (e.g. Kaufman et al., 2012; Saunila & Ukko, 2013; Sušanj, 2000).

- *Processes.* Rao and Weintraub's (2013a) building block of processes supports what
a majority of the research in the field of innovation management prescribes – that systematic processes to *ideate* (generate ideas, filter and prioritize ideas), *shape* (prototype,
iterate with quick feedback loops, etc.) and *capture* (processes tailored to context and easy
to move quickly to scale or to market) produce innovation in organizations. As much of the
practitioner literature has focused on how to deploy such processes within organizations
(e.g. Christensen et al., 2009; Dyer et al., 2011; O'Sullivan & Dooley, 2009; Rao, 2014;
Zairi & Al-Mashari, 2005), much research has been conducted regarding the effectiveness
of such models. Slater et al.'s (2014) extensive review of the literature identified that one

of the key contributors to radical product innovation capability in an organization is the innovation process involving discovery, incubation, and acceleration. While the theory that resulted from this literature review has not yet been tested, other empirical works identified that such processes indeed contribute to opportunities for innovation (e.g. Enzing et al., 2011; McAdam et al., 2007, O'Connor et al., 2007; Saunila & Ukko, 2013; Shahin & Zeinali, 2010; Sharifirad & Ataei, 2012; Steiber & Alänge, 2013). Researchers who have developed instruments to measure culture of innovation, as previously described, have also identified innovation management processes as critical enough a factor to incorporate into their respective measurement models (e.g. Hoe, 2011; Humphreys et al., 2005; Sušanj, 2000; Tohidi et al., 2012).

- *Success.* Operating from the assumption that innovation activities must be perceived as successful to encourage employees to engage in continued use, organizations should assess the extent to which they experience success with their innovation efforts, which can be reflected in the three factors of *external, enterprise,* and *individual* success (Rao & Weintraub, 2013a). Organizations that track the external market orientation and/or customer focus of their products may be more likely to develop products that are innovative, and can therefore be financially successful as well (Brettel & Cleven, 2011; Dobni, 2008; Herrmann et al., 2007; Kuščer, 2013; Lee et al., 2014; Remneland-Wikhamn & Wikhamn, 2011; Sarros et al., 2008).

Rao and Weintraub (2013b) posit that a carefully designed survey such as the InnoQuotient instrument can serve as a great starting point for helping organizations identify next steps to developing a culture of innovation. The InnoQuotient instrument was developed with this intention in mind, and is intended to serve as a practitioner-oriented and managerially actionable model for diagnosing and informing strengths and opportunities for improvement for organizations of all sectors, but most particularly in for-profit industries. The instrument consists of six building blocks (*values, behaviors, climate, resources, processes,* and *success*), each of which are represented by three first-order factors (see Figure 12.1). The instrument contains a total of 54 indicators, referred to as elements, across these six blocks, which were assessed using an ordinal, Likert-style scale where 1 = Not at all, 2 = To a small extent, 3 = To a moderate extent, 4 = To a great extent, and 5 = To a very great extent. In addition to the instrument, additional demographic questions are usually solicited to form relevant grouping variables that leaders might be interested in using to segment results, such as employee levels, functional roles, etc.

VALIDATION OF THE INNOQUOTIENT INSTRUMENT

In 2017, Danks et al. (2017a, 2017b) published the findings from their two-part investigation of the validation of the InnoQuotient instrument. The purpose of the investigation was to demonstrate evidence for the content and discriminant validity of the six-factor measurement model, as well as demonstrate the extent to which the findings were reliable across organizational groups, including countries, industries, employee levels, functional roles, and the languages of instrument administration. The investigation took place in two stages using a split sample design – first to confirm the proposed six-factor model, and secondly to explore alternative models, as necessary. The lead investigator for the validation study (Danks) identified that the instrument's lead author (Rao) had already executed a detailed, multi-faceted administration of the instrument to just under 20,000 participants from 138 companies across 24 industries in 13 countries.

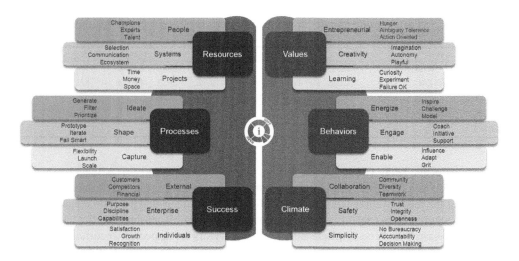

Figure 12.1   The InnoQuotient innovation culture model

Table 12.2   Participating countries

Country	n1	n2	Country	n1	n2
Spain	5,237	5,192	Mexico	70	69
Chile	2,346	2,410	Germany	69	55
Colombia	797	837	Scotland	21	31
United States	447	430	United Kingdom	25	26
Panama	385	407	Saudi Arabia	12	18
El Salvador	356	349	Belgium	9	4
Portugal	86	93			

Table 12.3   Participating industries

Industry	n1	n2	Industry	n1	n2
Financial and Insurance	2,404	2,442	IT – Software and Electronics	238	244
Telecommunications	1,053	1,128	Retail	239	236
Professional Services	841	911	Education	221	213
Industrial Machinery and Equipment	802	836	Public and State Administration	203	210
Health Care and Social Services	665	619	Transport and Logistics	206	179
Aerospace and Defense	647	567	Pharmaceuticals	161	171
Food and Beverages	435	420	Biotechnology and Research	42	30
Construction and Building Materials	396	389	Media and Publication	40	28
Industrial Metals and Mining	384	393	Agriculture and Fisheries	20	14
Automobile and Parts	315	308	NGOs	14	8
Oil and Chemicals	283	304	Distributors	7	5
Energy – Electricity and Gas	241	263	Hotels, Restaurants, Lodging	3	3

Many firms had participated through a partnership with the Spanish Society for Quality in 2015. Hence, this existing dataset was used for the validation study. The final dataset used for the validation study consisted of a total sample size of N = 19,781 participants, where the total dataset was randomly split in two (n1 = 9,860, n2 = 9,921) (see Tables 12.2–12.4).

Table 12.4   Participating functional roles, organizational levels, and languages

Role	n1	n2	Level	n1	n2	Language	n1	n2
Operations	4,164	4,127	Staff, without direct reports	5,991	5,953	Spanish	9,027	9,105
Commercial	1,942	1,986	Manager, with direct reports	2,793	2,833	English	833	816
Support	1,878	1,948	Director or executive	1,076	1,135			
Others	956	928						
R&D/Inn.	920	932						

In part one of the study (Danks et al., 2017a), the researchers found that while each of the six models showed acceptable model fit with strong item loadings, the structure coefficients for each of the models' three latent factors were also high, suggesting a possible lack of discriminant validity across factors – a finding that is not a significant threat to the validity of practitioner-based instruments where many of these factors are expected to correlate. It was also identified that while most of these first-order factor estimates of reliability, as measured by coefficient alpha, exceeded Nunnally's (1978) recommended threshold of 0.70, not all of the estimates met the desired threshold. Lastly, it was also found that while estimated variance inflation factors did not produce evidence for multicollinearity, each measurement model failed Harman's single common factor test (Podsakoff et al., 2003), suggesting that common method variance could threaten the accuracy of the factor and item correlations. Table 12.5 illustrates the findings from the confirmatory factor analyses for each of the six measurement models.

Additional investigation of alternative models was needed. In part two of the investigation Danks et al. (2017b) used an exploratory factor analysis to explore and propose additional models, including the specification of a single, global six-factor (block) model of innovation culture. Using a multi-step process of item elimination and model re-specification, an integrated five-factor model comprised of 37 indicators (elements) was identified as the best model fit (χ^2 = 21,984.960, df = 614, CFI = 0.919, AGFI = 0.996, SRMR = 0.032), RMSEA = 0.060 (0.060; 0.060). This alternate model demonstrated a similar adequacy of model fit than that of the six separate measurement models, but improved the reliability estimates across all organizational groups, where all reliability estimates exceeded Nunnally's (1978) recommended threshold of 0.70, with many of them higher than 0.90 for the alternate model, and many of which surpassed the estimates identified in previous literature (e.g. Aiman-Smith et al., 2005; Anderson & West, 1998; Dobni, 2008; Kuščer, 2013; Remneland-Wikhamn & Wikhamn, 2011; Tohidi et al., 2012). While this integrated model still did not reduce structure coefficients to improve evidence for discriminant validity – a finding that is, again, not a significant threat – the model did produce evidence of common method variance. This finding led to lessons learned at the measurement, factor, and item level. The authors of the instrument have identified the needed changes and are in the process of establishing a plan to modify the instrument, re-deploy the updated instrument with new samples, run the additional analyses, and publish the results. However, this work is still in development at this time.

Table 12.5   *Model fit estimates for the six measurement models*

Model	Spec	χ^2	df	CFI	AGFI	RMSEA	RMSEA CI90	SRMR
Values	3 factor	1117.818*	24	0.960	0.996	0.097	(0.094; 0.100)	0.029
Resources	3 factor	883.691*	24	0.980	0.997	0.060	(0.057; 0.064)	0.021
Behaviors	3 factor	1903.178*	24	0.975	0.998	0.090	(0.087; 0.094)	0.022
Processes	3 factor	924.771*	24	0.983	0.998	0.062	(0.058; 0.065)	0.019
Climate	3 factor	1755.376*	24	0.962	0.995	0.086	(0.082; 0.089)	0.030
Success	3 factor	982.654*	24	0.983	0.998	0.064	(0.060; 0.067)	0.019

Note: *$p < 0.001$. χ^2 = Satorra-Bentler (1988) scaled chi-square; CFI = comparative fit index; AGFI = adjusted goodness of fit index; RMSEA = root mean-square error of approximation; SRMR = standardized root mean square.
Source: Adapted from Danks et al. (2017a).

Note: For more information about the validation study, including a detailed description of tests for factor discrimination, reliability estimates by role and sector, use of the CMV latent factor model to test for common method variance, and the test for a higher level six factor model and a second order model, please see Danks et al. (2017a, 2017b).

THE INNOQUOTIENT MODEL: A USEFUL DIAGNOSTIC OF ORGANIZATIONAL CULTURE OF INNOVATION

In addition to this validation investigation, the utility validity of the InnoQuotient instrument has been identified through a succession of practitioner reports from multiple companies who have collaborated with the instrument's author (Rao) to implement the tool to assess their culture of innovation, and have reported its potency as a launching pad for identifying opportunities for strategic improvements. As of 2018, the InnoQuotient instrument has been utilized by 333 firms with 54,987 participants from 25 countries across 26 different industry sectors – a powerful sample against which all subsequent administrations can be benchmarked and compared, further supporting interpretation and the identification of next steps. The instrument has been administered in nine different languages, is fully automated and takes about ten minutes for the respondents to complete. Additional demographic questions such as firm size, industry classification, age, gender, education level, number of years at the firm, and innovation training have been embedded into the design, as well as the inclusion of customized grouping variables, such as functional, divisional, geographic areas, and organizational level (executives, managers, individual contributors) within the firm – all of which can be solicited to support additional segmentation and analysis. In addition, the survey can also be tailored to solicit two additional, open-ended questions to provide additional context to participant responses and support interpretation. These questions include: (1) What one to two things does your firm do well in its innovation efforts? and (2) What one to two things should your firm do to improve its innovation?

FROM ASSESSMENT TO ACTION AND IMPROVEMENT – A CASE SUMMARY AND LESSONS LEARNED

In this section we present a case summary from a recent application of the InnoQuotient instrument to demonstrate how it can be used to assess the culture of innovation, support decision-making, and initiate action planning and improvement. We also share key lessons learned from experiences in its broad use, and recommendations for how to support interpretation of results.

Case Summary

Following several years of low growth, a global medical devices firm headquartered in the US had recently appointed a new CEO, who had also brought with him a new group of executives into the firm as well. The executive team knew that there was significant talent and know-how for innovation within this well-known, multi-national firm. Yet, there was lack of concrete evidence of its strengths and organizational gaps. The executive team opted to use the InnoQuotient survey to identify areas where growth could take place.

In this case sample, the instrument was randomly administered via email to nearly 3,000 of 46,000 employees in a global healthcare firm, garnering a 29 percent response rate. Results from this administration were analyzed and were returned to the organization's senior leadership team, who received reports in the form of an executive summary, a comparative report, and a detail report. The reports represented the averages and the comparative ranking of all the six building blocks, the 18 factors and the 54 elements of the model. Figure 12.2 illustrates a sample report of average scores and rankings across each of the blocks, factors, and elements that is presented in the executive summary. The results demonstrate that this firm scored a global average of $x = 2.85$ on a 5-point scale, which was lower than the average score for all firms in the database, at $x = 3.20$. Comparative performance against all other firms in the database are also provided for each block, factor, and element to support further discussion.

Average scores and rankings are also reported for the 54 elements, ranked high to low, and segmented by organizational functions, geographic regions, and levels, for example (Figure 12.3). These results can illuminate bright spots and opportunities for improvement inside the organization, as well as reveal areas of consensus or disagreement from inside the firm on each of the elements. Executives are often surprised to see the variation in perception between leaders, mid-level managers, and employees in their organizations, and as expected, it has frequently been noted that respondents with higher roles in the organization report higher scores.

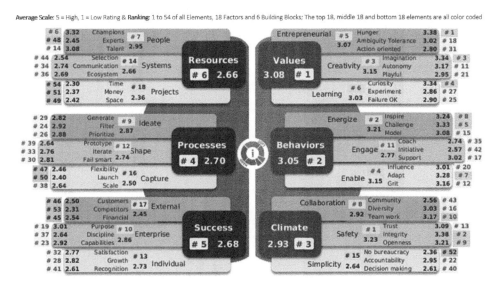

Figure 12.2   Average scores and rankings for sample healthcare organization

In this sample case study, senior leaders were provided feedback that some employees felt that their leaders inspired and challenged them to innovate – in this instance, the new CEO in the firm, who had brought with him/her a few new executives, all of whom were focused on messaging the importance of innovation. This recent effort seemed to be corroborated by the assessment results as well.

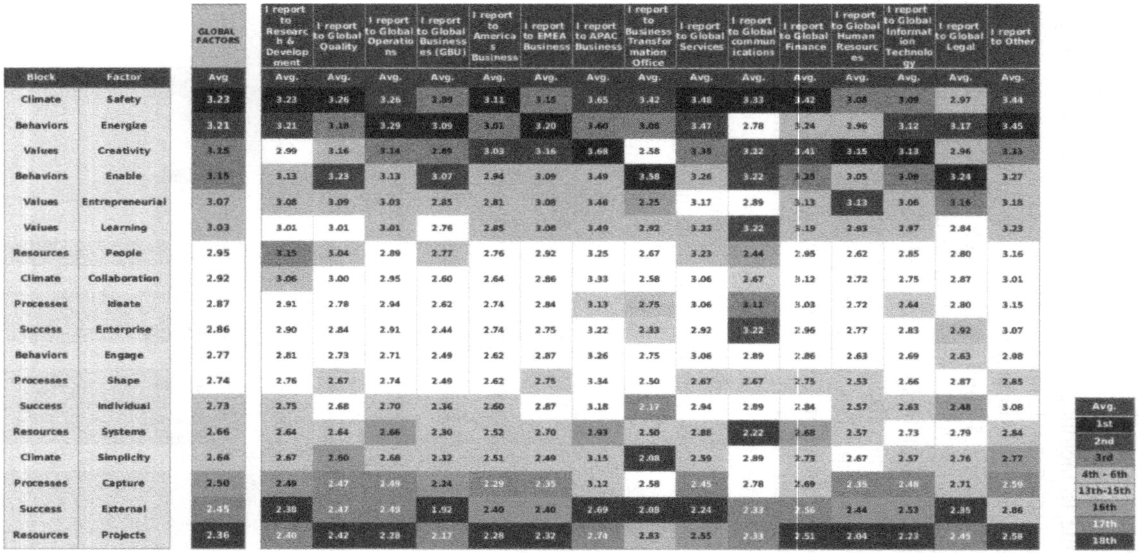

Block	Factor	GLOBAL FACTORS Avg	I report to Research & Development Avg.	I report to Global Quality Avg.	I report to Global Operations Avg.	I report to Global Businesses (GBU) Avg.	I report to Americas Business Avg.	I report to EMEA Business Avg.	I report to APAC Business Avg.	I report to Business Transformation Office Avg.	I report to Global Services Avg.	I report to Global communications Avg.	I report to Global Finance Avg.	I report to Global Human Resources Avg.	I report to Global Information Technology Avg.	I report to Global Legal Avg.	I report to Other Avg.
Climate	Safety	3.23	3.23	3.26	3.26	2.89	3.11	3.15	3.65	3.42	3.48	3.33	3.42	3.08	3.09	2.97	3.44
Behaviors	Energize	3.21	3.21	3.18	3.29	3.09	3.01	3.20	3.60	3.08	3.47	2.78	3.24	2.96	3.12	3.17	3.45
Values	Creativity	3.15	2.99	3.16	3.14	2.89	3.03	3.16	3.68	2.58	3.35	3.22	3.41	3.15	3.13	2.96	3.33
Behaviors	Enable	3.15	3.13	3.23	3.13	3.07	2.94	3.09	3.49	3.58	3.26	3.22	3.25	3.05	3.09	3.24	3.27
Values	Entrepreneurial	3.07	3.08	3.09	3.03	2.85	2.81	3.08	3.46	2.25	3.17	2.89	3.13	3.13	3.06	3.16	3.18
Values	Learning	3.03	3.01	3.01	3.01	2.76	2.85	3.08	3.49	2.92	3.23	3.22	3.19	2.93	2.97	2.84	3.23
Resources	People	2.95	3.15	3.04	2.89	2.77	2.76	2.92	3.25	2.67	3.23	2.44	2.95	2.62	2.85	2.80	3.16
Climate	Collaboration	2.92	3.06	3.00	2.95	2.60	2.64	2.86	3.33	2.58	3.06	2.67	3.12	2.72	2.75	2.87	3.01
Processes	Ideate	2.87	2.91	2.78	2.94	2.62	2.74	2.84	3.13	2.75	3.06	3.11	3.03	2.72	2.64	2.80	3.15
Success	Enterprise	2.86	2.90	2.84	2.91	2.44	2.74	2.75	3.22	2.33	2.92	3.22	2.96	2.77	2.83	2.92	3.07
Behaviors	Engage	2.77	2.81	2.73	2.71	2.49	2.62	2.87	3.26	2.75	3.06	2.89	2.86	2.63	2.69	2.63	2.98
Processes	Shape	2.74	2.76	2.67	2.74	2.49	2.62	2.75	3.34	2.50	2.67	2.67	2.75	2.53	2.66	2.87	2.85
Success	Individual	2.73	2.75	2.68	2.70	2.36	2.60	2.87	3.18	2.17	2.94	2.89	2.84	2.57	2.63	2.48	3.08
Resources	Systems	2.66	2.64	2.64	2.66	2.30	2.52	2.70	2.93	2.50	2.88	2.22	2.68	2.57	2.73	2.79	2.84
Climate	Simplicity	2.64	2.67	2.60	2.68	2.32	2.51	2.49	3.15	2.08	2.59	2.89	2.73	2.67	2.57	2.76	2.77
Processes	Capture	2.50	2.49	2.47	2.49	2.24	2.29	2.35	3.12	2.58	2.45	2.78	2.69	2.35	2.48	2.71	2.59
Success	External	2.45	2.38	2.47	2.49	1.92	2.40	2.40	2.69	2.08	2.24	2.33	2.56	2.44	2.53	2.35	2.86
Resources	Projects	2.36	2.40	2.42	2.28	2.17	2.28	2.32	2.74	2.83	2.55	2.33	2.51	2.04	2.23	2.45	2.58

Figure 12.3 *Average factor scores and rankings by functional area and reporting relationship*

The employees and executives were in agreement that neither the firm's customers nor competitors thought their organization was innovative. However, the employees felt that their leaders exhibited decent coaching behaviors and the employees proactively took initiative towards innovation.

The final reports also illustrate performance relative to external benchmarks – the norms for similar size firms and firms in their industry (see Figure 12.4). This report benchmarks the specific firm's averages and rankings on each of the 54 elements with the following: (1) Maximum – the best score for a firm for that element in the database, (2) Average – the average/ranking for that element for all firms in the database, (3) Minimum – the worst rating for a firm for that element among all firms in the database, (4) Sector score – the average for all firms in the same sector as the specific firm, (5) Size score – the average for all firms of the same size (small, medium or large) as the specific firm, and (6) "You"– the averages/ranking for the specific firm.

Lessons Learned

To support interpretation for the results reported in Figure 12.4, senior leaders are often briefed on the most frequent strengths and challenges that are commonly experienced by nearly all firms in the norming group. One of these lessons learned is that the three most common top factors that usually receive the highest scores include *entrepreneurial* mindset, *creativity*, and psychological *safety* for employees. Drilling down to some of the elements behind these factors, independent of the industry or country or size, it is commonly observed that firms are filled with employees that have a burning desire to explore opportunities for innovation and create new things (the *hunger* element). Employees are also good at questioning and pursuing opportunities, and most respondents believe that their firm has the *talent* required for pursuing innovation opportunities. In general, firms have a climate of *openness*, where the employees are free to express their opinions and speak their mind. Firms also seem to encourage new ways of thinking and solutions from a variety of perspectives.

Another lesson learned from past uses is that in spite of the above strengths, employees and firms experience significant hurdles that have the potential to impede hunger and abilities for innovation. At the factor level, *managing their innovation projects* usually ranks dead last, followed by lack of *rewards* for participating in innovation projects, and a lack of *engagement* from employees. The reasons behind these poor rankings can be hypothesized through deeper investigation into the elements behind these factors. Bureaucracy is the number one challenge that employees most frequently report, typically ranking dead last in large firms. It is not surprising that this might result in the employees' lack of interest in proactively initiating innovation activities. It is also hypothesized that the lack of time to participate in innovation projects can be a significant constraint for employees. In most large firms, a lack of *resources* is usually not an impediment, but the lack of the employees' dedicated time to innovation projects can become a key bottleneck within firms. Finally, while almost all firms have innovation champions within their firms, employees do not see their immediate superiors as exhibiting coaching behaviors that are conducive for innovation, perhaps resulting in employee disengagement, as firms tend to lack innovation experts that can guide and support their innovation projects.

While the above conclusions are based on the investigation of common rankings of the factors and elements among organizations, leadership *behaviors* consistently ranks in the middle third of the 54 elements. Past investigations into the leadership behavior results, such as ranges, averages, standard deviations, correlations and the qualitative responses, revealed more findings around leaders' behaviors. In the more innovative firms, it has been identified that there were committed leaders (champions) who seemed to exhibit the right behaviors that were needed for an innovative culture. Firstly, the better firms had a great resource – innovation champions. These innovation champions were great at energizing, engaging and enabling their employees. Champions energized their employees by inspiring them with an articulation of innovation opportunities. They frequently challenged them to think and act entrepreneurially and modeled the right innovation behaviors for others to follow. The champions engaged the employees by devoting time to coach them, pushed them to take initiative, provided feedback and supported innovation project team members. Finally, these leaders enabled employees by helping them navigate (*influence*) around bureaucratic obstacles, take action to change course (*adapt*) when needed, and persist (*grit*) in their innovation efforts even when there were setbacks.

Unfortunately, in a majority of the firms in the database, the above behaviors were not the norm. Having innovation champions, modeling and coaching innovation behaviors, inspiring and challenging the employees had some of the largest standard deviations, meaning that the difference between higher-performing firms and lower-performing firms was quite wide.

Average Scale: 5 = High, 1 = Low Rating and Ranking: 1 to 54 of all Elements
Max = Maximum for a firm in the Database; Avg = Average of all firms in the Database; Min = Minimum for a firm in the Database
Sec = Average of all firms in Your Industrial Sector; Size = Average of all firms of Your Size; You = Your Firm Averages & Rankings

RATIONAL	Max	Avg	Min	Sec	Size	You	Max	Avg	Min	Sec	Size	You
Resources												
Champions	5.00	3.49	2.22	3.47	3.40	3.32	13	7	15	5	7	6
Experts	4.25	2.88	1.35	3.02	2.84	2.45	50	49	53	45	47	48
Talent	5.00	3.66	2.71	3.78	3.61	3.08	34	2	1	1	2	14
Selection	4.20	2.95	1.67	3.04	2.90	2.54	51	44	47	38	41	44
Communication	4.40	3.05	1.95	3.12	2.99	2.74	43	38	34	34	38	34
Ecosystem	4.43	3.30	2.21	3.26	3.17	2.69	40	21	17	25	22	36
Time	4.50	2.82	1.75	2.81	2.70	2.30	32	52	35	52	53	54
Money	4.29	2.89	1.33	2.93	2.88	2.37	45	47	54	48	44	51
Space	4.30	2.82	1.63	2.94	2.80	2.42	48	51	51	47	48	48
Processes												
Generate	4.50	3.14	1.88	3.19	3.07	2.62	35	32	36	30	32	29
Filter	4.80	3.12	2.00	3.24	3.10	2.92	22	34	30	26	29	24
Prioritize	4.50	2.95	2.00	3.04	3.02	2.88	34	41	31	37	35	26
Prototype	4.04	2.96	1.67	3.01	2.90	2.64	53	42	48	44	42	39
Iterate	4.92	3.07	1.88	3.04	2.99	2.76	47	36	37	37	33	33
Fail smart	3.69	2.92	1.80	3.01	2.88	2.61	54	46	38	45	43	30
Flexibility	5.00	2.95	1.67	2.80	2.71	2.46	15	43	49	53	52	47
Launch	4.80	3.05	1.79	2.91	2.87	2.40	36	37	40	49	45	50
Scale	4.50	3.04	2.05	3.04	2.91	2.64	36	40	24	35	39	38
Success												
Customers	5.00	3.36	2.00	3.33	3.17	2.50	16	17	32	17	23	46
Competitors	4.60	3.31	2.06	3.11	3.14	2.31	19	21	35	26	53	
Financial	4.46	3.21	1.8	3.14	3.15	2.54	38	27	41	33	24	45
Purpose	4.71	3.43	2.00	3.44	3.36	3.01	24	12	33	11	10	19
Discipline	5.00	3.20	1.71	3.22	3.12	2.64	17	28	43	28	27	37
Capabilities	4.67	3.50	2.13	3.46	3.43	2.92	27	5	19	6	6	23
Satisfaction	5.00	3.16	2.10	3.17	3.00	2.77	18	30	20	31	36	32
Growth	5.00	3.14	1.71	3.22	3.04	2.62	19	33	44	27	34	28
Recognition	4.50	2.89	1.71	3.08	2.80	2.61	37	48	46	41	49	41

EMOTIONAL	Max	Avg	Min	Sec	Size	You	Max	Avg	Min	Sec	Size	You
Values												
Hunger	1	1	7	1	1	1	5.00	3.86	2.38	3.92	3.78	3.38
Ambiguity Tolerance	2	10	26	13	14	18	5.00	3.44	2.08	3.44	3.31	3.02
Action oriented	41	26	18	29	25	31	4.40	3.24	2.13	3.20	3.14	2.80
Imagination	30	4	3	3	5	3	4.56	3.52	2.33	3.59	3.47	3.34
Autonomy	3	11	11	14	11	11	5.00	3.43	2.33	3.39	3.35	3.17
Playful	23	9	16	12	13	21	4.71	3.47	2.21	3.44	3.32	2.95
Curiosity	44	6	6	4	4	4	4.38	3.49	2.42	3.52	3.48	3.34
Experiment	45	24	35	20	20	27	4.33	3.26	1.88	3.30	3.22	2.86
Failure OK	4	18	10	21	21	25	5.00	3.33	2.33	3.30	3.17	2.90
Behaviors												
Inspire	20	22	23	22	17	8	4.80	3.29	2.03	3.29	3.26	3.24
Challenge	25	23	25	19	19	5	4.67	3.27	2.01	3.31	3.22	3.33
Model	5	29	22	32	30	15	5.00	3.18	2.04	3.16	3.07	3.08
Coach	6	50	42	51	50	35	5.00	2.84	1.75	2.88	2.77	2.74
Initiative	52	53	50	51	42		4.17	2.82	1.63	2.89	2.71	2.57
Support	7	25	13	23	28	17	5.00	3.24	2.25	3.29	3.12	3.02
Influence	42	35	27	36	31	20	4.40	3.11	2.00	3.09	3.07	3.01
Adapt	9	16	12	16	16	7	5.00	3.36	2.32	3.35	3.28	3.28
Grit	26	13	5	15	15	12	4.67	3.42	2.45	3.32	3.28	3.16
Climate												
Community	39	45	46	46	46	43	4.43	2.92	1.70	3.01	2.86	2.56
Diversity	9	20	14	18	18	16	5.00	3.30	2.22	3.32	3.25	3.03
Team work	21	15	8	5	9	10	4.80	3.41	2.38	3.54	3.36	3.17
Trust	28	14	3	16	12	13	4.60	3.42	2.56	3.45	3.33	3.09
Integrity	10	8	2	4	3	2	5.00	3.48	2.69	3.54	3.49	3.38
Openness	11	3	4	7	8	9	5.00	3.54	2.48	3.52	3.40	3.21
No Bureaucracy	31	54	52	54	54	52	4.50	2.80	1.99	2.63	2.56	2.36
Accountability	12	31	28	28	33	22	5.00	3.16	2.00	3.27	3.04	2.99
Decision making	46	39	29	42	40	40	4.32	3.04	2.00	3.03	2.91	2.61

Figure 12.4   Average scores and rankings, compared with industry and firm benchmarks

RECOMMENDATIONS: MOVING FROM ASSESSMENT TO ACTION

By using the InnoQuotient instrument to review performance for each of the building blocks, discuss variation across critical organizational segments, and compare to other organizations of a similar industry or size, organizations can gain better insight into where to begin their work of improving their culture to foster innovative activity. The InnoQuotient instrument, when utilized as a diagnostic tool, can help produce the information and evidence needed to understand, in a sequential, step-by-step manner, and with a trained feedback consultant, additional context and support to uncover the richness of the varied possibilities for action. Senior leaders or facilitators who wish to lead organizations through a similar process may consider the following guidelines to help their organizations move from assessment to action:

1. *Use Diagnosis to Start Dialogue*. This instrument has the potential to serve as a key first step to starting the dialogue among the executives within the firm. First, it may confirm existing perceptions and feelings and make them more concrete. Second, the analysis of the results may actually expose persisting myths. For instance, employees and executives of a newly acquired US subsidiary of a European company voiced complaints about differences between the values and behaviors of their firm and their new parent organization. Yet, the InnoQuotient results revealed that on many important variables, there were no statistically significant differences between the two. Hence, the group was able to sustain action and limit perpetuating misconceptions.

2. *Challenge for Change*. It is often hard to predict how executives might interpret the instrument and how they may act upon the insights. The CEO of the case summary presented in this narrative shared the data with his top 200 executives during the firm's annual meeting. He identified variation between his firm and their competitors for the factor of bureaucracy. This CEO had the information he needed to challenge his leaders to start working on initiatives – a message which quickly reverberated throughout the firm globally. Without access to such evidence of the firm's performance, it would have been difficult for the CEO to throw down the gauntlet for the leaders in the firm.

3. *Benchmark Close to Home*. Comparisons with firms of similar size within the same industry are useful for benchmarking performance, but internal benchmarking can be one of the best places to start to initiate dialogue. If managers and employees notice that their division or function is performing poorly compared to others in the firm, they are more inclined to change. People change when they see their peers prosper, and usually elicits much less resistance from the employees to participate in actions to drive change.

4. *Start from Strength*. While it may be tempting to first attend to weakness as a focal point for action, better results often come when leaders clarify their strengths and build around them. For example, employees of a Latin American family business scored their firm highly for openness to learning and questioning the unknown, but scored their leaders poorly for lack of engagement, citing inadequate coaching and feedback behaviors. After hosting discussions to listen to employees to identify potential solutions, the executive team focused on their learning mindset to develop the next management layer through a series of training programs on leadership and coaching that included both the leaders and their direct reports.

5. *Start Small to Show Success*. Leaders are often impatient and urgent for immediate change that they can see throughout the organization; but culture is extremely resilient. Barring extreme threats – external or internal – it can be quite difficult work to change mindsets and behaviors. It is recommended that leaders select no more than three of the 54 elements and engage two or three friendly groups to start initiatives to demonstrate success quickly. Early successes help convert skeptics, who have the potential to convert others within the enterprise.

6. *Do Not Ignore Hidden Issues*. Repeatedly, we see average firms rank individual accountability right in the middle of all the 54 elements. Hence, executives do not raise this as a concern or strength in their discussions. Yet, in high performing firms, accountability is usually ranked very high. Innovation requires high levels of collaboration and strong accountability, barring which innovation teams can get mired in endless consensus building and bureaucracy. Usually high performing innovation teams take the risks – organizational and market – and good leaders are accountable for failures. That is how trust is built within enterprises; a key ingredient for enrolling others into projects involving uncertainty.

7. *Re-Evaluate Again for Sustainability*. Sustaining the ongoing journey towards a stronger culture of innovation is a huge challenge for most firms. In our experience, very few firms take concrete steps towards action that lead to lasting change. Further, fewer firms persist in their initiatives over several years. A small number of leaders will conduct a second iteration of the instrument to be able to measure efforts of improvement in the key building blocks of innovation culture. Leaders who repeat the diagnostic assessment demonstrate the right commitment to resources, and are able to initiate change and initiatives with some success. Without proper accountability that such measurement provides, it can be easy for firms to backslide and worsen performance with minimal effort.

CONCLUSION

The importance of an enterprise culture of innovation as a key differentiator is well understood in today's competitive landscape. In this chapter we have summarized the key developments in the measurement and assessment of organizational culture of innovation, presented the InnoQuotient model as an example of a practitioner-oriented measurement model for such assessment, and illustrated how organizations can utilize results from its assessment to drive action and improvement. We have also presented a list of key lessons learned from experiences in facilitating leaders to review their organizational performance on the InnoQuotient instrument, and recommendations for how to move from assessment to action. By taking the time to systematically diagnose its performance for each of the key building blocks of culture of innovation, and review segmented results from both within and beyond its own walls, organizations can take the necessary steps to hone in on where resources could be best applied to catalyze all leaders and employees toward action and innovative activity.

REFERENCES

Aiman-Smith, L., Goodrich, N., Roberts, D., & Scinta, J. (2005). Assessing your organization's potential for value innovation. *Research-Technology Management*, *48*(2), 37–42.
Anderson, N. R., & West, M. A. (1998). Measuring climate for work group innovation: Development and validation of the team climate inventory. *Journal of Organizational Behavior*, *19*(3), 235–258.
Bakovic, T., Lazibat, T., & Sutic, I. (2013). Radical innovation culture in Croatian manufacturing industry. *Journal of Enterprising Communities: People and Places in the Global Economy*, *7*(1), 74–80.
Barsh, J., Capozzi, M. M., & Davidson, J. (2008). Leadership and innovation. *McKinsey Quarterly*, *1*, 36.
Brettel, M., & Cleven, N. J. (2011). Innovation culture, collaboration with external partners and NPD performance. *Creativity and Innovation Management*, *20*(4), 253–272.

Chen, W. J. (2011). Innovation in hotel services: Culture and personality. *International Journal of Hospitality Management, 30*(1), 64–72.

Christensen, C. M, Grossman, J. H., & Hwang, J. (2009). *The innovator's prescription: A disruptive solution for health care.* New York, NY: McGraw-Hill.

Crossan, M. M., & Apaydin, M. (2010). A multi-dimensional framework of organizational innovation: A systematic review of the literature. *Journal of Management Studies, 47*(6), 1154–1191.

Danks, S., Rao, J., & Allen, J. M. (2017a). Measuring culture of innovation: A validation study of the Innovation Quotient instrument (Part one). *Performance Improvement Quarterly, 29*(4), 427–454.

Danks, S., Rao, J., & Allen, J. M. (2017b). Measuring culture of innovation: A validation study of the Innovation Quotient instrument (Part two). *Performance Improvement Quarterly, 30*(1), 29–53.

Denison, D. R. (1996). What is the difference between organizational culture and organizational climate? A native's point of view on a decade of paradigm wars. *Academy of Management Review, 21*(3), 619–654.

Dobni, C. B. (2008). Measuring innovation culture in organizations: The development of a generalized innovation culture construct using exploratory factor analysis. *European Journal of Innovation Management, 11*(4), 539–559.

Dyer, J., Gregersen, H., & Christensen, C.M. (2011). *The innovator's DNA: Mastering the five skills of disruptive innovators.* Boston, MA: Harvard Business Review Press.

Enzing, C. M., Batterink, M. H., Janszen, F. H., & Omta, S. O. (2011). Where innovation processes make a difference in products' short- and long-term market success. *British Food Journal, 113*(7), 812–837.

Francis, D.L. (2000). Assessing and Improving Innovation Capability in Organisations. PhD Thesis, The University of Brighton.

Herrmann, A., Gassmann, O., & Eisert, U. (2007). An empirical study of the antecedents for radical product innovations and capabilities for transformation. *Journal of Engineering and Technology Management, 24*(1), 92–120.

Hoe, S.L. (2011). Measuring an organization's innovation climate: A case study from Singapore. *Development and Learning in Organizations, 25*(6), 13–15.

Hofstede, G. (1991). *Cultures and organizations: Software of the mind.* London: McGraw-Hill Book Company.

Humphreys, P., McAdam, R., & Leckey, J. (2005). Longitudinal evaluation of innovation implementation in SMEs. *European Journal of Innovation Management, 8*(3), 283–304.

Hurley, R. F., & Hult, G. T. (1998). Innovation, market orientation, and organizational learning: An integration and empirical examination. *Journal of Marketing, 62*(3), 42–54.

Jaruzelski, B., Loehr, J., & Holman, R. (2011). Why culture is key. *Strategy and Business, 65*(1), 1–17.

Kaufman, H.R., Tsangar, H., & Vrontis, D. (2012). Innovativeness of European SMEs: Mission not yet accomplished. *Ekonomska istraživanja, 25*(2), 333–360.

Kimberlin, C. L., & Winterstein, A. G. (2008). Validity and reliability of measurement instruments used in research. *American Journal of Health System Pharmacists, 65*(23), 2276–2284.

Kuščer, K. (2013). Determining factors of mountain destination innovativeness. *Journal of Vacation Marketing, 19*(1), 41–54.

Lee, C. S., Chen, Y. C., Tsui, P. L., & Yu, T. H. (2014). Examining the relations between open innovation climate and job satisfaction with a PLS path model. *Quality & Quantity, 48*, 1705–1722.

McAdam, R., Keogh, W., Reid, R. S., & Mitchell, N. (2007). Implementing innovation management in manufacturing SMEs: A longitudinal study. *Journal of Small Business and Enterprise Development, 14*(3), 385–403.

Nunnally, J. C. (1978). *Psychometric theory* (2nd ed.). New York: McGraw-Hill.

O'Cass, A., & Ngo, L. V. (2007). Market orientation versus innovative culture: Two routes to superior brand performance. *European Journal of Marketing, 41*(7/8), 868–887.

O'Connor, A., Roos, G., & Vickers-Willis, T. (2007). Evaluating an Australian public policy organization's innovation capacity. *European Journal of Innovation Management, 10*(4), 532–558.

O'Reilly, C. A. (1989). Corporations, culture and commitment: Motivation and social control in organizations. *California Management Review, 31*, 9–25.

O'Sullivan, D. & Dooley, L. (2009). *Applying innovation.* Thousand Oaks, CA: Sage Publications.

Panuwatwanich, K., Stewart, R. A., & Mohamed, S. (2009). Validation of an empirical model for innovation diffusion in Australian design firms. *Construction Innovation: Information, Process, Management, 9*(4), 449–467.

Podsakoff, P. M., MacKenzie, S. B., Lee, J. Y., & Podsakoff, N. P. (2003). Common method biases in behavioral research: A critical review of the literature and recommended remedies. *Journal of Applied Psychology, 88*(5), 879.

Rao, J. (2014). Stop the nonsense! Innovation is a discipline. *European Business Review*, January–February, 24–27.

Rao, J., & Weintraub, J. (2013a). How innovative is your company's culture? *MIT Sloan Management Review, 54*(3), 28–37.

Rao, J. & Weintraub, J. (2013b). Becoming a more innovative culture: From assessment to action. *European Financial Review*, October–November, 15–18. Retrieved from http://www.europeanfinancialreview.com/?p=659

Remneland-Wikhamn, B., & Wikhamn, W. (2011). Open innovation climate measure: The introduction of a validated scale. *Creativity and Innovation Management, 20*(4), 284–295.

Sarros, J. C., Cooper, B. K., & Santora, J. C. (2008). Building a climate for innovation through transformational leadership and organizational culture. *Journal of Leadership & Organizational Studies, 15*(2), 145–158.

Satorra, A., & Bentler, P. M. (1988). Scaling corrections for chi-square statistics in covariance structure analysis. ASA 1988 Proceedings of the Business and Economic Statistics, Section 308–313. Alexandria, VA: American Statistical Association.

Saunila, M., & Ukko, J. (2013). Facilitating innovation capability through performance measurement: A study of Finnish SMEs. *Management Research Review, 36*(10), 991–1010.

Schein, E. H. (1990). Organizational culture. *American Psychologist, 45*(2), 109–119.

Scott, S. G., & Bruce, R. A. (1994). Determinants of innovative behavior: A path model of individual innovation in the workplace. *Academy of Management Journal, 37*(3), 580–607.

Shahin, A., & Zeinali, Z. (2010). Developing a relationship matrix for organizational learning and innovativeness with a case study in a manufacturing company. *International Journal of Business & Management, 5*(7).

Sharifirad, M. S., & Ataei, V. (2012). Organizational culture and innovation culture: Exploring the relationships between constructs. *Leadership & Organization Development Journal, 33*(5), 494–517.

Slater, S. F., Mohr, J. J., & Sengupta, S. (2014). Radical product innovation capability: Literature review, synthesis, and illustrative research propositions. *Journal of Product Innovation Management, 31*(3), 552–566.

Steiber, A., & Alänge, S. (2013). A corporate system for continuous innovation: The case of Google Inc. *European Journal of Innovation Management, 16*(2), 243–264.

Sun, H., Wong, S. Y., Zhao, Y., & Yam, R. (2012). A systematic model for assessing innovation competence of Hong Kong/China manufacturing companies: A case study. *Journal of Engineering and Technology Management, 29*(4), 546–565.

Sušanj, Z. (2000). Innovative climate and culture in manufacturing organizations: Differences between some European countries. *Social Science Information, 39*(2), 349–361.

Switzer, G. E., Wisniewski, S. R., Belle, S. H., Dew, M. A., & Schultz, R. (1999). Selecting, developing, and evaluating research instruments. *Social Psychiatry and Psychiatric Epidemiology, 34*(8), 399–409.

Tellis, G. J., Prabhu, J. C., & Chandy, R. K. (2009). Radical innovation across nations: The preeminence of corporate culture. *Journal of Marketing, 73*(1), 3–23.

Tohidi, H., Seyedaliakbar, S. M., & Mandegari, M. (2012). Organizational learning measurement and the effect on firm innovation. *Journal of Enterprise Information Management, 25*(3), 219–245.

Velasco, E., Zamanillo, I., & Del Valle, T. G. (2013). Mobilizing company members' full innovative potential. *Human Factors and Ergonomics in Manufacturing & Service Industries, 23*(6), 541–559.

Xerri, M. J., & Brunetto, Y. (2011). Fostering the innovative behaviour of SME employees: A social capital perspective. *Research & Practice in Human Resource Management, 19*(2), 43.

Zairi, M., & Al-Mashari, M. (2005). Developing a sustainable culture of innovation management: A prescriptive approach. *Knowledge and Process Management, 12*(3), 190–202.

13. Corporate entrepreneurship culture

Jenna Campton

WHAT IS CORPORATE ENTREPRENEURSHIP?

Before the definitions of corporate entrepreneurial culture, measurement methods, and issues can be discussed in this chapter, it is important that the reader understands what corporate entrepreneurship is, as this is still a debated topic in academic literature (see: Åmo, 2010; Blanka, 2019). The concept of corporate entrepreneurship was introduced in the 1980s, with several researchers investigating the process of entrepreneurial activity within organisations. This included the strategic process of how to encourage entrepreneurial activity (Burgelman, 1983; Rule & Irwin, 1988), organisational and managerial challenges (Kanter & Richardson, 1991), and how to sustain corporate entrepreneurship (McKinney & McKinney, 1989). Broadly speaking, corporate entrepreneurship involves promoting, having, and transforming organisations through innovation, enterprise, and initiative (Kanter, 1984). Corporate entrepreneurship comprises how companies can increase transformation through strategic renewal, implement new ideas, create new businesses within a firm, undertake new corporate ventures, and foster innovative initiatives where management is in charge of the process (Dess et al., 1999; Hornsby et al., 2002; Morris et al., 2011; Zahra, 1991).

There are several different levels at which corporate entrepreneurship can be measured and it is easy to confuse these, as even the academic literature uses some of the concepts interchangeably. Corporate entrepreneurship is also known as, and commonly swapped with the following terms: intrapreneurship, exopreneurship, corporate venturing, business renewal, entrepreneurial organisations, employee innovation behaviour, and management of innovation (see Åmo, 2010; Åmo & Kolvereid, 2005; Blanka, 2019; Christensen, 2004). Several reviews of academic literature have pointed out how these concepts are used interchangeably; for example Åmo (2010) highlights a paper by Christensen (2005) which used qualitative interviews to identify five enabling factors of intrapreneurship. However, the paper draws exclusively from literature and terminology concerning corporate entrepreneurship. Similarly, an article by Fitzsimmons et al. (2005) has a literature review overviewing corporate entrepreneurship, then proposes intrapreneurship hypotheses and utilises an intrapreneurship scale (see: Åmo, 2010). This is an important issue to consider as there is a difference between the many concepts when measured at the different levels of the organisational activity.

The concept of corporate entrepreneurship is considered to be an organisational level activity, whereas intrapreneurship is at the individual level, and exopreneurship is external to the company. Corporate entrepreneurship in essence concerns the transformation of an organisation through strategic renewal, innovation, or the creation of new ventures within an organisation (Åmo, 2010; Kanter, 1984; Dess et al., 1999; Zahra, 1991). The fundamental principle of corporate entrepreneurship is change management and innovation practices. Corporate entrepreneurship is generally initiated top down, with management levels leading the change, innovation or new initiative/venture (Åmo, 2010). The intended outcome of corporate entrepreneurship strategy is then improved for sustainable competitive advantage, performance, capability development and strategic repositioning (Kuratko, 2007). Therefore, it is from the upper levels of the corporation that the entrepreneurship is driven (top-down).

On the other hand, intrapreneurship is a broad process of innovation driven by employees usually from a bottom-up perspective. Intrapreneurship is focused on the individual human capital of an organisation and is a process through which the employees pursue business opportunities or potential innovation (Antoncic, 2007; Blanka, 2019). Intrapreneurship is therefore focused on an individual-level approach from the Schumpeterian innovation concept of entrepreneurship (Antoncic & Hisrich, 2003; Block et al., 2017). Schumpeterian entrepreneurs are those who turn novel ideas into innovative products and services to create new economic opportunities (Block et al., 2017). Intrapreneurship should then be measured at the individual level, involving personality traits including innovation, risk-taking behaviour, openness to change, autonomy, proactiveness and other characteristics/traits of innovative individuals who are harnessed in a corporate environment (Åmo, 2010; Antoncic & Hisrich, 2003). The outcomes of successful intrapreneurship commonly include behavioural outcomes, intrapreneurial activity, and organisational performance (for an overview of research see Blanka, 2019). So, clearly intrapreneurship occurs at the level of individuals, teams, and workgroups.

Exopreneurship is then the opportunities available outside of the boundaries of an organisation. Exopreneurship is acquiring innovation through external networks, such as joint ventures, external venture capital, subcontracting, franchises, strategic and cooperative alliances (Chang, 2000; Christensen, 2004). The focus of exopreneurship is on obtaining innovation from sources external to the organisation (Danyliuk, 2019). It is considered to be a process that is entirely external to the organisation and distinct from corporate entrepreneurship and intrapreneurship (Chang, 2001). Therefore, it is dissimilar from corporate entrepreneurship and intrapreneurship, as it is considered to be entrepreneurial activity outside of the organisation.

These definitions of corporate entrepreneurship, intrapreneurship, and exopreneurship are across multiple levels of an organisation, from how upper management and management encourage the entrepreneurial activities, to how, at the team and individual level, this is promoted and maintained, the values and underlying norms, and also external innovation. The issue with much of the current empirical research is occurring at the construct level of each identified term which makes it difficult to tease apart at the measurement level. Even now researchers are drawing on mixed definitions to justify their constructs and questionnaire items, scales, and factors (Blanka, 2019). The distinctions between corporate entrepreneurship, intrapreneurship, and exopreneurship are important as culture can occur at the level of the organisation, the team, the individual, and in how an organisation portrays itself to external agents. The focus of this chapter is on corporate entrepreneurship culture as portrayed in a top-down approach and measured at the level of the organisation and/or the individuals' perceptions of culture.

WHAT IS CORPORATE ENTREPRENEURIAL CULTURE?

The majority of the literature currently treats organisational culture and corporate entrepreneurial culture as being separate concepts. The idea is that an organisation will encourage innovation and risk taking, deemed the primary elements of entrepreneurship, and that this leads to corporate entrepreneurship occurring or being supported (e.g. Behram & Özdemirci,

2014; Chung & Gibbons, 1997; Paunovic & Dima, 2014; Umrani et al., 2018). Corporate entrepreneurial culture does not appear to exist as a specific measurable term/construct in the majority of research articles (Umrani et al., 2018). There is currently a noticeably large gap in the literature concerning corporate entrepreneurial culture.

However, there are several textbooks which have proposed how to create a corporate entrepreneurial culture. These textbooks recommend that the corporate entrepreneurial culture is reinforced through the management practices and policies of the company (Morris et al., 2011; Salama, 2011). Some empirical case studies, such as one on Google, also support that corporate entrepreneurship comes from the policies and culture of the organisation, which suggests a top-down approach (e.g., Finkle, 2012). The underlying values of innovation, risk taking, autonomy and utilising human capital are of prime importance (e.g. Paunovic & Dima, 2014; Wang et al., 2005). The proposed idea is that an organisation is attempting to create an entrepreneurial culture that is somewhat separate to the overall organisation's culture.

> An adequate organizational culture that includes referent values of entrepreneurial culture as well as motivational factors that support effective implementation of these values in the corporate environment and foster entrepreneurship to grow and flourish. (Paunovic & Dima, 2014, p. 269)

However, the issue is that the academic books cite other journal articles and academic textbooks that examine elements of individual entrepreneurial culture, without any empirical proof that there are links, or differences, between an individual culture and organisational corporate entrepreneurial culture (e.g., Behram & Özdemirci, 2014; Morris et al., 2011). If entrepreneurship can be considered a culture, then why is there not a culture of corporate entrepreneurship when the elements are a part of the organisation's culture? If corporate entrepreneurship is primarily considered an organisational strategy, as such, corporate entrepreneurial culture should be a shared set of values and norms as created by the organisation to promote this strategy.

Further, there is much variation in how studies have measured culture at different organisational levels. Some have measured intrapreneurial culture (individual/team level: e.g., Kuratko et al., 1990), others have measured entrepreneurial orientation (individual/firm level: e.g., Engelen et al., 2015), while others have not measured culture at all (e.g., Bau & Wagner, 2015). It appears that corporate entrepreneurship within a firm is measured mostly through entrepreneurial orientation at the team and individual level (e.g. Kloepfer, 2020; Soomro & Shah, 2019). There is limited research about whether there is a culture of corporate entrepreneurship at the firm level (Umrani et al., 2018). Culture for the most part is either measured as a general organisational culture, or by using existing organisational theories of culture.

CULTURE AND CORPORATE ENTREPRENEURSHIP AS SEPARATE CONSTRUCTS

Generally organisational culture research is utilised as a framework to identify the different dimensions and typologies of organisations (Arz, 2017). Organisational culture is interdisciplinary and encompasses many different concepts. Largely, organisational culture consists of artefacts, values, beliefs, and phenomena that are seen, heard, or felt – it is a part of the organisational psychology that forms the values, norms, and beliefs (Arz, 2017; Schneider, 1990; Schneider et al., 2013; Umrani et al., 2018). Over time, several scales have been created to measure culture at the organisational level (see Arz, 2017 for a review).

In terms of the corporate entrepreneurial culture, there is currently no direct measure in academic research. This is because most research proposes that corporate entrepreneurship and entrepreneurship in general is a separate concept/construct that is encouraged by the culture of the organisation (e.g., Behram & Özdemirci, 2014; Umrani et al., 2018). Much of the research states that as an organisation strives towards corporate entrepreneurship, it is through its separate organisational culture that it fosters the key elements of corporate entrepreneurship (Behram & Özdemirci, 2014; Covin & Wales, 2019; Umrani et al., 2018). Corporate entrepreneurial process is considered to be a top-down phenomenon that is driven through management and leaders (Morris et al., 2011). The main tenets of corporate entrepreneurship include corporate venturing through innovation and creation of new ventures, services, and products, risk-taking, innovativeness and proactiveness, and competitive aggressiveness and autonomy (Arz, 2017). These can be measured at different levels of the firm, for example entrepreneurial orientation can be measured at the individual and firm level (Fellnhofer, 2016). Therefore, research treats corporate entrepreneurship and organisational culture as separate measures.

Examples of Studies that use Culture Tools and Corporate Entrepreneurship Measures

Undoubtedly there is much confusion in the literature as to whether corporate entrepreneurial culture is a separate and distinct concept/construct, and whether organisational culture exists entirely separate to corporate entrepreneurship within an organisation (Arz, 2017; Covin & Wales, 2019). There are several empirical studies which have measured organisational culture separately from corporate entrepreneurship. Overall, these studies offer interesting insights into some common theories of culture and what dimensions corporate entrepreneurship could consist of. There are apparent themes which occur across these studies including management support, organisational structure, new business venturing and whether organisations encourage innovation and proactiveness (see Table 13.1). However, even these studies have notable issues concerning the measurement of corporate entrepreneurship.

One of the seminal older studies which may have added to the confusion concerning corporate entrepreneurship and intrapreneurship was conducted by Kuratko et al. (1990). In this study the premise of the literature review was corporate entrepreneurship, however, the paper deviates and then proposes a measure of intrapreneurship (Table 13.1). Kuratko et al.'s (1990) literature review gives little justification as to how an intrapreneurial culture is formed and cites much of the literature for corporate entrepreneurship. The measures that were chosen by Kuratko et al. (1990) are based on common ideas within the mixed literature of corporate entrepreneurship and intrapreneurship. Measures included management support for intrapreneurship, organisational structure, risk taking, time availability, and reward and resource availability (Kuratko et al., 1990). Some of these concepts are cited in later work by Morris et al. (2011) and Kuratko's later work (2007). In summary, intrapreneurial culture is measured in an ambiguous way as the measures are a mixture of concepts drawn from corporate entrepreneurship and intrapreneurship.

Overall organisational culture has also been measured through the Competing Values Framework (CVF). The CVF has been used in several research papers and consists of four culture types (Kloepfer, 2020). The first is a controlling dimension – Clan culture – which consists of the collective membership of shared values and common goals (Beus et al., 2020; Yu & Wu, 2009). The Adhocracy culture concerns growth, innovation, risk taking, and adaptability (Beus et al., 2020). The Hierarchy culture concerns rule-following, adherence, routines, predictability and efficiency (Beus et al., 2020). The Market culture is externally focused values that emphasise achievement, productivity, rewards, and goals through market competition (Beus et al., 2020; Yu & Wu, 2009). Overall, the CVF is generally used to look at how leadership behaviour produces competencies and values.

Behram and Özdemirci (2014) utilised corporate entrepreneurship as a mediator between the relationship between organisational culture (CVF) and environmental conditions on firm performance. The study was conducted in Turkey with medium-sized and large firms that employed 50 or more people. The 561 surveys included three levels of management and were collected from 187 companies. The measures were developed from previous authors – *corporate entrepreneurship* from Antoncic and Hisrich (2003) and Özdemirci (2011), *environmental conditions* from Hart and Banbury (1994) and Özdemirci (2011), *corporate culture* from Cameron and Quinn (2011), and *firm performance* created by the authors. Three factors were utilised to measure corporate entrepreneurship: management support for intrapreneurship, organisational structure, and resource availability (see Table 13.1). It should be noted that the corporate entrepreneurship measure was based on the paper by Antoncic and Hisrich (2003) which is actually a review of intrapreneurship literature. Similarly, the conference paper by Özdemirci (2011) which is the other quoted source for the corporate entrepreneurship measure actually cites Antoncic and Hisrich (2003) as the source of its measure. Although the authors claim to be measuring corporate entrepreneurship, the items are from a paper concerning intrapreneurship, which further muddles whether it is a clear measure of corporate entrepreneurship and organisational culture (CVF).

Another example of utilising a theorised measure of organisational culture and corporate entrepreneurship was conducted by Yildiz (2014). Hofstede's five cultural dimensions were utilised, including power distance, masculinity versus femininity, uncertainty avoidance, individualism versus collectivism, and long-term versus short-term orientation (Hofstede and Bond, 1988). Power distance is the relationship between those in authority, and subordinates, and how the power distribution is viewed – either as equal or unequal (Hofstede, 1984, 1997, 2001). Masculinity versus femininity is the degree of masculine traits, such as achievement, assertiveness and material rewards, versus feminine traits of cooperation, modesty and caring in the organisation (Hofstede, 1984, 1997, 2001). Uncertainty avoidance is measured from weak to strong in terms of risk and change. Individualism versus collectivism is the degree of self-interest versus the interests of the group. Lastly, long-term versus short-term orientation regards goal setting and strategic planning (Hofstede, 1984, 1997, 2001). The relationship between Hofstede's five cultural dimensions and corporate entrepreneurship was explored.

Yildiz (2014) utilised two different scales to measure corporate entrepreneurship. The first scale – ENTERSCALE – developed by Khandwalla (1977) and refined by Covin and Slevin (1989), measured the factors of innovation and proactiveness. The reference for Khandwalla is actually a book concerning organisational theory. In addition, the cited paper by Covin and Slevin (1989) contains no measures of corporate entrepreneurship, and it is possible that this might have been the incorrect reference. The second scale was adapted from Zahra (1991) and consisted of nine items that measured new business venturing, innovativeness, and strategic- or self-renewal. These examples highlight the need for clear, easily accessible references and sources of measures.

More recent work by Umrani et al. (2018) states that even organisational culture as a construct is still debated by the literature, adding further to the potential confusion of attempting to operationalise two constructs – organisational culture and corporate entrepreneurship – which still have no consistent scales. Umrani et al. (2018) have also highlighted the inconsistencies of research in the operationalising of corporate entrepreneurship at the organisational level. It is unfortunate then that the paper has little information concerning their adoption of a corporate entrepreneurship scale from the works of Hornsby et al. (2002). The paper states that 48 items were adapted, but the final measurement model has only 24 items. Little to no information concerning how the items were handled by Umrani et al. (2018) just adds to the general inconsistencies seen in the literature.

When digging deeper into how measures and instruments are used, there appear glaring inconsistencies in terms of the original purpose of the scales and how they are utilised by other studies. Umrani et al. (2018) cite that the measure of corporate entrepreneurship adapted from Hornsby et al. (2002) was utilised as it has been successful in two other articles by Hancer et al. (2009), and Umrani and Mahmood (2015). On further investigation, these articles also cite other authors and adaptations of scales, creating even more bewilderment for the reader as to exactly what scale was used. For example, Hancer et al. (2009) state they used a questionnaire from Miller and Friesen's (1982) index which, when further investigated, is a questionnaire concerning innovation which compares two groups – conservative firms versus entrepreneurial firms – in how they use innovation (i.e. not corporate entrepreneurship). This highlights how recent research is drawing on older scales which had a different purpose but have been inappropriately adapted for current research.

The second reference is to Umrani and Mahmood (2015) who cite an instrument from Hornsby et al. (2002) – the Corporate Entrepreneurship Assessment Instrument (CEAI). This instrument was designed to assess a firm's internal entrepreneurial environment through assessing the organisational factors that foster corporate entrepreneurial activity within a company through middle managers. It is important to note that the organisational level for which this instrument was developed was middle management. The five identified factors were management support, organisational structure, risk taking, time availability, and reward and resource availability (Hornsby et al., 2002). In summary, Hornsby et al. (2002) propose that future research should test the CEAI with other organisational levels of management, such as CEOs. Umrani and Mahmood (2015) used a sample of 265 operations and branch managers of banks, and the article by Umrani et al. (2018) does use 106 middle-level managers from 11 hotels. Thankfully, both Umrani papers are using the correct organisational level for the use of the CEAI instrument; however, it is curious as to why Umrani et al. (2018) do not just clearly state the use of the CEAI instrument when it aligns to the reported factors used by the research, albeit with different titles.

More recent research continues to have ambiguous references to where the measures have originated from. For example, Nguyen and Pham (2020) have cited their measure of corporate entrepreneurship to come from Umrani and Mahmood (2015), with no reference to the original source as mentioned previously – the Corporate Entrepreneurship Assessment Instrument (CEAI) (Hornsby et al., 2002). Nguyen and Pham (2020) analysed the results of 96 surveys from 100 chemical companies. No information is given concerning the participants' level of management within the organisation, e.g. middle or upper level managers. Hornsby et al. (2002) clearly indicated that future research should test the CEAI with other organisational levels of management, such as CEOs. There is clearly an issue when even recent research does not publish the details of the sample.

Overall, these reviewed examples were chosen to demonstrate how some researchers have elected to research overall organisational culture as separate to a culture of corporate entrepreneurship. The reviewed papers highlight the underlying issues of utilising literature which confuses corporate entrepreneurship and intrapreneurship as the basis of operationalising measures. The research further shows the need to clearly identify which corporate entrepreneurship scale is utilised and at what level of the organisation it is measured. Overall, each study has shown some critical errors in the fundamental design of the study measures, from operationalising the constructs, to the choice of sample and measurement level within the firm, e.g. middle vs upper management. However, as shown in Table 13.1 these studies do have some common themes for what concepts could be included in a measure of corporate entrepreneurship in future research.

ENTREPRENEURIAL ORIENTATION AS A MEASURE OF CORPORATE ENTREPRENEURSHIP

Although this chapter has so far reviewed only a few papers where corporate entrepreneurial culture is measured separately from organisational culture, it should be noted that corporate entrepreneurship has been researched for over 50 years and there are over 2,000 journal articles on the subject (see Glinyanova et al., 2021, for a recent review). The issue is that very few papers have looked at corporate entrepreneurship as a form of culture, with even the most recent review not mentioning the term "culture" (Glinyanova et al., 2021). As discussed previously, there has been much debate concerning how to measure corporate entrepreneurial culture, with a key issue being at what level culture should be measured – individual versus firm (Covin & Wales, 2019). This results in several studies which have mixed items measuring both firm and individual level concepts. Again, this reinforces the larger issue that the concept of corporate entrepreneurship culture is not clearly defined as it has been treated as a separate construct to organisational culture but also considered as an internal/individual culture.

Promoting entrepreneurial orientation within a firm is another way in which organisational culture and corporate entrepreneurship have been measured. Entrepreneurial orientation is considered to be a strategic position in which organisations promotive innovation, proactiveness, and risk taking (Covin & Slevin, 1989). However, entrepreneurial orientation and corporate entrepreneurship have many conceptual overlaps, which is highlighted in the recent work of Covin and Wales (2019). Entrepreneurial orientation is considered to be an attribute of the organisation with differing levels across business units (Covin & Wales, 2019).

In their editorial about research guidance, Covin and Wales (2019) recommend considering entrepreneurial orientation as an attribute which the organisation supports. Sustained entrepreneurial behaviour reflects proactive new entry, in terms of product, service, technology, market or model innovation (Covin & Wales, 2019). This suggests that entrepreneurial orientation is measured at the level of the individual. By contrast, corporate entrepreneurship exists as a discrete activity that occurs within an organisation, leading to the concepts being interlinked. This is due to entrepreneurial orientation being considered a behavioural construct which is defined by the organisation's actions, whereas corporate entrepreneurship refers to firm-level discrete activities in various forms of innovation and venturing (Covin & Wales, 2019). The argument seems to centre around at which level the behaviour is occurring and whether there is proactive new entry.

Table 13.1   *Comparison of studies that used culture tools with corporate entrepreneurship measures*

Study	Organisational culture	Corporate entrepreneurship measure	Scale/sub-scales and dimensions	Example items
Kuratko et al. (1990)	N/A – defined corporate entrepreneurship culture then an entrepreneurial instrument was developed.	The intrapreneurial assessment instrument (IAI)	A five-point scale, with 1 being very descriptive of their workplace and 5 being not at all descriptive. Three factors: Management support for intrapreneurship α = 0.76 (nine items) Organisational structure α = 0.75 (six items) Resource availability α = 0.68 (six items)	Management support for intrapreneurship, e.g. "Senior managers encourage bending the rules." "Risk-taker is considered a positive attribute." "Individual risk-takers are often recognised whether eventually successful or not." Organisational structure: "Second chances after mistakes." "Defining turf is important." "Difficult to form teams." Reward and research availability: "Options for financial support." "Problems with company budget process."
Behram and Özdemirci (2014)	Competing Values Framework (also, environmental conditions: dynamism, ambiguity, and munificence)	Corporate Entrepreneurship Measure developed by the authors.	No information concerning scale points. Three factors: Innovativeness α = 0.84 (six items) New Business Venturing and Self-Renewal α = 0.85 (five items) Proactiveness α = 0.84 (3 items)	Innovativeness: "Openness for employee's ideas." "Flexible organizational structure." New Business Venturing and Self-Renewal: "Pursuing new businesses in new industries." "Aggressive and competitive behaviors." Proactiveness: "Adventurous characteristics of top managers." "Tendency to apply risky projects."

Study	Organisational culture	Corporate entrepreneurship measure	Scale/sub-scales and dimensions	Example items
Yildiz (2014)	Organisation culture scale developed by Hofstede (1984, 1997, and 2001). Five dimensions (power distance, uncertainty avoidance, individualism versus collectivism, masculinity versus femininity, long-term versus short-term orientation). Each of the cultural dimensions was measured by four items, α = 0.76.	Combined two scales: ENTERSCALE – two dimensions: innovativeness and proactiveness and a Corporate Entrepreneurship Scale – three dimensions (new business venturing, innovativeness, and strategic- or self-renewal)	7-point rating scales (1 = strongly disagree to 7 = strongly agree) The four overall dimensions of the corporate entrepreneurship scale (consisted of 19 items). Innovation (five items), new business venturing (five items), strategic renewal (four items), and proactiveness (five items), α = 0.81	Innovation: "Has initiated several programs to improve the productivity of business units." "Has pioneered the development of breakthrough innovations in its industry." New business venturing: "Has acquired many companies in very different industries." "Has acquired significantly more patents than its major competitors."
Umrani et al (2018)	Organisational culture adapted from Denison (2000). 18 item 5-point Likert scale. Sample item: "Cooperation across different parts of the organization is actively encouraged".	Adapted 48 items from Hornsby et al. (2002). Five factors: Management support Organisational boundaries Reward reinforcement Time availability Work discretion	5-point Likert scale (1 = strongly disagree to 5 = strongly agree). 24 items in final model reported – no information on item reduction/ reasoning: Management support (six items) Organisational boundaries (four items) Reward reinforcement (six items) Time availability (three items) Work discretion (five items) No Cronbach alpha's reported	One example item reported: "In my organisation, developing one's own ideas is encouraged for the improvement of the firm."

Further, Covin and Wales (2019) suggest that entrepreneurial orientation can be conceptualised as a form of corporate entrepreneurship. However, entrepreneurial orientation must be the attribute of the organisation's form of corporate entrepreneurship. Essentially the basis of the distinction is dependent on the firm itself, whether it is sustained corporate entrepreneurship, or episodic, such as business model innovation within a firm (Covin & Wales, 2019). This distinction is then blurred and arbitrary if the firm has constant entrepreneurial action which comes from the directive of top-down management (Covin & Wales, 2019). Therefore, the entrepreneurial orientation scale could possibly be altered and utilised to measure corporate entrepreneurship but appears to be mostly used in research as being separate to corporate entrepreneurship culture.

Previous research has used the entrepreneurial orientation scale by changing the questions to measure characteristics at the firm level. Engelen et al. (2015) explored the relationship between entrepreneurial orientation and performance to see if it was changed by transformational leadership style. Transformational leaders generally have six behaviours, including articulating a vision, providing an appropriate role model, facilitating acceptance of group goals, having high expectations, showing supportive leader behaviour, and offering intellectual stimulation (Engelen et al., 2015). Transformational leadership is considered to be a top-down effect that shapes the work environment of an organisation (Engelen et al., 2015).

Entrepreneurial orientation was measured using an eight-item Likert scale composed of three innovation items from Dess and Lumpkin (2005), and two proactiveness items and three risk-taking items from Lee and Sukoco (2007). The three dimensions of innovativeness, proactiveness, and risk taking were aggregated together to measure entrepreneurial orientation. Items were worded at the firm level, e.g. "In general, the top managers of our firm have a strong tendency to be ahead of others in introducing novel products or ideas" (Engelen et al., 2015, p. 1092). Thus, the entrepreneurial orientation scale can be used to measure entrepreneurial orientation at the firm level. However, more research needs to identify if this is a reliable and valid measure of corporate entrepreneurial orientation and can be used as a measure of corporate entrepreneurial culture, which the research by Covin and Wales (2019) alludes to.

OVERALL ISSUES IN MEASURING CORPORATE ENTREPRENEURSHIP AND CULTURE AND THE CULTURE OF CORPORATE ENTREPRENEURSHIP

By now it should be apparent that research concerning corporate entrepreneurial culture is currently lacking in the literature (Arz, 2017; Glinyanova et al., 2021). Perhaps the issue is not why is there no direct measure of corporate entrepreneurial culture, rather, it is a matter of how/when the corporation decided to become more entrepreneurial, as highlighted by Covin and Wales (2019). Did the firm have a pre-existing corporate culture which they chose to change to a corporate entrepreneurial one? This could have occurred due to an opportunity or for competitive advantage (Covin & Wales, 2019). So, managers and workgroups were formed to capitalise on their human capital and then trained in entrepreneurship tactics. Or did the corporate entrepreneurial culture form naturally, as some of the work on entrepreneurial orientation suggests (Wales et al., 2011). Was the culture disseminated as a strategy from the top down, or did it naturally occur vertically and horizontally across work units? (Wales et al., 2011). Or is the firm using a strategy-making process with a basis for entrepreneurial action, as entrepreneurial orientation suggests (as it is a strategy-making process that is used for the firm's purpose, vision, and competitive advantage) (Rauch et al., 2009). These examples emphasise how the firm-level definition of corporate entrepreneurship needs to be considered when finding samples.

The primary issue concerning the measurement of corporate entrepreneurial culture would be at what level a study would need to measure this phenomenon. Corporate entrepreneurial culture would need to be measured where the phenomenon of entrepreneurship is occurring. As discussed previously there is no current research which has attempted to establish whether a corporate entrepreneurial firm has a corporate entrepreneurship culture or whether the firm's culture is separate to this. More research is needed which uses other research designs, for example, qualitative research could be used to identify how the different levels of management view the use of corporate entrepreneurship – is it separate to the organisation's culture, or embedded?

This chapter has also emphasised the many measurement issues when there is no clear definition of culture, corporate entrepreneurship, and corporate entrepreneurial culture. The examples of studies which used both culture tools and corporate entrepreneurship measures underscore this issue. The reviewed studies show how the items can be a mixture of intrapreneurship and corporate entrepreneurship with no consideration for the different measurement levels of individual vs management level vs organisational level (e.g. Behram & Özdemirci, 2014; Kuratko et al., 1990). This leads to many problems with the outcomes of the studies and how they apply to an organisation when the measures are across the different levels of the organisation.

Further, the reviewed research in this chapter highlights the underlying issues of transparency in the use of scales and items. Several papers were found which did not clearly identify the source of the items, or else they appeared to adapt items but provide insufficient information concerning how and why the items where adapted or removed (e.g. Behram & Özdemirci, 2014; Nguyen & Pham, 2020; Umrani et al., 2018; Yildiz, 2014). This could possibly be due to the journal guidelines and word count limiting the authors. Regardless, it does underline the need for future research to be clear concerning where items and scales are adapted from. This further emphasises the need to consistently use a measure and develop it over time.

In measuring corporate entrepreneurial culture, several problems were identified in a recent editorial for research guidance by Covin and Wales (2019). Essentially the editorial highlighted the need to use samples of organisations that have sustained corporate entrepreneurship in order to identify if the organisational culture is separate from a culture of corporate entrepreneurship. If the firm has constant entrepreneurial action, then the entrepreneurial orientation scale could be adapted to measure corporate entrepreneurial orientation, as it was by Engelen et al. (2015). However, the items would need to be further adapted to include culture items. This would require more exploratory research to identify how to do this and if this would be a valid and reliable measure of corporate entrepreneurial culture.

Overall, each study has shown some critical errors in the fundamental design of the study, from operationalising the constructs, to the choice of sample and measurement level within the firm, for example middle vs upper management. This suggests many avenues for future research which could utilise some of the previous measures, such as an entrepreneurial orientation scale at different levels of the firm to establish whether entrepreneurial orientation is indeed a measure of culture or could be altered to capture the culture of firms that have a strong corporate entrepreneurship manifestation. Alternatively, a new measurement scale could be constructed by first using qualitative research (interviews, case studies) to identify the phenomenon of corporate entrepreneurial culture. Notably, the majority of studies that have been identified which include corporate entrepreneurship culture or organisational culture and corporate entrepreneurship have all utilised the same research design – surveys. Future research should consider qualitative methods to explore the phenomenon of corporate entrepreneurial culture further. This could then guide quantitative research in the creation or adaptation of measures.

CONCLUSIONS

There are many pathways for future research to take concerning corporate entrepreneurship culture, the most important being how to measure corporate entrepreneurial culture across each level of the organisation, from the firm level, to management, to teams, and individuals. Much of the focus of research is still at the team/individual level, leaving a large research gap concerning corporate entrepreneurial culture at the firm level. Future research should aim to identify if there is a difference between the organisational culture and corporate entrepreneurship, or whether the values and norms of corporate entrepreneurship have been integrated into the overall firm level culture in order to promote a strategic response.

REFERENCES

Åmo, B. W. (2010). Corporate entrepreneurship and intrapreneurship related to innovation behaviour among employees. *International Journal of Entrepreneurial Venturing*, 2(2), 144–158.

Åmo, B. W., & Kolvereid, L. (2005). Organizational strategy, individual personality and innovation behavior. *Journal of Enterprising Culture*, 13(01), 7–19.

Antoncic, B. (2007). Intrapreneurship: A comparative structural equation modelling study. *Industrial Management & Data Systems*, 107(3), 309–325.

Antoncic, B., & Hisrich, R. D. (2003). Clarifying the intrapreneurship concept. *Journal of Small Business and Enterprise Development*, 10(1), 7–24.

Arz, C. (2017). Mechanisms of organizational culture for fostering corporate entrepreneurship: A systematic review and research agenda. *Journal of Enterprising Culture*, 25(04), 361–409.

Bau, F., & Wagner, K. (2015). Measuring corporate entrepreneurship culture. *International Journal of Entrepreneurship and Small Business*, 25(2), 231–244.

Behram, N. K., & Özdemirci, A. (2014). The empirical link between environmental conditions, organizational culture, corporate entrepreneurship and performance: The mediating role of corporate entrepreneurship. *International Journal of Business and Social Science*, 5(2), 264–276.

Beus, J. M., Solomon, S. J., Taylor, E. C., & Esken, C. A. (2020). Making sense of climate: A meta-analytic extension of the competing values framework. *Organizational Psychology Review*, 27(1), 10–17.

Blanka, C. (2019). An individual-level perspective on intrapreneurship: A review and ways forward. *Review of Managerial Science*, 13(5), 919–961.

Block, J. H., Fisch, C. O., & Van Praag, M. (2017). The Schumpeterian entrepreneur: A review of the empirical evidence on the antecedents, behaviour and consequences of innovative entrepreneurship. *Industry and Innovation*, 24(1), 61–95.

Burgelman, R. A. (1983). Corporate entrepreneurship and strategic management: Insights from a process study. *Management Science*, 29(12), 1349–1364.

Cameron, K. S., & Quinn, R. E. (2011). *Diagnosing and Changing Organizational Culture Based on the Competing Values Framework*. New York: John Wiley & Sons.

Chang, J. (2000). Model of corporate entrepreneurship: intrapreneurship and exopreneurship. *International Journal of Entrepreneurship*, 4, 69–104.

Chang, J. (2001). Intrapreneurship and exopreneurship in manufacturing firms: an empirical study of performance implications. *Journal of Enterprising Culture, 9*(2), 153–171.

Christensen, K. S. (2004). A classification of the corporate entrepreneurship umbrella: Labels and perspectives. *International Journal of Management and Enterprise Development, 1*(4), 301–315.

Christensen, K. S. (2005). Enabling intrapreneurship: The case of a knowledge-intensive industrial company. *European Journal of Innovation Management, 8*(3), 305–322.

Chung, L. H., & Gibbons, P. T. (1997). Corporate entrepreneurship: The roles of ideology and social capital. *Group & Organization Management, 22*(1), 10–30.

Covin, J. G., & Slevin, D. P. (1989). Strategic management of small firms in hostile and benign environments. *Strategic Management Journal, 10*(1), 75–87.

Covin, J. G., & Wales, W. J. (2019). Crafting high-impact entrepreneurial orientation research: Some suggested guidelines. *Entrepreneurship Theory and Practice, 43*(1), 3–18.

Danyliuk, M., Babenko, V., Krykhivska, N., & Oryshchyn, T. (2019, October). Forming an innovative exopreneurship model to achieve strategic goals. In 2019 7th International Conference on Modelling, Development and Strategic Management of Economic Systems (MDSMES 2019). Atlantis Press.

Denison, D. R. (2000). Organizational culture: Can it be a key lever for driving organizational change. In Cartwright, S. and Cooper, C. (Eds), *The Handbook of Organizational Culture*. London: John Wiley and Sons.

Dess, G. G., & Lumpkin, G. T. (2005). The role of entrepreneurial orientation in stimulating effective corporate entrepreneurship. *Academy of Management Perspectives, 19*(1), 147–156.

Dess, G. G., Lumpkin, G. T., & McGee, J. E. (1999). Linking corporate entrepreneurship to strategy, structure, and process: Suggested research directions. *Entrepreneurship Theory and Practice, 23*(3), 85–102.

Engelen, A., Gupta, V., Strenger, L., & Brettel, M. (2015). Entrepreneurial orientation, firm performance, and the moderating role of transformational leadership behaviors. *Journal of Management, 41*(4), 1069–1097.

Fellnhofer, K. (2016). The organizational pervasiveness of entrepreneurial orientation across hierarchical levels. *International Journal of Entrepreneurship and Innovation, 17*(4), 217–227.

Finkle, T. A. (2012). Corporate entrepreneurship and innovation in Silicon Valley: The case of Google, Inc. *Entrepreneurship Theory and Practice, 36*(4), 863–887.

Fitzsimmons, J. R., Douglas, E. J., Antoncic, B., & Hisrich, R. D. (2005). Intrapreneurship in Australian firms. *Journal of Management and Organization, 11*(1), 17–27.

Glinyanova, M., Bouncken, R. B., Tiberius, V., & Ballester, A. C. C. (2021). Five decades of corporate entrepreneurship research: Measuring and mapping the field. *International Entrepreneurship and Management Journal*, 1–27.

Hancer, M., Ozturk, A. B., & Ayyildiz, T. (2009). Middle-level hotel managers' corporate entrepreneurial behavior and risk-taking propensities: A case of Didim, Turkey. *Journal of Hospitality Marketing & Management, 18*(5), 523–537.

Hart S. and Banbury C. (1994). How strategy-making processes can make a difference. *Strategic Management Journal, 15*, 251–269.

Hofstede, G. (1984). *Culture's Consequences: International Differences in Work-Related Values*. Thousand Oaks, CA: Sage.

Hofstede, G. (1997). *Cultures and Organizations: Software of the Mind*. New York: McGraw Hill.

Hofstede, G. (2001). *Culture's Consequences: Comparing Values, Behaviors, Institutions, and Organizations across Nations*. Thousand Oaks, CA: Sage.

Hofstede, G., & Bond M.H. (1988). The Confucius connection: From cultural roots to economic growth. *Organizational Dynamics, 1*, 4–21.

Hornsby, J. S., Kuratko, D. F., & Zahra, S. A. (2002). Middle managers' perception of the internal environment for corporate entrepreneurship: assessing a measurement scale. *Journal of Business Venturing, 17*(3), 253–273.

Kanter, R. M. (1984). *The Change Masters*. New York: Simon & Schuster.

Kanter, R. M., & Richardson, L. (1991). Engines of progress: Designing and running entrepreneurial vehicles in established companies – The Enter-prize program at Ohio Bell, 1985–1990. *Journal of Business Venturing, 6*(3), 209–229.

Khandwalla, P. N. (1977). *The Design of Organization*. New York: Harcourt Brace Jovanovich.

Kloepfer, K. (2020). *Entrepreneurial Orientation: The Good, the Bad, and the Interesting* (Order No. 27957708). Available from ProQuest One Academic. ProQuest Dissertations Publishing (2413335960).

Kuratko, D. (2007). Corporate entrepreneurship. *Foundations and Trends® in Entrepreneurship, 3*(2), 151–203.

Kuratko, D. F., Montagno, R. V., & Hornsby, J. S. (1990). Developing an intrapreneurial assessment instrument for an effective corporate entrepreneurial environment. *Strategic Management Journal, 11*, 49–58.

Lee, L. T., & Sukoco, B. M. (2007). The effects of entrepreneurial orientation and knowledge management capability on organizational effectiveness in Taiwan: The moderating role of social capital. *International Journal of Management, 24*(3), 549–572.

McKinney, G., & McKinney, M. (1989). Forget the corporate umbrella – entrepreneurs shine in the rain. *MIT Sloan Management Review, 30*(4), 77–82.

Miller, D., & Friesen, P. H. (1982). Innovation in conservative and entrepreneurial firms: Two models of strategic momentum. *Strategic Management Journal, 3*(1), 1–25.

Morris, M. H., Kuratko, D. F., & Covin, J. G. (2011). *Corporate Entrepreneurship & Innovation* (3rd Ed.). Cengage Learning.

Nguyen, T., & Pham, T. (2020). The effect of corporate entrepreneurship, organizational culture on supply chain management and business performance in chemical industry. *Uncertain Supply Chain Management, 8*(1), 67–76.

Özdemirci, A. (2011). Corporate entrepreneurship and strategy process: A performance based research on Istanbul market. *The Proceedings of 7th International Strategic Management Conference, Procedia – Social and Behavioral Sciences, 24*, 611–626.

Paunovic, S., & Dima, I. C. (2014). Organizational culture and corporate entrepreneurship. *Annals of the University of Petroşani. Economics, 14*(1), 269–276.

Pinchot, G. (1985). *Intrapreneuring.* New York. NY: Harper and Row.

Rauch, A., Wiklund, J., Lumpkin, G. T., & Frese, M. (2009). Entrepreneurial orientation and business performance: An assessment of past research and suggestions for the future. *Entrepreneurship Theory and Practice, 33*(3), 761–787.

Salama, A. (2011). *Creating and Re-creating Corporate Entrepreneurial Culture.* Gower Publishing, Ltd.

Rule, E.G., and Irwin D.W. 1988. Fostering intrapreneurship: The new competitive edge. *Journal of Business Strategy, 9*(3), 44–47.

Schneider, B. (1990). *Organizational Climate and Culture.* San Francisco: Jossey-Bass. Schneider, B., Ehrhart, M. G. and Macey, W. H. (2013). Organizational climate and culture. *Annual Review of Psychology,* 64, 361–388.

Soomro, B. A., & Shah, N. (2019). Determining the impact of entrepreneurial orientation and organizational culture on job satisfaction, organizational commitment, and employee's performance. *South Asian Journal of Business Studies, 8*(3), 266–282.

Umrani, W. A., & Mahmood, R. (2015). Examining the dimensions of corporate entrepreneurship construct: A validation study in the Pakistani banking context. *Mediterranean Journal of Social Sciences, 6*(6), 278–278.

Umrani, W. A., Kura, K. M., & Ahmed, U. (2018). Corporate entrepreneurship and business performance. *PSU Research Review, 2*(1), 59–80.

Wales, W., Monsen, E., & McKelvie, A. (2011). The organizational pervasiveness of entrepreneurial orientation. *Entrepreneurship Theory and Practice, 35*(5), 895–923.

Wang, Z., Chen, J., Zhu, Z., & Anquan, W. (2005). A system model for corporate entrepreneurship. *International Journal of Manpower, 26*(6), 529–543.

Yildiz, M. L. (2014). The effects of organizational culture on corporate entrepreneurship. *International Journal of Business and Social Science, 5*(5), 35–44.

Yu, T., & Wu, N. (2009). A review of study on the competing values framework. *International Journal of Business and Management, 4*(7), 37–42.

Zahra, S. A. (1991). Predictors of financial outcomes of corporate entrepreneurship: An exploratory study. *Journal of Business Venturing, 6*(4), 259–286.

14. Measuring and developing an ethical organizational climate

Niel J. Christensen, Nathanael J.N. Lee and John B. Bingham

The recognition of the importance of ethics in organizations has progressed greatly in the last two decades. Widespread scandals, such as Enron in 2001 and WorldCom in 2002, have alerted many to the sober realities that unethical behavior in organizations is not only prevalent, but destructive. These scandals gave rise to the Sarbanes–Oxley Act of 2002, which required organizations to adopt ethical codes of conduct (Martin & Cullen, 2006). The global impact of such scandals contributes to economic instability, such as the global financial crisis of 2008, as well as general distrust for businesses and institutions. Thus, ethics became a relevant concept affecting policy, operations, and culture, rather than an abstract concept hidden in the background of organizations. More recently, the prominent 'Me Too' scandals regarding workplace sexual harassment have further emphasized ethical decision-making by individuals, and ethical policies in organizations, as key organizational priorities.

Because the ethical norms of the workplace influence ethical practices of employees (Simha & Cullen, 2012; Treviño, 1986), scholars and practitioners are devoting more attention to the climate in which ethical or unethical behavior flourishes within organizations (Martin & Cullen, 2006; Simha & Cullen, 2012). Further, scholars have called for greater emphasis on ethics and broader understanding of the contexts in which employees make ethical decisions (Martin & Cullen, 2006; Newman et al., 2017; Simha & Cullen, 2012). Arnaud (2010) defines ethical work climate as the 'organizational context in which ethical and unethical activities occur' (p. 345). Ethical climate also appears to guide what behaviors are considered right and thus becomes a mechanism through which ethical issues are managed (Martin & Cullen, 2006, p. 177).

In addition to the ethical behavior of organizational members, ethical climate has also been associated with a variety of outcomes at both individual and organizational levels. Some scholars have examined ethical climate as a predictor of attitudes, job satisfaction, and organizational commitment (Demirtas & Akdogan, 2015; Erben & Guneser, 2008; Martin & Cullen, 2006). Other studies have examined ethics from a resource-based view, theorizing that an ethical climate contributes to individual-level performance and competitive advantage for the firm (Manroop, 2015; Manroop et al., 2014). For example, Shin et al. (2015) found that ethical climate predicted increased organizational citizenship behavior and increased financial performance of an organization. Demirtas and Akdogan (2015) found that ethical climate contributed to decreased turnover intention. Other studies show that ethical climate predicts industry culture differences (Duh et al., 2010; Venezia et al., 2010) and ethical differences across countries (Laratta, 2009; Parboteeah et al., 2014). Thus, the benefits of understanding and developing an ethical organizational climate appear to be well established.

Although extant research suggests understanding the antecedents to ethical climate is important, 'the literature investigating the determinants of ethical climate is both fragmented and under-researched' (Martin & Cullen, 2006, p. 179). The purpose of this chapter is to provide a broader understanding of the antecedents of ethical climate by summarizing recent research on the topic, and to facilitate ongoing research on the measurement and development of ethical organizational climates.

TYPOLOGIES OF ETHICAL CLIMATE

Research on ethical climate has increased in recent years (Newman et al., 2017, p. 475) making it arguably one of the most influential conceptual foundations in the business ethics domain (Martin & Cullen, 2006). The concept of ethical climate focuses on the organizational-level perceptions of ethical climate, rather than on unaggregated individual perceptions. Ethical climate 'differs from other moral constructs such as moral identity and moral awareness in that it looks at how the social context in organizations influences ethical behavior of employees through fostering their collective moral reasoning' (Newman et al., 2017, p. 479). Scholars have debated and studied ethical climate for at least three decades. In past years, some scholars viewed ethical climate and ethical culture synonymously. Recently, however, ethical culture has been defined as the 'subset of organizational culture that captures the organization's systems and practices of behavioral control that promote ethical or unethical behavior' (Newman et al., 2017, p. 480). Conversely, ethical climate is the broader focus on 'perceived organizational values that shape ethical decision making' (Newman et al., 2017, p. 480). Both ethical climate and ethical culture focus on explaining behavior in the context of ethical environments and scholars continue to debate the predictive or sequential nature of which construct precedes the other. Due to the considerable overlap between ethical climate and ethical culture, and the more common use of the term 'ethical climate', this chapter will combine research undertaken on ethical climate and ethical culture under the umbrella of ethical climate.

A framework for measuring ethical climate was originally introduced by Victor and Cullen (1987, 1988). In 1987, Victor and Cullen defined ethical climate as 'the shared perception of what is correct behavior and how ethical situations should be handled in an organization' (p. 51). In 1988, Victor and Cullen redefined ethical climate as 'prevailing perceptions of typical organizational practices and procedures that have ethical content' (p. 101). These broad definitions are useful in conceptualizing the ethical climate construct. Additionally, Victor and Cullen (1988) created a typology for different kinds of ethical climate. The typology shown in Figure 14.1 contrasts two dimensions: locus of analysis and ethical theory.

The loci of analysis were derived from sociological theories of roles and reference groups (Victor & Cullen, 1988). The 'individual' level represents individual perceptions of ethics within an organization, the 'local' level represents ethical reasoning at the organizational or work-group level, and the 'cosmopolitan' level represents sources of organizational reasoning external to the focal organization, such as overarching industry codes or legal systems (Victor & Cullen, 1988).

The ethical theory dimension comprises three distinct types of organizational ethical climate: 'egoism', 'benevolence', and 'principle'. These three categories organize the majority of moral philosophy (Fritzche & Becker, 1984) and resemble the criteria used to organize moral development (Kohlberg, 1969). Together, the dimensions of 'locus of analysis' and of 'ethical theory' form Victor and Cullen's (1988) 'five common empirical derivatives of ethical climate'. Although Victor and Cullen (1987) originally conceptualized nine different types of ethical climate, the five common empirical derivatives shown in Figure 14.1 were the only climate types that were found to exist under Victor and Cullen's (1988) empirical studies.

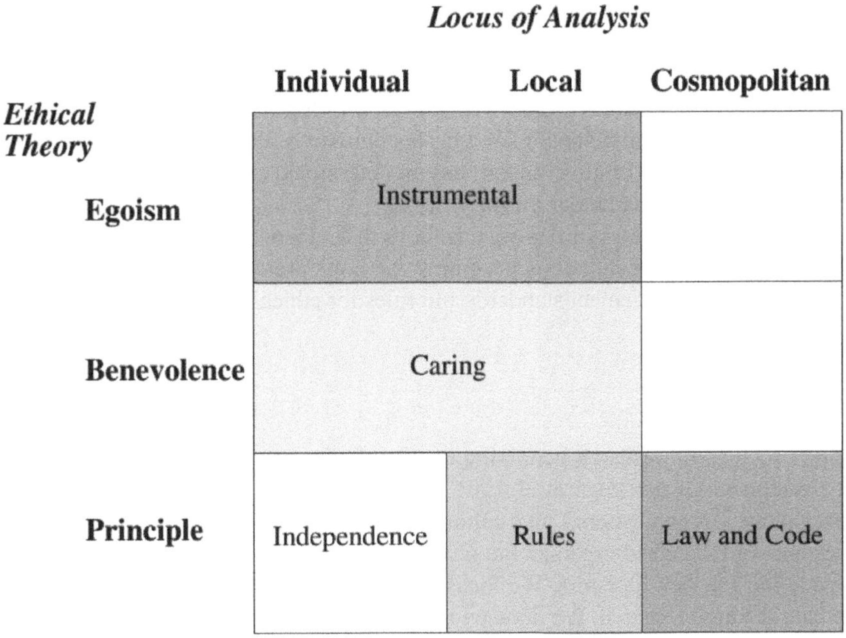

Locus of Analysis

Note: The figure shows Victor and Cullen's (1987) five common empirical derivatives of ethical climate, derived from moral ethical theory (shown as rows at the left) and the locus of analysis showing different levels of environment (shown as columns at the top).
Source: Victor and Cullen (1987, 1988).

Figure 14.1   Five common empirical derivatives of ethical climate

Understanding this typology is critical for ethical climate research because the majority of researchers use these five commonly observed ethical climates (Newman et al., 2017). This typology, either in its entirety or with modifications (abbreviated versions), is the most favored method of measuring ethical climate (Lemmergaard & Lauridsen, 2008). It is important to understand Victor and Cullen's (1988) typology to assist in conceptualizing the large amount of subsequent research using the same typology. Martin and Cullen's (2006) 'Continuities and extensions of ethical climate theory: A meta-analytic review' adopted this typology and defined each of the five common empirical derivatives as follows.

1. The 'instrumental' ethical climate is characterized by norms and expectations that encourage ethical decision-making from an egoistic perspective (Martin & Cullen, 2006, p. 178). Self-interest guides behavior and decisions are made to provide personal benefits. Martin and Cullen's (2006) review concluded that instrumental ethical climates are the least preferred (p. 179).

2. In 'caring' climates, individuals make decisions with the wellbeing of others, and society as the priority (Martin & Cullen, 2006, p. 179). Consideration for others is the goal of every part of the organization's operations. Employees prefer caring climates (ibid.).
3. The 'independence' climate emphasizes personal moral beliefs as the basis for ethical decision-making (ibid.). Organizations with an independence climate support carefully considered individual moral beliefs before being influenced by external moral ideals (ibid.).
4. The 'law and code' climate is present in organizations that adhere to an external set of rules and principles for ethical behavior (ibid.). This climate is often found in industries where an external force (e.g., the government) has predetermined certain rules to be followed by each organization in a particular industry (ibid.).
5. Finally, the 'rules' climate typifies organizations that adhere to an internally designed code of conduct (ibid.). This climate is becoming the most prevalent ethical climate as many modern companies implement standards and rules for ethical behavior (ibid.).

METHODOLOGY

This chapter focuses on research pertaining to ethical climates between 2008 and 2018. We adopt the categories of Newman et al. (2017): leadership and managerial practices, organizational practices, organizational and cultural contexts, and individual differences. These categories are well suited to organize the research on ethical climate and allow for a useful categorization of relevant literature. We focus primarily on articles we believe hold the greatest potential for future research. We draw on research from different cultural contexts in order to create a more comprehensive view of the antecedents to ethical climate. The following two methods were used to find pertinent articles.

First, we selected three extensive literature reviews: two books and one meta-analysis. We draw primarily on Newman et al.'s (2017) 'Ethical climates in organizations: A review and research agenda' and Agle et al.'s (2014) *Research Companion to Ethical Behavioral in Organizations: Constructs and Measures*. These two sources provide a thorough review of the current state of research on ethical climate theory. We also draw from Martin and Cullen's (2006) 'Continuities and extensions of ethical climate theory: A meta-analytic review', which summarizes key findings before 2008.

For comprehensiveness, we reviewed articles from EBSCO's 'Academic Search Ultimate' and 'JSTOR'. In EBSCO, we searched by the years 2014–2018 using keywords 'ethical climate' and 'ethical culture'. (Relevant articles from before 2014 are found in Agle et al.'s (2014) *Research Companion to Ethical Behavioral in Organizations: Constructs and Measures*.) The JSTOR keyword search was conducted from the years 2014–2018, using the keywords 'ethical and climate' and 'ethical and culture'. We filtered the JSTOR search by the 'business' and 'management and organizational behavior' categories.

Findings from the *Research Companion to Ethical Behavioral in Organizations: Constructs and Measures* and the EBSCO and JSTOR searches were refined to focus on articles specifically related to ethical climate. This focus narrowed our total to 92 articles, which were further filtered to include only articles that discussed direct antecedents of ethical climate. Relevant articles from Newman et al. (2017) that fit our criteria were added to the final filtered results, for a total of 26 articles. This chapter examines 22 seminal articles concerning the antecedents of ethical climate and four articles concerning the measurement of ethical climate in the last decade.

MEASURING ETHICAL CLIMATE

In addition to developing the foundational theory on ethical climate, including the five common empirical derivatives of ethical climate (Victor & Cullen, 1987, 1988), Victor and Cullen (1987) also created an Ethical Climate Questionnaire (ECQ) as a measurement tool. The original ECQ tool was a 26-question survey that asked respondents to rate their work culture on a 6-point Likert scale.

Cullen et al. (1993) revisited the original ECQ and added ten items to the 26-item survey, resulting in a total of four questions for each of the nine climate types (p. 670). Cullen et al. (1993) also conducted a review of the application of the ECQ since its inception. They found reliable evidence that ethical climates are perceived at the psychological level (p. 673). Seven of the original nine theoretical climate types are identified in research, leaving only two of the hypothesized climates unsubstantiated (Cullen et al., 1993, p. 673).

Since 1993, the ECQ tool has been used and adapted in several other studies, including many of the studies on antecedents of ethical climate outlined below. Researchers have continued to use the ECQ because it has been widely validated (Dark & Rix, 2015). In addition to the ECQ, other methods of measuring dimensions of ethical climate have been developed, most notably the Ethical Leadership Scale, developed by Brown et al. (2005), and the Ethical Work Climate measure, developed by Babin et al. (2000). However, this section focuses on measurement approaches developed since 2008 (Table 14.1).

Table 14.1   Ethical climate measures developed and tested between 2008–2018

Author	Date	Developed Tested	Measurement Tool	Description
Arnaud	2006 2010	Developed Tested	Ethical Climate Index	36-item survey enabling researchers to study multiple aspects of ethical climate beyond Victor and Cullen's work.
Lennick & Kiel Martin & Austin	2005 2010	Developed Tested	Moral Competency Index	40-item survey measuring ten competencies within a moral framework deemed in need of further refinement.
Schwepker	2013	Developed & Tested in 7 studies	Ethical Climate Measure	7-item survey measuring perceptions of practices and values that govern ethical decisions.
Ardichvili & Jondle	2009	Developed	Center for Ethical Business Cultures Model	35-item questionnaire modeled from five ethical characteristics identifying an organization's ethical state.
Jondle et al.	2014	Developed & Tested	Ethical Business Culture Survey	12-item survey that evolved from the Center for Ethical Business Cultures identifying areas for ethical culture improvement.

The Ethical Climate Index (ECI)

Arnaud (2006, 2010) explored an alternative method of measuring ethical climate by developing and testing a six-factor model of individual-level ethical decision-making and behavior. The model is called the Ethical Climate Index (ECI). The six factors of the ECI are (1) collective moral awareness, (2) norms of empathetic concern, (3) collective moral judgment focus on self, (4) collective moral judgment focus on others, (5) collective moral motivation, and (6) collective moral character. All six ECI factors are rated on a 5-point scale ranging from 1 ('describes my department very well'), to 5 ('does not describe my department at all') (Arnaud, 2006, pp. 195–196). Arnaud (2006) conducted three studies using the Ethical Climate Index (ECI). Each study further refined the ECI survey down to a 36-item questionnaire that was administered to MBA students at a large public university in the United States in the final study (Arnaud, 2006, p. 195). Arnaud (2006) concluded that the three independent surveys validated the ECI as a useful measure of ethical climate (p. 216). Arnaud (2010) further confirmed the ECI's validity and reliability. Although the ECI affords scholars an additional method to measure ethical climate, it has only been used once in a 2016 study by Salamon and Melsko (2016). The ECI allows researchers to study multiple aspects of ethical climate beyond Victor and Cullen's (1987, 1988) work, which examines only the moral reasoning aspect of ethical climates (Newman et al., 2017, p. 481). Because relatively few studies have focused on it, the ECI provides an avenue for future testing and research to further extend its application and generalizability.

The Moral Competency Index (MCI)

Martin and Austin (2010) conducted a survey at a medium-sized university in the United States to test the validity of Lennick and Kiel's (2005) moral competency index (MCI), which is presented in Lennick and Kiel's book *Moral Intelligence: Enhancing Business Performance and Leadership Success* (2005). The MCI contains 40 questions and measures ten competencies within a moral framework on a 5-point Likert scale (Martin & Austin, 2010, pp. 441–442).

The results of a factor analysis (ibid., p. 443) indicated variable factors rather than the ten competencies hypothesized by Lennick and Kiel (2005). Martin and Austin's Principal Factor Analysis also revealed that the constructs the MCI attempts to measure do not seem to exist outside of the philosophical domains (as cited in Lennick & Kiel, 2005, p. 444). Martin and Austin concluded that the MCI is not a valid measurement tool of ethics in organizations without further refinement.

Ethical Climate Measure

Schwepker's (2013) measure of ethical climate is based on Qualls and Puto's (1989) theories about ethical climate. This ethical climate measure 'assesses individuals' perceptions of those practices, procedures, norms, and values that govern ethical decisions in their organizations' (Schwepker, 2013, p. 394). The ethical climate measure has seven items on a 5-point Likert scale where 1 = 'strongly disagree' and 5 = 'strongly agree'. Newman et al. (2017) found that Schwepker's scale has been used in seven studies and that an abbreviated form of the scale has been used in three studies (p. 481). Schwepker (2013) also used Singh and Rhoads's (1991) ethical ambiguity scale, which is a 5-point scale ranging from 1 ('very certain') to 5 ('very uncertain').

Center for Ethical Business Cultures (CEBC) & Ethical Business Culture Survey (EBCS)

Ardichvili and Jondle (2009) developed an ethical measurement tool called the Center for Ethical Business Cultures survey (CEBC). Ardichvili and Jondle's model incorporated five characteristics: 'values-driven', 'leadership effectiveness', 'stakeholder balance', 'process integrity', and 'long-term' (as cited in Jondle et al., 2014). The survey used in conjunction with the model had 35 questions on a Likert scale ranging from 1 ('strongly disagree') to 7 ('strongly agree'). The survey measured the perceived strength of each individual characteristic within organizations.

Jondle et al. (2014) refined the CEBC 35-item survey to a 30-item survey which was administered to MBA students in the United States (p. 33). The survey was then refined to a 24-item survey and distributed to another group of MBA students (ibid., p. 34). A final revision was made, limiting the survey to ten questions associated with Ardichvili and Jondle's (2009) five characteristics of ethical culture. Jondle et al. also drew on Brown et al.'s (2005) Ethical Leadership Scale to add two additional items to the survey. The resulting survey was named the Ethical Business Culture Survey (EBCS). Data was then collected by administering the updated 12-item survey at a large multinational company (Jondle et al., 2014, p. 37). Evidence from this study supported the existence of each of Ardichvili and Jondle's (2009) five characteristics of ethical culture (Jondle et al., 2014, p. 41). Jondle et al. pointed out that while the EBCS can identify parts of ethical culture that need to be improved, the EBCS does not explain the source of ethical problems (2014, p. 42). They suggest the survey should be used for a first-stage detection of problems. Jondle et al. also advocate for the continued testing and refinement of the EBCS and CEBC constructs to prove their validity.

ANTECEDENTS OF ETHICAL CLIMATE

Newman et al. (2017) categorized the antecedents of ethical climate into four categories: 'leadership and managerial practices', 'organizational practices', 'organizational and cultural context', and 'individual differences'. While Newman et al.'s review was intended to be exhaustive, citing a greater number of articles with short summaries, we investigate deeper into seminal articles, some included in Newman et al.'s review and some in additional articles. We discuss these articles and potential for future research at a more granular level. We also classify the articles examined in this chapter according to Victor and Cullen's (1988) five common empirical derivatives of ethical climate. Many of the articles in this chapter intentionally or unintentionally explored how antecedents of ethical climate affect the instrumental, caring, independence, law and code, and rules climates of organizations. Both Newman et al.'s (2017) four classifications and Victor and Cullen's (1988) five derivatives of ethical climate are used to organize articles in Tables 14.2, 14.3, 14.4, and 14.5. Newman et al.'s categories organize antecedent research, while Victor and Cullen's categories structure the particular kinds of ethical climates that result from different antecedents.

Leadership and Managerial Practices

Strong ethical leadership is one of the most cogent antecedents for ethical climate in the workplace. In studies done by Mulki et al. (2009) and Neubert et al. (2009), ethical leadership was shown to be positively correlated with ethical climate. New hires assimilate to their organization's ethical climate or choose to leave because the culture is not fit for them. Ethical climate is largely developed through the behavior of top management and the choices that are made in regard to the policies and procedures of the firm (Mayer et al., 2009). In Table 14.2, we summarize studies classified by Newman et al.'s (2017) 'leadership and managerial practices' as antecedents for ethical climate while using Victor and Cullen's categories to structure the particular kinds of ethical climates that result from these leadership and managerial practices.

Summary of key studies measuring ethical leadership's impact

Mayer et al. (2009)
These researchers used Social Learning Theory (Bandura, 1977, 1986) to hypothesize about the influence of ethical leadership on ethical climate. Social Learning Theory explains that individuals learn appropriate ways to act through a role-modeling process by observing the behaviors of others (Bandura, 1977, 1986). Leaders in organizations are representative models of an organization's behavioral norms and ethics. Mayer et al. (2010) developed their own scale for measuring ethical climate with six items. The path coefficient between ethical leadership and ethical climate was positive and significant (Mayer et al., 2010, p. 12). These findings indicate that when leaders act ethically, they create a more ethical climate. Mayer et al. (2010) also found evidence that ethical climate acts as a mediator between ethical leadership and employee misconduct. This suggests that when leaders create an ethical climate, workers in that climate are more likely to act ethically.

Shin (2012)
Shin led one of the foremost studies investigating how CEO leadership influences ethical climate, analyzing data from 223 CEOs and 6,021 employees in South Korea. The study focused mainly on the 'rules climate' and the 'law and code' climate from Victor and Cullen's (1988) five dimensions. The study found that CEO ethical leadership is indeed positively related to ethical climate and collective organizational citizenship behavior. Shin (2012) suggested that future researchers gather data from CEOs' immediate subordinates to increase validity, and that different climates be tested to allow the results to become more widely representative. These results could be further validated by conducting a similar study in different geographies.

Shin et al. (2015)
This study gathered data from 4,468 employees at 147 Korean companies that spanned a variety of industries, to measure how the ethical leadership of top managers affected ethical climate. The results showed that top management ethical leadership was a strong predictor of ethical climate (Shin et al., 2015). This, in turn, increased organizational citizenship behavior and was related to increased financial performance (ibid.). Again, to further extend the results of this study, it could be reexamined in other geographies.

Lu and Lin (2014)
Ethical leadership has a significant impact on ethical climate and the ethical behavior of employees. In order to measure that impact, Lu and Lin (2014) developed a three-part questionnaire for 400 employees working in the Taiwan International Port Corporation. The three parts of the questionnaire were 'ethical leadership', 'ethical climate', and 'ethical behavior'.

Table 14.2   Leadership and managerial practices (based on Newman et al.'s 'leadership and managerial practices' classification)

Author	Date	Constructs	Victor and Cullen Five Empirical Derivatives	Measurement Tool
Parboteeah et al.	2010	Communication & Empowerment	Instrumental, Caring, Rules	Ethical Climate Questionnaire (Victor and Cullen, 1987, 1988)
Shin	2012	CEO Leadership	Rules, Law & Code	Ethical Leadership Scale (Brown et al., 2005)
Demirtas & Akdogan	2015	Ethical Climate, Turnover Intention & Affective Commitment		Ethical Leadership Scale (Brown et al., 2005), Ethical Climate Questionnaire (Victor and Cullen, 1987, 1988), Affective Organizational Commitment Scale (Meyer & Allen, 1991), Turnover Intention Scale (Rosin and Korabik, 1991)
Ötken & Cenkci	2012	Paternalistic Leadership	Caring, Independence	Ethical Climate Questionnaire (Cullen et al., 1993), Paternalistic Leadership Questionnaire (Cheng et al., 2004), Trust in Leader Questionnaire (Börü, 2001)
Lu & Lin	2014	Ethical Leadership, Ethical Climate, Ethical Behavior		Ethical Leadership Scale (Brown et al., 2005), Ethical Climate Questionnaire (Victor and Cullen, 1987, 1988), Ethical Behavior Questionnaire (developed from Ferrell et al., 2000).
Mayer et al.	2010	Social Learning Theory, Ethical Climate	Rules/NA	Ethical Leadership Scale (Brown et al., 2005), Ethical Climate Questionnaire (Mayer et al., 2010), Social Learning Theory (SLT; Bandura, 1977, 1986)
Zehir et al..	2014	Charismatic Leadership, Organizational Citizenship Behavior		Ethical Climate Scale (Schwepker, 2001), Charismatic Leadership Scale (Conger & Kanungo, 1994),
Shin et al.	2015	Top Managers' Ethical Leadership		Ethical Climate Questionnaire (Victor and Cullen, 1987, 1988), Ethical Leadership Scale (Brown et al., 2005)
Mulki et al.	2009	Instrumental Leadership	Instrumental	Leaders Behavior Questionnaire (House, 1971), Ethical Climate Scale (Schwepker, 2001)
Ghosh	2015	Benevolent Leadership, Organizational Citizenship Behavior		Benevolent Leadership Questionnaire (Karakas and Sarigollu, 2012), Ethical Climate Questionnaire (Victor and Cullen, 1987, 1988)
Erben & Guneser	2008	Paternalistic Leadership, Organizational Commitment	Caring, Independence	Paternalistic Leadership Scale (Cheng et al., 2004), Ethical Climate Questionnaire (Victor and Cullen, 1987, 1988)

The study endeavored to make up for the lack of research in the port, transportation and maritime realms and showed positive influences for ethical leadership and ethical climate on employee behavior and evidence that ethical climate mediates ethical leadership and employee ethical behavior (Lu & Lin, 2014). The study also suggests that future researchers define the relationship between ethical climates and organizational culture and their impact on employee performance, specifically 'how ethical leadership and ethical climate influence individual behaviors or attitudes, particularly behaviors or attitudes that may lead to misconduct, and try to define the characteristics of such ethical behaviors' (p. 221). Additionally, other studies could focus on religion, cultural background, and social status at the individual and aggregate level. Finally, the authors suggest potential benefit of a longitudinal study to examine the long-term effects of ethical leadership and ethical climate (p. 221).

Demirtas and Akdogan (2015)
A cycle of positive ethical climate can be established through ethical leadership behavior. Demirtas and Akdogan (2015) exemplified this relationship through utilizing Brown et al.'s (2005) 10-item ethical leadership scale, Victor and Cullen's (1988) ECQ, Meyer and Allen's (1991) Affective Organizational Commitment scale, and Rosin and Korabik's (1991) Turnover Intention scale. The 5-point Likert-scale survey was administered to 500 employees from three different aviation companies in Turkey (Demirtas & Akdogan, 2015). The results were deemed statistically significant for ethical leadership as a strong antecedent for ethical climate, increased affective commitment, and decreased turnover intention (ibid.).

Demirtas and Akdogan's (2015) study is unique in that it examined the direct and indirect effects of ethical leadership within the manufacturing industry. The study suggests that companies should look for and promote managers who have the capacity to perpetuate a positive ethical climate. Demirtas and Akdogan (2015) suggest that future researchers conduct studies to assess the impact of ethical leadership on group-level climates and other behavioral variables.

Ethical leadership attributes
What leader attributes influence an organization's ethical climate? The four studies reviewed in this section explore various leadership styles – benevolent, authoritarian, paternalistic, and charismatic, along with their associated attributes – in a variety of cultures. In general, benevolent leadership, with attributes such as genuine concern for others, high moral standards, and unselfishness, has been associated with ethical leadership and ethical climate in organizations. Authoritarian styles of leadership were shown to be negatively correlated with ethical climate unless employees had a strong relationship of trust in their leader's ethical standards. Authoritarian leadership styles are more likely to motivate employees to obey rules and procedures out of fear, whereas benevolent leadership styles are more likely to influence employees to emulate their leaders and endeavor to behave more like them at work and outside of work. Paternalistic leadership, which involves a strong authority figure who treats employees as members of a large family, was studied in Turkey and India, where paternalistic styles of leadership may be more common and perhaps more effective than in western countries.

Summary of key studies on important ethical leadership attributes

Ötken and Cenkci (2011)

By examining the specific benefits of individual traits, such as paternalistic leadership, in Turkey, Ötken and Cenkci (2011) claimed that in eastern cultures, paternalistic leadership can contribute to ethical climate. A small survey was administered to 154 MBA students working in organizations in Istanbul and to 73 online participants. The survey contained the following four sections: an introduction to the survey and demographic questions; Cullen et al.'s (1993) 36-item questionnaire; a paternalistic leadership questionnaire developed by Cheng et al. (2004) with 26 questions focusing on three dimensions of paternalistic leadership (authoritarianism, benevolence, and morality); and a trust-in-leader questionnaire (Ötken & Cenkci, 2011). The trust-in-leader questionnaire consisted of ten items specific to characteristics of trust found within Turkish society (ibid.).

Results from the study showed that leaders who were either authoritative or who held to a high moral standard created an ethical climate of obedience out of either fear or respect (Ötken & Cenkci, 2011). Although the preliminary results were promising, the study had many limitations. Aside from the limitations associated with the small sample size, results were generalized and the data for the independent and dependent variables were gathered from the same source. The researchers admitted that this type of methodology 'may lead to the issue of same source bias or common method variance' (p. 535). Finally, the researchers' sample was taken from many different workers in various organizations with differing ethical climates and leadership styles. In order to further this realm of research, researchers could develop a method of measuring ethical climate impact that allows results from different countries to be compared and general principles to be identified.

Zehir et al. (2014)

Zehir et al. (2014) examined the influence of charismatic leadership on ethical climate and organizational citizenship behavior, measuring ethical climate with Schwepker's (2001) seven-item scale. This scale used a 5-point Likert scale ranging from 1 ('strongly disagree') to 5 ('strongly agree') (Zehir et al., 2014, p. 1369). Charismatic leadership was measured with Conger and Kanungo's (1994) Charismatic Leadership Scale, comprised of 25 items that measure the following six behavioral dimensions of charismatic leadership: sensitivity to the environment, sensitivity to members' needs, strategic vision and articulation, personal risk, unconventional behavior, and status quo (p. 1369). These surveys were administered to 600 Turkish workers in a variety of industries (p. 1368). The results showed that two of the six behavioral dimensions of charismatic leadership – 'sensitivity to the environment' and 'strategic vision and articulation' – explained the variance in creating an ethical climate (p. 1372). When a leader exhibited more ethical behavior through these two behavioral dimensions, employees generally perceived a more ethical climate. This survey's generalizability is accentuated by its sampling from a variety of work industries. To further enhance this survey's usefulness and generalizability, different cultures and geographies should be explored under the same conditions.

Ghosh (2015)

Ghosh (2015) examines four dimensions of benevolent leadership – ethical sensitivity, spiritual wisdom, positive engagement, and community responsiveness – as antecedents of ethical climate. Using Karakas and Sarigollu's (2012) survey with ten items for each of the four dimensions of benevolent leadership, Ghosh surveyed senior leaders, as well as middle and junior employees, at eight different non-profit firms in India (Ghosh, 2015, pp. 600–601). Victor and Cullen's (1988) Ethical Work Climate scale was adapted to a 16-item survey to measure ethical climate (Ghosh, 2015, p. 601). Ghosh's analysis showed that each of the four dimensions of benevolent leadership was related to the development of ethical climate, which in turn predicted increased organizational citizenship behavior. It was unclear whether benevolent leadership directly affected organizational citizenship behavior.

Erben and Guneser (2008)

Erben and Guneser's (2008) study analyzed the relationship of paternalistic leadership and organizational behavior, with ethical climate as a mediator. Erben and Guneser measured paternalistic leadership with Cheng et al.'s (2004) Paternalistic Leadership Scale: a 26-item survey with a 6-point Likert scale ranging from 1 ('strongly disagree') to 6 ('strongly agree'). The Paternalistic Leadership Scale examines authoritarian, benevolent, and moral types of leadership. Ethical climate was measured with Victor and Cullen's (1988) 36-item ECQ. Erben and Guneser's findings focused on the benevolent and authoritarian leadership dimensions. The benevolent style was characterized by concern for others both within and without the organization. Moral leaders showed superior personal virtues, self-discipline, and unselfishness (Cheng et al., 2004). Authoritarian-style leaders exhibited absolute authority and control over subordinates, even to the point of conflicting with Victor and Cullen's (1988) rules climate, which advocated following the predetermined rules of the organization rather than simply leadership (Erben & Guneser, 2008, p. 965). Ethical climate was found to be positively related to benevolent and moral paternalistic leadership and negatively related to authoritarian paternalistic leadership. Organizational commitment is not the focus of this chapter, but Erben and Guneser also found that benevolent paternalistic leadership was associated with both affective and continuance organizational commitment. This can be described by benevolent leaders' tendency to 'personalize' the work environment and create emotional attachments with workers.

Summary of key study on ethical actions and skills

Parboteeah et al. (2010)

When studying the effect of managerial practices, Parboteeah et al. (2010) focused on two specific managerial practices and their effect on the three possible ethical climates outlined by Victor and Cullen's (1987) local organization level of analysis: the egoistic, the benevolent, and the principled. Parboteeah et al. (2010) hypothesized that communication and empowerment would positively relate to the benevolent and the principled local ethical climates while being negatively related to the egoistic local ethical climate. Employees from 83 high-technology companies within Taiwan's top 100 patent-owning companies responded 'yes' or 'no' when asked whether they perceived communication and empowerment as being present in their work environment. The study also used Victor and Cullen's (1988) ECQ with a six-point Likert-type scale.

The results from the study provide evidence that the managerial principle of communication is positively related to the 'principled' local type and that empowerment is negatively related to the 'egoistic' local type and positively related to the 'benevolent' local type (Parboteeah et al., 2010, pp. 604–605). Parboteeah et al. suggest that future researchers find a more sophisticated questionnaire design to more accurately assess empowerment and communication and to administer these surveys in different countries and different industries to get a more universally applicable result.

Summary of key study contradicting conventional findings

Mulki et al. (2009)

Mulki et al.'s (2009) study explored the role of instrumental leadership of salespeople on ethical climate. Instrumental leaders establish clear guidelines, reduce role ambiguity, and make the relationship between achievements and rewards clear (p. 127). Mulki et al. measured leadership style with House's (1971) 13-item Leaders Behavior Description Questionnaire (Mulki et al., 2009, p. 130). Ethical climate was measured with Schwepker's (2001) scale because of its simplicity and applicability to salespeople (Mulki et al., 2009, p. 130). The results indicate a positive, significant relationship between instrumental leadership style and ethical climate (p. 133). Ethical climate, in turn, positively influences supervisor satisfaction, job satisfaction, and employee effort (Mulki et al., 2009). The implications of this study support Mulki et al.'s theory that the reduced uncertainty caused by instrumental leadership improves salesperson performance (ibid.). This study counters traditional theory that leadership styles associated with support and caring are usually associated with ethical climate more than authoritarian styles of leadership (Erben & Guneser, 2008). The unique nature of the sales environment may account for this difference.

Organizational Practices

Considerable research has been undertaken on the effects of leadership on ethical climate. It seems reasonable that the way organizations function would also strongly influence employees' perspective about ethics. Nonetheless, research on how different types or approaches to organizing, such as human resource management practices, influence ethical climate remains largely unexplored. Guerci et al.'s (2015) study is the only empirical study to date that examines organizational practices as an antecedent to ethical climate. Their work suggests that human resource management is related to ethical climate in a number of ways. For instance, human resource practices focused on rewards and punishments were found to be correlated with an egoistic ethical climate – which is a climate characterized by self-interest (Guerci et al., 2015). Alternatively, human resource practices that screen new hires for ethical aptitude were correlated with caring and principled climates (ibid.). Given the variety of human resource management practices in organizations, especially in light of outsourcing, globalization, and changing demographics, there are many future research opportunities to better understand ethical climate. In Table 14.3, we summarize studies classified by Newman et al.'s (2017) 'organizational practices' as antecedents for ethical climate while using Victor and Cullen's (1987) categories to structure the particular kinds of ethical climates resulting from different organizational practices.

Table 14.3   *Organizational practices (based on Newman et al.'s 'organizational practices' classification)*

Author	Date	Constructs	Victor and Cullen Five Empirical Derivatives	Measurement Tool
Guerci et al.	2015	Human Resources Systems	All Five Dimensions	Modified Ethical Climate Questionnaire (Victor and Cullen, 1987, 1988)
Manroop et al.	2014	Human Resources Systems	All Five Dimensions	Ethical Climate Questionnaire (Victor and Cullen, 1987, 1988)
Manroop	2015	Human Resources Systems	Caring, Independence, Law & Code	

Summary of key study on organizational practices

Guerci et al. (2015)

We agree with Newman et al. (2017) that only Guerci et al. (2015) have empirically examined the influence of human resource management on ethical climates. Guerci et al. examined the three possible ethical climates using Victor and Cullen's (1987) local (organizational) level of analysis: the egoistic, the benevolent, and the principled. A survey was administered in six European countries: Italy, Germany, Poland, the United Kingdom, Spain, and France (Guerci et al., 2015). This survey included a modified ECQ focusing on the local level of analysis and used a 6-point Likert scale to determine perceptions of ethical climate (ibid.). Another questionnaire with a 5-point Likert scale was administered to examine the rate at which employers implemented certain human resource management (ibid.). The results indicated that ability- and opportunity-enhancing human resource practices were positively correlated with benevolent and principled climates, while motivation-enhancing practices were positively correlated with egoistic climates (ibid.).

Frameworks of how human resource systems can influence ethical climate

Manroop et al. (2014)

These scholars consider human resource systems from a resource-based view by positing that human resource systems play a key role in shaping ethical climate (Manroop et al., 2014, p. 797). Manroop et al. did not conduct a quantitative study that showed clear antecedents of ethical climate, but they did produce a useful framework for understanding how human resource systems fit into Victor and Cullen's (1988) five empirical derivatives of ethical climate. Manroop et al.'s (2014) framework used human resource system components as rows: recruitment and selection, training, compensation, and performance management. These rows were contrasted with the five empirical derivatives of ethical climate as columns (ibid.). Manroop et al. theorized that an ethical climate can create a competitive advantage for the firm.

Manroop (2015)

In 2015, Manroop further elaborated on how human resource systems act as antecedents to ethical climate. He classified human resource systems as either climate enhancing or climate destroying. Beginning with the instrumental ethical climate, Manroop argued that human resource systems that foster self-interest in employees rather than organizational interest will destroy an instrumental ethical climate. Next, he theorized about the caring ethical climate, theorizing that human resource systems that emphasize concern for the welfare of others will develop a positive caring ethical climate (Manroop, 2015, p. 192). Conversely, systems that foster behavior such as lying, deception, and deviance will destroy a caring ethical climate (p. 9). The independence climate will be supported by systems that encourage behaviors that are guided by deeply held, personal moral convictions (p. 194). An independence climate will be destroyed by human resource systems that require organization members to act contrary to their deeply held, personal moral convictions (p. 195). Law and code ethical climates will be destroyed by encouraging behaviors that an incongruent to legal and professional standards and supported by the opposite (p. 196). Similarly, rules climates are destroyed by encouraging behaviors that conflict with institutional rules and standards and are supported by the inverse (p. 198). Manroop's (2015) qualitative study thus highlights specific areas where human resource systems can either create or destroy certain ethical climate types.

Organizational and Cultural Context

Beyond leadership and human resource practices within an organization, the organizational and cultural context is a key predictor of ethical climates (Martin & Cullen, 2006). Public and private organizations exhibit different ethical climates (Venezia et al., 2010; Weber & Gerde, 2011), as do family and nonfamily businesses (Duh et al., 2010), and nonprofit and for-profit organizations (Laratta, 2009). Even the industry and nationality of a company influence ethical climate (Parboteeah et al., 2014; Venezia et al., 2010). We acknowledge that perceptions of ethical climate will vary based on these different aspects. Only recently has research been extended to consider the overarching cultural context as an antecedent of ethical climate (Newman et al., 2017, p. 485). We select diverse organizational contexts that are discussed in the articles below. Exploring the effects of culture on ethical climate appears to be the next phase of research in this area. In Table 14.4, we summarize studies classified by Newman et al.'s (2017) 'organizational and culture context' as antecedents for ethical climate and use Victor and Cullen's categories to structure the particular kinds of ethical climates found by measuring these contexts.

Table 14.4   *Organizational and culture context (based on Newman et al.'s 'organizational and cultural context' classification)*

Author	Date	Constructs	Victor and Cullen Five Empirical Derivatives	Measurement Tool
Weber & Gerde	2011	Military Groups	Instrumental, Caring	Ethical Climate Questionnaire (Victor and Cullen, 1987, 1988)
Duh et al.	2010	Family Enterprises		OCAI method for closed ended questions. Ethical Climate Questionnaire (Victor and Cullen, 1987, 1988)
Venezia et al.	2010	Public vs. Private Sector Accountants		Ethical Climate Questionnaire (Victor and Cullen, 1987, 1988)
Laratta	2009	Nonprofit & Government Sectors		Modified Ethical Climate Questionnaire (Victor and Cullen, 1987, 1988)
Parboteeah et al.	2014	Human Resources Management, Africa	All Five Dimensions	Corruption Perception Index, Individual Interviews

Summary of key studies on organizational and industry context

Laratta (2009)

Laratta (2009) compared the ethical climates of nonprofit and government organizations in Japan and the United Kingdom. He administered a survey to 500 respondents in nonprofit organizations and 500 respondents in government organizations in each country, for a total of 2,000 potential respondents. The survey was a modified version of Victor and Cullen's (1988) ECQ with 6-point Likert scale that measured eight climate types identified for this study: self-interest, organizational interest, efficiency, friendship, team interest, stakeholder orientation, personal morality, and rules and law (Laratta, 2009, pp. 364–365). In the United Kingdom, stakeholder orientation (social caring), friendship, and self-interest climates were found to be perceived similarly by nonprofit and government sectors (Laratta, 2009). In Japan, all eight climate types were also found to be perceived similarly by nonprofit and government sectors (ibid.). Laratta's study implies that Japan's government accountability demands on nonprofit organizations are potentially unnecessary because government contracts between nonprofit and government organizations will be fulfilled with the same ethical rigor. He suggests the lack of similarity among UK nonprofit and government organizations highlights areas where both groups can build on commonalities.

Laratta (2009) not only explored the difference between ethical climates in nonprofits and governments, but also highlighted the potential cultural antecedents of ethical climate in Japan and the United Kingdom. This research could be extended into and across different cultures.

Duh et al. (2010)

This team of researchers examined the degree of involvement of family in an enterprise and a family's influence on the enterprise's core values, culture, and ethical climate. A four-part questionnaire was used (Duh et al., 2010). The first part collected demographic data on the enterprises used in the study: legal form, main activity, number of owners, and percentage of family ownership. The second part presented respondents with close-ended questions used to assess the importance of a set of core values originally proposed by García-Marzá (2005). In the third part, Cameron and Quinn's (1999) Organizational Culture Assessment Instrument method was used in four close-ended questions to examine enterprise culture. In the fourth part, Victor and Cullen's (1988) ECQ was used with a 6-point Likert scale.

The findings showed that both family and nonfamily enterprises had a positive attitude toward core values related to ethical content (Duh et al., 2010, p. 484). However, a statistically significant difference between family and nonfamily businesses for the core value 'dignity' indicated that family enterprises are generally more eager than nonfamily businesses for respect and encouragement of human rights and the values involved in reciprocal recognition between individuals (p. 484). The results also indicated that the caring climate was the prevailing ethical climate in family enterprises, while law and code was the prevailing climate in nonfamily enterprises (p. 485).

This study revealed that both family and nonfamily organizations value ethics to similar but slightly different degrees (Duh et al., 2010). Possible antecedents of these differences should be explored in future research. Duh et al.'s research could also be expanded by exploring whether family and nonfamily enterprises perceive ethical climate in the same way.

Venezia et al. (2010)

Venezia et al. (2010) compared ethical climates of public- and private-sector accountants in the Philippines and Taiwan. A revised version of Victor and Cullen's (1988) ECQ with 36 questions was used to evaluate the accountants' perceptions of ethical climate (Venezia et al., 2010). They then used factor analysis to evaluate the results with Cullen et al.'s (1993) seven dimensions of ethical climate: rules/codes, caring, self-interest, social responsibility, efficiency, instrumentalism, and personal morality. The public sector perceived rules/codes, caring, self-interests, social responsibility, and instrumentalism climates as most prevalent, while efficiency and personal morality were more prevalent in the private sector (Venezia et al., 2010). Venezia et al. theorized that private accountants are encouraged to be more entrepreneurial in solving clients' problems. This resulted in greater perceived efficiency and lower proclivity toward strict rules. Public accountants, by contrast, were governed more closely by public standards and civil rules. These differences resulted in a greater emphasis on the personal morality climate among private accountants. This study could be expanded by researching accountants outside of Asia. Contrasting the ethical perceptions of public and private professions beyond accounting would also add further validity to Venezia et al.'s theories.

Weber and Gerde (2011)

Using Victor and Cullen's (1988) ECQ with ten different military work groups, Weber and Gerde analyzed ethical work climate. Each respondent was asked to rate the 26 statements on the ECQ as to how descriptive each statement was of the employee's decision-making process (Weber & Gerde, 2011). Respondents rated each statement on a 7-point scale, with a '7' being most descriptive.

Weber and Gerde (2011) found three different situations where military workgroups were more likely to have instrumental or caring ethical work climates: military workgroups in organizational environments of greater risk or magnitude of consequences, workgroups with high levels of task interdependence, and workgroups in organizational environments of greater environmental uncertainty (p. 605). Weber and Gerde's (2011) study provided a foundation for studying different work environments as antecedents to ethical climate. Studies exploring ethical climate in organizational environments of greater risk or magnitude of consequences, high levels of task interdependence, or environmental uncertainty should be conducted in civilian organizations to further this research.

Summary of key study on organizational cultural context

Parboteeah et al. (2014)

Parboteeah et al. (2014) highlighted the lack of research ethics research in the African context. Their study qualitatively analyzed three companies in Nigeria and two companies in South Africa. Across the five organizations, 29 interviews were conducted, and the perceptions of an egoistic, benevolence, or principled ethical climate were assessed. Parboteeah et al. hypothesized that in Nigeria, an egoist climate would be positively related to ethnic diversity and corruption. (Nigeria is home to 250 different ethnic groups, and the Transparency International 2012 Corruption Perception Index ranked Nigeria as one of the most corrupt countries in the world; South Africa in comparison is ranked as only moderately corrupt [Parboteeah et al., 2014, p. 991]). The results indicated that one company in Nigeria had a dominant egoist ethical climate with a focus on self-interest. Another company in Nigeria and a company in South

Africa had perceptions of both egoistic and benevolent climates, and the third company in Nigeria and another company in South Africa had benevolent ethical climates.

Parboteeah et al. (2014) suggested that human resource management may moderate the relationship between self-interested ethnic diversity/corruption and egoistic climate. They conclude that Nigeria's political climate of corruption and extreme diversity can be mitigated by equally staunch human resource practices. Although much research remains regarding ethics in Africa, future research could focus on an empirical study on the effect of human resource management as an antecedent of ethical climate within Africa.

Individual Differences

We agree with Newman et al. (2017) that in comparison to other areas, research into individual differences and ethical climate is not as advanced. Martin and Cullen (2006) also stated that the majority of research on the ethics of individuals has focused on the effects of ethical outcomes of an individual's behavior. There is need for future research on individual-level variables acting as antecedents of ethical climate. Two of the three studies outlined below examined nurses' individual differences as antecedents to ethical climate (Filipova, 2009; Goldman & Tabak, 2010). Factors such as job tenure and position strongly affected perceptions of ethical climate (Newman et al., 2017, p. 485). Because the aggregate perceptions of ethics in an organization are the foundation for an ethical climate (Newman et al., 2017, p. 479), individual differences should be explored further in the business context. In Table 14.5, we summarize studies classified by Newman et al.'s (2017) 'individual differences' as an antecedent for ethical climate while using Victor and Cullen's categories to structure the specific kinds of ethical climates found by measuring differences between individuals.

Table 14.5   Individual differences (based on Newman et al.'s 'individual differences' classification)

Author	Date	Constructs	Victor and Cullen Five Empirical Derivatives	Measurement Tool
Goldman & Tabak	2010	Nurses, Israel	Instrumental, Independent	Ethical Climate Questionnaire (Victor and Cullen, 1987, 1988)
Filipova	2009	Nurses	Law & Code, Rules	Ethical Climate Questionnaire (Victor and Cullen, 1987, 1988)
Domino et al.	2015	Accountants	Independent	Ethical Climate Scale (Victor and Cullen, 1988), Modified Work Locus of Control Scale (Spector, 1988)

Summary of key studies on individual differences

Filipova (2009)
Filipova studied antecedents of ethical climate among nurses. A survey was administered to licensed and registered nurses in a midwestern state (Filipova, 2009). Data on ethical climates were collected via the 26-item ECQ, with additional questions concerning demographic and employment characteristics. As suggested by Victor and Cullen (1988), the nurses were asked

to respond to questions in terms of what the climate of their organization actually was and not what they would like it to be. Items were measured on a 6-point Likert scale (Filipova, 2009, p. 578).

Overall, nurses most often perceived their climate as a 'law and code' ethical climate, with a 'rules' climate being second-most common (p. 583). The strict management of medical facilities logically affirmed these findings. Filipova found that Licensed Practical Nurses (nurses with lower responsibility) perceived less of an independence climate than Registered Nurses (nurses with greater responsibility) (p. 583). This affirmed Goldman and Tabak's (2010) theory that nurses with higher job position and greater responsibility prefer 'independence' ethical climates. Future research could further investigate how ethical climates change according to mixture of roles and responsibilities of nurses found in different hospitals.

Goldman and Tabak (2010)

Goldman and Tabak (2010) conducted a study on job satisfaction among nurses in Israel. They first examined how the demographic differences of nurses influence their perception of ethical climate and then analyzed how the perception of ethical climate affects job satisfaction. For the purposes of this review, we will focus on how the demographics of nurses influence their perception of ethical climate. Goldman and Tabak used a 22-item ECQ based on the work by Victor and Cullen (1988). Independent demographic variables, measured using 11 items, were gender, age, level of education, professional seniority, seniority on the ward (length of employment), and ethnic origin and religion (p. 238).

The results showed that nurses with more years of practice have a higher preference for instrumental and independent ethical climates as compared to those who have worked for less time (p. 241). Independent ethical climates are characterized by having a high degree of professional autonomy (p. 241). Goldman and Tabak also theorized that nurses with more years of experience are exposed to a variety of technology and complex ethical dilemmas. In order to solve these problems most effectively and provide the highest level of patient care, nurses with longer tenure preferred independent ethical climates. While this study was not grounded in the business context, its implications are relevant, and similar studies should be conducted in the business context.

Domino et al. (2015)

Domino et al. (2015) explored individual accountants' perceptions of the ethical climate within their organization and the extent to which these professionals will tolerate unethical behavior and accept it as the norm. To measure how well an individual aligns with the ethical norms of an organization (ethical climate fit), four items were adapted from the independence dimension of Victor and Cullen's (1988) Ethical Climate Scale (Domino et al., 2015). Locus of control was measured with an adapted form of Spector's (1988) Work Locus of Control Scale (Domino et al., 2015, p. 459). All measurements were made with a 6-point Likert scale.

Domino et al. (2015) found three antecedents of ethical climate fit: higher internal levels of locus of control (a sense of control over reward and reinforcement); greater numbers of prior job changes; and higher perceptions of an increasingly better fit with the firm's ethical climate (e.g., fit trend) suggesting that individual differences among accountants affected their ability to fit into an organization's ethical climate (p. 453). Thus, individual differences do interact with ethical climate. Future studies could investigate how ethical climate fit affects ethical climate.

RESEARCH AND THEORETICAL IMPLICATIONS

Despite ethical climate research having been introduced more than 30 years ago, there are still fruitful opportunities for research on the measurement and development of ethical climate. First, when considering the measurement of ethical climate, Victor and Cullen's (1988) ECQ still remains the most commonly used tool for measuring ethical climates. Many studies use adapted versions of the ECQ. Arnaud's (2006, 2010) Ethical Climate Index examines the collective morals of an organization through a similar survey. The six factors tested by Arnaud's (2006, 2010) Ethical Climate Index allow for a potentially broader conceptualization of ethical climate than Victor and Cullen's (1988) ECQ. Future improvements to the Ethical Climate Index and ECQ are recommended. Additionally, new measures that accommodate the increasingly complex global economy would expand research on measuring ethical climate.

Second, when considering developing ethical climate, the studies outlined in this chapter are a helpful starting point. Social Learning Theory is used to explain how ethical leaders directly create ethical climates (Mayer et al., 2010). CEO ethical leadership is indeed positively related to ethical climate and collective organizational citizenship behavior (Shin, 2012). Ethical managers also increased affective commitment to the organization and decreased turnover intention (Demirtas and Akdogan, 2015; Erben & Guneser, 2008). However, other studies on ethical leadership that do not directly address antecedents of ethical climate also provide opportunities for future research. For instance, the degree of ethical leadership predicted unethical pro-organizational behavior in a curvilinear pattern (Miao et al., 2012). This suggests that the level of ethical leadership is variable and reaches an inflexion point and thus may affect ethical climate. Another consideration is that ethical leadership is found to cascade across hierarchical levels, not just directly down from leader to follower (Schaubroeck et al., 2012). Thus, leaders from geographically dispersed departments, or even organizations, could potentially act as influential antecedents to ethical climate. Organizational change such as mergers, acquisitions, restructuring, or layoffs also presents unique contexts for ethical leadership and ethical climate (Sharif & Scandura, 2013). Finally, individual-level factors such as personality and early life exposure to ethical role models should be explored as antecedents to ethical leadership (Brown & Treviño, 2013).

Extant research on organizational practices yields promising areas of future research. As discussed above, motivation-, ability-, and opportunity-enhancing human resource management predicted egoistic, benevolent, or principled ethical climates (Guerci et al., 2015). Guerci et al. opened several new avenues for research. Longitudinal studies of how human resource management impacts ethical climate have yet to be conducted. Other research on organizational practices found that ethical training by human resource professionals improves ethical behavior (Yazdani & Murad, 2014). Additionally, the existing ethical climate of an organization could potentially affect human resource practices. That is, research is needed to determine to what extent ethical (or unethical) financial management, cultural norms, leadership styles, and decision-making approaches influence human resource practices such as selection, performance management, incentive systems, and training programs. These reciprocal relationships should be examined. Further, different stages of human resource management implementation (not all human resource practices are implemented with the same rigor, complexity, or effectiveness) should be examined. The emerging and evolving role of human resource management suggests that examining different internal views (e.g., the views of human resource professionals about their role in influencing ethical climate) may be helpful in future research.

Organizational and cultural context present additional areas for future research. Organizational environments with greater risk of consequences, higher levels of task interdependence, and greater environmental uncertainty are likely to affect certain types of ethical climates more than more stable environments (Weber & Gerde, 2011). Cross-national studies showed how culture affects ethical climate among different countries (Laratta, 2009; Parboteeah et al., 2014). Industry norms also predicted certain ethical climates (Duh et al., 2010; Laratta, 2009; Venezia et al., 2010). The following three factors create a matrix of numerous possibilities for future research: organizational environment, cultural context, and industry context. Cultural context is not easily quantified, and as Robertson and Fadil (1999) suggested, subcultures exist within each national culture. While daunting, examining the effect of cross-cultural and sub-cultural contexts on ethical climate would greatly help multinational organizations improve their ethical climates. For example, research on ethical climates in the countries of the African continent is underdeveloped and ripe for research opportunities (Parboteeah et al., 2014).

Numerous studies have shown how individual differences predict ethical outcomes, but individual differences also act as antecedents to ethical climate. The collective perception of ethical climate is built by individuals within an organizational context but occurs at the individual level. While empirical research supporting this logical theory is sparse, individual differences do influence how members of an organization perceive an ethical climate (Goldman & Tabak, 2010). For example, nurses of greater tenure preferred different ethical climates from those preferred by nurses with less job experience (ibid.). Similar circumstances most likely exist in a variety of other industries but have yet to be examined. The demographic characteristics, personalities, status differences, and other characteristics of employees are potential areas for future research concerning ethical climate. Future studies could also investigate how ethical climate fit affects ethical climate (Domino et al., 2015). Other individual differences, such as religiosity, gender, job position, tenure, and age, could also affect ethical perceptions (Conroy & Emerson, 2004).

In this chapter, we have focused on antecedents to ethical climate. However, to suggest that there is not also a relationship between antecedents and outcomes, would be untrue. The extent to which ethical climate moderates or mediates antecedents and outcomes should be explored. The complexity of these relationships has yet to be discovered fully. For instance, while ethical leadership's influence on ethical behavior has been studied thoroughly, there is evidence that ethical climate mediates ethical leadership effects on behavior (Mayer et al., 2010, p. 13). Thus, antecedents of ethical climate may sometimes affect climate directly and at other times predict ethical climate more strongly, which then predicts outcomes.

PRACTICAL IMPLICATIONS

Our hope in writing this chapter is to help both researchers and practitioners understand extant research on ethical climate, its measurement and limitations, and how it can be applied in organizational settings. Our examination of the literature suggests useful principles, tools, and approaches for the practical application of ethical climates in organizational contexts today.

First, the development of an ethical climate must start with the leader of the company. Leaders are in a position where what they say and do influence how their employees work. Even managers who lead smaller teams within in a department have influence. Numerous studies have shown that employees look to their leaders for how they should act and behave. A manager's actions can often be a rationalization for what employees consider appropriate.

Second, while the impact of leaders can develop an ethical climate, human resource management also maintains and improves an ethical climate. Human resource departments control important aspects of ethical climate, such as choosing who to hire, how to present training, and how to compensate employees based on their progress and performance. A strong human resource team can greatly enhance a company's ethical climate by bringing attention to positive examples of ethical behavior and rewarding and supporting employees. An effective human resource team can help employees feel cared for, which is an important part of ethical climate (Victor & Cullen, 1987). Cultural and industry context also have an effect on ethical climate. Each culture and industry may have different ethical norms. Human resource professionals and organizational leaders should be aware of these overarching contexts and implement programs to compensate accordingly.

Finally, each individual in a company will have his or her own perception of ethics. This perception is developed through each individual's background, work experience, and job role. A strong ethical climate will help individuals align their ethical perceptions with the goals of the organization.

Research about how ethical climate is developed, maintained, and improved is still in its infancy. We call for future researchers to further this field of study and for business professionals to implement the ideas and principles that are available to improve the ethics of the world's organizations.

REFERENCES

Agle, B. R., Hart, D. W., Thompson, J. A., & Hendricks, H. M. (2014). *Research Companion to Ethical Behavior in Organizations: Constructs and Measures.* Cheltenham, UK: Edward Elgar.

Ardichvili, A., & Jondle, D. (2009). Ethical business cultures: A literature review and implications for HRD. *Human Resource Development Review, 8*(2), 223–244.

Arnaud, A. (2006). *A New Theory and Measure of Ethical Work Climate: The Psychological Process Model (PPM) and the Ethical Climate Index (ECI).* (Doctoral dissertation). Retrieved from Electronic Theses and Dissertations. (742) University of Central Florida, Orlando.

Arnaud, A. (2010). Conceptualizing and measuring ethical work climate: Development and validation of the Ethical Climate Index. *Business and Society, 49*(2), 345–358.

Babin, B. J., Boles, J. S., & Robin, D. P. (2000). Representing the perceived ethical work climate among marketing employees. *Journal of the Academy of Marketing Science, 28*(3), 345–358.

Bandura, A. (1977). Self-efficacy: Toward a unifying theory of behavioral change. *Psychological Review, 84*(2), 191–215.

Bandura, A. (1986). *Social Foundations of Thought & Action.* Englewood Cliffs, NJ: Prentice-Hall.

Börü, D. (2001). Örgütlerde Güven Ortamının Yaratılmasında İlk Adım…Güvenilir İnsanlar Kim? Proceedings of the 9th Management and Organization Conference in Istanbul, Turkey (pp. 189–204).

Brown, M. E., & Treviño, L. K. (2013). Do role models matter? An investigation of role modeling as an antecedent of perceived ethical leadership. *Journal of Business Ethics, 122*(4), 587–598.

Brown, M. E., Treviño, L. K., & Harrison, D. A. (2005). Ethical leadership: A social learning perspective for construct development and testing. *Organizational Behavior and Human Decision Processes, 97*(2), 117–134.

Cameron, K., & Quinn, R. (1999). *Diagnosing and Changing Organizational Culture: Based on the Competing Values Framework.* New York, NY: Addison-Wesley.

Cheng, B., Chou, L. F., Tsung, Y. W., Huang, M., & Farh, J. (2004). Paternalistic leadership and subordinate responses: Establishing a leadership model in Chinese organizations. *Asian Journal of Social Psychology*, *7*(1), 89–117.

Conger, J. A., & Kanungo, R. N. (1994). Charismatic leadership in organizations: Perceived behavioral attributes and their measurement. *Journal of Organizational Behavior*, *15*(5), 439–452.

Conroy, S. J., & Emerson, T. L. (2004). Business ethics and religion: Religiosity as a predictor of ethical awareness among students. *Journal of Business Ethics*, *50*(4), 383–396.

Cullen, J. B., Victor, B., & Bronson, J. W. (1993). The Ethical Climate Questionnaire: An assessment of its development and validity. *Psychological Reports*, *73*(2), 667–674.

Dark, D., & Rix, M. (2015). Back to the future: Using the Ethical Climate Questionnaire to understand ethical behaviour in not for profits. *Asia Pacific Journal of Health Management*, *10*(3), SI22–SI31.

Demirtas, O., & Akdogan, A. A. (2015). The effect of ethical leadership behavior on ethical climate, turnover intention, and affective commitment. *Journal of Business Ethics*, *130*(1), 59–67.

Domino, M. A., Wingreen, S. C., & Blanton, J. E. (2015). Social cognitive theory: The antecedents and effects of ethical climate fit on organizational attitudes of corporate accounting professionals – a reflection of client narcissism and fraud attitude risk. *Journal of Business Ethics*, *131*(2), 453–467.

Duh, M., Belak, J., & Milfelner, B. (2010). Core values, culture and ethical climate as constitutional elements of ethical behaviour: Exploring differences between family and non-family enterprises. *Journal of Business Ethics*, *97*(3), 473–489.

Erben, G. S., & Guneser, A. B. (2008). The relationship between paternalistic leadership and organizational commitment: Investigating the role of climate regarding ethics. *Journal of Business Ethics*, *82*(4), 955–968.

Ferrell, O. C., Fraedrich, J., & Ferrell, L. (2000). *Business Ethics: Ethical Decision Making and Cases* (4th ed.). New York, NY: Houghton Mifflin.

Filipova, A. A. (2009). Licensed nurses' perceptions of ethical climates in skilled nursing facilities. *Nursing Ethics*, *16*(5), 574–588.

Fritzche, D. J., & Becker, H. (1984). Linking management behavior to ethical philosophy. *Academy of Management Journal*, *27*(1), 166–175.

García-Marzá, D. (2005). Trust and dialogue: Theoretical approaches to ethics auditing. *Journal of Business Ethics*, *57*(3), 209–219.

Ghosh, K. (2015). Benevolent leadership in not-for-profit organizations. *Leadership & Organization Development Journal*, *36*(5), 592–611.

Goldman, A., & Tabak, N. (2010). Perception of ethical climate and its relationship to nurses' demographic characteristics and job satisfaction. *Nursing Ethics*, *17*(2), 233–246.

Guerci, M., Radaelli, G., Siletti, E., Cirella, S., & Shani, A. B. R. (2015). The impact of human resource management practices and corporate sustainability on organizational ethical climates: An employee perspective. *Journal of Business Ethics*, *126*(2), 325–342.

House, R. J. (1971). A path goal theory of leader effectiveness. *Administrative Science Quarterly*, *16*(3), 321.

Jondle, D., Ardichvili, A., & Mitchell, J. (2014). Modeling ethical business culture: Development of the Ethical Business Culture Survey and its use to validate the CEBC model of ethical business culture. *Journal of Business Ethics*, *119*(1), 29–43.

Karakas, F., & Sarigollu, E. (2012). Benevolent leadership: Conceptualization and construct development. *Journal of Business Ethics*, *108*(7), 537–553.

Kohlberg, L. (1969). Stage and sequence: The cognitive-development approach to socialization. In D. A. Goslin (Ed.), *Handbook of Socialization Theory and Research* (pp. 347–480). Chicago, IL: Rand McNally.

Laratta, R. (2009). Ethical climate in nonprofit organizations: A comparative study. *International Journal of Sociology and Social Policy*, *29*(7/8), 358–371.

Lemmergaard, J., & Lauridsen, J. (2008). The ethical climate of Danish firms: A discussion and enhancement of the ethical-climate model. *Journal of Business Ethics*, *80*(4), 653–675.

Lennick, D., & Kiel, F. (2005). *Moral Intelligence: Enhancing Business Performance and Leadership Success*. Upper Saddle River, NJ: Wharton School.

Lu, C. S., & Lin, C. C. (2014). The effects of ethical leadership and ethical climate on employee ethical behavior in the international port context. *Journal of Business Ethics*, *124*(2), 209–223.

Manroop, L. (2015). Human resource systems and competitive advantage: An ethical climate perspective. *Business Ethics: A European Review, 24*(2), 186–204.

Manroop, L., Singh, P., & Ezzedeen, S. (2014). Human resource systems and ethical climates: A resource-based perspective. *Human Resource Management, 53*(5), 795–816.

Martin, D. E., & Austin, B. (2010). Validation of the moral competency inventory measurement instrument: Content, construct, convergent and discriminant approaches. *Management Research Review, 33*(5), 437–451.

Martin, K. D., & Cullen, J. B. (2006). Continuities and extensions of ethical climate theory: A meta-analytic review. *Journal of Business Ethics, 69*(2), 175–194.

Mayer, D. M., Kuenzi, M., & Greenbaum, R. L. (2010). Examining the link between ethical leadership and employee misconduct: The mediating role of ethical climate. *Journal of Business Ethics, 95*(1), 7–16.

Mayer, D. M., Kuenzi, M., Greenbaum, R., Bardes, M., & Salvador, R. (2009). How low does ethical leadership flow? Test of a trickle-down model. *Organizational Behavior and Human Decision Processes, 108*(1), 1–13.

Meyer, J. P., & Allen, N. J. (1991). A three-component conceptualization of organizational commitment. *Human Resource Management Review, 1*(1), 61–98.

Miao, Q., Newman, A., Yu, J., & Xu, L. (2012). The relationship between ethical leadership and unethical pro-organizational behavior: Linear or curvilinear effects? *Journal of Business Ethics, 116*(3), 641–653.

Mulki, J. P., Jaramillo, J. F., & Locander, W. B. (2009). Critical role of leadership on ethical climate and salesperson behaviors. *Journal of Business Ethics, 86*, 125–141.

Neubert, M. J., Carlson, D. S., Kacmar, K. M., Roberts, J. A., & Chonko, L. B. (2009). The virtuous influence of ethical leadership behavior: Evidence from the field. *Journal of Business Ethics, 90*(2), 157–170.

Newman, A., Round, H., Bhattacharya, S., & Roy, A. (2017). Ethical climates in organizations: A review and research agenda. *Business Ethics Quarterly, 27*(4), 475–512.

Ötken, A. B., & Cenkci, T. (2012). The impact of paternalistic leadership on ethical climate: The Moderating role of trust in leader. *Journal of Business Ethics, 108*(4), 525–536.

Parboteeah, K. P., Chen, H. C., Lin, Y. T., Chen, I. H., Lee, A. Y. P., & Chung, A. (2010). Establishing organizational ethical climates: How do managerial practices work? *Journal of Business Ethics, 97*(4), 599–611.

Parboteeah, K. P., Seriki, H. T., & Hoegl, M. (2014). Ethnic diversity, corruption and ethical climates in sub-Saharan Africa: Recognizing the significance of human resource management. *International Journal of Human Resource Management, 25*(7), 979–1001.

Qualls, W. J., & Puto, C. P. (1989). Organizational climate and decision framing: An integrated approach to analyzing industrial buying decisions. *Journal of Marketing Research, 26*(2), 179–192.

Robertson, C., & Fadil, P. A. (1999). Ethical decision making in multinational organizations: A culture-based model. *Journal of Business Ethics, 19*(4), 385–392.

Rosin, H. M., & Korabik, K. (1991). Workplace variables, affective responses, and intention to leave among women managers. *Journal of Occupational Psychology, 64*(4), 317–330.

Salamon, T., & Mesko, M. (2016). Can an ethical work climate influence payment discipline? *Journal of Industrial Engineering and Management, 9*(1), 73–89.

Schaubroeck, J. M., Hannah, S. T., Avolio, B. J., Kozlowski, S. W., Lord, R. G., Treviño, L. K., . . . Peng, A. C. (2012). Embedding ethical leadership within and across organization levels. *Academy of Management Journal, 55*(5), 1053–1078.

Schwepker, C. H. (2001). Ethical climate's relationship to job satisfaction, organizational commitment, and turnover intention in the salesforce. *Journal of Business Research, 54*(1), 39–52.

Schwepker, C. H. (2013). Improving sales performance through commitment to superior customer value: The role of psychological ethical climate. *Journal of Personal Selling & Sales Management, 33*(4), 389–402.

Sharif, M. M., & Scandura, T. A. (2013). Do perceptions of ethical conduct matter during organizational change? Ethical leadership and employee involvement. *Journal of Business Ethics, 124*(2), 185–196.

Shin, Y. (2012). CEO ethical leadership, ethical climate, climate strength, and collective organizational citizenship behavior. *Journal of Business Ethics, 108*(3), 299–312.

Shin, Y., Sung, S. Y., Choi, J. N., & Kim, M. S. (2015). Top management ethical leadership and firm performance: Mediating role of ethical and procedural justice climate. *Journal of Business Ethics*, *129*(1), 43–57.

Simha, A., & Cullen, J. R. (2012). Ethical climates and their effects on organizational outcomes: Implications from the past and prophecies for the future. *Academy of Management Perspectives*, *26*(4), 20–34.

Singh, J., & Rhoads, G. K. (1991). Boundary role ambiguity in marketing-oriented positions: A multidimensional, multifaceted operationalization. *Journal of Marketing Research*, *91*(3), 328–338.

Spector, P. E. (1988). Development of the work locus of control scale. *Journal of Occupational Psychology*, *61*(4), 335–340.

Treviño, L. K. (1986). Ethical decision making in organizations: A person–situation interactionist model. *Academy of Management Review*, *11*(3), 601–617.

Venezia, G., Venezia, C., & Hung, C. (2010). A comparative study of ethical work climates among public and private sector Asian accountants. *International Business and Economics Research Journal*, *9*(4), 77–85.

Victor, B., & Cullen, J. B. (1987). A theory and measure of ethical climate in organizations. In W. C. Frederick (Ed.), *Research in Corporate Social Performance and Policy* (pp. 51–71). Greenwich, CT: JAI Press.

Victor, B., & Cullen, J. B. (1988). The organizational bases of ethical work climates. *Administrative Science Quarterly*, *33*(1), 101–125.

Weber, J., & Gerde, V. W. (2011). Organizational role and environmental uncertainty as influences on ethical work climate in military units. *Journal of Business Ethics*, *100*(4), 595–612.

Yazdani, N., & Murad, H. S. (2014). Toward an ethical theory of organizing. *Journal of Business Ethics*, *127*(2), 399–417.

Zehir, C., Müceldili, B., Altindağ, E., Şehitoğlu, Y., & Zehir, S. (2014). Charismatic leadership and organizational citizenship behavior: The mediating role of ethical climate. *Social Behavior and Personality: An International Journal*, *42*(8), 1365–1375.

15. Measuring nonprofit organisational culture: key issues and insights
Ruth Knight

Nonprofit organisations are founded and developed for the public good, with charitable or social impact goals. Given their distinct set of objectives and values, it is important to understand the organisational culture within this sector, in order to support the nonprofit workforce and achieve organisational outcomes.

THE SIGNIFICANCE OF THE THIRD SECTOR

The "third sector" is a widely accepted term to describe an array of nonprofit and charitable organisations, including human service organisations, associations, cooperatives, companies limited by guarantee, and social enterprises that are independently run entities governed by a board of directors. Third-sector organisations are distinct from for-profit (private) companies as they do not report, or distribute profits, to shareholders. Instead, they reinvest surplus revenue back into their mission and report to a range of stakeholders, including beneficiaries, regulators, donors and funders. Organisations in this sector range in size and legal structure, but all seek social change, often by raising funds so they can work towards their social, environmental or cultural objectives – including strengthening economic and social participation (Productivity Commission, 2016).

Support for, and investment in, the third sector continues to grow considerably with the activity and influence of the sector in almost every country in the world growing exponentially (Casey, 2016). Countries in Asia have a strong third sector and a rich tradition of philanthropy, with religious institutions and community development organisations playing a key role in advancing some of the largest third-sector organisations in the world (Lyons & Hasan, 2002). In Europe, America and Australia, the third sector not only influences policy, philanthropic giving and social innovation, but is also a major employer of professional workforces.

Salamon and Sokolowski (2018, p. 49) have reported that the European third sector is "an enormous economic force, outdistancing most major industries in the scale of its workforce". The European third sector employed slightly more than 13 percent of the total workforce in Europe in 2014, but continues to grow as nonprofits provide a vehicle for giving expression to a host of interests and values and have developed diverse revenue sources. The increased acknowledgement of the economic and social impact of the third sector is helping to support robust third-sector development.

In America, the third sector includes member-serving organisations and public-serving organisations that contributed an estimated $1,047.2 trillion to the US economy in 2016, comprising 5.6 percent of the country's GDP (Urban Institute, 2020). Organisations range in size and have a diverse range of organisational objectives, but display a distinctiveness and basic character as they aim to "enrich human existence and contribute to the social and cultural vitality of American life" (Salamon & Sokolowski, 2015, p. 15).

In Australia, the Australian Charities and Not-for-profits Commission (ACNC) report that the revenue of charities who submit their financial statements to this national regulator was $155.4 billion in 2018 (ACNC, 2018). This income is sourced from government grants, investors, sponsorship and social enterprise, as well as philanthropic sources such as charitable giving from individuals and from trusts and foundations. Around $1.3 billion is raised through fundraising events and charity gambling (McGregor-Lowndes et al., 2017). Another $12.8 billion is given in-kind by 3.3 million volunteers each year (Deloitte Access Economics, 2017; McCrindle, 2019). These volunteers and a paid workforce of more than one million employees work to organise, implement and report on the sector's activities.

The third sector has been called the "cornerstone of civil society" (McGregor-Lowndes et al., 2017), reflecting the major economic and social role that nonprofit organisations play in every community. For this reason, it is important to research and understand sector activities, organisational theory, workforce development, management and culture.

THIRD-SECTOR CULTURE

Historically and globally, the third sector has been built on philanthropy, volunteerism and community action. For this reason, despite the perception (which is often true) that nonprofit employees earn less than their private or public counterparts, nonprofits offer meaningful opportunities to contribute to the well-being of society (Ballart & Rico, 2018; Bright, 2016). The sector was founded on these cultural values and beliefs that are still considered the values that make the sector unique. However, over the years nonprofit organisations have faced unprecedented change due to an increased focus on innovation, public accountability, organisational effectiveness, financial sustainability and organisational growth. These demands may be changing these organisations' cultural values as nonprofits operate in more for-profit and business-like ways (McDonald, 2007).

Let us consider Australia as an example of the issues and trends affecting organisational culture. Lyons (2001) explains that colonisation brought immigrants with a set of religious and secular ideologies, beliefs and values concerning who should offer health and social services. Colonial governments were reluctant to run nonprofit organisations, but philanthropists, entrepreneurs and people motivated by a strong sense of social justice created a diverse and thriving sector founded on a strong commitment to nonprofit values, community support and social change. Today, the Australian third sector is vibrant in every community, with over 600,000 nonprofits that include many Aboriginal and Torres Strait Islander community organisations, striving to support the environmental and social development of their communities (Australian Government, 2018; Sullivan, 2010).

Over the years, the third sector in Australia has grown significantly and while still diverse, many changes have influenced a large cultural shift in the way organisations see their ability to transform the sector and achieve its full potential to change lives and society (Ógáin et al., 2012). These changes include evolving government–nonprofit relationships, a more educated and regulated workforce, new technology, increased competitive tendering and commercial activity, taxation and law reform, the establishment of a national regulator, new standards of governance, and significant pressure to have an increased focus on innovation, public accountability, organisational effectiveness and excellence, financial success and growth (Connolly & Klein, 1999; Cornelius & Corvington, 2012; Hoag & Cooper, 2006; McGregor-Lowndes, 1998; O'Connell et al., 2013; Pagnoni, 2013; Pettijohn & Boris, 2018; Phillips & Smith, 2011; Shilbury & Moore, 2006).

An altered funding landscape with "more competition for the community purse" (Scaife et al., 2003, p. 3) has led to organisations becoming more entrepreneurial and commercialised (Burston, 2020; Hadley & Goggin, 2019; Maier et al., 2016; Valentinov, 2010). Some commentaries have suggested that whereas traditionally the sector heavily relied on donor goodwill and philanthropy, nonprofit organisations today are increasingly seeking new revenue streams and using sophisticated branding and storytelling as an effective tool for attracting and retaining donors (Deloitte, 2021; Ko and Liu, 2021; Merchant et al., 2010). This suggests that the sector is becoming more competitive and innovative, and organisations are motivated by shared value, efficiency and achieving results (e.g. Crane, 1995; Goerke, 2003; Linnenluecke & Griffiths, 2010; Social Enterprise Alliance, 2010; Wanberg & Banas, 2000; Willems et al., 2014).

This summary of the changing political and funding environment indicates that organisational culture within the third sector is changing and impacting the way organisations fund, design and evaluate their services, allocate resources, manage their workforce, and report to stakeholders. Clearly in what is an ever-changing environment, understanding organisational culture is critically important because it guides decision making and affects performance and the propensity for innovation.

THE ROLE AND IMPACT OF ORGANISATIONAL CULTURE

Organisational culture describes the way people within the organisation collectively think, speak and behave in the workplace. It is influenced by shared values, assumptions, customs, beliefs and attitudes, and ultimately determines the behavioural norms, functioning and outcomes of the organisation (Bik, 2010; Deshpande & Webster, 1989; Fenton & Inglis, 2007; Schein, 2004; Warrick, 2017). Culture affects job satisfaction, stress, organisational commitment, employee turnover and change readiness (e.g. Appelbaum et al., 2008; Dennis & Bocarnea, 2005; Emery & Barker, 2007; Gifford et al., 2002; Gioia et al., 2000; Rosenfeld et al., 2004; Zafft et al., 2009). Importantly, a supportive organisational culture has been found to be critical to organisational commitment, which is important for nonprofit organisations who want to engage and retain employees (and other stakeholders) more effectively (Banaszak-Holl et al., 2013). Other researchers suggest that organisational culture works as a complement to leadership, helping employees solve problems, interpret their work and innovate (Bowers et al., 2017; Fiordelisi et al., 2019; Proctor, 2013; Yanti & Dahlan, 2017).

Innovation is an important function of nonprofit organisations that culture has been found to influence. The public and funders expect the sector to solve complex and major social challenges, and innovation is often associated with "a willingness to find out what achieves most impact" (Mulgan, 2019, p. 231). Yet studies have found that organisational culture can either encourage or discourage innovative thinking and practice (Hull & Lio, 2006; Jaskyte & Dressler, 2005). It seems intuitive that nonprofit organisations would have the values that encourage creativity and innovation so they can achieve their social purpose, but this cannot always be assumed as organisational culture can reduce an organisation's risk-taking propensity and ability to become more efficient and/or effective (McDonald, 2007).

MEASURING NONPROFIT CULTURE: KEY ISSUES AND EVIDENCE

Measuring culture is increasingly being seen as an important tool in efforts to create more productive and innovative cultures within organisations. Like other organisations, nonprofits need to make a methodological choice about how they measure culture and decide whether to measure values and/or behaviours, and which elements of culture need to be examined (Taras et al., 2009). Historically, research on this topic has been in the domain of anthropology, meaning that researchers observing culture lean towards an emic approach involving inquiry and observation within each unique organisational culture. This approach focusses on learning about the culture through active participation and critical observation (Flinn, 2011). Some foundational organisational culture researchers (e.g. Schein, 1992) consider this methodology a way of empowering organisations to feel ownership about the process because the culture of organisations is too complex to be reduced to just another variable or feature of organisational performance (Siehl & Martin, 1990, as cited in Denison, 1996).

A qualitative approach using conversational and observational styles of information gathering can be appropriate for organisations that wish to integrate the assessment and exploration of culture into everyday conversations in team meetings, workshops or focus groups. This method of enquiry can expose the rituals, shared perceptions and assumptions that tend to be more abstract, yet powerfully shape beliefs, values and behaviour patterns (Schein & Schein, 2017). These cultural assessments can also review organisational data such as policies, strategies, service delivery performance and outcomes to supplement the stories and opinions collected from employees. This process helps explore the leadership, funding, political and other environmental factors that might be influencing the culture within a nonprofit organisation. Qualitative approaches have been used by researchers such as Owczarzak, Broaddus, and Pinkerton (2016) to understand how the evaluation and accountability mandates of organisations funded to provide a public health intervention influenced their "audit culture". Interviewing employees allowed the researchers to uncover how obligations to funders can impact on service delivery and evaluation reporting. Spencer and Skalaban (2018) also used qualitative methods to identify how national and local context can shape the culture of nonprofit organisations and influence potential partnerships and organisational sustainability.

In contrast, researchers who take a neopositivist, etic stance tend to use prior theory and research to determine the cultural norms on which they ask organisational members to report. This stance is taken by researchers less concerned about issues of depth (Martin, 2002), but who prefer comparing and contrasting organisations. Researchers from the business and social science disciplines tend to favour the etic stance using self-report questionnaires to gather data about personal or work values and behaviours because qualitative approaches can be more expensive, time-consuming, and make comparative studies difficult (Ashkanasy et al., 2000; Taras et al., 2007; Tucker et al., 1990).

Using a quantitative survey approach has its advantages, and questionnaires can be a valuable tool in diagnosing cultures (Maslowski, 2006) as it is easy to gather perceptions from a large workforce, and it is possible to benchmark findings alongside those from similar organisations. However, the potential disadvantages of surveys include the possibility that participants' responses may be influenced by a range of emotional, psychological, social and environmental pressures such as power, conflict and social exchange (Flynn et al., 2011; Lucas et al., 2012; Parzefall & Salin, 2010). To address these risks, organisations should be aware of the pressures that employees and/or volunteers face when completing a culture assessment and take particular care when communicating to employees the rationale for conducting a culture assessment.

A mixed methods approach is also possible. For example, Livorsi et al. (2016) started with a survey and then interviewed staff to gather "rich feedback that may not have been obtainable through standard means" (p. 375). A mixed methods approach was also taken by Milbourn et al. (2019), who used telephone interviews and online surveys to examine the motivations of volunteers leaving a nonprofit organisation. The study did not aim specifically to understand the organisational culture, yet the findings revealed that cultural values and practices were key factors that reduced feelings of belonging and autonomy, and ultimately influenced respondents' decisions to cease their engagement with the organisation (p. 280).

There is also the question about who should conduct a culture assessment. Assessments can be conducted either in-house by a dedicated person or team, or they can be conducted by an independent researcher or consultant. Many organisations seek independent advisors to assist them, given that in some cultures it is difficult or impossible for employees to feel they can speak up or provide information that might impact on their relationship with leadership or the organisation (Constandt & Willem, 2019). Potentially, there may be risks that the wrong approach could even harm the existing culture by making informants feel disempowered or negatively confronted. Staff may fear retaliation or procedural unfairness if they are asked to expose misconduct or toxic elements of the culture. Some assessments could lead to the exposure of poor leadership and unethical or bullying behaviours, which need to be addressed, so leaders must be accountable when weaknesses in the culture are exposed. Exposing a culture that is having a negative impact on the workforce or beneficiaries can erode public confidence in the nonprofit sector and have an impact on donor trust and support (Rhode & Packel, 2009). Using independent researchers can also be useful if an analysis of assumptions and routines is required. A strong propensity to conform to the dominant culture means people are remarkably resistant to the existence of information that is costly or uncomfortable for them. Organisations may not be aware of cultural concerns or feel the need to change unless an independent review is conducted (Manzoni, 2012).

Despite the risks and limitations, there are many benefits to measuring organisational culture in nonprofit organisations. Participatory learning and reflection can yield valuable insight into people's values and behaviours at work and how this affects employee-related outcomes, organisational performance, and other areas of importance to nonprofit leaders.

METHODS TO ASSESS CULTURE IN NONPROFIT ORGANISATIONS

Some theoretically sound and validated tools have been adapted for third-sector organisations even though they were originally designed for public or private organisations. An example is the Competing Values Framework (CVF) tool (Quinn & Rohrbaugh, 1983), a popular framework used by private and public organisations to assess organisational culture (Newton,

2006). The CVF has four organisational culture typologies, and within these cultures, sets of value dimensions, reflecting the understanding of organisational effectiveness among experts, theorists and researchers. The four cultures reflect what organisations value, and their criteria for effectiveness (Quinn & Rohrbaugh, 1983):

1. The human relations culture, which values cohesion and morale, employee consultation and participation, belonging and trust.
2. The open systems culture, which values flexibility and growth, adaptability and change capacity.
3. The internal process culture, which values information and communication, procedures, stability and security.
4. The rational goal culture, which values productivity, profitability, goal setting and efficiency.

Each culture type has different behaviours and beliefs that organisations display, depending on the comparative importance of processes (*means*) and final results (*ends*). The CFV also has sets of competing values that lie within each of these four cultures. The first is *flexibility* versus *control*. Flexibility refers to values such as adaptability, individual initiative and diversity, with control values referring to authority, structure and coordination (Quinn & Rohrbaugh, 1983, p. 370). The other pair of competing values is *internal* versus *external*. These values reflect whether an organisation focuses its attention inwards toward its internal dynamics, or outward towards its external environment. Ideally, organisations have a mix of these competing values, but often some values are more dominant than others, depending on leadership, the organisation's life cycle, and/or the nature of the organisation's work.

Using the CVF to assess the organisational culture of nonprofit human service organisations, Newton and Mazur (2016) asked employees and volunteers from an organisation delivering human services whether their organisation had any of the 16 values identified by the CVF. They also included an additional five values (community spirit, improving others' quality of life, compassion for others, respect for all people, and ethical behaviour), collectively referred to as "altruistic culture", that were not included in the CVF. Several limitations are discussed in the paper, but the research provided interesting insights about culture and its impact on employee perceptions and outcomes.

In order to test the CVF in another nonprofit context, Knight (2014) conducted a study to investigate the relationship between organisational culture, change readiness, and employee attitudes and outcomes. Employees (direct service providers, management, administration and finance staff) from three large nonprofit human service organisations experiencing organisational change and growth participated. The four CVF cultural typologies were measured using a 16-item instrument adapted from Kalliath et al. (1999) to suit the nonprofit sector context. Four items described by Newton (2007) as altruistic culture values were also measured, creating in total a 20-item assessment instrument. Respondents were asked to indicate how much each value was demonstrated by their organisation. Statistical analysis showed that the five cultures were correlated. This provided an opportunity to conduct further analysis to examine if the five cultures could be overarched by even more general factors. As a result of this second-level analysis, the previous five cultures were grouped into just two new factors – *flexible* (human relations, open systems and altruistic) and *control* (rational goal and internal process) as suggested by the CVF.

In an extension of the same study, Knight (2014) tested and validated the CVF model with nonprofit human services organisations. Data analysis once again confirmed the validity of a 16-item CVF instrument and a two-factor structure related to perceptions of workplace *flexible* and *control* cultural values. This model was used to investigate if perceptions of different organisational cultures were related to the change-related variables and job-related attitudes and outcomes under investigation in the study, such as change readiness and job satisfaction (Knight, 2014, p. 135).

It is worth noting that the CVF does not determine which specific culture or values can improve organisational effectiveness, but rather it provides an organisation with the ability to explain organisational behaviour and self-determine which values and culture are important for it. However, using the CVF to explore nonprofit employees' perceptions of organisational culture found some helpful insights for nonprofit leaders and those responsible for employee performance and engagement.

The study (Knight, 2014) concluded that employees working in the Australian human service nonprofit organisations under examination had higher job satisfaction when the organisation valued cohesion, teamwork, morale, trust and respect (characterised by human relations, open systems and altruistic values). Those organisations that placed greater importance on goal attainment, productivity and profitability (characterised by rational goal and internal process values) had employees with lower job satisfaction and higher intention to leave, especially when implementing change. That does not imply that the rational goal and internal process values should not be valued by nonprofit organisations as nonprofit employees are interested and motivated by achievement and results. However, these employees are more likely to have higher job satisfaction if these achievements are in the context of maintaining social networks and gaining self-efficacy so that they can embrace the constant changes that are common within nonprofit organisations (Knight, 2014). Therefore, to retain a vibrant and committed workforce, nonprofit leaders should consider creating and fostering a culture where people feel cared about and supported to achieve personal and organisational goals. This may be more so for human service employees where the work is demanding, and the workforce often experience stress, trauma or change (Schuler et al., 2016). The findings of this study suggest that there are situations where the organisational culture may need to be trauma-informed and a workforce that experiences regular stress may need to be supported. This type of organisation may need to ensure that the culture supports the workforce to feel a collective responsibility to create and maintain a culture that promotes ethical practice and psychological safety (Edmondson & Mogelof, 2005).

The study also highlighted that leadership may be the key to fostering job satisfaction in flexible-oriented cultures (Knight, 2014). Leadership's ability to think culturally, promote sensemaking and courage have all been noted as characteristics that can positively influence change efforts (Brooks, 1996). Meanwhile, poor leadership, lack of trust and poor communication have been blamed as reasons why change efforts fail so often (Gilley et al., 2012). The literature suggests that leaders influence organisational culture, but the culture also influences leaders' decision-making and ability to support change (Martínez et al., 2021) Leaders, therefore, have an important opportunity and responsibility to foster good culture and reduce employee turnover, which is one of the major factors affecting organisational sustainability (Knight, 2014, p. 165).

In summary, culture emerges from collective behaviour because it is fostered and maintained by the people within the organisation. The CVF tool originally developed by Quinn and Rohrbaugh (1983) is a quantitative assessment of organisational culture. It has been tested and validated in nonprofit organisations by Knight (2014), who confirmed that perceptions of organisational culture influence employee attitudes and behaviours, and that the role of leaders is critical when maintaining particular types of culture and fostering change readiness.

PHILANTHROPIC CULTURE

The word "philanthropy" has Greek origins. Sulek (2010) explains that the word *philanthropia* began as a specialised theological and philosophical term to express the concepts of love for humankind. Over the years, the word was used to describe a range of public values and virtues, but since the 20th century it has been used almost exclusively to refer to charitable giving (p. 398). Philanthropic giving of time (volunteering) and money (donations and funding) have always been the cornerstone of the nonprofit sector and while "it is not simply the consequence of a universal altruistic impulse" (Zunz, 2012, p. 294), philanthropy has become an activity in which many people participate as it has mutual benefits for those that give, and those who are beneficiaries of philanthropy.

Philanthropy is so important to the third sector that the cultural typology *philanthropic culture* describes specific cultural values and behaviours that impact on charitable giving policies and practices, and ultimately fundraising success. A philanthropic culture describes the set of shared beliefs and goals an organisation has about giving and fundraising, how fundraisers and donors are valued, how the joy of giving is fostered throughout the workforce and community, and how the organisation celebrates philanthropic gifts: "A culture of philanthropy means that everyone accepts and celebrates the beauty of philanthropy and donors, no matter the type or size of the gift" (Joyaux, 2011, p. 11).

Understanding and measuring philanthropic culture is a new area of research, but it is gaining considerable interest as emerging trends have identified that globalisation, accountability and social media have impacted on giving perspectives and practices. To date, qualitative methods have been used by researchers such as Gallo (2014), Meyer (2015), Sargeant and Bryant (2020), and Smith (2013). Organisations interested in assessing their own philanthropic cultural typology are encouraged to learn what people throughout the organisation think about fundraising, their level of involvement in nurturing donor relationships and expressing donor appreciation, how often program staff refer potential donors to the fundraising team, and how staff and volunteers share the organisation's case for support (Chell, 2016; Crumpton, 2016; Sargeant, 2017; Sargeant & Woodliffe, 2007). Evaluations should also consider how actively engaged board members are with donor identification and stewardship, whether fundraising and fund development is a strategic discussion at board meetings, and whether the CEO effectively communicates fundraising innovation goals and objectives that inspire and engage employees and volunteers. Regular (at least annual) culture assessments should review if and how the organisation supports its fundraisers, provides them with training and leadership development, and ensures they adhere to fundraising codes of conduct. Strategies that effectively support fundraisers can boost an organisation's fundraising capacity and increase philanthropic returns and organisational sustainability (Scaife et al., 2013).

CONCLUSION

Plentiful evidence suggests that the organisational culture of nonprofit organisations is critical, and should be part of the growing dialogue about how these organisations govern themselves, foster social innovation, improve fundraising approaches and service delivery, create shared value, and use philanthropy to achieve organisational effectiveness (Hill & Addis, 2017; Scott, 2014). Organisational culture has a significant role to play in determining the job satisfaction of employees and the performance of an organisation (Bartlett & Bartlett, 2011; Burnes, 1997; Guerra et al., 2005; Tian et al., 2018), so learning what influences culture and whether there are cultural attributes that create productive workplaces and organisational effectiveness is a worthwhile endeavour (Schein & Schein, 2017).

Despite the challenges and limitations, measuring organisational culture is extremely beneficial. Measuring the culture offers an opportunity to the third sector to monitor changes and the perceived balance of efficiency, achieving goals and getting the job done, with the nonprofit values of community service, social impact and philanthropy. It provides organisations with the ability to make strategic decisions concerning employee and organisational outcomes. Leaders and managers can use culture assessments to plan and measure the organisation's ability to attract and retain employees, provide quality services, and attract support. Nonprofit leaders can use culture assessments to guide the allocation of resources, their communication and workforce development strategies, and innovation priorities. The third sector continues to play an important role in society, and, given the changes nonprofit organisations are experiencing, it is imperative that leaders take strategic actions to influence the culture positively, support their workforce, and achieve the organisation's goals.

REFERENCES

ACNC (2018). *Australian Charities Report*. Australian Government. Australian Charities and Not-for-profits Commission (ACNC). Retrieved from https://www.acnc.gov.au/tools/reports/australian-charities-report-2018

Appelbaum, S. H., Berke, J., Taylor, J., & Vazquez, J. A. (2008). The role of leadership during large scale organizational transitions: Lessons from six empirical studies. *Journal of American Academy of Business, Cambridge, 13*(1), 16.

Ashkanasy, N. M., Broadfoot, L. E., & Falkus, S. (2000). Questionnaire measures of organizational culture. In N. M. Ashkanasy, C. P. M. Wilderom, & M. F. Petersen (Eds.), *Handbook of Organizational Culture and Climate* (pp. 131–145). Thousand Oaks: Sage Publications.

Australian Government (2018). *Strengthening for Purpose: Australian Charities and Not-For-Profits Commission Legislation Review 2018*. Commonwealth of Australia. Retrieved from https://treasury.gov.au/publication/p2018-t318031

Ballart, X., & Rico, G. (2018). Public or nonprofit? Career preferences and dimensions of public service motivation. *Public Administration (London), 96*(2), 404–420. doi:10.1111/padm.12403

Banaszak-Holl, J., Castle, N. G., Lin, M., & Spreitzer, G. (2013). An assessment of cultural values and resident-centered culture change in U.S. nursing facilities. *Health Care Management Review, 38*(4), 295–305. doi:10.1097/HMR.0b013e3182678fb0

Bartlett, J. E., & Bartlett, M. E. (2011). Workplace bullying: An integrative literature review. *Advances in Developing Human Resources, 13*(1), 69–84. doi:10.1177/1523422311410651

Bik, O. P. G. (2010). *The Behavior of Assurance Professionals: A Cross-Cultural Perspective*. Delft: Euburon.

Bowers, M. R., Hall, J. R., & Srinivasan, M. M. (2017). Organizational culture and leadership style: The missing combination for selecting the right leader for effective crisis management. *Business Horizons*, *60*(4), 551–563. doi:10.1016/j.bushor.2017.04.001

Bright, L. (2016). Is public service motivation a better explanation of nonprofit career preferences than government career preferences? *Public Personnel Management*, *45*(4), 405–424. doi:10.1177/0091026016676093

Brooks, I. (1996). Leadership of a cultural change process. *Leadership & Organization Development Journal*, *17*(5), 31–37.

Burnes, B. (1997). Organizational choice and organizational change. *Management Decision*, *35*(10), 753–759.

Burston, M. A. (2020). A complex matter: Charitable organisation or corporate institution? A reflection on charity and its applicability in an era of market-driven higher education in Australia. *Critical Studies in Education*, *61*(1), 115–132. doi:10.1080/17508487.2017.1333520

Casey, J. (2016). Comparing nonprofit sectors around the world: What do we know and how do we know it? *Journal of Nonprofit Education and Leadership*, *6*(3). doi:10.18666/JNEL-2016-V6-I3-7583

Chell, K. W. (2016). *Giving and Sharing: The Predictors and Outcomes of online Donor Appreciation.* (Doctor of Philosophy), Queensland University of Technology, Brisbane, Australia.

Connolly, P., & Klein, L. C. (1999). Good growth, bad growth and how to tell the difference. *Nonprofit World*, *17*(3), 32.

Constandt, B., & Willem, A. (2019). The trickle-down effect of ethical leadership in nonprofit soccer clubs. *Nonprofit Management & Leadership*, *29*(3), 401–417. doi:10.1002/nml.21333

Cornelius, M., & Corvington, P. (2012). Nonprofit workforce dynamics. In L. Salamon (Ed.), *The State of Nonprofit America*. Washington, DC: Brookings Institution Press.

Crane, A. (1995). Rhetoric and reality in the greening of organizational culture. *Greener Management International*, *12*, 49–62.

Crumpton, M. A. (2016). Cultivating an organizational effort for development. *The Bottom Line*, *29*(2), 97–113. doi:10.1108/BL-02-2016-0010

Deloitte (2021). Current and Future Context for Social Sector Decision-Makers: A toolkit for understanding and responding to COVID-19's impact to nonprofits and social enterprises. https://www2.deloitte.com/content/dam/Deloitte/us/Documents/about-deloitte/us-deloitte-d2i-current-and-future-context-for-social-sector-decision-makers-june2021.pdf

Deloitte Access Economics (2017). *Economic Contribution of the Australian Charity Sector.* Retrieved from https://www.acnc.gov.au/sites/default/files/Download%20the%20report%20for%20Economic%20contribution%20of%20the%20Australian%20charity%20sector%20%5BPDF%202MB%5D.pdf

Denison, D. R. (1996). What is the difference between organizational culture and organizational climate? A native's point of view on a decade of paradigm wars. *Academy of Management Review*, *21*(3), 619.

Dennis, R. S., & Bocarnea, M. (2005). Development of the servant leadership assessment instrument. *Leadership & Organization Development Journal*, *26*(7/8), 600.

Deshpande, R., & Webster, F. (1989). Organizational culture and marketing: Defining the research. *Journal of Marketing*, *53*(1), 3. doi:10.2307/1251521

Edmondson, A. C., & Mogelof, J. P. (2005). Explaining psychological safety in innovation teams: Organizational culture, team dynamics, or personality? In L. L. Thompson & H.-S. Choi (Eds.), *Creativity and Innovation in Organizational Teams* (pp. 109–136). Mahwah, NJ: Lawrence Erlbaum Associates.

Emery, C. R., & Barker, K. J. (2007). The effect of transactional and transformational leadership styles on the organizational commitment and job satisfaction of customer contact personnel. *Journal of Organizational Culture, Communication and Conflict*, *11*(1), 77.

Fenton, N. E., & Inglis, S. (2007). A critical perspective on organizational values. *Nonprofit Management and Leadership*, *17*(3), 335–347. doi:10.1002/nml.153

Fiordelisi, F., Renneboog, L., Ricci, O., & Lopes, S. S. (2019). Creative corporate culture and innovation. *Journal of International Financial Markets, Institutions & Money*, *63*. doi:10.1016/j.intfin.2019.101137

Flinn, J. (2011). Ethnographic methods in nonprofit management. *Nonprofit and Voluntary Sector Quarterly*, *40*(3), 420–434. doi:10.1177/0899764009346334

Flynn, F. J., Gruenfeld, D., Molm, L. D., & Polzer, J. T. (2011). Social psychological perspectives on power in organizations. *Administrative Science Quarterly*, *56*(4), 495–500. doi:10.1177/0001839212440969

Gallo, M. L. (2014). Creating a culture of giving in Irish higher education: An education in direct(ing) philanthropic giving in Ireland. *European Journal of Higher Education*, *4*(4), 373–387. doi:10.1080/21568235.2014.912948

Gifford, B. D., Zammuto, R. F., Goodman, E. A., & Hill, K. S. (2002). The relationship between hospital unit culture and nurses' quality of work life. *Journal of Healthcare Management*, *47*(1), 13–26.

Gilley, A., Thompson, J., & Gilley, J. W. (2012). Leaders and change: Attend to the uniqueness of individuals. *Journal of Applied Management and Entrepreneurship*, *17*(1), 69–83.

Gioia, D. A., Schultz, M., & Corley, K. G. (2000). Organizational identity, image, and adaptive instability. *Academy of Management Review*, *25*(1), 63.

Goerke, J. (2003). Taking the quantum leap: Nonprofits are now in business. An Australian perspective. *International Journal of Nonprofit and Voluntary Sector Marketing*, *8*(4), 317–327.

Guerra, J., Martinez, I., Munduate, L., & Medina, F. (2005). A contingency perspective on the study of the consequences of conflict types: The role of organizational culture. *European Journal of Work and Organizational Psychology*, *14*(2), 157–176.

Hadley, B., & Goggin, G. (2019). The NDIS and disability arts in Australia: Opportunities and challenges. *Australasian Drama Studies*, *74*, 9–38.

Hill, R., & Addis, R. (2017). *Views from the Impact Investing Playing Field in Australia on What's Happening and What's Needed Next*. Retrieved from http://www.australianadvisoryboard.com/wp-content/uploads/2017/12/20171215_Views-from-the-Field-2017_FINAL.pdf

Hoag, B., & Cooper, C. L. (2006). *Managing Value-Based Organizations: It's Not What You Think*. Cheltenham, UK and Northampton, MA, USA: Edward Elgar Publishing.

Hull, C. E., & Lio, B. H. (2006). Innovation in non-profit and for-profit organizations: Visionary, strategic, and financial considerations. *Journal of Change Management*, *6*(1), 53–65. doi:10.1080/14697010500523418

Jaskyte, K., & Dressler, W. W. (2005). Organizational culture and innovation in nonprofit human service organizations. *Administration in Social Work*, *29*(2), 23–41.

Joyaux, S. P. (2011). *Strategic Fund Development: Building Profitable Relationships that Last* (3rd ed.). Hoboken, NJ: John Wiley & Sons.

Kalliath, T. J., Bluedorn, A. C., & Gillespie, D. F. (1999). A confirmatory factor analysis of the competing values instrument. *Educational and Psychological Measurement*, *59*(1), 143–158.

Knight, R. L. (2014). *Organisational Culture, Change Readiness and Retention: A Human Services Perspective*. Queensland University of Technology.

Ko, W. W., & Liu, G. (2021). The transformation from traditional nonprofit organizations to social enterprises: An institutional entrepreneurship perspective. *Journal of Business Ethics*, *171*(1), 15–32. https://doi.org/10.1007/s10551-020-04446-z

Linnenluecke, M. K., & Griffiths, A. (2010). Corporate sustainability and organizational culture. *Journal of World Business*, *45*(4), 357–366.

Livorsi, D., Knobloch, M. J., Blue, L. A., Swafford, K., Maze, L., Riggins, K., . . . Safdar, N. (2016). A rapid assessment of barriers and facilitators to safety culture in an intensive care unit. *International Nursing Review*, *63*(3), 372–376. http://dx.doi.org/10.1111/inr.12254

Lucas, J. W., Baxter, A. R., & Huffman, M. (2012). Power, influence, and diversity in organizations. *Annals of the American Academy of Political and Social Science*, *639*(1), 49–70.

Lyons, M. (2001). *Third Sector: The Contribution of Non-profit and Cooperative Enterprise in Australia*. Sydney: Allen & Unwin.

Lyons, M., & Hasan, S. (2002). Researching Asia's third sector. *VOLUNTAS: International Journal of Voluntary and Nonprofit Organizations*, *13*(2), 107–112. doi:10.1023/A:1016091620849

Maier, F., Meyer, M., & Steinbereithner, M. (2016). Nonprofit organizations becoming business-like: A systematic review. *Nonprofit And Voluntary Sector Quarterly*, *45*(1), 64–86. doi:10.1177/0899764014561796

Manzoni, J. F. (2012). Building and nurturing a high-performance–high-integrity corporate culture. *Studies in Managerial and Financial Accounting*, *25*, 41–63. doi:10.1108/S1479-3512(2012)0000025005

Martin, J. (2002). *Organizational Culture: Mapping the Terrain*. Thousand Oaks, CA: Sage Publications.

Martínez, C., Skeet, A. G., & Sasia, P. M. (2021). Managing organizational ethics: How ethics becomes pervasive within organizations. *Business Horizons*, *64*(1), 83–92. doi:10.1016/j.bushor.2020.09.008

Maslowski, R. (2006). A review of inventories for diagnosing school culture. *Journal of Educational Administration*, *44*(1), 6–35. doi:10.1108/09578230610642638

McCrindle (2019). *Australian Community Trends Report National Research Study*. McCrindle Research, Norwest, NSW. Retrieved from https://clarety-acf.s3.amazonaws.com/userimages/Resources/ACT _Report_McCrindle_Feb2019.pdf

McDonald, R. E. (2007). An investigation of innovation in nonprofit organizations: The role of organizational mission. *Nonprofit and Voluntary Sector Quarterly*, *36*(2), 256–281.

McGregor-Lowndes, M. (1998). An examination of recent taxation amendments, corporate law reforms and Queensland legislative reforms affecting nonprofit organisations. Working Paper.

McGregor-Lowndes, M., Crittall, M., Conroy, D., Keast, R., Baker, C., Barraket, J., & Scaife, W. (2017). *Individual Giving and Volunteering: Giving Australia 2016*. Commissioned by the Australian Government Department of Social Services. Brisbane, Queensland: The Australian Centre for Philanthropy and Nonprofit Studies, Queensland University of Technology, Centre for Social Impact Swinburne, Swinburne University of Technology and the Centre for Corporate Public Affairs.

Merchant, A., Ford, J. B., & Sargeant, A. (2010). Charitable organizations' storytelling influence on donors' emotions and intentions. *Journal of Business Research*, *63*(7), 754–762. doi:10.1016/j.jbusres .2009.05.013

Meyer, M. (2015). Perceived role of registered nurses in advancing a culture of philanthropy in a healthcare environment (Order No. 3687603). Available from ProQuest Central; ProQuest Dissertations & Theses Global, 1668381758.

Milbourn, B., Black, M. H., & Buchanan, A. (2019). Why people leave community service organizations: A mixed methods study. *VOLUNTAS: International Journal of Voluntary and Nonprofit Organizations*, *30*(1), 272–281. doi:10.1007/s11266-018-0005-z

Mulgan, G. (2019). *Social Innovation in the 2020s*. Park Hill, Bristol, UK: Policy Press.

Newton, C. J. (2006). *An Exploration of Workplace Stressors and Employee Adjustment: An Organisational Culture Perspective*. Doctor of Philosophy, University of Queensland, Brisbane.

Newton, C. J. (2007). Organizational culture and value congruence in a human service nonprofit organization: A work stressor–employee adjustment perspective. Paper presented at the Association for Research on Nonprofit Organizations and Voluntary Action, Atlanta, GA.

Newton, C. J., & Mazur, A. K. (2016). Value congruence and job-related attitudes in a nonprofit organization: a competing values approach. *International Journal of Human Resource Management*, *27*(10), 1013–1033. doi:10.1080/09585192.2015.1053962

O'Connell, A., Martin, F., & Chia, J. (2013). Law, policy and politics in Australia's recent not-for-profit sector reforms. *Australian Tax Forum*, *28*(2), 289–315.

Ógáin, E. N., Lumley, T., & Pritchard, D. (2012). *Making An Impact: Impact Measurement Among Charities and Social Enterprises in the UK*. Retrieved from http://www.managingforimpact.org/sites/ default/files/resource/ni_ogain_2012_making-an-impact.pdf

Owczarzak, J., Broaddus, M., & Pinkerton, S. (2016). Audit culture: Unintended consequences of accountability practices in evidence-based programs. *American Journal of Evaluation*, *37*(3), 326–343. doi:10.1177/1098214015603502

Pagnoni, L. A. (2013). *The Nonprofit Fundraising Solution: Powerful Revenue Strategies to Take You to the Next Level* (1st ed.). New York: AMACOM.

Parzefall, M., & Salin, D. (2010). Perceptions of and reactions to workplace bullying: A social exchange perspective. *Human Relations*, *63*(6), 761–780.

Pettijohn, S., & Boris, E. (2018). Testing nonprofit state culture: Its impact on the health of the nonprofit sector. *Nonprofit Policy Forum*, *9*(3). doi:10.1515/npf-2018-0012

Phillips, S. D., & Smith, S. R. (2011). *Governance and Regulation in the Third Sector: International Perspectives*. New York: Routledge.

Proctor, T. (2013). *Creative Problem Solving for Managers: Developing Skills for Decision Making and Innovation* (4th ed.). Florence, KY, USA: Routledge.

Productivity Commission. (2016). *Introducing Competition and Informed User Choice into Human Services: Identifying Sectors for Reform*. Study Report. Retrieved from https://www.pc.gov.au/

inquiries/completed/human-services/identifying-reform/report/human-services-identifying-reform
.pdf

Quinn, R. E., & Rohrbaugh, J. (1983). A spacial model of effectiveness criteria: Towards a competing values approach to organizational analysis. *Management Science, 29*(3), 363–377.

Rhode, D., & Packel, A. (2009). Ethics and nonprofits. *Stanford Social Innovation Review, 7*(3), 29–35.

Rosenfeld, L. B., Richman, J. M., & May, S. K. (2004). Information adequacy, job satisfaction and organizational culture in a dispersed-network organization. *Journal of Applied Communication Research, 32*(1), 28.

Salamon, L. M., & Sokolowski, S. W. (2015). *The Resilient Sector Revisited: The New Challenge to Nonprofit America* (2nd ed.). Washington, DC: Brookings Institution Press.

Salamon, L. M., & Sokolowski, W. (2018). The size and composition of the European third sector. In B. Enjolras, L .M. Salamon, K. H. Sivesind, & A. Zimmer (Eds.), *The Third Sector as a Renewable Resource for Europe: Concepts, Impacts, Challenges and Opportunities* (pp. 49–94). Cham: Springer International Publishing.

Sargeant, A. (2017). *Fundraising Principles and Practice* (2nd ed.). Hoboken: Wiley.

Sargeant, A., & Bryant, E. (2020). *Towards a Philanthropic Orientation*. Institute for Sustainable Philanthropy. Devon, UK. Retrieved from https://www.philanthropy-institute.org.uk/

Sargeant, A., & Woodliffe, L. (2007). Gift giving: An interdisciplinary review. *International Journal of Nonprofit and Voluntary Sector Marketing, 12*(4), 275–307. doi:10.1002/nvsm.308

Scaife, W. A., Williamson, A., & McDonald, K. (2013). *Who's Asking for What? Fundraising and Leadership in Australian Nonprofits*. Australian Centre of Philanthropy and Nonprofit Studies, QUT. Retrieved from https://eprints.qut.edu.au/59196/

Schein, E. (1992). *Organizational Culture and Leadership* (2nd ed.). San Francisco: Jossey-Bass Publishers.

Schein, E. (2004). *Organizational Culture and Leadership* (3rd ed.). San Francisco: Jossey-Bass Publishers.

Schein, E., & Schein, P. (2017). *Organizational Culture and Leadership* (5th ed.). Hoboken, NJ: Wiley & Sons.

Schuler, B. R., Bessaha, M. L., & Moon, C. A. (2016). Addressing secondary traumatic stress in the human services: A comparison of public and private sectors. *Human Service Organizations: Management, Leadership & Governance, 40*(2), 94–106. doi:10.1080/23303131.2015.1124060

Scott, M. A. (2014). *Organisational Factors that Drive Fundraising Effectiveness in Australian Health Charities.* Queensland University of Technology.

Shilbury, D., & Moore, K. A. (2006). A study of organizational effectiveness for national olympic sporting organizations. *Nonprofit and Voluntary Sector Quarterly, 35*(1), 5–38. doi:10.1177/0899764005279512

Smith, J. M. (2013). Philanthropic identity at work: Employer influences on the charitable giving attitudes and behaviors of employees. *International Journal of Business Communication, 50*(2), 128–151. doi:10.1177/0021943612474989

Social Enterprise Alliance. (2010). *Succeeding at Social Enterprise: Hard-Won Lessons for Nonprofits and Social Entrepreneurs* (1st ed.). San Francisco: Jossey-Bass.

Spencer, S. B., & Skalaban, I. A. (2018). Organizational culture in civic associations in Russia. *VOLUNTAS: International Journal of Voluntary and Nonprofit Organizations, 29*(5), 1080–1097. doi:10.1007/s11266-017-9925-2

Sulek, M. (2010). On the classical meaning of philanthrôpía. *Nonprofit and Voluntary Sector Quarterly, 39*(3), 385–408. doi:10.1177/0899764009333050

Sullivan, P. (2010). *The Aboriginal Community Sector and the Effective Delivery of Services: Acknowledging the Role of Indigenous Sector Organisations*. DKCRC Working Paper 73. Desert Knowledge CRC. Alice Springs.

Taras, V., Rowney, J., & Steel, P. (2009). Half a century of measuring culture: Review of approaches, challenges, and limitations based on the analysis of 121 instruments for quantifying culture. *Journal of International Management, 15*(4), 357–373. doi:10.1016/j.intman.2008.08.005

Taras, V., Rowney, J., & Steel, P. D. G. (2007). *Half a Century of Measuring Culture: Approaches, Challenges, Limitations and Suggestions Based on the Analysis of 121 Instruments for Quantifying Culture*. Paper presented at the Academy of Management.

Tian, M., Deng, P., Zhang, Y., & Salmador, M. P. (2018). How does culture influence innovation? A systematic literature review. *Management Decision, 56*(5), 1088–1107. doi:10.1108/MD-05-2017-0462

Tucker, R. W., McCoy, W. J., & Evans, L. C. (1990). Can questionnaires objectively assess organisational culture? *Journal of Managerial Psychology, 5*(4), 4–11.

Urban Institute (2020). *The Nonprofit Sector in Brief 2019*. Retrieved from https://nccs.urban.org/publication/nonprofit-sector-brief-2019#the-nonprofit-sector-in-brief-2019

Valentinov, V. (2010). Internal organization and governance. In B. A. Seaman & D. R. Young (Eds.), *Handbook of Research on Nonprofit Economics and Management*. Cheltenham, UK and Northampton, MA, USA: Edward Elgar Publishing.

Wanberg, C. R., & Banas, J. T. (2000). Predictors and outcomes of openness to changes in a reorganizing workplace. *Journal of Applied Psychology, 85*(1), 132.

Warrick, D. D. (2017). What leaders need to know about organizational culture. *Business Horizons, 60*(3), 395-404. doi:10.1016/j.bushor.2017.01.011

Willems, J., Boenigk, S., & Jegers, M. (2014). Seven trade-offs in measuring nonprofit performance and effectiveness. *VOLUNTAS: International Journal of Voluntary and Nonprofit Organizations, 25*(6), 1648–1670. doi:10.1007/s11266-014-9446-1

Yanti, S., & Dahlan, J. (2017). The effects of organizational culture, leadership behavior, and job satisfaction on employee organizational committment. *Journal of Positive Management, 8*(4), 80–96. doi: 10.12775/JPM.2017.132

Zafft, C. R., Adams, S. G., & Matkin, G. S. (2009). Measuring leadership in self-managed teams using the competing values framework. *Journal of Engineering Education, 98*(3), 273–282.

Zunz, O. (2012). *Philanthropy in America: A History*. Princeton, NJ: Princeton University Press.

16. Leadership capabilities: the influence of organizational purpose and culture in the nonprofit sector

Adelle J. Bish, Karen Becker and Bernd Irmer

INTRODUCTION

Leadership has been shown to have a strong influence on the culture of nonprofit organizations and therefore a focus on understanding and enhancing effectiveness of leadership in this context is critical. However, the nonprofit sector is not homogenous, and in this chapter it is argued that the underlying organizational purpose may impact on the organizational culture and therefore the leadership capabilities required. In the nonprofit sector, a growing emphasis in recent years on improved governance and accountability, and balancing competing stakeholder demands has intensified the focus on leadership capabilities. Despite this, the examination of leadership capabilities and the extent to which they may vary depending on nonprofit organization purpose or type has been limited.

This chapter draws on a comparative case study of the similarities and differences in leadership capabilities that are required in different types of nonprofit organizations. This study illustrates how two different types of nonprofits, established to serve differing purposes and missions, with differing culture and values, subsequently require different leadership capabilities. The research adopted a user-centered approach to understand the participants' mental models about leadership and culture, and the value and contribution of this research technique is also highlighted.

A SECTOR WITH DIVERSE LEADERSHIP NEEDS

The nonprofit sector is experiencing significant disruption in relation to governance, management, business models and funding structures (Anheier, 2014; Paton et al., 2007). In turn, these changes have had substantial impact on the expectations of leaders in nonprofit organizations (Paton et al., 2007) and fueled research interest in appropriate models for organizational culture (Langer & LeRoux, 2017), governance and management (McClusky, 2002; Paton et al., 2007; Stid & Bradach, 2009). Research indicates that leadership in a nonprofit organization is challenging due in part to the characteristics of the sector including "centrality of values; complexity of resource generation; reliance on volunteers; difficulties in judging organizational performance; lack of clarity about accountability" (Lyons, 2001, p. 22), together with a scarcity of resources and increasing demand for services (Anheier, 2014; Hamlin et al., 2011). In light of these challenges there has been intensified interest in investigating how to be an effective leader in this particular context (e.g., Hamlin et al., 2011; Thach & Thompson, 2007).

Now, with continued expansion and impact of the nonprofit sector, we argue that the consideration of context needs to delve deeper to develop a greater appreciation of the diversity *within* the nonprofit sector. Leadership capability models need to be able to differentiate between the diverse requirements of different *types* of nonprofit organizations (Anheier, 2014). As shown in emerging literature in the nonprofit field, leadership capabilities may differ not only from those in other sectors (Bish & Becker, 2016) but also within the sector based on the purpose of the nonprofit (Hamlin et al., 2011; Thach & Thompson, 2007). Therefore, this study aimed to better understand the differences in leadership requirements *within* the sector, derived from the influence of the type of nonprofit organization in question and its organizational purpose and objectives.

In addition to organizational purpose, leadership has a strong influence on the culture within nonprofit organizations (Jaskyte, 2004). As nonprofits increasingly need to be agile and responsive to changing needs there is increased demand for nonprofit leaders to be proficient in establishing and sustaining an organizational culture that meets these needs (Langer & LeRoux, 2017; McMurray et al., 2013). Indeed, Jaskyte's (2004) exploration of the influence of leadership practices on levels of nonprofit innovation closely examined the role of the leader in creating organizational culture. Jaskyte (2004) found that the answer to how the leader influences innovative behaviors is complicated and connected to the interplay between leadership and culture as leader behaviors create and sustain alignment with core values and practices that support behaviors required for organizational effectiveness. Similarly, Schein (1985) argued that leadership and culture are weaved together. A leader's beliefs, values and assumptions have a major impact on the formation of culture and on the transmission of this culture through human resource management practices such as recruitment and selection, development and rewards to support desired behaviors (Schein, 2010).

In a nonprofit environment, it would be expected that an effective leader uses their understanding of the purpose, mission and external operating environment to determine appropriate organizational responses. This includes consideration of culture. For example, Langer and LeRoux's (2017) study of nonprofit executives found that leaders in nonprofits are cognizant of the need to shape organizational culture in order to effectively perform essential activities to serve the nonprofit purpose. The influence of culture also extends to ensuring the continued attraction and retention of employees and volunteers who are specifically motivated to work in this sector because of their values (LeRoux & Feeney, 2013; Schepers et al., 2005), and career growth aspirations, and to stay within a nonprofit while these needs are met (Peachey et al., 2013).

Therefore, we know that any consideration of leadership performance within the nonprofit sector needs to acknowledge the dynamic relationship between leadership and organizational culture. Nonprofit leaders need to both understand organizational culture and its role in shaping desired behaviors (Schein, 2010) and have the capabilities required to act on this knowledge. Furthermore, we acknowledge the interconnectedness of the parts within the system, particularly in relation to purpose, strategy and managing organizational culture (Kilmann, 2003). In this chapter, we are specifically interested in how differences in nonprofit purpose, mission and organizational culture may have a corresponding influence on the knowledge, skills and experience (the capabilities) required of leaders within this sector.

THE INFLUENCE OF PURPOSE AND CULTURE

The nonprofit sector is diverse and includes different types of nonprofits operating as formal organizations that are independent of government (Lyons, 2001), including "private, voluntary, nonprofit organizations and associations" established to achieve varied outcomes (Anheier, 2014, p. 4). At the most fundamental level, Anheier (2014) separates nonprofit organizations into either member-serving or public-serving. Typically, member-serving nonprofits, such as cooperatives, trade unions and advocacy groups, exist to provide benefits to their members, while public-serving nonprofits are focused on providing services to the community in general, such as medical research, human services programs, education and health services. The diversity within the sector is also shaped by geographical region, history, politics and culture (Boris, 1999). This diversity creates corresponding variety in strategy, forms and foci (Anheier, 2014; Moore, 2000), and approaches to managing people and culture (Ridder & McCandless, 2010; Ridder et al., 2012) in order to achieve objectives. Increased competition for funding sources, and the challenges associated with exploring new avenues of funding, has also altered business models within the sector. As leaders navigate this changing landscape they face "operational and cultural challenges in the pursuit of commercial funding" in order to achieve their mission (Dees, 1998, p. 56). Indeed, there is continued demand in this sector for leaders who are able to align purpose and strategy with improved execution in order to create sustainable futures, where each nonprofit can continue to serve their purpose and meet stakeholder needs (Weerawardena et al., 2010). In an effort to further advance investigation of the diversity within the nonprofit sector, this research explores how differences in purpose, strategy and culture may also impact the leadership capabilities that are required in these organizations.

NONPROFIT LEADERSHIP CAPABILITIES

The nonprofit sector has many passionate individuals in leadership positions. However, questions persist about what leaders need to be able to do in the sector, particularly in terms of balancing competing strategic demands (Stid & Bradach, 2009), and delivering core services in a manner consistent with organizational values (Cheverton, 2007; McMurray, et al., 2013). Furthermore, the central focus on values evident in nonprofit cultures results in intense scrutiny of the degree of alignment between management behaviors and organizational values in achieving objectives (Coultas et al., 2012; McMurray et al. 2010). In addition, nonprofit leaders must respond to the expectations of multiple stakeholders with diverse and not necessarily complementary needs (Kong, 2007). It is not surprising then that nonprofit executives report that managing in this sector means working within a "complicated and ambiguous world" (Wilensky & Hansen, 2001, p. 223). Indeed, the complexity of managing in the nonprofit environment is exacerbated by changes in funding and governance structures and business models requiring nonprofits to be more agile and responsive. Nonprofit leaders are increasingly required to facilitate organizational change and foster cultures of creativity and innovation (Lutz Allen et al., 2013), in addition to developing financial management and strategic planning skills (Wang & Ashcraft, 2012).

Table 16.1   Comparison of case organizations

	Case A	Case B
Focus of organization	Public-serving	Member-serving
Purpose	Service provider and fund-raising body for people affected by a particular medical condition	Advocacy and provision of information and advice to member organizations
Employees	Approximately 250	Approximately 70
Volunteer workforce	Yes, approximately 2000	No
Funding source	Philanthropy, fund-raising initiatives, donations	Membership fees, fee-for-service work

These significant changes are likely to alter and broaden the capabilities required to be an effective nonprofit leader, raising questions about what capabilities leaders need, whether they have them, and how such capabilities can be developed.

Yukl (2012) proposed a framework of leadership capabilities consisting of the meta-categories of task-oriented behaviors, relations-oriented behaviors, change-related behaviors and externally-focused behaviors. Subsequent research has applied the framework developed by Yukl and colleagues (Yukl, 2012; Yukl et al., 2002) to the study of managers in the nonprofit sector and expanded its components to acknowledge the nonprofit context (Bish & Becker, 2016). It was reported that nonprofit managers do indeed engage in behaviors relating to tasks, relationships, change and external issues as identified in the Yukl (2012) framework, but additional behaviors were added within these meta-categories. There were also two additional meta-categories identified: nonprofit orientation and personal knowledge and experience (Bish & Becker, 2016).

Taken collectively, there is a growing body of evidence that the nonprofit sector has distinctive leadership capability requirements compared to the private and public sectors (Bish & Becker, 2016; Hamlin et al., 2011; Thach & Thompson, 2007) and that these unique aspects must be considered when attempting to adopt leadership approaches from other sectors (Cheverton, 2007). The study reported in this chapter takes a necessary step to compare leadership capability requirements between two types of nonprofit organizations, with the possibility that differences are interwoven with organizational culture.

COMPARATIVE CASE STUDIES

A qualitative comparative case study approach (Yin, 2013) was employed for this study, given the dearth of research into leadership capabilities in different types of nonprofit organizations. Our focus was on in-depth analysis, comparing two types of nonprofit organizations. Based on the classification framework presented earlier, a purposive sampling strategy (Yin, 1999) was utilized to select organizations that varied in terms of purpose, strategy and focus (a member-serving and a public-serving nonprofit organization), as we expected corresponding differences in terms of leadership capabilities. Both organizations were located within one Australian state. Table 16.1 provides a summary of the key differences between the two cases. Case A is a public-serving, charitable organization relying on private donations and philanthropy to fund its research and support activities focusing on a specific disease in the community. Case A employs medical specialists to provide advice to patients and families and a range of program employees to create, coordinate and manage fundraising activities. The organization has approximately 250 employees as well as a regular volunteer workforce of approximately 2000. In Case A, 21 participants were interviewed, representing 42 percent of the leaders in the organization.

Case B is a member-serving advocacy group employing a range of specialists (approximately 70 employees) with technical knowledge to provide advocacy, policy and informational services to member organizations. This type of nonprofit is classified as a member-serving nonprofit and is a private association, where membership is non-compulsory. In Case B, 15 participants were interviewed, representing 94 percent of the leaders in the organization.

Data Collection and Analysis

One-on-one interviews were conducted with the participants using three core questions: "what should a leader *know* in order to be a good leader in this organization?", "what should a leader be able *to do* in order to be a good leader in this organization?" and "think of someone in this organization that you believe is very capable as a leader – what is it about them that makes you consider them a good leader?". In addition to these three interview questions, the interviewer applied a user-centered research method of card sorting. Card sorting is a form of methodology referred to as Q methodology and was developed in 1935 by William Stephenson, a physicist-psychologist (Brown, 1996). Q methodology typically refers to a form of factor analysis that considers differences between individuals rather than between variables. In this case, the method sought to look at the differences between the participants' perspectives on leadership capabilities. This method involves the provision of a set of cards as stimulus, each showing a single word or construct. Card sort has been advocated as a valuable method for leadership studies that focus on capabilities or competencies (Jahrami et al., 2009), although reporting on its use in recent studies is limited. Card sort allows for the participant to consider each stimulus separately and rank these based on level of importance (Santos, 2006). In this research, card sort was used to vary the activities within the data collection stage and engage the participants in a meaningful way with the leadership concepts under consideration.

Cards were designed with a single capability listed for consideration by the participant. To develop the list of capabilities, we started with the fifteen leadership behaviors from Yukl's (2012) taxonomy of leadership behaviors. The HR representative from each organization was asked to assist in contextualizing the words and terms to capabilities adequately covering each of the meta-categories whilst also being meaningful to the employees in their organization. Table 16.2 shows the words used in the two case organizations. Participants were asked to consider each of the cards in turn, and to identify the most critical capabilities for leaders in their organization.

At the conclusion of the data collection phase, all interviews were recorded and transcribed verbatim. The data were analyzed applying theoretical thematic analysis (Braun & Clarke, 2006) to classify the data according to the taxonomy of leadership behaviors (Yukl, 2012) and the extended framework (Bish & Becker, 2016).

Table 16.2   Capabilities in card sort for each case organization

Change management
Client focus
Communication
Community engagement
Compliance with policies and legislation
Conflict management/resolution
Continuous improvement
Decision making
Goal setting/results oriented
Innovation and creativity
Managing diversity
Managing safety and health
Managing teams
Mentoring
Negotiation and influencing
Performance management
Problem solving
Project management
Relationship building/collaboration
Resilience
Self-awareness
Managing volunteers (Case A only)
Promotes [company] values and vision (Case B only)
Stakeholder engagement (Case B only)
Strategic planning (Case B only)

FINDINGS OF CASE STUDY ANALYSIS

Findings are presented in two sections. First, we present the analysis of responses to the open-ended interview questions relating to the expectations of leaders in the organization. Second, the card sort results are shown, highlighting the differences in leadership capability requirements between the two case organizations. Discussion of these findings explores the extent to which the nonprofit's purpose and culture impacts on the expectations of leadership capabilities.

Interview Findings

Task-oriented meta-category
Yukl (2012, p. 68) argues that the primary objective of this meta-category is to "accomplish work in an efficient and reliable way". In both cases, we found evidence of the seven task-oriented capabilities, with Table 16.3 presenting examples of how these capabilities were described by the participants in each case.

Table 16.3   *Task-oriented knowledge and capabilities*

Behavior	Example interview quotes	
	Case A	Case B
Clarifying	Often it's somebody who can direct and guide people so that they then don't focus on trivial types of things that tend to take up more of their time than it should. (A5)	And then they have got to have good … skills to form the narrative with those people, "This is what we are doing. This is why we are doing it. This has got value. If we do this, this is the pay-off" (B2)
Planning	To be always on the ball and thinking and come up with initiatives and ideas that are on a more specific level than the strategic plan but would support that plan (A11) You need to know that you have got appropriate resources and timing and be able to give timeframes for when that work can be done (A13)	We obviously do a lot of planning at the start of year and budget process. Set the agenda for the 12 months. And that is a collective type of process because it can be a little bit competitive around resources and things like that (B4)
Monitoring operations	So being able to operate and keep the finger on the pulse when you have got eight/ten people across the state doing all sorts of different things, which is quite a challenge (A21)	In terms of nipping it in the bud and dealing with it on a daily basis, to make sure that we don't an escalation and things becoming performance problems (B4)
Problem solving	Deal with challenges, themselves, and sort out the problems that might arise, for them to be equipped enough to deal with those challenges and things (A12)	Dealing with issues as they come up (B7)
Navigating organizational politics	They have been around a lot and they know where/ who they need to go and speak to, to get things (A9) [you need a manager] who understands the game of – I don't know what it is – the territory of the hierarchy (A10)	It is part of all those soft skills; to know when you can do things and when you can't (B4)
Implementing policies and procedures	It's about having structure and having the appropriate policies and procedures in place … (A4)	Doing recruitment properly [according to the policy] is really, really important (B7)
Managing projects	I think they need to be able to project manage; they need to be able to manage small teams of staff and they need to have project and program leadership skills (A19)	I also undertake a number of internal projects as a sort of internal project manager (B5)

Whilst there was evidence of all task-oriented capabilities in both organizations, we compared the extent to which participants emphasized *particular* capabilities as important and this comparison shows a number of key differences. In Case A, the capability that was most mentioned was that of clarifying; however, in Case B the focus was most heavily on planning. The sense in Case A was that most planning was done by a few senior managers in the organization and therefore the overall focus was predominantly on ensuring fostering an understanding of organizational plans; that is clarifying rather than planning per se. However, in Case B, most of the leaders were responsible for the planning within their area. Those in Case B believed that their lean organizational context made it more difficult to work 'on' the business because as a leader they are heavily engaged 'in' the business, and this may explain in part their need to consciously focus on planning. This particular difference may be more directly related to differences in organizational structure and size than type of nonprofit (public-serving vs.

member-serving), however, it could also be suggested that Case B has also developed a culture that emphasizes the importance of daily planning for all leaders, rather than being seen to drive planning efforts through key individuals.

The other major point of difference was the fact that managing projects and navigating organizational politics (two of the capabilities in the extended framework) were much less likely to be raised by those in Case B than those in Case A. This may reflect the different focus of Case B with less project work and more ongoing advocacy and support, together with a heavy focus externally on members. This difference in focus appeared to remove the attention from internal politics and service to reinforce a culture that emphasized the importance of building positive external stakeholder relationships.

Table 16.3   *Task-oriented knowledge and capabilities*

Behavior	Example interview quotes	
	Case A	Case B
Supporting	So knowing how to deal with each individual employee to get the most out of each (A1)	I do promote the sense of connectedness and family (B2)
Developing	Certainly let me know if there are any training deficits within the team, so that we can seek support for that (A13)	As a manager, it's that ability to help people grow or help people grow themselves (B6)
Recognizing	I think it's really important that everybody feels that what they do is really valuable and really – just important. Because I think everything fits (A17)	Again, apart from handing out an award, I am linking it back to our corporate objectives …. So what I have been trying do is shine a light, I suppose, on, "Look at this great outcome that we have been able to get for our members" (B1)
Empowering	Not having that solution in the head, not actually fixing it, but saying, "Okay, what do we need to do to fix it?" (A4)	What can we be doing to ensure that the staff and team are participative in the processes of identify customer need; participative in the process of being creative around what sort of solutions and things we might be able to deliver in that space (B1)
Relating	Understanding those communication styles and how can you understand your team to know how are they going to respond best, so that your outcomes can be achieved. (A2)	I think it comes from those sort of skills in relation to communication, listening, all the things that you need to lead people into providing that two-way street (B4) Get up and talk. I am old-school. You have a relationship first and everything else flows from it. You have got to work at it (B6).
Collaborating	…and how to engage and promote communication and collaboration across the team (A21) A bit more collaborative with other departments in the organization, to make sure that everything aligns (A18)	…work with others to do things (B5) Obviously, the communication and skills that everyone brings to the table in terms of communicating with their peers across – they have similar skills (B4)
Managing conflict	…they [the team] really had no idea of half the stuff that was actually going on and if ever there was any little conflict or whatever, I would deal with that particular person but usually in private sort of thing, so not in front of the team (A17) They are great at managing people and dealing with conflict (A12)	They don't need to be managed but people who don't need to be managed have issues from time to time that need to be resolved (B5)

Table 16.5   Change-oriented knowledge and capabilities

Behavior	Example interview quotes	
	Case A	Case B
Advocating change	I think that's what we are charged with; being able to see the opportunities for the organization and go out and do that kind of "look across all the different organizations as a benchmark and see what we can bring back to [organization] and how we can grow things" (A6)	So I am more the sort of ring leader, I suppose, and identifying the opportunities within the teams and making it real, I suppose (B1)
Envisioning change	They need to set the vision for the business. Be very clear on what it is they want this place to look like in one, three, ten years from now; and be able to communicate that effectively to my group (A7)	You have got to be a bit more forward-looking for the organization … You have got to look at "where do we want to be in ten years' time?" (B6)
Encouraging innovation	They suggest encouraging us to talk about each other's business which I agree is the way to go and being open and accountable and being able to look at each other's areas and see opportunities (A6)	What's a more creative way that we can respond to that? (B4)
Facilitating collective learning	A willingness to learn from others and teach others at the same time; an openness to being challenged or questioned and a fearlessness to question upwards as well if they need to (A5)	That is part of the workforce planning; about benchmarking, collecting metrics, benching against others; so knowing how well you are travelling and the sharing of ideas with the organization (B6)

Relations-oriented meta-category

The primary objective of the relations-oriented meta-category is to "increase the quality of human resources and relations" (Yukl, 2012, p. 68). Again, in both cases we found evidence of all seven relations-oriented capabilities. The examples shown in Table 16.4 illustrate that leaders are expected to have a primary focus on developing and supporting people.

Both cases placed the heaviest emphasis on developing people; however, after this, we found differences in terms of the emphasis placed on the particular relations-oriented capabilities. In Case A, the capability that was next highest cited was managing conflict. This is in stark contrast to Case B, where this capability was the least mentioned. It appears that leaders in Case A may be more likely to encounter conflict, perhaps due to the more political nature of this organization. As noted previously, leaders in Case A need to be able to navigate internal politics to be effective in their task-related capabilities, while this was not a highly identified aspect of leadership behavior or culture in Case B.

Change-oriented meta-category

The primary objectives of the change-oriented meta-category are to "increase innovation, collective learning and adaptation to the external environment" (Yukl, 2012, p. 68), and we found evidence of the importance of change-related capabilities in both cases. Specifically, to manage change, leaders must be able to advocate for change, envision change and encourage innovation, as well being able to explain the impact of change and appropriate responses to it. Participants expressed the need for leaders to be both agile and responsive to change as well as proactive in initiating required changes. Table 16.5 presents examples of these capabilities in each case.

Table 16.6   *External knowledge and capabilities*

Behavior	Example interview quotes	
	Case A	Case B
Networking	Media, and people, and communities. It's just that stakeholder management stuff. So an ability to do that (A20)	The roles require a very high level of relationship management both internally and externally (B5)
	A lot of public health is based on relationships/ partnerships with different industries and stuff like that (A18)	The managers in the policy area, the people who deal directly with membership, they have to have the capacity to engage with people at different levels … it is extremely diverse. And from a positional point of view, you are dealing with mayors, councils, who are elected on not competency but popularity; some extremely capable, some worldly, some extremely incapable and tunnel vision (B1).
External monitoring	They need to be aware of what's going on in the outside world and how it kind of measures up or how it's trending and that kind of thing. (A13)	…have to have a very good understanding of what's happening across all of our members and what's happening across the industry and Local Government (B4)
Representing	So someone you trust to be your advocate … So I have confidence that what we are trying to achieve will be well-represented and thoughtfully represented, to give it the best chance of coming into reality (A10)	…the GMs [General Managers] play a role in being, for want of a better word, figureheads or representatives of the organization as a whole (B4)

As with the previous meta-categories a comparison of the emphasis placed on particular capabilities shows some key differences. Case A has a focus on envisioning change, followed by facilitating collective learning about the change process, and encouraging innovation. On the other hand, encouraging innovation was the most highly identified capability in Case B, followed by envisioning change. This disparity could be a result of Case B operating in a member-services nonprofit environment, where members demand innovative solutions. Conversely, leaders in Case A are driven by a different focus in the field of health, where they are facing increased fundraising competition and demands to rapidly adjust to changing donation behaviors. In this environment, it appears that the role of a leader is more about helping staff to understand the change and to "paint a picture" of what it will be like in order to manage the change processes effectively for staff and volunteers and to providing consistency in terms of services provided to those in need.

External meta-category

Yukl (2012, p. 68) identifies that the primary objectives of the external meta-category are to "acquire necessary information and resources, and to promote and defend the interests of the team or organization". In both cases leaders are expected to liaise with relevant stakeholders outside of the organization, and be able to build strategic partnerships and influence the direction being taken within their relevant part of the nonprofit sector. The complexity of the stakeholder environment is evident, and this heightens the need to be able to engage and sustain relationships outside the organization. Table 16.6 presents examples of identification of these capabilities by participants.

Table 16.7   Nonprofit orientation

Behavior	Example interview quotes	
	Case A	Case B
Nonprofit commitment	I suppose it's about, for me personally, seeing the impact the organization has and wanting to be part of that (A4)	You need to be able to grow the pie year on year because as a not-for-profit, the more money you can create inside the business, the more services and tools and support you can ultimately deliver to the members (B1)
	They need to have contextual awareness of people, not just in the not-for-profit sector but general commercial businesses; because I could pick my team up and put it into a commercial organization but they don't operate like a not-for-profit (A7)	
Managing volunteers	Especially when they are working with volunteers which pretty much all the staff are…(A6)	NA
	I guess the working with volunteers, I see that as an important – and it is a skill and awareness (A10)	

Comparatively, with Case A, we found that the emphasis was upon establishing broad networks so that the organization can be better informed about services, availability of resources and to gain further recognition for their health-related cause. On the other hand, Case B had an emphasis on representing the business externally, requiring leaders to be highly effective in terms of representing their members, beyond the nonprofit sector in the for-profit and public sector domains. Furthermore, in Case B, the need appears to be more akin to stakeholder management including the ability to adapt the message and its delivery for different types of members (i.e., association members varied based on size, location and organizational complexity) and member representatives (i.e., senior and middle managers, plus operational staff), and also to manage upwards (e.g. different levels of government), and sideways (e.g. with other advocacy groups).

Nonprofit orientation meta-category

The primary objective of this category relates to the leader's understanding of the broader nonprofit context and how this information is used to enhance decision-making, communication methods and overall approach to leadership and management (Bish & Becker, 2016). In the analysis of Case A this included two nonprofit-oriented behaviors: nonprofit commitment and managing volunteers. In Case B, as there were no volunteers utilized by the organization, this capability did not emerge in the data. Participants across both cases identified the need for leaders to know, understand and be committed to the purpose of the nonprofit, as illustrated in the comparative examples shown in Table 16.7.

The data suggests the need to be adaptive and agile (consistent with the competitive pressures in the for-profit sector), to manage the tension between fit and flexibility, as well as meeting competing stakeholder demands. The demands differ in each case due in part to the organizational objectives, operating environment and culture. Leaders in Case A do not have the same level of influence in their environment but rather are required to change their strategy to respond to environmental factors, particularly in relation to changes in public sentiment and behavior towards charities and donations. On the other hand, Case B leaders are involved in formulating a position and advocating on behalf of the membership organizations, and their leadership actions shape the strategic agenda beyond the bounds of their organization as they play a key role in shaping the political landscape. In addition to advocating on behalf of its membership, Case B also advises and assists members on a broad range of issues such as governance, compliance, industrial relations and stakeholder communication.

Personal knowledge and experience meta-category

The primary objective of this meta-category is the assimilation of what has been previously learned and the application of this knowledge to the current nonprofit context (Bish & Becker, 2016). In both cases we found an emphasis on the need for leaders to be able to think strategically, followed by the need for discipline-based knowledge and then self-awareness. Table 16.8 presents examples of identification of these capabilities by participants in each case organization.

Table 16.8   *Personal knowledge and experience*

Behavior	Example interview quotes	
	Case A	Case B
Self-awareness	Definitely, there's communication skills and the ability to be really self-aware and that self-disclosure, so we don't look like we are really removed (A6)	A person who knows the type of manager they are is comfortable with it and can operate within that, in a positive sense (B6)
Thinking strategically	A good ability to think more broadly, so more strategically about the unit within think they work and where it sits within the broader organizational framework (A16)	They need to have a solid understanding of what's happening across the business because so many of our issues impact on other areas. So that's a really critical thing (B7)
Discipline-based knowledge	They are specialized areas and some of the things that I admire about them is that they are experts around that …. So when they say something or contribute something to meetings/conversations, you know that you are getting a high quality contribution. They come from a place of knowledge and in-depth knowledge (A15)	Oh, well, it has been the fact that you are an expert. So it's that leadership by expertise. So you happen to know more about whatever the subject matter is than most people on the planet (B2)

Comparatively however, in Case B the discipline-related knowledge was heavily emphasized as participants identified two groups of leaders: those who have a focus on managing people and those who also need specific technical knowledge. A number of those identified as leaders in Case B had small teams and were responsible for technical tasks as well as having management responsibilities and therefore, in these cases, their technical expertise was seen as vital for success in their role.

Card Sort Findings

At the end of the interviews, the card sort activity was conducted, asking participants to prioritize the most important capabilities for leaders in the organization. The top six results of this activity for each organization are presented in Table 16.9.

Table 16.9   *Comparing the emphasis placed on each capability in each organization*

Priority	Case A	Case B
1	Communication	Communication
2	Innovation and creativity	Managing teams
3	Self-awareness	Negotiation and influencing
4	Negotiation and influencing	Performance management
5	Managing teams	Promotes [company] values and vision, and Stakeholder engagement (TIE)
6	Mentoring	Goal setting/results oriented, and strategic planning (TIE)

The card sort findings reflected and verified the overall pattern of the results from the interviews. The capabilities that were prioritized were the ones which aligned with the organization's purpose and associated organizational culture. In Case A, leadership capabilities focused on developing and executing organizational strategy to efficiently and effectively deliver services were emphasized. In Case B, leadership capabilities which were prioritized were more focused on those enabling senior leaders to effectively engage in high profile advocacy work on behalf of the membership, and inspiring staff to support them in these efforts. In addition to verifying the findings of the interviews, the card sort provided the interviewees an opportunity to extend and clarify comments made earlier. One participant noted at the conclusion of the interview that the tactical act of ranking capabilities comparative to each other based on importance, resulted in her providing more in-depth consideration and deeper justification for which capabilities were most important and why.

CONCLUSION AND CONTRIBUTIONS

The objective of the study reported in this chapter was to explore the diversity of leadership needs within the nonprofit sector. We acknowledged the complexities within the sector in terms of what nonprofits are created to do, their scale, scope and overall missions, and used this as our starting point to consider leadership needs. Specifically, we took a closer look at whether the type of nonprofit, its purpose and enabling culture, may influence the required leadership capabilities, and if so, in what ways. A secondary objective was to enhance our knowledge of data collection methods by adopting the use of card sort methodology. We wanted to test the suitability of this methodology for investigating leadership capabilities, specifically as a tool for guided reflection. Overall, we found support for both the proposal that type of nonprofit can influence the emphasis placed on the need for particular leadership capabilities, and that the card sort methodology had utility in examining the importance of leadership capabilities.

Both nonprofits studied required leadership capabilities consistent with the leadership framework, however, the *importance* placed on each area is altered due in part to the inherent differences in organizational purpose, objectives and culture. The public-serving nonprofit emphasized leadership capabilities such as problem-solving and conflict management, often linked to the fact that they were challenged with an environment where program-based teams were fundamental to their operations. Being able to manage projects and take an organization-wide perspective were likewise highly valued capabilities in this organizational culture, as delivering on their outcomes for public stakeholders required working across organizational boundaries in project teams. In the member-serving nonprofit, planning and representing were highly valued leadership capabilities. These capabilities were seen as important as the organization was less team- and project-based but structured around individual subject matter experts providing professional services directly to members in targeted areas of advocacy or advice within their own sphere of expertise. Both organizations placed significant value on leaders being able to develop their people and clarify roles and expectations.

In practice, for talent management and development, our findings highlight the importance of considering the influence of the particular organizational purpose, mission and culture on what leaders are expected to do. This enhanced appreciation of contextual factors improves the design of appropriate talent management processes (e.g., for recruiting and selecting leaders, managing and rewarding performance and leadership development programs) to meet these organizational needs (Akingbola, 2013) and to ensure consistent application by the leadership team (McMurray et al., 2010) to support desired culture and values.

From a methodological perspective, the card sort activity proved to be an effective and meaningful tool to facilitate a detailed discussion of leadership. Interviewees clearly engaged with this task; they took it seriously, reflecting upon leaders' behaviors and what was important for the success of the organization. In addition to the content (data) that this activity provided, it is also relevant to reflect on the *process* of card sort as a research technique. The interviewers observed that the card sort activity fostered conscious deliberation of each capability individually and prompted an in-depth discussion about and reflection on leadership capability requirements. The shift in focus from answering interview questions to physically holding and sorting cards, engaging in a tactile, multi-sensory task, prompted individual reflection and, in terms of data collection, kept participants engaged with the use of tangible stimuli. Rather than considering the list of capabilities as a group, as might occur if they were provided with the full list, the participants took time with each card to consider what each statement meant to them and then to rule it "in" or "out" based on their judgment of its importance for leaders in the organization. The inclusion of this activity provided a valuable dimension to the data-collection process, adding momentum to the conversation and providing the interviewer with greater insights about the interviewee, as well as the required capabilities. Of added benefit, these insights were gained in an unobtrusive manner.

We highly recommend consideration of card sort methodology for future research designs. As illustrated here, the card sort activity served its purpose well in terms of data collection, facilitating deliberate consideration of leadership in a tactile and engaging manner. It allowed interviewers to move beyond general leadership concepts to grapple with perceptions of specific capabilities and their importance to obtaining organizational objectives within the context of culture. In conclusion, the card sort methodology may also be useful in studying organizational culture and values by assisting participants to make deliberate consideration of the nature of these constructs within their organizational context.

REFERENCES

Akingbola, K. (2013). Context and nonprofit human resource management. *Administration and Society*, *45*(8), 974–1004. DOI 10.1177/0095399712451887

Anheier, H. K. (2014). *Nonprofit Organizations: Theory, Management, Policy* (2nd ed.). London: Routledge.

Bish, A. J. & Becker, K. (2016). Exploring management capabilities for the nonprofit sector. *Nonprofit and Volunteer Sector Quarterly, 45*(3): 437–457.

Boris, E. T. (1999). The nonprofit sector in the 1990s. In C. T. Clotfelter and T. Ehrlich (Eds), *Philanthropy and the Nonprofit Sector in a Changing America* (pp. 1–33). Bloomington, IN: Indiana University Press

Braun, V., & Clarke, V. (2006). Using thematic analysis in psychology. *Qualitative Research in Psychology, 3*, 77–101. DOI 10.1191/1478088706qp063oa

Brown, S. R. (1996). Q methodology and qualitative research. *Qualitative Health Research, 6*(4), 561–567.

Cheverton, J. (2007). Holding our own: Value and performance in nonprofit organisations. *Australian Journal of Social Issues, 42*, 427–436. DOI 10.1002/j.1839-4655.2007.tb00068.x

Coultas, C. W., Kindel, B., Zajac, S., & Salas, E. (2012). Nine empirical guidelines for top leadership teams in nonprofit organizations. In R. Burke and C. Cooper (Eds), *Human Resource Management in the Nonprofit Sector: Passion, Purpose and Professionalism* (pp. 117–143). Cheltenham, UK and Northampton, MA, USA: Edward Elgar Publishing.

Dees, J. G. (1998). Enterprising nonprofits. *Harvard Business Review, 76*, 54–69.

Hamlin, R. G., Sawyer, J., & Sage, L. (2011). Perceived managerial and leadership effectiveness in a non-profit organization: An exploratory and cross-sector comparative study. *Human Resource Development International, 14*(2), 217–234. DOI 10.1080/13678868.2011.558318

Jahrami, H., Marnoch, G., & Gray, A. M. (2009). Use of card sort methodology in the testing of a clinical leadership competencies model. *Health Services Management Research, 22*(4), 176–183.

Jaskyte, K. (2004). Transformational leadership, organizational culture, and innovativeness in nonprofit organizations. *Nonprofit Management and Leadership, 15*(2), 153–168.

Kilmann, R. H. (2003). *Beyond the Quick: Managing Five Tracks to Organizational Success*. Washington, DC: Beard Books.

Kong, E. (2007). The strategic importance of intellectual capital in the non-profit sector. *Journal of Intellectual Capital, 8*, 721–731. DOI 10.1108/14691930710830864

Langer, J., & LeRoux, K. (2017). Developmental culture and effectiveness in nonprofit organizations. *Public Performance & Management Review, 40*(3), 457–479.

LeRoux, K., & Feeney, M. K. (2013). Factors attracting individuals to nonprofit management over public and private sector management. *Nonprofit Management & Leadership, 24*, 43–62.

Lutz Allen, S., Smith, J. E., & Da Silva, N. (2013). Leadership style in relation to organizational change and organizational creativity: Perceptions from nonprofit organizational members. *Nonprofit Management & Leadership, 24*, 23–42. DOI 10.1002/nml.21078

Lyons, M. (2001). *Third Sector: The Contribution of Nonprofit and Cooperative Enterprises in Australia*. St Leondards, NSW: Allen and Unwin.

McClusky, J. E. (2002). Re-thinking nonprofit organization governance: Implications for management and leadership. *International Journal of Public Administration, 25*, 539–559. DOI 10.1081/PAD-120013255

McMurray, A. J., Islam, M. M., Sarros, J. C., & Pirola-Merlo, A. (2013). Workplace innovation in a non-profit organization. *Nonprofit Management & Leadership, 23*, 367–388. DOI 10.1002/nml.21066

McMurray, A. J., Pirola-Merlo, A., Sarros, J. C., & Islam, M. M. (2010). Leadership, climate, psychological capital, commitment, and wellbeing in a non-profit organization. *Leadership & Organization Development Journal, 31*, 436–457. DOI 10.1108/01437731211253000

Moore, M. H. (2000). Managing for value: Organizational strategy in for-profit, nonprofit, and governmental organizations. *Nonprofit and Voluntary Sector Quarterly, 29*(suppl 1), 183–208.

Paton, R., Mordaunt, J., & Cornforth, C. (2007). Beyond nonprofit management education: Leadership development in a time of blurred boundaries and distributed learning. *Nonprofit and Voluntary Sector Quarterly, 36*(4 suppl), 148S–162S. DOI 10.1177/0899764007305053

Peachey, J. W., Lyras, A., Cohen, A., Bruening, J. E., & Cunningham, G. B. (2013). Exploring the motives and retention factors of sport-for-development volunteers. *Nonprofit and Voluntary Sector Quarterly, 43*(6), 1052–1069.

Ridder, H. G., & McCandless, A. (2010). Influences on the architecture of human resource management in nonprofit organizations: An analytical framework. *Nonprofit and Voluntary Sector Quarterly, 39*, 124–141. DOI 10.1177/0899764008328182

Ridder, H. G., Piening, E. P., & Baluch, A. M. (2012). The third way reconfigured: How and why nonprofit organizations are shifting their human resource management. *VOLUNTAS: International Journal of Voluntary and Nonprofit Organizations*, *23*(3), 605–635.

Santos, G. J. (2006). Card sort technique as a qualitative substitute for quantitative exploratory factor analysis. *Corporate Communications: An International Journal*, *11*(3), 288–302.

Schein, E. (1985). *Organizational Culture and Leadership*. San Francisco: Jossey-Bass.

Schein, E. H. (2010). *Organizational Culture and Leadership* (Vol. 2). London, UK: John Wiley & Sons.

Schepers, C., Gieter, S. D., Pepermans, R., Bois, C. D., Caers, R., & Jegers, M. (2005). How are employees of the nonprofit sector motivated? A research need. *Nonprofit Management & Leadership*, *16*, 191–208

Stid, D., & Bradach, J. (2009). How visionary nonprofits leaders are learning to enhance management capabilities. *Strategy & Leadership*, *37*, 35–40.

Thach, E., & Thompson, K. J. (2007). Trading places: Examining leadership competencies between for-profit vs. public and non-profit leaders. *Leadership & Organization Development Journal*, *28*, 356–375. DOI 10.1108/01437730710752229

Wang, L., & Ashcraft, R. F. (2012). Needs assessment and curriculum mapping: Enhancing management skills of the nonprofit workforce. *Nonprofit Management & Leadership*, *23*, 121–136. DOI 10.1002/nml.21058

Weerawardena, J., McDonald, R. E., & Mort, G. S. (2010). Sustainability of nonprofit organizations: An empirical investigation. *Journal of World Business*, *45*(4), 346–356.

Wilensky, A.S., & Hansen, C. D. (2001). Understanding the works beliefs of nonprofit executives through organizational stories. *Human Resource Development Quarterly*, *12*(3), 223.

Yin, R. K. (1999). Enhancing the quality of case studies in health services research. *Health Services Research*, *34*(5 Pt 2), 1209–1224.

Yin, R. K. (2013). *Case Study Research: Design and Methods* (5th ed.). Thousand Oaks, CA: Sage Publications.

Yukl, G. (2012). Effective leadership behavior: What we know and what questions need more attention. *Academy of Management Perspectives*, *26*, 66–85. DOI 10.5465/amp.2012.0088

Yukl, G., Gordon, A., & Taber, T. (2002). A hierarchical taxonomy of leadership behavior: Integrating a half century of behavior research. *Journal of Leadership & Organizational Studies*, *9*, 15. DOI 10.1177/107179190200900102

17. Deciphering "bad" organizational cultures[1]

Sonja A. Sackmann

INTRODUCTION

At the beginning of this century, a series of scandals and fraudulent business practices made practitioners and scholars alike question how these could happen. How could Enron – according to *Fortune Magazine*, America's most innovative company – over the period of six years (Stein, 2000), forge their balance sheets, leading eventually to many job losses, losses in retirement accounts and a $74 billion loss for shareholders? How could WorldCom inflate its assets by as much as $11 billion, with its bankruptcy resulting in 30,000 lost jobs and a $180 billion loss for shareholders? How could Freddie Mac misstate $5 billion in earnings? How could Bernard Madoff create the greatest Ponzi scheme ever, tricking investors out of almost $65 billion? How could Parmalat cover its increasing debt for years and report non-existing assets?

In addition to these drastic business scandals, briberies and Dieselgate, recent studies reveal that an increasing number of employees experience high levels of stress resulting in sick-leave, burnouts and, hence, losses of productivity both for the organization (Schaufeli, 2018; Wigert & Agrawal, 2018) and for the economy. How can organizations become toxic to their employees and how can that be detected so that employees recognize the toxic potential in time and have the option to leave before their health is compromised, and job applicants realize that they had better not sign the work contract?

To find answers to these questions, scholars and practitioners have turned to the concepts of organizational or corporate climate and culture.[2] While organizational climate is an individual-level construct (e.g., Key, 1999; Kish-Gephard et al., 2010; Parboteeah et al., 2011), referring to a person's perception of an organization's climate, the concept of culture refers to shared or commonly-held beliefs that influence organizational members' thinking, feeling and behavior (Sackmann, 1991, 2006, 2021). Hence, culture is a collective or group phenomenon rooted in organizational members' minds and expressed in different kinds of manifestations including behavior that is typical for the group or organization.

Corrupt organizations expect their employees to behave in corrupt or unethical ways in order to attain the organizations' goals (Pinto et al., 2008). The culture of an organization plays a vital role in developing corrupt behavior (Sackmann & Horstmann, 2009). Thus, corrupt or unethical behavior is part of their daily work-life and considered the normal way of behaving. It is part of the organization's culture that influences the behavior of organizational members (Ashford et al., 2008; Beenen & Pinto, 2009; Dahling et al., 2012; Kaptein, 2011). Because of these corrupt behaviors, organizations expect a benefit vis-à-vis their competitors or they consider this type of behavior necessary for their survival. Organizational members may also expect positive rewards from their corrupt or unethical actions or they may be afraid of negative consequences in case they do not follow the corrupt or unethical way of working. Because of the division of labor, employees may only be involved in a small part of the entire corruption process. Furthermore, Campbell and Göritz (2014, p. 292) distinguish between active and passive corrupt behavior. Active corrupt behavior involves deliberate unethical or illegal activities such as transferring money for bribes or destroying compromising documents. Passive corrupt behavior implies no actual corrupt actions but tolerating those as a part of work-life. Once corrupt and unethical behavior has become part of an organization's culture, this behavior tends to be perpetuated and the culture may be evaluated as *toxic* or *bad*.

Given that it is unlikely that an organization officially commits to corrupt or unethical behavior, the question remains how one can detect, understand or even measure a corrupt or unethical organizational culture. In the following sections, organizational culture is defined with its various components and its potential qualities. This is followed by characterizations of the qualities of corrupt and unethical organizational cultures and an exploration of how these *bad* organizational cultures can be deciphered. Uncovering early situations of business fraud or stressed employees can eventually help prevent the perpetuation of bad cultures.

THE CONCEPT OF CULTURE

Culture as a concept in management and organization studies was borrowed from anthropology, the original domain of culture and its exploration. Hence, the different conceptualizations and definitions of culture, and approaches to its study, were adopted as well (Sackmann, 1991; Smircich, 1983). Despite their many differences, existing conceptualizations of culture share a few characteristics: they consider culture a collective multi-level phenomenon created in social interactions to solve the group's internal and external problems (Schein, 2010). Organizational culture is rooted in its members' minds and expressed in their behavior and artifacts that they have created. Hence, the discussion in this chapter is based on the following definition of organizational culture:

> The core of culture consists of a set of commonly-held basic beliefs of a group of organizational members, developed and acquired in social interactions. This set of commonly-held beliefs influences their thinking, feeling and behavior, it is passed on to new members of the group and may find expression in the group members' values, norms and artifacts. (Sackmann, 1991)

The various components of culture can be visualized in the form of levels (e.g., Sackmann, 2021; Schein, 2010) (see Figure 17.1).

Artifacts are created by organizational members such as products, architecture, interior design, documents, showcases, etc. Even though they are visible manifestations of a culture, their meaning is not always easy to decipher and it also may have shifted over time. Formal rules and standards for behavior are frequently expressed in written documents such as guidelines for behavior or a code of conduct, accounting standards, rules for handling expenditures, and many more. Once developed in the interaction of organizational members, these formal rules and standards are distributed and thus accessible to internal members. Informal rules are, however, only known to insiders and verbally passed on to those who are considered part of the trustworthy in-group. They serve as standards for behavior and may refer to how to speed up a certain process or decisions, what it takes to be considered a *good* organizational member in a given organization, what should be avoided if one wants to stay in the organization, and so on. In the case of organizations with a corrupt or unethical culture, the informal norms may also include how to circumvent formal procedures and get things done for the benefit of the organization – even if it is unethical or corrupt. In regard to organizational values, two kinds exist: those that are officially expressed in documents such as an organization's printed value statement and those that are lived and only observable during daily work behavior. Corrupt or unethical cultures tend to have a wide gap between officially expressed values and those that are lived in day-to-day work and interactions. For understanding an existing culture, the informal rules and lived values are important as they are rooted in the set of commonly-held basic beliefs that invisibly influence organizational members' thinking, feeling and behavior.

These components are generic to every organizational culture. Their specific content and expression can contribute to a culture that is high performing (e.g., Sackmann, 2008), innovative (Ernst, 2003), generative (Sackmann, 2018), one that may enable a corporation's sustained performance (Kotter & Heskett, 1992; Sackmann, 2006), or one that may lead to an organization's crisis (Sackmann, 2013). Depending on its particular imprint, an organizational culture may also be toxic or community-centered (Gilbert et al., 2011), ethical or unethical (Armenakis et al., 2011; Warren et al., 2014) and corrupt (Campbell & Göritz, 2014). In the following section, I will explore those factors that may contribute to a corrupt and unethical organizational culture.

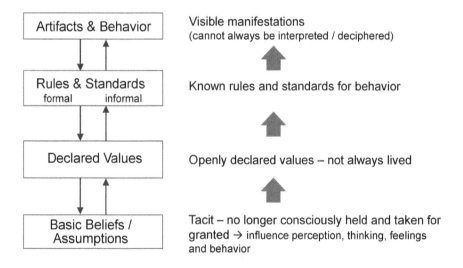

Figure 17.1   Levels of organizational culture

CHARACTERISTICS OF A CORRUPT AND UNETHICAL ORGANIZATIONAL CULTURE

Corrupt and unethical are general terms that refer to different kinds of conditions. In regard to culture, *corruption and unethical behavior* may result from either illegal conduct or general misconduct that is considered unethical in our Western world.[3] The business scandals mentioned previously, such as Enron, WorldCom and Freddie Mac, are based on fraudulent accounting practices of either an individual or a group of individuals and thus represent illegal business behavior that may lead to or be an expression of a toxic or generally bad culture.

Other illegal business behavior cases resulting in or being a product of *corrupt* cultures may be based on corporate fraud (Tan et al., 2017), corruption (Campbell & Göritz, 2014; Lanier & Kirchner, 2018; Pinto et al., 2008), unethical business behavior (Ross & Benson, 1995) or corporate wrongdoing (Solas, 2019).

In their analysis of 14 interviews conducted with experts in the field of organizational corruption, Campbell and Göritz (2014) identified a set of interlocking norms, values and assumptions at the managerial and the employee level, characterizing corrupt cultures. At both levels, the basic assumption is that the end justifies the means. At the managerial level, values of performance, results orientation, security and success are prevalent, influencing the norms for goal setting as well as rewards and punishment. The employee level is characterized by additional assumptions appealing to higher loyalties, a low level of awareness that corruption is unlawful but rather is a matter of course, and that they (the organization) were always corrupt but have a strong sense that they are a team competing against "the others". Resulting values are team spirit and security, leading to norms of coercion, punishment, organizational silence, separation and corrupt behavior being an open secret in the organization.

Unethical cultures may not necessarily entail illegal behavior but organizational members may engage in behavior that is considered unethical (Key, 1999), abusive (Buchko et al., 2017; Lutgen-Sandvik & McDermott, 2008; Powell, 1998) or unhealthy, with eventually toxic and harmful effects for both organizational members and the organization. A wide range of collective behavior may fall into this category of misconduct or unethical behavior such as widespread mistrust in an organization resulting in excessive monitoring and organizational controls. Other forms of misconduct are social loafing (Mihelič & Culiberg, 2019), breach of psychological contracts (Coyle-Shapiro et al., 2019), mobbing, bullying (Sprigg et al., 2018) or different kinds of abusive exploitation such as sexual harassment (Goldberg et al., 2019), abuse of power, labor, time and/or the environment (e.g., Mighty Earth, 2019). High-pressure workplaces such as reported from Amazon (Kantor & Streitfeld, 2015) or Microsoft (Eichenwald, 2012), as well as being considered some of the worst companies to work for (Stebbins, 2019), may also be viewed by many organizational members as having an unethical, toxic, *bad* and ultimately unhealthy culture.

Individual cases of these kinds of unhealthy, unethical, abusive, toxic or illegal behaviors may not necessarily lead to or be an expression of a corrupt or unethical culture (Buchko et al., 2017; Kish-Gephart et al., 2010) if they are identified early and eliminated. For a culture to be corrupt or unethical, these behaviors are part of its DNA; that is, they are typical for the organizational unit and based on a set of collectively-held basic beliefs that are considered unethical or corrupt according to our Western standards and that are observable in the respective group of organizational members over an extended period of time. These two types of illegal and unethical or abusive behavior may pertain to one of the subcultures of an organization and thus be a subset of an organization, or the *corrupt/unethical* phenomenon may be spread in the entire organization. Examples of these two general categories of *bad* organizational cultures and their different conduct are listed in Figure 17.2.

Despite potential short-term benefits pointed out above, these kinds of behaviors will eventually have negative and harmful effects both for organizational members and for the entire organization. Organizational members may experience high levels of stress and the need for emotional labor that may ultimately lead to illness, burnout or depression. Even if organizations may benefit from these corrupt or unethical behaviors in the short term, they will experience increasing levels of sick leave from their employees and a loss of trust from their customers, suppliers and the wider public once the corrupt or unethical behavior becomes publicly known. This will eventually result in reduced earnings or a decline in the organization's value. The firm may have to seek protection from its creditors under Chapter 11 according to US law or may eventually have to file for bankruptcy. Society may be affected by job and financial losses and a feeling of being cheated.

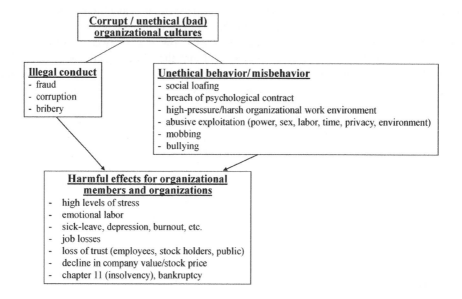

Figure 17.2   Classification and examples of corrupt/unethical organizational cultures and potential implications for organizational members and organizations

CHALLENGES ASSOCIATED WITH MEASURING CORRUPT/ UNETHICAL ORGANIZATIONAL CULTURES

Two major challenges exist in measuring corrupt or unethical organizational cultures. One pertains to the concept of culture and the other to the characteristics of a corrupt/unethical culture. As shown in Figure 17.1, culture is a multifaceted phenomenon consisting of various components located at different levels that are more or less visible. A wide range of questionnaire instruments exist to analyze different components at different levels of an organization's culture, with a focus on a range of dimensions all considered to be relevant for understanding the specific quality of a given culture (Sackmann, 2010).[4] None of these questionnaires can, however, unravel the deepest level of collective beliefs or assumptions. This requires a qualitative methodology. To reveal potential gaps between officially declared and lived culture requires a combination of qualitative methods such as documentary analysis, interviews and observations. Ethnography, the method of choice by anthropologists, sets out to understand the relevant dimensions of culture from the insiders' perspective rather than applying theory-derived dimensions by an outside researcher.

The challenge of analyzing corrupt or unethical cultures is that insiders are unlikely to openly talk about the corrupt or unethical qualities of their culture to an outsider for several reasons. Firstly, once acquired, culture is taken for granted by members of an organization and drops out of awareness (Schein, 2010). Hence, it is difficult to consciously address those guiding rules that influence thinking, emotions and behavior in one's daily work life – both in answering a questionnaire and in an interview. Since the unethical or corrupt behavior has become part of their daily work life routines, organizational members consider this type of behavior as the normal way to go about work (Campbell & Göritz, 2014). Secondly, being part of the system, organizational members may not want to talk about unethical or corrupt behavior for fear of negative sanctions and repression, since talking about this kind of behavior would fall into the category of whistleblowing (as in the case of Sherron Watkins at Enron (McLean & Elkind, 2003)), with the consequence of becoming an adversary to the organization and an outcast. Furthermore, organizational members may feel compelled to keep the corrupt or unethical system going because they identify with the organization and have a psychological commitment to it (Buchko et al., 2017). They may also feel economically dependent on it and not address critical issues for fear of the company's failure and/or for fear of losing their job. And finally, not all organization members may know about the corrupt or unethical behavior occurring in their organization since they are not part of that specific subculture (Armenakis & Lang, 2014). Hence, for an outsider, it is extremely difficult to uncover unhealthy, unethical or corrupt behavior.

With these caveats in mind, the following will explore methods to uncover corrupt or unethical organizational cultures.

EXISTING METHODS TO UNCOVER CORRUPT OR UNETHICAL ORGANIZATIONAL CULTURES

In the fields of management, organization and social sciences, measurement is different from the natural sciences. No thermometer exists that can measure the temperature of an organization's culture and, hence, give an indication of its degree of health, corruptness or *badness*. The social and organizational sciences use proxies or indices for assessing a phenomenon such as culture. Given its different levels indicated in Figure 17.1, different kinds of instruments exist to assess various components and dimensions of culture at the organizational level (Sackmann, 2010). These range from highly unstructured to highly structured methods addressing one or multiple levels of culture and using one or multiple data collection methods. Their approach varies from trying to unravel the culture as perceived by its members, including the dimensions that are relevant for its characterization, to applying instruments that were developed on the basis of theoretical considerations or empirical evidence, using a set of specific dimensions considered relevant by outsiders. However, no instrument currently exists to specifically assess a *bad* culture which may consist of different elements and facets contributing to its *badness* (as shown in Figure 17.2). Hence, to assess a corrupt or an unethical culture, one may have to be creative in developing and combining possible approaches to tap its essence.

Figure 17.3 shows several data collection methods that can be used in gathering information about the quality of an organizational culture, with a focus on corrupt or unethical conduct.

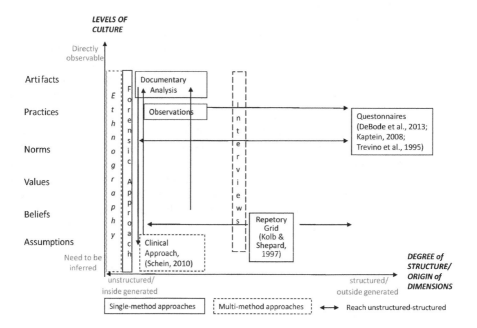

Figure 17.3   Possible data collection methods for analyzing corrupt/unethical organizational cultures

The left-hand side of Figure 17.3 shows the different levels of culture on the vertical axis, and on the horizontal axes, the degree of structure of an analysis method combined with the origin of dimensions. Methods listed on the left-hand side are highly unstructured with the goal to generate the insiders' views about the quality of a given culture. Methods listed on the right-hand side are highly structured, such as a questionnaire that provides a set of specific questions developed by an outsider to be answered by organizational members. Arrows pointing to the left and/or right indicate that a data collection method may be designed in a more or less structured or unstructured way. Arrows pointing up or down indicate the culture levels that can be tapped with the specific data collection method.

Questionnaires

A few questionnaires exist that can be used to get a first impression of the degree of ethicality of an organization's culture. Trevino et al. (1995) developed the Ethical Culture Questionnaire that was modified by Key (1999). The modified version contains 18 statements that need to be rated on a scale ranging from 1 to 6 with 1 meaning completely false and 6 meaning completely true. Kaptein (2008) measures ethical organizational culture on eight dimensions using 58 questions. DeBode et al. (2013) developed a shorter version using 32 questions for measuring the same eight dimensions considered relevant to the degree of ethicality of an organization's culture. The eight dimensions are: clarity, congruency of supervisors, congruency of management, feasability, supportability, transparency, discussability and sanctionability.

When using this questionnaire, DeBode et al. (2013, p. 479) caution that it may not be able to tap all relevant dimensions of an ethical culture and suggest also using qualitative research methodologies. Interpretation of obtained results is also a challenge since there is no clear cut-off pointing to an ethical or unethical culture.

Repertory Grid

The repertory grid (e.g., Kolb & Shepard, 1997) is a technique in which a set of bipolar constructs are developed on the basis of interviews conducted with selected organizational members (on the insider end of the axis) or chosen from the relevant literature about, for example, corrupt/unethical behavior in organizations (outsider end of the axes). These constructs are then either transformed into a questionnaire or presented in person for organizational members, to be answered on a scale from −3 to +3. The resulting data can be entered into a computer program to facilitate the analysis and compare different organizational units. The repertory grid is a highly flexible instrument that forces respondents to make a choice between two opposing constructs (see Sackmann, 2010, pp. 96–104). Depending on the chosen constructs, one may assume that respondents could be lured into revealing parts of an unethical or corrupt organization's culture. The question remains, however, as to whether organizational members are open and/or honest enough to talk to an outsider and address the critical issues of their corrupt or unethical culture – even when they are probed in a personal conversation and assured their responses will be treated with anonymity.

Interviews

Interviews are a highly flexible means to collect data. They may be rather unstructured, exploring issues as they come up in a conversation with the interviewee, and probing further into these issues. In this case, the quality and depth of data collection depends on the interviewers' flexibility during the interview. Interviews may also be structured using a guideline of preselected questions. Even though an interview is a single method, the interviewer can make observations during the interview, checking for consistencies and inconsistencies between verbal accounts and nonverbal behavior such as body language. Hence, interviews are listed as multi-method approach in Figure 17.3. Nevertheless, despite probing by the interviewer, interviewees may avoid addressing issues of corruption or unethical behavior. In this case, former employees could be identified and interviewed. A potential problem in interviews is that interviewees may use a coded language that is not familiar to interviewers coming from the outside. In such a case, the interviewer may not be able to understand the connotations and underlying meanings of the spoken words.

Observations

Observations are always possible if one has access to an organization and its various locations, production areas, offices and/or meetings. Similar to interviews, observations may range from highly unstructured to highly structured data gathering. Unstructured observations may be conducted during a first visit of a company location, while encountering interactions among organizational members, for example while waiting in the reception area, during lunch in the organization's premise or during meetings. An example of a highly structured observation is the Bales interaction system (Bales, 1950) that can be used to observe specific interpersonal interactions using predefined dimensions, but these are unlikely to reveal unethical behavior. Observations may tap into highly rich data sources that are happening in the "here and now" without involving potential recall and selective perception and information biases of an interviewee. However, there are four major problems associated with observations. Firstly, an observer may not be able to record the observed data during the observation process, thus having to rely on memory when charting down critical observations. Secondly, observers may be distracted during their observational process and/or overwhelmed by the abundance of data, thus may only pay selective attention. Thirdly, observers may not be able to decipher the underlying cultural meanings in the process of interpreting their observations. And finally, the choice of observation time and place may not reveal unethical behavior.

Documentary Analysis

Documents of an organization can be analyzed in any stage of a culture assessment. A large number of external data sources exist, including the internet, providing a wide range of documents to outsiders. These range from company websites giving information geared to investors, customers, suppliers and (potential) employees, to information provided by newspapers, magazines, investment companies, employees (e.g., Kununu: www.kununu .com), rating companies or non-governmental agencies such as Greenpeace or Mighty Earth. Hence, without even physically entering the door of an organization's site, rich data sources are available that may give insights into an organization's culture (e.g., Armenakis & Lang, 2014). If it is possible to access an organization, a wide range of internal documents may complement, enrich and potentially correct any analysis based on externally obtained information. Documents of interest include business reports, corporate guidelines, value statements, codes of conduct, leadership guidelines, documents about internal rules and regulations, employee surveys, internal statistics, and accounting documents. Comparing information gained from various sources such as employee statements from Kununu, reports from non-governmental agencies and company official material may also be helpful for validation purposes and in discovering critical issues. Depending on the depth of the analysis, documents can reveal insights about all levels of culture. The problems associated with the analysis of documents pertain to their availability, their abundance and their interpretation. The massive amount of documents available both from external and internal sources may cover or blur critical issues of corruption and unethical behavior. In addition, internal documents that may reveal issues of corruption or unethical behavior will most likely not be made available to an outsider unless s/he has informal sources that want to uncover the wrongdoing. And, similar to observations, it may be difficult for an outsider to uncover the critical issues from the available documents. Natural language processes (NLP) can be used to analyze large amounts of printed material such as emails or spoken language from chats in social networks regarding bad or unethical conduct. The challenge will be to identify the critical key words or phrases.

Forensic Diagnosis

The forensic diagnosis conducted and reported by Armenakis and Lang (2014) is entirely based on documents that were available to outsiders. The researchers used Schein's (2010) three-level framework of artifacts, espoused values and underlying assumptions and the stakeholder theory of management regarding legal, economic, moral and philanthropic responsibilities to describe the fraudulent conduct of a healthcare company in England using a wide range of documents covering events from 1984 to 2011. It may be argued that what they identified as underlying assumptions may pertain more to guiding beliefs, but underlying assumptions could have been extracted from the documents as well. This kind of diagnostic endeavor shows the potential richness of documentary data and its usefulness in deciphering a corrupt culture. However, the authors analyzed the case retrospectively after 16 executives had been found guilty of a $2.7 billion fraud. The question remains as to whether such a forensic analysis can detect corrupt or unethical behavior before it is known to the public.

Clinical Approach

Schein (2010) describes ways to uncover a corrupt or unethical culture from the outside, in the role of a customer, job applicant, journalist or researcher. Six steps are suggested (Schein, 2010, p. 178):

1. Visit and observe.
2. Identify artifacts and processes that are puzzling.
3. Ask insiders why things are done that way.
4. Identify espoused values that are appealing, and ask how they are implemented in the organization.
5. Look for inconsistencies, and ask about them.
6. Consider on all that was said and reflect on what deeper assumptions actually determine the observed behavior.

Schein considers a clinical approach most adequate in deciphering the deepest level of culture (Schein, 2010, p. 183) based on his own work and experience. This approach consists of open, deep level conversations with people giving information *voluntarily*, combined with observations and comparison of the different kinds of data. The insights gained from the analysis of this data is then fed back to the organization and discussed. In the case of corrupt or unethical cultures, it is, however, unlikely that organizational members will ask a consultant/researcher into the organization to help them – unless they want to deliberately change their culture.

Ethnography

Ethnography (Fetterman, 2009; Spradley, 1979) is anthropologists' method of choice to uncover and understand a given culture and its internal meaning systems. An ethnographer typically stays with an organization for an extended period of time – either in the role of an employee (e.g., Flik, 1990; Sharpe, 1997) or in the role of a researcher (e.g., Azevedo, 2011; Schumacher, 1997; Tukiainen, 2011). Ethnographers engage extensively in the field, using a combination of methods such as participant observations, informal conversations, interviews and documentary analysis to explore culture with a specific focus. They gather data that are available during daily work-life, thus observing work practices, listening to what organization members say and what happens during the course of a work day. During or at the end of the day, field notes are typically taken and analyzed on an ongoing basis by comparing and contrasting all obtained information. The resulting insights form the basis for further probing into puzzling issues. As insiders, ethnographers have the opportunity to check underlying meanings of artifacts and observed behavior and thus can validate their interpretations. However, it is unlikely that an organization with an undisclosed corrupt or unethical culture will allow a researcher access to their organization. Ethnographers may either apply for a regular job and disguise their intentions (with the associated ethical concerns) or turn into a whistleblower.[5] Nevertheless, ethnography could be considered the most promising approach for uncovering nondisclosed unethical or corrupt organizational cultures.

The above discussion shows that several data collection methods are available to potentially uncover a corrupt, unethical or bad culture, but that it is not easy in the case of an undisclosed case. The final section summarizes the major challenges in uncovering a corrupt or unethical culture.

DECIPHERING A "BAD" CULTURE – SOME CONCLUDING COMMENTS

Organizational culture, especially a corrupt or unethical culture, is difficult to decipher, as evidenced by known fraudulent business cases that all had external auditors testifying as to their proper business behavior. Given that undisclosed corrupt or unethically acting organizations are likely trying to cover up their illegal and wrongdoing behavior, creative approaches are needed to uncover corrupt and unethical behavior, combining different data types and data sources in a triangulation approach (Flick, 2014). At the level of artifacts (see Figure 17.1), an outsider can obtain a large amount of documentation from external sources (Armenakis & Lang, 2014). In the case of a multinational company, the Corruption Perception Index (Transparency International, 2018) can give first insights into the extent of potentially existing corruption in a specific country. Comparing information obtained from different externally available sources such as *The Worst Companies To Work For*, employee blogs (e.g., Kununu), Mighty Earth, investigative journalism, and former employees, can yield valuable information and first insights about an organization's reputation and its potential wrongdoing. Resulting assumptions and hypotheses can be tested using practice level data from observations, documents, emails, chats and conversations with organizational members. Outsiders may search for a meeting place of current and former employees, mingle with them and engage them in conversations about their (former) employer.

If access is possible in the role of a visitor, job applicant, potential investor or external auditor, all senses need to be used for observations of potential manifestations and behaviors that may indicate problematic practices. These may include all kinds of documents as well as working practices, interactions among employees, interactions between employees and management and interactions with outsiders. In general, the six steps suggested by Schein (2010) listed above are helpful in guiding data collection on site. Of particular interest are inconsistent documents, behaviors that appear to be strange, as well as practices that are not in line with the official work practices declared in formal documents such as the corporate values statement, leadership guidelines, code of corporate ethics, etc. Further indicators are mistrust, an abundance of controls and control systems, a sense of secretive behavior, hesitant discussions, little willingness to open up and share information, strict procedures in dealing with outsiders that make no sense in the given context, different cliques of employees, whispering, high levels of competition and high performance pressure, lack of respect for people, stressed and overworked employees, lack of communication and team spirit, humiliations, bad habits, micromanagement, large amounts of gossip and sarcasm, lack of empathy, high or no level of turnover, and the kind of reward systems. A comparison of all information gained from the external and internal data sources, as well as a comparison between formal organizational documents, emails, chats and the organization's ways of behaving may reveal issues for further probing and eventually help uncover lived norms and values as well as behavior-guiding beliefs and assumptions.

As such, visitors, job applicants or external auditors should consider themselves antennae for collecting all kinds of different cues during their stay in the organization. Uncovering a corrupt or unethical culture is like searching for small pieces of a puzzle and putting them together to finally reveal the entire picture – similar to the detective Columbo's inductive approach rather than Sherlock Holmes' deductive style (Sackmann, 1990, p. 359). The central features of the inductive approach are open, curious, attentive observations keeping all senses open, asking so-called "stupid" questions, questioning apparently clear facts, and constantly questioning, comparing and interpreting the data. Once detective Columbo has developed a hypothesis on the basis of the collected data, he also conducts small experiments to finally elicit a confession from the suspect. Columbo's detective style demonstrates that despite all difficulties in uncovering a corrupt or unethical culture in the absence of a valid measurement instrument, it is feasible, but requires an imaginative, creative multiple methods approach. Existing questionnaires can be used by organizations to detect early undesirable developments to prevent the development of corrupt and unethical organizational culture.

NOTES

1. This research was supported by the Estonian Research Council Grant PRG1107.
2. While organizational culture is the more general concept including for-profit and not-for-profit organizations, corporate culture pertains to for-profit companies.
3. Since jurisdictions as well as national cultures may differ from nation to nation, the judgment of what is considered illegal and unethical/misbehavior may also differ to some extent (e.g., Bicker & Sackmann, 2019; Chhokar et al., [2008] 2013; Hofstede, 2001).
4. Sackmann (2010) discusses 25 different ways to analyze organizational culture with their pros and cons. These include single and multiple method approaches.
5. Well known whistleblowers are Sherron Watkins in the case of Enron or the character McDeere played by Tom Cruise in the movie *The Firm* (1993) directed by Sydney Pollack.

REFERENCES

Armenakis, A., & Lang, I. (2014). Forensic diagnosis and transformation of an organizational culture. *Journal of Change Management, 14*(2), 149–170.

Armenakis, A., Brown, S., & Mehta, A. (2011). Organizational culture: Assessment and transformation. *Journal of Change Management, 11*(3), 305–328.

Ashford, B. E., Gioia, D. A., Robinson, S. L., & Trevino, L. K. (2008). Introduction to the special topic forum: Re-viewing organizational corruption. *Academy of Management Review, 33*(3), 670–684.

Azevedo, G. (2011). Intercultural integration in Sino-Brazilian joint ventures. In H. Primecz, L. Romani & S. Sackmann (Eds.), *Cross-Cultural Management in Practice. Culture and Negotiated Meanings* (pp. 112–124). Cheltenham, UK and Northampton, MA, USA: Edward Elgar Publishing.

Bales, R. F. (1950). *Interaction Process Analysis: A Method for the Study of Small Groups*. Oxford, UK: Addison-Wesley.

Beenen, G., & Pinto, J. (2009). Resisting organizational-level corruption: An interview with Enron whistle-blower Sheron Watkins. *Academy of Management Learning and Education, 8*(2), 275–289.

Bicker, E., & Sackmann, S. (Eds.) (2019). *Compliance bei M&A-Transaktionen.* Stuttgart, Germany: Schäffer-Poeschel.

Buchko, A. A., Buscher, C., & Buchko, K. J. (2017). Why do good employees stay in bad organizations? *Business Horizons, 60*(5), 729–739.

Campbell, J.-L., & Göritz, A. S. (2014). Culture corrupts! A qualitative study of organizational culture in corrupt organizations. *Journal of Business Ethics, 120*(3), 291–311.

Chhokar, J. S., Brodbeck, F. C., & House, R. J. (Eds.) ([2008] 2013). *Culture and Leadership Across the World. The GLOBE Book of In-depth Studies of 25 Societies.* New York, NY: Taylor & Francis.

Coyle-Shapiro, J. A.-M., Pereira Costa, S., Doden, W., & Chang, C. (2019). Psychological contracts: Past, present, and future. *Annual Review of Organizational Psychology and Organizational Behavior, 6*(1), 145–169.

Dahling, J. J., Chau, S. L., Mayer, D. M., & Gregory, J. B. (2012). Breaking rules for the right reasons? An investigation of prosocial rule breaking. *Journal of Organizational Behavior, 33*(1), 21–42.

DeBode, J. D., Armenakis, A. A., Feild, H. S., & Walker, A. G. (2013). Assessing ethical organizational culture: Refinement of a scale. *Journal of Applied Behavioral Science, 49*(4), 460–484.

Eichenwald, K. (2012). Microsoft's lost decade. *Vanity Fair, 624,* 108–117.

Ernst, H. (2003). Unternehmenskultur und Innovationserfolg: Eine empirische Analyse. *Zeitschrift für betriebswirtschaftliche Forschung, 55*(1), 23–44.

Fetterman, D. (2009). *Ethnography: Step by Step* (3rd ed.). Thousand Oaks, CA: Sage.

Flick, U. (2014). *An Introduction to Qualitative Research* (5th ed.). Los Angeles, CA: Sage.

Flik, H. (1990). The Ameba concept … organizing around opportunity within the GORE culture. In H. Simon (Ed.), *Herausforderung Unternehmenskultur* (pp. 91–129). Stuttgart, Germany: Schäffer.

Gilbert, J. A., Carr-Ruffino, N., Ivancevich, J. M. & Konopaske, R. (2011). Toxic versus cooperative behaviors at work: The role of organizational culture and leadership in creating community-centered organizations. *International Journal of Leadership Studies, 7*(1), 29–46.

Goldberg, C. B., Rawski, S. L., & Perry, E. L. (2019). The direct and indirect effects of organizational tolerance for sexual harassment on the effectiveness of sexual harassment investigation training for HR managers. *Human Resource Development Quarterly, 30*(1), 81–100.

Hofstede, G. (2001). *Culture's Consequences. Comparing Values, Behaviors, Institutions and Organizations Across Nations* (2nd ed.). Thousand Oaks, CA: Sage.

Kantor, J., & Streitfeld, D. (2015, August 15). Inside Amazon: Wrestling big ideas in a bruising workplace. *The New York Times.* Retrieved March 12, 2020, from www.nytimes.com/2015/08/16/technology/inside-amazon-wrestling-big-ideas-in-a-bruising-workplace.html.

Kaptein, M. (2008). Developing and testing a measure for the ethical culture of organizations: The corporate ethical virtues model. *Journal of Organizational Behavior, 29*(7), 923–947.

Kaptein, M. (2011). From inaction to external whistleblowing: The influence of the ethical culture of organizations on employee responses to observed wrongdoing. *Journal of Business Ethics, 98*(3), 513–530.

Key, S. (1999). Organizational ethical culture: Real or imagined? *Journal of Business Ethics, 20*(3), 217–225.

Kish-Gephard, J. J., Harrison, D. A. & Trevino, L. K. (2010). Bad apples, bad cases, and bad barrels: Meta-analytic evidence about sources of unethical decisions at work. *Journal of Applied Psychology, 95*(1), 1–31.

Kolb, D. G., & Shepard, D. M. (1997). Concept mapping organizational cultures. *Journal of Management Inquiry, 6*(4), 282–295.

Kotter, J. P., & Heskett, J. L. (1992). *Corporate Culture and Performance.* New York, NY: Free Press.

Lanier, C., & Kirchner, M. (2018). Corruption and culture: Empirical analyses of long-term indulgence and corrupt systems. *Review of Business: Interdisciplinary Journal on Risk and Society, 38*(2), 30–43.

Lutgen-Sandvik, P., & McDermott, V. (2008). The constitution of employee-abusive organizations: A communication flows theory. *Communication Theory, 18*(2), 304–333.

McLean, B., & Elkind, P. (2003). *The Smartest Guys in the Room: The Amazing Rise and Scandalous Fall of Enron.* New York, NY: Portfolio.

Mighty Earth (2019, July 11). *Cargill: The Worst Company in the World*. Retrieved March 12, 2020, from www.mightyearth.org/wp-content/uploads/Mighty-Earth-Report-Cargill-The-Worst-Company -in-the-World-July-2019.pdf.

Mihelič, K. K., & Culiberg, B. (2019). Reaping the fruits of another's labor: The role of moral meaningfulness, mindfulness, and motivation in social loafing. *Journal of Business Ethics, 160*(3), 713–727.

Parboteeah, K. P., Martin, K. D., & Cullen J. B. (2011). An international perspective on ethical climate. In N. M. Ashkanasy, C. P. M. Wilderom & M. F. Peterson (Eds.), *The Handbook of Organizational Culture and Climate* (pp. 600–616). Thousand Oaks, CA: Sage.

Pinto, J., Leana, C. R., & Pil, F. K. (2008). Corrupt organizations or organizations of corrupt individuals? Two types of organization-level corruption. *Academy of Management Review, 33*(3), 685–709.

Powell, G. N. (1998). The abusive organization. *Academy of Management Perspectives, 12*(2), 95–96.

Ross, D. L., & Benson, J. A. (1995). Culture change in ethical redemption: A corporate case study. *Journal of Business Communication, 32*(4), 345–362.

Sackmann, S. A. (1990). Diagnose von sozialen Systemen. In G. Fatzer & C. D. Eck (Eds.), *Supervision und Beratung* (pp. 341–361). Bergisch Gladbach, Germany: Edition Humanistische Psychologie.

Sackmann, S. A. (1991). *Cultural Knowledge in Organizations: Exploring the Collective Mind*. Newbury Park, CA: Sage.

Sackmann, S. A. (2006). *Success Factor: Corporate Culture. Developing a Corporate Culture for High Performance and Long-term Competitiveness*. Gütersloh, Germany: Bertelsmann Stiftung.

Sackmann, S. A. (2008). Hochleistungsorganisationen aus unternehmenskultureller Perspektive. In P. Pawlowski & P. Mistele (Eds.), *Hochleistungsmanagement: Leistungspotenziale in Organisationen gezielt fördern* (pp. 181–206). Wiesbaden, Germany: Gabler.

Sackmann, S. A. (2010). *Assessment, Evaluation, Improvement: Success through Corporate Culture*. Gütersloh, Germany: Bertelsmann Stiftung (Print 2006 1st ed.; Print 2007 2nd ed.; E-book 2010). Retrieved March 12, 2020, www.bertelsmann-stiftung.de/de/publikationen/publikation/did/ assessment-evaluation-improvement-success-through-corporate-culture.

Sackmann, S. A. (2013). Die Rolle der Unternehmenskultur bei Unternehmenskrisen. In F. Richter (Ed.), *Effizientes Sanierungsmanagement* (pp. 43–62). Stuttgart, Germany: Schäffer-Poeschel.

Sackmann, S. A. (2018). Generative Organisationskulturen und Führungsaufgaben – Ansätze zur zukunftsfähigen Gestaltung von Prozessen der Organisationsentwicklung. In A. Metzner-Szigeth (Ed.), *Zukunftsfähige Entwicklung und generative Organisationskulturen. Wie wir Systeme anders wahrnehmen und Veränderung gestalten können* (pp. 122–135). München, Germany: Oekom.

Sackmann, S. A. (2021). *Culture in Organizations. Development, Impact and Culture-Mindful Leadership*. Springer Nature.

Sackmann, S. A. & Horstmann, B. (2009). The role of corporate culture in developing and preventing corruption. In A. Stachowicz-Stanusch (Ed.), *Organizational Immunity to Corruption: Building Theoretical and Research Foundations* (pp. 261–277). Katowice: The Katowice Branch of the Polish Academy of Sciences.

Schaufeli, W. B. (2018). *Burnout in Europe: Relations with National Economy, Governance, and Culture*. Research Unit Occupational & Organizational Psychology and Professional Learning (internal report). KU Leuven, Belgium. Retrieved March 12, 2020, from www.wilmarschaufeli.nl/ publications/Schaufeli/500.pdf.

Schein, E. (2010). *Organizational Culture and Leadership* (4th ed.). San Francisco, CA: Jossey Bass.

Schumacher, T. (1997). West Coast Camelot: The rise and fall of an organizational culture. In S. A. Sackmann (Ed.), *Cultural Complexity in Organizations: Inherent Contrasts and Contradictions* (pp. 107–132). Thousand Oaks, CA: Sage.

Sharpe, D. R. (1997). Managerial control strategies and subcultural processes: On the shop floor in a Japanese manufacturing organization in the United Kingdom. In S. A. Sackmann (Ed.), *Cultural Complexity in Organizations: Inherent Contrasts and Contradictions* (pp. 228–251). Thousand Oaks, CA: Sage.

Smircich, L. (1983). Concepts of culture and organizational analysis. *Administrative Science Quarterly, 28*(3), 339–358.

Solas, J. (2019). Conscientious objections to corporate wrongdoing. *Business and Society Review, 124*(1), 43–62.

Spradley, J. P. (1979). *The Ethnographic Interview*. New York, NY: Holt, Rinehart & Winston.

Sprigg, C. A., Niven, K., Dawson, J., Farley, S., & Armitage, C. J. (2018). Witnessing workplace bullying and employee well-being: A two-wave field study. *Journal of Occupational Health Psychology*, *24*(2), 286–296.

Stebbins, S. (2019, June 12). *The Worst Companies to Work For*. 24/7 WallSt. online. Retrieved March 12, 2020, from https://247wallst.com/special-report/2019/06/12/the-worst-companies-to-work-for-4.

Stein, N. (2000). The world's most admired companies. How do you make the most admired list? Innovate, innovate, innovate. The winners on this year's list, compiled by the Hay Group consultancy, tell how they do it. *Fortune Magazine*, October 2, 183–186. Retrieved March 12, 2020, from http://archive.fortune.com/magazines/fortune/fortune_archive/2000/10/02/288448/index.htm.

Tan, D. T., Chapple, L. & Walsh, K. D. (2017). Corporate fraud culture: Re-examining the corporate governance and performance relation. *Accounting and Finance*, *57*(2), 597–620.

Transparency International (2018). Corruption Perceptions Index 2018. Retrieved March 12, 2020, from www.transparency.org/cpi2018.

Trevino, L., K., Butterfield, K. D., & McCabe, D. L. (1995). *Contextual Influences on Ethics-related Outcomes in Organizations: Rethinking Ethical Climate and Ethical Culture.* Paper presented at the Annual Meeting of the Academy of Management, San Diego, CA, August 1995.

Tukiainen, S. (2011). Dynamics of ethnocentrism and ethnorelativism: A case study of Finnish–Polish collaboration. In H. Primecz, L. Romani & S. Sackmann (Eds.), *Cross-cultural Management in Practice: Culture and Negotiated Meanings* (pp. 29–40). Cheltenham, UK and Northampton, MA, USA: Edward Elgar Publishing.

Warren, D. E., Gaspar, J. P., & Laufer, W. S. (2014). Is formal ethics training merely cosmetic? A study of ethics training and ethical organizational culture. *Business Ethics Quarterly*, *24*(1), 85–117.

Wigert, B., & Agrawal, S. (2018, July 12). Employee burnout, part 1: The 5 main causes. Gallup online. Retrieved March 12, 2020, from www.gallup.com/workplace/237059/employee-burnout-part-main-causes.aspx.

18. Measuring organizational culture in Christian churches

Angela J. Ward

ORGANIZATIONAL PARAMETERS: DEFINING "CHURCH"

Before exploring the unique characteristics of churches and their effect on attempts at measurement of their organizational culture, it is necessary to define what is meant by the term "church." Colloquially, the term "church" usually conjures an image of a material structure at a physical address, a "meeting place" where people participate in religious services. This material structure may have been originally constructed for this purpose (such as a cathedral); it could be a physical space that was originally constructed for another purpose but has since been retrofitted for regular religious activities (such as repurposed retail space in a strip mall); or it could be a temporary gathering place that is borrowed or rented but without lasting material changes to the structure's design or decoration (such as a public facility like a school, community center, or park shelter).

However, modern technology has expanded the notion of what may be considered a gathering place for church attenders. Many large churches now offer online "locations" where the faithful can participate in (or at least watch) religious services and programs via the internet. Some of these online sites even provide live chat rooms, where visitors can interact with pastors or other organizational employees. In addition, there are church services offered in virtual environments, utilizing virtual reality (VR) software and equipment (Ward, 2008; Bettis, 2018). Already, defining "church" is complicated.

Add to this the fact that the word "church" did not even appear in the original biblical manuscripts. The word later translated "church" was the Greek word *ekklēsia*, which means gathering or assembly (Chapman, 1984, p. 28). *Ekklēsia* first appears in Matthew 16:18, which is when Christians believe Jesus foretold his establishment of the church through Peter. As the church itself expanded, so did the understanding of the Greek word used to denote it. By late New Testament times, *ekklēsia* had four primary meanings:

1. All Christians in one geographic area, e.g., "the church of God that is in Corinth" (1 Cor 1:2).
2. All Christians on earth.
3. A small Christian group that regularly meets together in a home (Rom 16:5, 1 Cor 16:19, Phlm 2).
4. A group of Christians actually assembled (Giles, 1995, pp. 115–118).

So, again: what is a church? For purposes of this discussion regarding its organizational culture, the researcher suggests that a church be quantified as *a local, physical, formal, specific, regular gathering of religious adherents*. It is local, in that there is a geographic proximity among its participants. It is physical, in that participants interact in real time and space. It is formal, in that the gathering meets specifically for designated religious practices and observances. It is specific, in that its location is differentiated from other gatherings in the same geographic area. And it is regular, in that gatherings are repeated with an agreed-upon frequency.

The remainder of this chapter will assume the researcher's definition when using the word "church," and will focus in particular on churches that identify as "Christian."

UNIQUE CHARACTERISTICS OF CHRISTIAN CHURCHES

Even after defining the parameters of what constitutes a "church" as an organization, churches present unique characteristics, and therefore unique challenges, to attempts to measure their organizational culture. During the course of over 30 years as a participant and leader in Christian churches, the researcher has observed several characteristics specific to these organizations, which must be considered when undertaking church culture research.

Unique Classification

As a formal organization, a church would normally be classified sociologically as a "non-kinship group" (Collins, 1975, pp. 313, 358–59). However, the Bible teaches that believers in Christ share a *spiritual* kinship. Jesus and the Apostles write of brothers and sisters in the faith. Therefore, a Christian church is both a non-kinship (sociological) and a kinship (theological) group, which may also contain human kinship relationships. This unique combination results in different (and sometimes competing) types of organizational values, as the researcher will describe later in this chapter.

Unique Language

As in other sectors, Christian churches use unique language or apply different definitions to common words. For example, "family" could mean the church community, irrespective of kinship relationships. And while "member"—a term frequently used in the organizational culture literature—may have a clear definition in a business organization, in the church world it is a loaded term. Some churches maintain a formal membership process and roster, although that membership may include people who have not attended the church in years. Others use the term "member" to refer to regular attenders. Still others avoid the term entirely. In addition, the church's understanding of membership may not be accurately reflected in an individual member's (or participant's) language. Ask a person if they are a member of a particular church, and an affirmative answer may simply mean "*I* consider myself a part of," whether or not the church itself would consider that person a member. A researcher attempting to measure organizational culture in churches must therefore have a strong grasp of the unique language of the church milieu, in order to develop research tools and language that can accurately describe and measure the unique aspects of church organizational culture.

Unique Composition

Christian churches consist of several unique subgroups in regards to participation and authority. The two most recognized are clergy and laity, but among these categories there are also subgroups such as lay leaders, volunteers, and general attendees. The roles of these subgroups vary widely wide depending on size and ecclesial structure, which are based on theological beliefs and philosophical values. For example, a non-denominational church of 150 regular attenders might have a paid minister who works with a small group of "elders" (overseers) to govern and direct the church's activities, although the minister might be considered the primary spiritual leader of the congregation. Under this governing body, there might be volunteer committees, who in turn coordinate volunteer workers in various areas of activity such as children's programs and facility maintenance. If the church is a part of a denomination, the clergy will be accountable to a judicatory entity, such as a bishop or a district director, and the church's values and activities will be directed or at least informed by denominational beliefs and judicatory expectations.

All of these subgroups together form the local church, but each of them has different perspectives on the organization. Who, then, should be consulted to provide an accurate picture of the organizational culture in that church? The every-Sunday (but Sunday only) congregant? The volunteer lay leader who may have more in-depth perspective, but perhaps in only one area of the church's other activities? Paid clergy and other staff, who do not share the experience of the rank-and-file? Research must consider which perspective(s) should be included in an assessment of a church's organizational culture.

Unique Subcultures

Like any organization, a church can have both a dominant culture and any number of subcultures (Barnard, 1938, p. 115). In a larger church, participants—especially volunteer leaders—will identify primarily with their particular subgroup and its culture, more than with the church as a whole. For example, a woman who volunteers with a church's programs for the homeless may spend hours each week with that sub-ministry, but only one hour participating in religious observances with the entire church. Her perspective on the church's primary culture will be limited, even though she would be considered an active participant.

A similar issue arises with churches that hold services and programs on multiple sites or campuses, a phenomenon which is prevalent in evangelical Protestant congregations (Stetzer, 2014). The longer each site is in existence, the greater the likelihood that it will develop its own culture, instead of reflecting the culture of the "mother ship." In these cases, even though the gatherings are described by the flagship organization as extension sites, by the researcher's definition they function more like independent churches.

THE NEED FOR MEASUREMENT OF CHURCH ORGANIZATIONAL CULTURE

The specific characteristics and challenges of the church organizational context, along with the assumed spiritual importance of a church's work, make church organizational culture an important area for research. As in any organization, culture reflects and impacts every area of a church, including but not limited to leadership forms and structure, programming, communication, conflict management, purpose/mission, staffing, strategy, and external perception.

Clergy must understand that they are not just spiritual shepherds, but leaders of an organization that has its own culture and subcultures. Church leaders at all levels should seek to identify the culture in their particular church, and then develop a culture that fosters the greatest health and effectiveness at achieving its missional values. Church planters should be trained in the concept of church culture as it relates to the type of culture they are trying to create in their new works. Leaders who are trying to change their churches should recognize that lasting church change involves changing the culture of the organization, not just its behaviors, programs, or written statements of mission, vision, or values. Churches that are looking for new staff, and individuals seeking clergy positions, need to recognize the significance of cultural "fit" between a leader and the organization and should include assessments of organizational culture in the search process. Finally, an accurate instrument to measure organizational culture in churches might eventually serve a predictive function, perhaps helping to identify cultures that may foster or hide emotional, physical, and spiritual abuse by clergy or other leaders.

APPROACHES TO MEASUREMENT OF CHURCH ORGANIZATIONAL CULTURE

Like organizational culture in general, church organizational culture is a multi-dimensional construct. Therefore, it is only reasonable to assume that it is best studied using a multi-method approach. Jack Duncan proposes three dimensions that must be considered when devising a method for analyzing any type of organizational culture:

1. The objective/subjective dimension. An organization's objective aspects are those that exist outside the minds of organization members, and can be readily observed by outsiders. Examples of these objective aspects include stories, monuments, and pictures. Subjective aspects, on the other hand, cannot be directly observed but are nevertheless very real. Subjective aspects include shared assumptions, values, meanings, and understandings.
2. The qualitative/quantitative dimension. Organizational culture can be analyzed both quantitatively (i.e., by what can be concretely measured) and qualitatively (i.e., by noting the way people interpret the culture).
3. The observer (outsider)/native (insider) dimension. "Gaining an outsider's perspective on a culture is important because an observer can sometimes detect features that elude insiders. At the same time, outsiders impose their own perspectives on events, creating the danger that the meaning derived may not represent the meaning that the person being observed intended" (Duncan, 1989, pp. 229, 231).

In consideration of these three dimensions, Duncan sets the tone for the majority of researchers by advocating for what anthropologist Clifford Geertz described as a "thick description" (Geertz, 1973, p. 27) that incorporates a multi-method approach and utilizes both quantitative and qualitative research from internal and external perspectives (Duncan, 1989; Ott, 1989; Alvesson, 2002; Martin, 1992, 2002; Schein, 2000). While these methods are difficult to combine, the use of a variety of methods results in comprehensive and overlapping data that help give a complete picture of the organization under study.

The Case for Quantitative Research

However, while a multi-method research approach is the best way to arrive at a full-orbed understanding of an organization's culture, the reality remains that this type of approach is complex, expensive, and time-consuming (Ashkanasy et al., 2000, p. 131). In addition, qualitative methods are limited by the weaknesses inherent to that type of research, including observer bias and altered participant behavior (Mayo, 1933).

If organizational culture is indeed an organizational variable, then culture can be measured and mapped on a scale (Schultz, 1994, p. 11). Although Edgar Schein was highly critical of survey research for what he deemed to be its superficiality (Schein, 1991, p. 245), a majority of researchers agree that quantitative methods can be very useful. While the deepest levels of culture can only be investigated using qualitative methods, the shallower and more observable levels of organizational culture can be measured using quantitative methods. These representations and symbols can still give a researcher clues about the underlying assumptions behind the data (Ashkanasy et al., 2000, pp. 132–33).

Stephen McGuire points out additional advantages to survey-based culture studies over qualitative studies:

1. Surveys allow organizational members to report their perceptions of their organization's values, beliefs, and behavioral norms, without the biases that observers introduce. Because culture is socially constructed, it is indeed the perceptions of organizational members that are of interest, rather than a description of the organization by an outside observer.
2. Surveys allow for replication and assessment of culture (and changes in culture) over time. Quantitative methods allow for empirical tests of reliability of the instrument.
3. Surveys, which use a common format and can be completed by multiple informants, permit a quantification and explicit reporting of the degree to which values, beliefs and norms are *shared* by organizational members. This is important since culture is a socially shared phenomenon.
4. Surveys permit comparisons across organizations and among groups within an organization, which facilitate the identification of those characteristics that differentiate a given group from others.
5. Quantitative measures of culture can be used with multivariate statistics, thus permitting an analysis of underlying dimensions of culture, and the relationship between culture and organizational outcomes (McGuire, 2003, pp. 62–63).

Classification of Survey Measures

There are three classes of survey measures: behavior surveys, typing surveys, and profiling surveys. Behavior surveys attempt to identify patterns of organizational behavior. Typing surveys use instruments to assign organizations to a particular cultural "type." This designation also allows respondents to compare their organizations with others, and to track the cultural changes within an organization.

Profiling surveys are concerned with providing a description of an organization by measuring the strengths or weaknesses of a variety of dimensions. The resulting scores do not assign a type, but simply report a profile of organizational culture based on a set of behaviors, values, and beliefs that may not be mutually exclusive. Profiling surveys can be further divided into three types: effectiveness surveys, descriptive surveys, and fit profiles. Effectiveness surveys are concerned with links between particular values and measures of organizational effectiveness. Descriptive surveys, as the name implies, are concerned solely with measuring the organization's values, without evaluating their impact on organizational effectiveness. Fit profiles are concerned with the relationship between the organization's culture, and the "fit" or satisfaction of its individual members (Ashkanasy et al., 2000, p. 135).

CHURCH ORGANIZATIONAL CULTURE: LITERATURE REVIEW

The last three decades have seen a proliferation of research and writing on the topic of organizational culture in general and as it applies to business organizations. While the concept of organizational culture has made its way into professional resources for clergy and other church leaders, these references and tools are largely based on intuitive or anecdotal understanding, without a solid research foundation. Meanwhile, attempts at developing research-based tools have largely focused on adapting existing quantitative models and instruments for use in church contexts. However, this approach brings inherent limitations based on the unique characteristics noted earlier in this chapter.

Professional Understanding

One of the first known references to the concept of organizational culture within a church was made by R. Paul Stevens in the now out-of-print, *Complete Book of Everyday Christianity* (1997). Stevens cites Edgar Schein extensively in an article entitled, "Organizational culture and change" and defines culture as a "corporate 'feeling' or environment that communicates to new and old members what is important and what is permitted" (Stevens, 1997, p. 714). Spiritual formation director Ruth Haley Barton demonstrates an unreferenced understanding of organizational culture as a concept in an article about how to cultivate an organizational culture of spiritual transformation (Barton, 2004, p. 2). In 2005's *Culture Shift,* pastors Robert Lewis and Wayne Cordeiro attempt to elevate organizational culture in pastoral awareness. However, the authors do not include a clear definition of culture, or explain how they arrived at their understanding of the concept, instead referring only to its impact: "Culture is the most important social reality in your church" (Lewis and Cordeiro, 2005, p. 3).

This is not to say that all church leaders and pastors are unaware of the concept of organizational culture. At Mosaic Church in Los Angeles, lead pastor Erwin McManus carries the title of "Cultural Architect" (ErwinMcManus, 2009). Reverend Ray Johnston, founding pastor of Bayside Church in Granite Bay, California, has spoken about the need for churches to embed a priority for evangelism into their "DNA" (Johnston, 2004). On the other side of the country at Seacoast Community Church based in Charleston, South Carolina, founding pastors and brothers Greg and Geoff Surratt referred to their church's culture in explaining why their congregation has been open to many ministry innovations in its history (Surratt and Surratt, 2005, 33). Kevin Ford writes that each church has a unique "code" (Ford, 2007, p. 64). Megachurch pastor Andy Stanley of Northpoint Church in Atlanta, Georgia, has spoken often about the impact of "systems" and of operational values on the effectiveness of a church (Stanley, 2007).

In his 2010 book *Cracking Your Church's Culture Code*, church consultant Samuel R. Chand defines church organizational culture as the "personality" of a church and points out that culture trumps vision; that is, "Culture—not vision or strategy—is the most powerful factor in any organization. It determines the receptivity of staff and volunteers to new ideas, unleashes or dampens creativity, builds or erodes enthusiasm, and creates a sense of pride or deep discouragement about working or being involved there" (Chand, 2010, p. 2). Chand goes on to propose the acrostic CULTURE to describe seven keys of culture: control, understanding, leadership, trust, unafraid, responsive, and execution. In addition, Chand offers churches a free online culture survey to diagnose organizational culture on a scale based on five proposed types of culture: inspiring, accepting, stagnant, discouraging, or toxic. While Chand is to be commended for trumpeting the importance of organizational culture in the church, his book and survey lack any evidence of scholarly research and instead use anecdotal evidence and professional intuition to support his theory.

The most comprehensive popular work to date on the topic of organizational culture in churches is Aubrey Malphurs's 2013 book, *Look Before You Lead: How to Discern and Shape Your Church Culture*. Malphurs, a church consultant and seminary professor, asserts that "a primary responsibility of today's strategic church leaders is to create, implement, and re-implement an organizational culture that rewards and encourages movement toward the church's mission and vision" (Malphurs, 2013, p. 7). He defines church culture as "its unique expression of its shared beliefs and values" (p. 19) and likens congregational culture to an apple, consisting of a skin (the church's outward behavior), flesh (the church's values), and core (the church's beliefs). This three-level understanding directly mirrors Edgar Schein's iceberg metaphor, with its levels of artifacts, espoused beliefs and values, and underlying assumptions, as depicted in Figure 18.1.

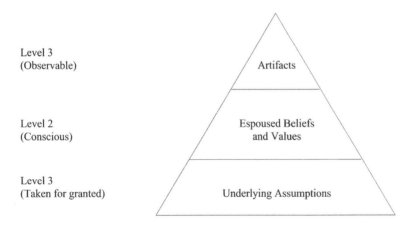

Level 3
(Observable)   Artifacts

Level 2
(Conscious)   Espoused Beliefs
and Values

Level 3
(Taken for granted)   Underlying Assumptions

Source: Adapted from Schein (2004, p. 26).

Figure 18.1   Levels of organizational culture

In extensive appendixes, Malphurs provides a series of "audits" or surveys to help church leaders assess their organization's culture. These audits include a behaviors audit, a core values audit, a beliefs audit, and a spiritual maturity audit, along with scoring guides for several audits, presumably developed by Malphurs based on his consulting experience, as no citations are given or research protocols described.

Malphurs's book is an excellent resource, the most comprehensive popular work to date. It is based in part on Schein's reputable model. The audits are worthwhile tools to help clergy and other church leaders think about their church's culture. However, like the other popular books on this subject, Malphurs writes from his experience, intuition and observation as a pastor and consultant. While his understanding possesses face validity, his work is not rooted in rigorous scholarship. Malphurs seems unaware of scholarly research on the subject of church organizational culture, again highlighting the scholarly/popular separation in ministry-related writing and resources.

Scholarly Research

A comprehensive search by this author revealed only a handful of research works on the topic of church organizational culture. All but one of these have been written within the last 15 years. Additionally, all but one used existing frameworks and instruments to attempt to assess organizational culture within a church context.

Hal Pettegrew

In 1993, doctoral student Hal Pettegrew of Trinity Evangelical Divinity School studied the relationship between organizational climate and volunteer motivation and satisfaction. Based on the literature at the time of his research, Pettegrew proposed ten organizational climate factors in a church setting: organization/structure, support, reward/recognition, trust, care/concern, warmth/friendliness, standards, purpose/cause, communication, and ownership/identity. These ten factors were incorporated into a 30-item, 5-point response, Likert-type instrument. Pettegrew found a strong positive relationship between the presence of positive organizational climate factors and positive volunteer motivation and satisfaction (Pettegrew, 1993, p. 113).

Pettegrew describes climate as the personality of an organization that develops as the result of people's interaction within the organization (Pettegrew, 1993, p. 23). This description sounds similar to the contemporary understanding of organizational culture; and indeed, Pettegrew discusses this climate/culture question in his dissertation.

Overviewing the organizational literature, one sees that one of the predominant themes in the 1960s through the early 1980s has been the organizational climate theme. This theme did not disappear from discussion in the decade of the 1980s, but the concept of organizational culture has become more predominant with popular works written by Peters and Waterman (1982) and Deal and Kennedy (1982) and theoretical underpinnings by writers such as Edgar Schein (2004). Along the way, one wonders if some writers have simply not incorporated the concept of organizational climate into that of organizational culture. At any rate, basic definitions of culture would lead the reader to believe that organizational culture greatly influences organizational climate. Assuming organizational culture is an operative force beneath organizational climate, further research would be warranted in looking at organizational culture in relation to the institution of the church (Pettegrew, 1993, pp. 39–40).

W. Brady Boggs

It would be nearly a decade before Pettegrew's suggestion would be addressed in a doctoral dissertation authored by W. Brady Boggs of Regent University. Boggs's exploratory study examined the relationship between organizational culture and church effectiveness in Assemblies of God congregations in North Carolina. To measure organizational culture, Boggs chose to administer the Organizational Culture Assessment Index, which is based on the Competing Values Framework (CVF) developed by Kim S. Cameron and Robert E. Quinn

(Cameron and Quinn, 1999). Boggs modified the wording to adapt the instrument to a church context (Boggs, 2002, p. 109).

To measure church effectiveness, Boggs modified the Balanced Scorecard (Kaplan and Norton, 1996), which measures corporate performance in four areas: financial, customer, internal business, and innovation and learning. To use the scorecard with churches in his research, Boggs modified the four perspectives to include finance (growth rate of organization's annual income); constituent (growth rate of world missions support); operations (growth rate of Sunday morning worship attendance); and innovation and learning (growth rate of Sunday School attendance) (Boggs, 2002, pp. 44–46).

Boggs's study discovered positive relationships between various combinations of organizational cultures and measures of church performance, but not a correlation between one specific culture and all measures of church performance (Boggs, 2002, pp. 118–19). Nevertheless, Boggs's research is significant because it is the first study to measure the relationship between organizational culture and ministry performance. Although Boggs used existing measures for both factors, he recognized that the original wording of those instruments needed to be modified to reflect the unique properties of the church. It is also noteworthy that Boggs' search of the literature for his study revealed a lack of foundational research regarding church organizational culture, although he found a substantial body of literature for other types of organizations (Boggs, 2002, p. 109).

Thomas C. Davis

For his doctoral research at Asbury Theological Seminary in 2007, Thomas C. Davis studied the relationship between three independent variables: organizational culture, leadership style, and worship attendance growth. Davis's research sample consisted of United Methodist churches that were located in the fastest growing suburbs of Atlanta, and which had senior pastors who had been at those churches for five years or more (Davis, 2007, pp. 19–20).

Based on his research, Davis proposed that organizational culture is "a pattern of shared basic assumptions that have been learned by a local church." He further proposed eight types of church organizational culture: evangelizing, worshipping, teaching, community building, social consciousness raising, "blending" (high in three or more of the other cultures), King, and Father, the latter two which refer to the church's understanding of the nature of God. Davis then designed a questionnaire to determine the presence of these eight proposed culture types in his subject churches.

While Davis's definition of organizational culture reflects an understanding of several aspects of the construct, the eight types of church organizational culture that Davis proposes mix missional values and behaviors with theological orientation. In addition, the "blended" culture he proposes allows that a church may possess a number of equally high missional values and behaviors. Counting any combination of three or more values as a "blended" culture does not provide for adequate differentiation for reliable research.

Andreas Dietrich

In the same year, Andreas Dietrich, also at Asbury Theological Seminary, developed the Church Culture Survey (CCS) based on Geert Hofstede's four Cultural Value Dimensions (individualism/collectivism, high and low power-distance, strong and weak uncertainty avoidance, and masculine/feminine dimensions) (Hofstede, 2005). Dietrich further extrapolated themes from Hofstede's research into five subcategories for congregational assessment, including attitudes and behavior, theology, pastoral role, decision making, and communication patterns (Dietrich, 2007, 46). Dietrich's survey, consisting of 40 bipolar statement pairs with five possible responses to each pair, was administered to three congregations in a pilot study, then revised and administered to one posttest congregation, Dietrich's own church.

The Church Culture Survey passed statistical tests for face validity, content validity, inter-rater reliability, internal consistency, and inter-item correlation. At the same time, Dietrich acknowledged the weaknesses in directly applying Hofstede's model to congregational use.

Because Hofstede's findings are based largely on research in business settings, not all aspects of the Cultural Value Dimensions apply to the life of a congregation. Therefore, this study uses Hofstede's dimensions as broad parameters from which to extrapolate only those aspects of culture that have significant value for understanding congregations (Dietrich, 2007, p. 47).

Nevertheless, Dietrich's work provides a significant foundation for future efforts toward the design of an instrument to measure church organizational culture, although Dietrich also noted a lack of literature regarding the construct (Dietrich, 2007, p. 18).

Additional Research

The book *Shaped by God's Heart: The Passion and Practices of Missional Churches* reports the results of a two-year field study of 200 Protestant churches across the United States (Minatrea, 2004). Author Milfred Minatrea proposes nine "culture checkpoints" that correlate with a "missional culture," defined as "a reproducing community of authentic disciples, being equipped as missionaries sent by God, to live and proclaim His Kingdom in their world" (Minatrea, 2004, p. xvi). Minatrea's research led to the development of the Missional Culture Church Assessment, which seeks to measure the presence of the nine checkpoints in a church's behavior. The checkpoints include: high threshold for membership; real, but not real religious; teach to obey rather than simply to know; rewrite worship every week; live apostolically; expect to change the world from their own front porch; order their actions based upon their purpose; measure growth by capacity to release rather than retain; value beliefs and are passionate about the Kingdom of God (Minatrea, 2004, pp. 29–139). At the time of this writing, the Missional Church Cultural Assessment was only available in the book or online via a link from the web site xpastor.org to theculturetool.com, a sub-site of the church staffing firm Vanderbloemen (www.vanderbloemen.com).

In an article in the *Journal of Psychology and Christianity*, authors George M. Diekhoff, Susan K. Thompson and Ryan M. Denney of Midwestern State University developed a multi-dimensional scale of church climate, defined as "the collection of relatively enduring organizational characteristics that distinguish it from other organizations and affect the people within the organization" (Diekhoff et al., 2006, p. 18). The authors used several existing measures to locate subject churches on a four-quadrant map of church climates, including socially/emotionally supportive, spiritually stimulating, boring, and rigid (Diekhoff, Thompson and Denny, 2006, p. 18). While this study purported to measure church climate and not church culture, the terminology used reflected shared themes with the concept of organizational culture.

This review of the literature shows the relative lack of research on the subject of organizational culture in churches, as well as the weaknesses inherent to utilizing instruments and frameworks that have not been specifically designed around the unique construct and context of church organizational culture. With this understanding in mind, the author's research focused on the development of a new quantitative instrument to measure organizational culture in churches (Ward, 2011). To date, this remains the most comprehensive scholarly attempt to quantitatively define and measure this construct. While the researcher failed in efforts to produce a statistically valid and reliable instrument, the process yielded insights that should prove beneficial to future efforts to quantify and measure the construct.

CHURCH ORGANIZATIONAL CULTURE: CONSTRUCT DEFINITION AND INSTRUMENT DEVELOPMENT

The purpose of the author's doctoral research was to operationalize the construct, church organizational culture (COC), and to develop an instrument to measure the construct (Ward, 2011). The design of the study followed accepted protocols for construct validation (Hinkin, 1998; Ghiselli et al., 1981). The mixed-methods study included six components: precedent literature review, construct development, instrument design, pilot testing, survey revisions, and statistical analysis.

Throughout the study, the researcher utilized a panel of nine subject matter experts (SMEs). Panel members were selected for their recognized expertise in the areas of church leadership, theology, and Christian leadership education. Specifically, each member had to have at least five years of full-time experience in a significant leadership role within a local church. Additionally, the majority of panel members held a terminal degree in a field related to church ministry, practical theology, or leadership. It was the goal of the researcher to include both knowledge experts and skilled practitioners; therefore, the panel included a combination of scholars, pastors, and other church leaders.

Proposed Definition

Based on the review of precedent literature, the researcher proposed a definition for the new construct of church organizational culture; one that incorporated the common themes found in existing definitions of organizational culture yet used language specific to church ministry. The proposed definition stated: "Church organizational culture (COC) is the system of basic assumptions, values, and reinforced behavioral expectations that are shared by the people within a local church and tangibly reflected in their symbolic expressions and collective practices." The expert panel agreed that this served as an accurate definition for the COC construct.

Proposed Dimensions

Upon approval of the definition of church organizational culture, the researcher presented the expert panel with a list of 20 proposed dimensions of COC. This list was formulated by examining the list of 114 dimensions of organizational culture as identified in the literature (van der Post and de Coning, 1997, p. 155); noting common or overlapping themes as identified in precedent research (O'Reilly et al., 1991; Harrison and Stokes, 1992; Denison and Neale, 1996); and developing a new list of dimensions using language that would reflect the unique nature of the church and be familiar and understandable to those in church ministry.

Based on the responses of the expert panel, personal analysis of the original list, and the results of pilot testing and initial statistical analysis, the researcher reduced the initial list of twenty dimensions to sixteen, then to fifteen.

Table 18.1   Dimensions of church organizational culture—final revisions

#	Name of Dimension	Definition
1	Motivation	The extent to which the church views outsiders as an orienting and motivating factor for its missional activities.
2	Openness	The extent to which the church welcomes and accepts others.
3	Belonging	The extent to which the church is characterized by high personal commitment to the organization.
4	Conflict Management	The degree to which issues are handled openly and honestly in the church.
5	Empowerment	The extent to which insiders are encouraged and supported to contribute to the church's success.
6	Boldness	The extent to which the church values innovation and change in pursuit of its missional tasks.
7	Results	The degree to which the church is driven by measurable organizational accomplishment.
8	Teamwork	The degree to which the church values cooperation to accomplish organizational goals.
9	Leadership Trust	The extent to which insiders trust those in authority positions in the church.
10	Direction	The degree to which the church exemplifies a clear direction and strategy.

Instrument Design

Based on the results of the Delphi study, an initial set of questionnaire items for the church organizational culture (COC) instrument were generated. The researcher's intent was to design a descriptive study: a type of profiling study that does not assign value judgments to responses and that could be applied to Protestant Christian churches of all sizes, governance structures, denominational affiliations, demographics, and geographic locations. The initial questionnaire was presented to the expert panel for feedback on the wording of each item. In addition, the researcher enlisted the assistance of a naïve panel to confirm grouping of the items with the correct dimensions. Based on suggestions made by these panels, the researcher made revisions to the initial survey items.

The researcher performed several rounds of pilot testing, purposively sampling evangelical Protestant Christian churches in the United States to participate in pilot administration of the new instrument. For the purpose of the study, a key informant was defined as "an individual, male or female, who currently holds a position of oversight over a ministry or sub-ministry within the church, and who has regularly attended that church for at least eighteen months." This qualification represented an attempt to address the "unique composition" challenge and identify individuals who were involved in the church at a level that would facilitate knowledgeable responses regarding a church's culture.

Following the initial pilot test, the researcher made revisions to the instrument wording and format and again consolidated the list of dimensions, from 15 to ten. A list of the final revised collection of ten dimensions is displayed in Table 18.1. The revised instrument was then piloted at additional Protestant Christian churches in the United States.

Findings

According to the proposed church organizational culture construct, the COC Survey items should have grouped around the ten dimensions, or factors. Instead, exploratory factor analysis identified only one dominant factor, and the corresponding items did not appear to relate to each other in any meaningful way. There are several possible explanations for these results. First, the construct of Church Organizational Culture may actually consist of only one primary factor instead of clearly delineated dimensions, as originally proposed. Second, the construct may be too broad to be measured accurately using a quantitative instrument. Third, the construct may be measurable, but the dimensions were not accurate or clearly delineated enough for accurate measurement. Fourth, the proposed construct and dimensions may be accurate, but the wording of the items was not clear or focused enough to provide enough distinction between each dimension. It should be added that representatives from the pilot churches expressed during consultations that the survey results, while not statistically reliable or valid, were still very helpful for their organizations in understanding the complex construct of COC and the impact it has on ministry effectiveness.

As anticipated, this project yielded a wealth of helpful information. First, the construct of church organizational culture is indeed very broad and difficult to measure. The researcher began with a list of 20 dimensions and reduced this list to ten dimensions by the pilot stage of the process. However, while trying to reduce the number of dimensions for a more manageable survey, the researcher inadvertently ended up painting too broadly—trying to measure too much—with each of those ten dimensions. As a result, the questionnaire items were not focused enough to produce meaningful or statistically acceptable results. A shorter list of dimensions also minimizes the breadth and significance of the COC construct. In reality, COC may actually consist of many *more* dimensions, perhaps 15–20. Measuring these would require a complete redesign of the construct and of the COC Survey.

Second, it is to eliminate language that is subjective, or that reflects the biases of the researcher and/or the expert panel about the issues involved. The researcher also found it difficult to word the items so that they would measure values and assumptions, not just artifacts of organizational culture (Schein, 2004). In retrospect, some of the items could be answered by simple organizational observation, instead of a complex survey process. For example, questions about formal authority structures could be answered by a review of the church's constitution and bylaws. While these do affect church organizational culture, they are artifacts that reflect deeper values and assumptions, and it was difficult to write questions that could measure the underlying values.

Third, while the COC Survey was intended to measure overall church organizational culture, in reality it was most likely measuring organizational *leadership* culture; that is, the way a church's leadership operates in attempting to fulfill its missional tasks. Church leadership culture (CLC) is probably a subset of COC. In addition, the COC pilot survey was administered to church *leaders*, and the results would therefore reflect that level of individual involvement and awareness by respondents. A general attendee or congregant would probably not be able to answer many of the COC Survey questions with any authoritative knowledge, as s/he would not have a solid enough awareness of dimensions such as evaluation and direction, which are addressed at the organizational leadership level.

Finally, it became apparent from consultations with participating churches that the descriptive information provided by the survey was helpful to a point, but the real value to participating organizations rested in the *interpretation* of the results. Therefore, most participants expressed a desire for an interpretation guide that analyzed the results in terms of typing or fit. However, this kind of interpretation rests on all kinds of assumptions behind the survey and what constitutes a "good" or "bad," "strong" or "weak" result for a particular item or dimension. The COC Survey was designed to measure *church* organizational culture; that is, organizational culture within a church, *any* church or any style, without typing or judgment of the results. This kind of descriptive survey is different from a survey that purports to measure "churchy" or "religious" or "healthy" or "strong" organizational culture, or any other type of descriptor that assumes certain value judgments. Yet participants wanted some kind of standard, so that they could measure their organization against a predetermined set of values.

SUGGESTIONS FOR FURTHER RESEARCH

The formal development of the construct of church organizational culture opened an entirely new vein of research in the area of organizational studies. While churches could previously apply business and scholarly literature regarding organizational culture to ministry settings, the development of a specific definition for the construct of COC combines these domains and establishes church organizational culture as its own valid field of scholarly inquiry. However, there is much work to be done, and a database search in February 2019 revealed that no work has been published on this topic since the author's dissertation (Ward, 2011).

The first issue that must be remedied is the disconnect between scholarly and popular work on the topic of church organizational culture. The researcher attempted to bridge this gap by bringing the researcher's personal expertise as a church leader to the development of a reliable and valid instrument to measure COC. It would take a similarly qualified individual, ideally a scholar who also possesses significant previous clergy experience and a popular platform, to continue to narrow the divide.

The next step for further research would be continued development of the church organizational culture construct, specifically focusing on the component dimensions. With more time for qualitative research, a researcher might use grounded theory methods to collect data from which s/he could identify themes and extract possible dimensions of COC. From there, research could move to the development and testing of a completely revised instrument to measure the construct. Grounded theory research might also reveal a typological framework for COC, leading to the development of typing surveys (vs. purely descriptive) that would allow participants to compare their organizations with others, and to track the cultural changes within an organization.

CONCLUSION

After two decades of awareness, inquiry, and publication, the answer to the question, "How can organizational culture be quantitatively measured?" remains, "Not easily." COC is broad and complex, yet remains a worthwhile path of inquiry. At this writing, however, scholarly research on this topic has stalled. Leaders in Christian churches who seek tools to assess their organization's culture must therefore either look to the existing popular literature, utilize culture assessments that are not church-specific, or hire a consulting firm, which may or may not understand the specific nuances of church organizational culture. It is hoped that the next 20 years will bring greater awareness, continued research focus, increased communication between popular and scholarly leaders, and improved tools to measure this construct.

REFERENCES

Alvesson, Mats (2002). *Understanding Organizational Culture.* Thousand Oaks, CA: Sage.

Ashkanasy, Neal M., Broadfoot, Lynelle E., & Falkus, Sarah (2000). Questionnaire measures of organizational culture. In Neal M. Ashkanasy, Celeste P. M. Wilderom & Mark F. Petersen (eds), *Handbook of Organizational Culture and Climate* (pp. 131–45). Thousand Oaks, CA: Sage Publications.

Barnard, Chester I. (1938). *The Functions of the Executive.* Cambridge, MA: Harvard University Press.

Barton, Ruth H. (2004). A deeper calling: Cultivating an organizational culture of spiritual transformation. *Christian Management Report* (October): 1–4.

Bettis, Kara (2018). The embodied church in a digital age. *Christianity Today.* Retrieved from https://www.christianitytoday.com/pastors/2018/fall-state-of-church-ministry/embodied-church-in-digital-age.html.

Boggs, W. Brady (2002). An exploratory study of the relationship between organizational culture types and a balanced scorecard of effectiveness measures in the church. Ph.D. diss., Regent University.

Cameron, Kim S., & Quinn, Robert E. (1999). *Diagnosing and Changing Organizational Culture: Based on the Competing Values Framework.* Reading, MA: Addison-Wesley.

Chand, Samuel R. (2010). *Cracking Your Church's Culture Code: Seven Keys to Unleashing Vision and Inspiration.* San Francisco, CA: Jossey-Bass.

Chapman, Milo L. (1984). The church in the gospels. In Melvin E. Dieter & Daniel N. Berg (eds), *The Church: An Inquiry into Ecclesiology from a Biblical Theological Perspective.* Anderson, IN: Warner Press.

Collins, John J. (1975). *Anthropology: Culture, Society, and Evolution.* Englewood Cliffs, NJ: Prentice-Hall, Inc.

Davis, Thomas C. (2007). The relationship among organizational culture, pastoral leadership style, and worship attendance growth in United Methodist churches in rapidly growing suburbs of Atlanta (D.Min. dissertation). Asbury Theological Seminary.

Deal, Terrence E., & Kennedy, Allan A. (1982). *Corporate Cultures: The Rites and Rituals of Corporate Life.* Reading, MA: Addison-Wesley.

Denison, Daniel R., & Neale, William S. (1996). *Denison Organizational Culture Survey.* Ann Arbor, MI: Denison Consulting.

Diekhoff, George M., Thompson, Susan K., & Denney, Ryan M. (2006). A multidimensional scaling analysis of church climate. *Journal of Psychology and Christianity* 25 (1): 17–26.

Dietrich, Andreas (2007). Discerning congregational culture for pastoral ministry: The church culture survey (D.Min. dissertation). Asbury Theological Seminary.

Duncan, W. Jack (1989). Organizational culture: "Getting a fix" on an elusive concept. *Academy of Management Executive* 3 (3): 229–36.

ErwinMcManus (2009). Retrieved 27 May 2009 from http://erwinmcmanus.com/mosaic/.

Ford, Kevin G. (2007). *Transforming Church: Bringing out the Good to get to Great.* Wheaton, IL: SaltRiver Books.

Geertz, Clifford (1973). *The Interpretation of Cultures.* New York, NY: Basic Books.

Ghiselli, Edwin E., Campbell, John P., & Zedeck, Sheldon (1981). *Measurement Theory for the Behavioral Sciences.* San Francisco, CA: W. H. Freeman and Company.

Giles, Kevin (1995). *What on Earth is the Church? An Exploration in New Testament Theology.* Downers Grove, IL: InterVarsity Press.

Harrison, Roger, & Stokes, Herb (1992). *Diagnosing Organizational Culture.* San Francisco, CA: John Wiley and Sons.

Hinkin, Timothy R. (1998). A brief tutorial on the development of measures for use in survey questionnaires. *Organizational Research Methods* 1: 104–21.

Hofstede, Geert (2005). *Cultures and Organizations.* New York, NY: McGraw-Hill.

Johnston, Ray (2004). Developing a thriving church that reaches unchurched people. Workshop, National Pastors Convention, San Diego, CA. February 13.

Kaplan, R. S., & Norton, D. P. (1996). *The Balanced Scorecard*. Boston, MA: Harvard Business School Press.

Lewis, Robert, & Cordeiro, Wayne (2005). *Culture Shift*. San Francisco, CA: Jossey-Bass.

Malphurs, Aubrey (2013). *Look Before You Lead: How to Discern and Shape Your Church Culture*. Grand Rapids, MI: Baker Books.

Martin, Joanne (1992). *Cultures in Organizations: Three Perspectives*. New York, NY: Oxford University Press.

Martin, Joanne (2002). *Organizational Culture: Mapping the Terrain*. Thousand Oaks, CA: Foundations for Organizational Science.

Mayo, Elton (1933). *The Human Problems of an Industrial Civilization*. New York, NY: The Macmillan Company.

McGuire, Stephen J. J. (2003). Entrepreneurial organizational culture: Construct definition and instrument (Ph.D. dissertation). The George Washington University.

Minatrea, Milfred (2004). *Shaped by God's Heart: The Passion and Practices of Missional Churches*. San Francisco, CA: Jossey-Bass.

O'Reilly, C. A., Chatman, J. A. Chatman, & Caldwell, D. F. (1991). People and organizational culture: A profile comparison approach to person–organization fit. *Academy of Management Journal* 34 (3): 487–516.

Ott, J. Steven. (1989). *The Organizational Culture Perspective*. Chicago, IL: The Dorsey Press.

Peters, Thomas J., & Waterman, Robert H., Jr. (1982). *In Search of Excellence: Lessons from America's Best-Run Companies*. New York: Harper and Row.

Pettegrew, Hal K. (1993). The relationship of organizational climate factors and motivation and satisfaction among volunteers in evangelical Protestant churches. Ph.D. diss., Trinity Evangelical Divinity School.

Schein, Edgar (1991). What is culture? In Peter J. Frost, Larry F. Moore, Meryl Reis Louis & Craig C. Lundberg (eds), *Reframing Organizational Culture*. Newbury Park, CA: Sage Publications.

Schein, Edgar (2000). Sense and nonsense about culture and climate. In Neal M. Ashkanasy, Celeste P. M. Wilderom & Mark F. Petersen (eds), *Handbook of Organizational Culture and Climate* (pp. xxiii–xxxiii). Thousand Oaks, CA: Sage Publications.

Schein, Edgar (2004). *Organizational Culture and Leadership* (3rd ed.). San Francisco, CA: Jossey-Bass.

Schultz, Majken (1994). *On Studying Organizational Cultures: Diagnosis and Understanding*. New York, NY: Walter de Gruyter.

Stanley, Andy (2007). Systems. *Catalyst Conference*.

Stetzer, Ed (2014, February 24). Multisite churches are here, and here, and here to stay. *Christianity Today*. Accessed at https://www.christianitytoday.com/edstetzer/2014/february/multisite-churches -are-here-to-stay.html.

Stevens, R. Paul (1997). Organizational culture and change. In Robert Banks & R. Paul Stevens (eds), *The Complete Book of Everyday Christianity* (pp. 713–18). Downers Grove, IL: InterVarsity Press.

Surratt, Geoff, & Surratt, Greg (2005). Change makers. *Leadership* 26 (1): 33–35.

van der Post, W. Z., & de Coning, T. J. (1997). An instrument to measure organisational culture. *South African Journal of Business Management* 28 (4): 147–68.

Ward, Angela J. (2011). *Church Organizational Culture: Construct Definition and Instrument Development* (Doctoral dissertation). The Southern Baptist Theological Seminary.

Ward, Angie (2008, July 25). The First Church of Second Life. *Out of Ur*. Retrieved from https://www .christianitytoday.com/pastors/2008/july-online-only/first-church-of-second-life.html.

19. Rolling up our sleeves and pulling up our socks: a critical review of safety culture definitions and measures, and innovative ways to move the field forward

Tristan W. Casey, Xiaowen Hu, Chantelle Reid, Phuong Anh Tran and Frank W. Guldenmund

INTRODUCTION

Despite Schein's warning, safety culture continues to generate significant academic inquiry (Bye et al., 2020) and is responsible for a great amount of activity in the industrial consulting space (Le Coze, 2019). For better or worse, the concept of safety culture is firmly entrenched in the vernacular of high-risk and even less riskier organizations, as evidenced by numerous reviews that highlight the breadth and volume of safety culture research that has been done since the early 1990s (Bisbey et al., 2021; Guldenmund, 2000; Kalteh et al., 2021; Wiegmann et al., 2004). Hailed by some as a panacea for introducing step-change in safety management sophistication and increasing safety performance 'beyond the plateau' (Cooper, 2000; Hudson, 2007; Reason, 1996), and by others as a concept that should be rejected entirely (Dekker, as cited in Borys, 2014; Hopkins, 2019), safety culture has stimulated endless academic debate and much confusion among practitioners (Le Coze, 2019). To make things more complicated, safety culture research has also spawned a host of iterations such as patient safety culture (Fleming, 2005), road and traffic safety culture (Edwards et al., 2014), process safety culture (Olive et al., 2006), nuclear safety culture (Lee & Harrison, 2000), resilient safety culture (Adjekum & Tous, 2020; Pillay et al., 2010), and even 'emotional' safety culture (Wang et al., 2018).

A lack of conceptual clarity and implementation of misaligned measurement methods presents a critical challenge for academics and practitioners alike. For instance, when scholars fail to sharply define their focal constructs, it can have a profound adverse effect on measurement, such as reducing face validity and impacting item response quality (Voss et al., 2020); items that are either deficient in their measurement or contaminated by overlapping conceptually with other established concepts in the field, and poor overall construct validity (Podsakoff et al., 2003). In safety culture research, construct definitions tend to be poorly defined, all-encompassing, and/or lack clear conceptual boundaries (such as using safety culture and safety climate interchangeably). Poorly constructed definitions impair the development of psychometrically valid quantitative measures and make it difficult to code and analyze qualitative data accurately. All-encompassing definitions of safety culture that include behaviors, attitudes, perceptions, beliefs, knowledge, and many other psychological constructs, can make it impossible to discern the predictive relationship with outcome variables (i.e., safety accidents and injuries). Without a clear conceptual boundary, it will be difficult to disentangle exactly what should be measured and how it should be measured. Finally, using measures of a related concept such as safety climate to measure safety culture impairs advancement of both fields and could impact the efficacy of integrative reviews and meta-analyses.

Considering these challenges, in this book chapter we aim to advance safety culture research by providing a set of clear guidelines that improve conceptual clarity and deliver best practice recommendations to measure safety culture. We start by providing a brief tour of the safety culture literature and summarize the origins and aspirations of safety culture across three different streams of work: evaluative, descriptive, and practical. Then, based on a review of 74 articles, we assess the issue of conceptual clarity and measurement misalignment in depth. We then advance a manifesto of safety culture research to guide more robust practice in this area. Finally, we articulate some solutions to the conceptual and methodological mess that we find ourselves in and paint a picture of emerging innovations that could have utility for safety culture measurement.

SAFETY CULTURE

Schein (2010) defines organizational culture as implicit core assumptions that manifest in espoused values (priorities and perceptions) and artifacts (symbols, signs, behaviors). These implicit assumptions develop over time as members struggle with fundamental problems of internal integration (i.e., working together cohesively) and external adaptation (i.e., responding to threats that other groups, in particular competitors, might pose). Safety represents an integral challenge that organizations must manage and requires both environmental adaptation and internal cooperation and coordination to resolve effectively. These properties align the challenge of safety well with the potential solutions made possible by organizational culture: for example, by defining how hazards should be managed; what constitutes an unacceptable/acceptable risk and how unsafe acts should be dealt with—in other words, how safety should be understood and dealt with by members of the organization.

When it comes to measurement, a key conceptual distinction made in the organizational culture literature is the one between cultures as something organizations have versus something an organization is (Smircich, 1983). In the former case, emphasis is placed on normative ideas about what an organization should and shouldn't have, more tangible artifacts like systems and practices, and comparing, usually quantitatively, different organizations against one another. In the latter case, emphasis is placed on description and understanding, repressing or declaring any bias or judgment that may be cast over the cultural evaluation. Qualitative and inductive theory-building methods dominate this latter perspective. These distinctions have impacted safety culture research. We will provide a brief historical review on safety culture research, and then move onto the contemporary thinking.

Historically, safety culture research can be divided into three main streams of work: evaluative, descriptive, and practical. As shown by Figure 19.1, these streams of safety culture research are interdependent, influencing each other with many bridging or overlapping publications that facilitated transitions between the various literatures. Each of these streams is expanded in the following sections.

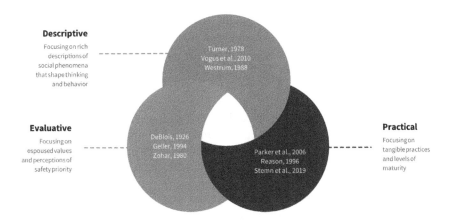

Descriptive

Focusing on rich descriptions of social phenomena that shape thinking and behavior

Turner, 1978
Vogus et al., 2010
Westrum, 1988

Evaluative

Focusing on espoused values and perceptions of safety priority

DeBlois, 1926
Geller, 1994
Zohar, 1980

Practical

Focusing on tangible practices and levels of maturity

Parker et al., 2006
Reason, 1996
Stemn et al., 2019

Figure 19.1   Visual representation of historical safety culture research

Evaluative

The evaluative perspective of safety culture aligns with the idea that culture is what an organization *should* have to maintain safety—in particular, a fundamental commitment to the importance of safety and joint responsibility across all employees. Key contributions to safety culture as a concept include: (a) it is comprised of a fundamental sense of safety's value and importance, which elevates safety issues above other competing priorities; (b) this value can be taught/conveyed to others either through specific human resource practices or leadership; and (c) it can be operationalized as a series of dimensions to reflect the values that organizational and leadership practices convey.

The earliest signs of safety culture are apparent in the work of DeBlois (1926) who described a phenomenon he called 'safety atmosphere' (Carsten Busch, personal communication); a sense of safety's value and priority that permeated an industrial worksite. DeBlois also goes on to talk about how new employees are subtly influenced by the practices of peers: while the employee will be taught specific safety practices as part of their induction, what really matters is what is actually done on the production floor in terms of shaping safety behavior.

This emphasis on the priority given to safety and peer practice is best captured in Zohar's (1980) seminal work on safety climate, defined as employees' shared perception about organizational policies and practices in relation to safety. A strong safety climate is one where all safety policies and practices reflected an absolute priority on safety assigned by the leaders in the organization. It is likely that this quantitative, normative, and dimensional nature of safety climate influenced safety culture research in profound ways. For a while, researchers seemed to equate the two terms, combining research from across these domains and using the concepts interchangeably (Glendon, 2008; Halligan & Zecevic, 2011). Burns et al. (2006) suggested that the most common way to measure safety culture is through safety climate surveys.

It was not until the 2000s that researchers started to converge on the idea that safety culture and safety climate are distinct, yet related concepts. Following from the proposition that safety climate represents a superficial representation of the underlying safety culture (Flin et al., 2000), Griffin and Curcuruto (2016) added further conceptual specificity by stating that safety climate is an indicator of safety culture—in other words, a proxy measure at a point in time that is suggestive of the molar state or nature of the safety culture.

Descriptive

The descriptive perspective aims to describe what culture is: a dynamic process of meaning-making in organizations. Safety culture emerges from the interactions among structures that seek to organize and coordinate people in high-risk environments, and involves the detection of threats, communication, and accurate interpretation/receipt of information that stimulates corrective action.

Turner (1978) was among the first to explicitly link organizational culture to safety accidents. Specifically, he argued that organizational beliefs about the nature of hazards, what constitutes a risk, and what should be done to manage them, can lead to the incubation of latent risks and draw attention away from dangers that really matter. Various concepts relating to this idea of the gradual and unnoticed normalization of risk such as small short-cuts, deviations from established rules and procedures (Dekker, 2016; Snook, 2000), and even decision making in the context of group dynamics like groupthink (Vaughan, 1996), all typify the descriptive stream.

Others extended this work and proposed that cultural assumptions and beliefs determined the style of responses to information and opportunities for innovation (Westrum, 1988). Indeed, scholars along this line of research argued that inherent within a 'safe' organization are social forces that elevate and emphasize risk-related information, particularly when it is anomalous (Antonsen, 2009; Kirk et al., 2005). Thus, safety culture was productive in the sense that a 'good' safety culture was one that promoted information flow between and within organizational levels (Westrum, 2004).

The area of high reliability organizing (HRO), which itself is sociological given its focus on how groups of people can work collaboratively and within socially-engineered structures to create nearly error-free performance (Weick, 1987), is a relatively recent development in safety culture research. Through five social organizing processes and structures, a cultural state of 'collective mindfulness' is achieved. Through this mindfulness, HROs are proposed to create capability to discover and manage unexpected events (Weick et al., 2008). Sense-making features heavily in contemporary models of HRO and is described as a collaborative process of social construction of meaning that elaborates the various safety practices that workers must show to deal effectively with threats (Vogus et al., 2010).

Finally, Hopkins's (2019) focus on organizational structures as the key to understanding how culture forms and shapes behavior is another key development in this stream. Hopkins vehemently disagrees with the values-based approach that typifies 'hearts and minds' safety culture programs, and instead argues for centralization of safety functions with direct-line reporting to management so safety issues are given immediate and adequate attention (Le Coze, 2020).

Practical

Following the Chernobyl nuclear disaster, the International Atomic Energy Agency (IAEA, 1991) defined safety culture as the 'assembly of characteristics, attitudes and behaviors in individuals, organizations and institutions which establishes that, as an overriding priority, protection and safety issues receive the attention warranted by their significance' (p. 1). Eventually, this sufficiently broad definition of safety culture essentially opened the floodgates for all manner of constructs to be included within the domain of the safety culture concept and contributed to the development of the practical view of safety culture. The practical view of safety culture sees it as something that can be improved to drive better safety outcomes. Using a more practice-driven approach, maturity models serve as a guide or roadmap to illuminate safety strategy and stimulate ongoing organizational development.

Safety culture maturity models are comprised of multiple dimensions and indicators organized by levels of effectiveness or stages of evolution (Goncalves Filho et al., 2010). Many safety culture maturity models are derived from Hudson's five-step ladder and it is widely regarded as one of the most influential safety culture models in existence (Goncalves Filho & Waterson, 2018). Developed by Hudson in collaboration with Reason (1996), the HSE culture ladder also drew on some of Westrum's ideas regarding information quality and sociological patterns of interpretation, sense-making, and social norms/practices in response to safety-related news, much to Westrum's (2014) chagrin. As organizations ascend the maturity ladder, social capital (trust) and informedness also increase, resulting 'automatically' in improved safety performance and greater employee safety proactivity and initiative. 'Automatically' because this is how the safety universe operates according to this model.

When applied diligently, safety culture maturity models can hold practical utility as tools to guide organizational safety development efforts through assisting with strategic planning, intervention design, and measurement (Goncalves Filho & Waterson, 2018). Further, they are customizable and able to reflect the nuances of local organizational contexts (e.g., the specific industry or established practices in place). Safety maturity models can even 'make us think' about the concept of safety culture, prompting greater understanding of the competing influences that shape safety practice, and various 'fads' or 'fashions' (Le Coze, 2019).

CONCEPTUAL ISSUES INHERENT IN EXISTING SAFETY CULTURE DEFINITIONS

To review the existing safety culture research, we consulted major databases including Scopus, Web of Science, PubMed, PsychInfo, and Google Scholar. A structured search string including variations of the safety culture label (e.g., WHS culture, SHES culture, HSE culture etc.) was implemented and publications were constrained to the year 2000 onwards, as well as English-only peer reviewed primary research articles. The related concept of safety climate was excluded from our review. A total of 5,125 articles were initially located. Following the removal of duplicates and out-of-scope articles, a total of 1,346 remained. After reviewing abstracts and removing articles that related to specific domains of safety culture (e.g., patient safety culture, process safety culture) 74 articles were retained for the final in-depth review and analysis.

Across these studies we found evidence of several issues within the safety culture literature, as summarized in Table 19.1 and explained further below. We outline firstly some issues with safety culture definition clarity, followed by issues related to ill-defined construct boundaries.

Table 19.1   Summary of issues identified in existing safety culture research

Issue	No. and % of Studies	Exemplar Study
No issues overall	6, 15.8%	Nævestad et al. (2018)
No issues with definitions only	14, 18.9%	Oxtoby et al. (2017)
No issues with construct boundaries only	38, 51.4%	Job et al. (2020)
Undefined/conflicted definition	26, 35.1%	Mustafa et al. (2017)
All-encompassing definition	34, 46.0%	Heckemann et al. (2019)
Confusion between safety climate and safety culture	11, 14.8%	McDiarmid & Condon (2005)
Confusion between organizational culture and safety culture	25, 33.8%	Mokarami et al. (2019)

Note: Total number of reviewed studies was 74.

Definitional Clarity

Undefined or conflicted

Surprisingly, 26 (35.1 percent) of reviewed studies failed to specify a clear definition of safety culture (e.g., Mustafa et al., 2017) or failed to define it at all (e.g., Nowrouzi et al., 2016). Within many of these studies' literature reviews, multiple and sometimes conflicting definitions of safety culture are presented without a clear synthesis and explicit statement of which one(s) have been adopted and/or adapted for the study. Without a clear definition, the development or selection of a suitable measure is impossible (MacKenzie, 2003).

Peppered throughout the reviewed articles were references to normative descriptions of safety culture, with all manner of labels applied without explanation. For instance, authors described safety cultures as good/bad, positive/negative, strong/weak, and even healthy/unhealthy (e.g., Ruan et al., 2012). These labels are problematic because they are reductionist and do a disservice to the richness and complexity inherent within safety culture (Bye et al., 2020). Further, scholars rarely specify what they mean by these labels, implying that it is assumed knowledge what a good or positive safety culture is actually comprised of. Finally, the use of such labels suggests that there is one ideal or 'gold standard' safety culture that all high-risk organizations should aspire to, and so ideal safety is achieved through homogeneity in thinking and behavior across industry; a questionable proposition that has yet to be convincingly supported by evidence (Antonsen et al., 2017). What is more, such a static view on safety assumes that when everybody is doing the 'right' thing all the time', safety is a certitude.

All-encompassing

Among many researchers there is a tendency to refer to 'safety practices' or behaviors collectively as safety culture. We found 34 (46.0 percent) studies with this issue. Indeed, the INSAG definition seems to equate all manner of safety-related characteristics as being part of the safety culture concept. Yet in practice, some aspects of organizational life will be culturally derived whereas others will not. An example is the practice of stopping work. Stopping work is an inherently difficult safety practice because there are many reasons why a worker may choose to stop or not (Weber et al., 2018). For instance, the worker may perceive that management will not support the decision (safety climate), or that the effort required to stop outweighs the benefits (motivational), or they may not be aware of the need to stop (knowledge and skills), and finally, that stopping work is not an accepted social norm among teammates (culture). The result is the same, namely, that the worker takes a risk, yet the underpinning pattern of reasoning is completely different. Furthermore, when asked to justify his or her actions, the worker can choose between any of these four arguments, depending on, indeed, what the group culture 'allows'. Thus, a critical challenge for researchers, particularly when working with observable artifacts or manifestations of culture like behavior, is to adequately justify and explain why the target practice should be included within the construct of safety culture.

Contaminating safety culture with other constructs means that the measurement model could be impaired and statistical relationships with outcome variables, such as safety behaviors, may either be attenuated or amplified. For example, Díaz-Cabrera et al. (2007) defined safety culture as meanings, interpretations, attitudes, values, beliefs, rules and procedures related to safety. The inclusion of 'rules and procedures related to safety' within the domain of safety culture would likely inflate associations with perceptions of safety management systems (either modeled as an antecedent or outcome of safety culture) across seven themes.

Ill-Defined Construct Boundaries

Safety culture versus safety climate

In our review of existing studies, 11 (14.8 percent) confused or equated the terms safety culture and safety climate. Safety culture and safety climate are comparable yet distinct constructs that are often used interchangeably (Griffin & Curcuruto, 2016). Safety climate has been positioned as: (a) a momentary snapshot of the underlying safety culture (a 'moment of culture in time'; Flin et al., 2000; Guldenmund, 2007); (b) a more superficial representation of deeper beliefs and assumptions (usually equated with espoused values; Sari & Dewi, 2021); and (c) as a construct that is equivalent to safety culture (climate-as-culture; Håvold, 2010). Equating safety culture and safety climate is especially problematic because safety climate is inherently normative, whereas safety culture is not. Further, this practice has direct implications for both constructs as it often reduces culture to a single number (usually an average across multiple questions) which raises the question what this number actually represents and to who it pertains. For instance, does this number, whatever it represents, apply to all members of the organization some of the time, or to some members all of the time? Working with single numbers as descriptors of large groups indeed erodes the conceptual clarity of safety climate.

Safety culture versus organizational culture

Others have attempted to define safety culture through its relationship with organizational culture, sometimes with mixed results. Indeed, we found evidence of 25 (33.8 percent) studies reviewed that unclearly or incorrectly differentiated safety culture for organizational culture. In sum, safety culture has been described as either (a) a subset of the broader organizational culture (Cooper, 2000), or (b) a specific type of organizational culture that high-risk organizations have (Leaver & Reader, 2019). In the former case, this proposition begs the question of where safety culture starts and organizational culture stops; in other words, how are the boundaries of these interrelated constructs delineated? In the latter case, safety culture is used as a qualifier, as something an organization either has, or has not. However, if high-risk organizations have a safety culture, do other organizations with different priorities have similarly conceptualized cultures? From these lines of research, we can quickly see why a whole host of different forms of safety culture have been generated (e.g., process safety culture, patient safety culture etc.).

Measurement Issues

Lack of theoretical base

Safety maturity models often suffer from criticisms regarding underspecified theory and detachment from contemporary ideas about the dynamic nature of organizational culture (Goncalves Filho & Waterson, 2018; Westrum, 2014). Maturity models seem to beguile any critical evaluation of their underlying theory through focusing more on indicators than the mechanism(s) that underly progression or evolution upwards through the various stages of development (Goncalves Filho & Waterson, 2018). Indeed, studies utilizing safety culture maturity models should report on what theories are being used to explain the process of change and how safety improvement is being generated. Moreover, such studies should explain why safety cultures can only grow into the direction they envision, as if cultures are bonsai trees, that can take the shape of the caretaker's liking.

Lack of empirical rigor

Only recently have scholars started to critically evaluate the validity of safety culture maturity models. Regarding validity and reliability, Goncalves Filho and Waterson (2018) found that 44 percent of reviewed studies failed to carry out any form of validity and reliability assessment on their models. Only one (Fleming, 2007) study to date has performed a comprehensive assessment of the model's validity and reliability. Overall, safety culture maturity models stimulated a great deal of positive action in industry (Le Coze, 2019) yet are often based on shaky theoretical ground. In sum, maturity models tend to be developed purely through small-scale qualitative studies consulting managers and/or safety-specific personnel (e.g., Parker et al., 2006). A notable example to address this issue is the work done by Stemn and colleagues (2019) across four Ghanaian gold mines using an integrated safety culture maturity model derived from several published sources (including Parker et al., 2006). Results showed that mines differed in their maturity scores, and importantly, correlated negatively with overall mine safety performance as measured by serious injury incident rates. Several dimensions within the model had stronger relationships with incidence rates, including 'care and respect', 'safety performance measurement', and 'learning from accidents'.

Misalignment Between Definitions and Methods

In practice, we find strong evidence of misalignment between definitions and methods. As shown in Table 19.2 below, instances of misalignment were prevalent across the articles reviewed for this research, with 59 (79.7 percent) exhibiting this shortcoming. Primarily, the issue of alignment concerned definitions that included difficult to quantify features such as beliefs or implicit assumptions yet used a quantitative generic safety survey to measure safety culture. For example, Díaz-Cabrera et al. (2007) defined safety culture as 'meanings, interpretations, attitudes, values, beliefs, rules, and procedures related to safety' yet measured it using the quantitative Safety Culture Values and Practices questionnaire. Focus was placed on measuring tangible practices that are thought to reflect underlying beliefs about safety.

Table 19.2   *Evidence of misalignment between safety culture definitions and measurement*

-	Aligned Definition/Measure	Misaligned Definition/Measure
	15, 20.3%	59, 79.7%
Exemplar Studies	Nævestad et al. (2020)	Atombo et al. (2017)

Similarly, Job et al. (2020) defined safety culture as a broad conglomerate of attitudes, values, perceptions, policies, rules, and behaviors related to safety, yet used a quantitative survey focusing primarily on safety management system elements and perceptions of safety behavior. Within the hospital setting, safety culture is commonly measured quantitatively using generic tools (Chen & Li, 2010; Singer et al., 2007; Sorra & Dyer, 2010). Such tools result in not only a 'flavorless' representation of safety culture but reduce its richness to a single number.

This clash between the ethnographic and social constructivist origins of organizational culture and the positivist methods used commonly by organizational and industrial psychologists seems to reflect an ontological and epistemological crisis in safety culture research. At a minimum, if a positivist approach is to be taken to measuring safety culture, then a correspondingly superficial and narrow definition of safety culture should also be used (e.g., focusing on espoused values or shared safety practices). Scholars could even consider talking instead about safety climate and using a corresponding validated measure.

An example alignment between measure and definition is evidenced by the work of Nævestad and colleagues (2019) in their exploration of road safety culture, which is defined and operationalized as shared behavioral norms regarding the expectations of others regarding acceptable road safety behaviors while driving (measured using a quantified survey).

WAYS FORWARD TO IMPROVE THE CONCEPTUALIZATION AND MEASUREMENT OF SAFETY CULTURE

To date, the most widely accepted approach to organizational culture by scholars and practitioners alike and of particular relevance to safety is Schein's work on organizational culture (Edwards et al., 2013; Guldenmund, 2000). Briefly, organizational culture may be considered as a layered phenomenon; the deeply held assumptions concerning the nature of time, space, and reality, which influence the values, goals, and priorities espoused by organizational members, and in turn, precipitate and encourage specific organizational member behaviors that express these underlying shared ways of thinking and reinforces these shared patterns over time. Reciprocally, it is widely recognized that practices and artifacts can also shape the underlying safety culture too (McDonald et al., 2000). Adopting a layered conceptualization of culture is helpful from the perspective of explaining how tangible aspects of organizations may foster or encourage certain shared beliefs and assumptions, as well as how deep shared thinking may in turn shape decisions around the nature of these artifacts and how they are implemented (Guldenmund, 2010).

Edwards et al. (2013) defined safety culture as the deep-seated assumptions and beliefs that interact with an organization's safety practices, to produce observable behaviors. Each of these aspects is measured through interpretivist, normative, and lastly, observational methods. Interestingly, Edwards and colleagues (2015) later applied this model in the Australian trucking industry and proposed that cultural beliefs should be explored and taken into account, using a human factors perspective, to design more effective and impactful safety practices such as reward and recognition programs. In essence, rather than managing the culture directly, *understand* the culture to manage the practices.

By simplifying safety culture to layers—assumptions/beliefs, values, and artifacts (essentially behavior)—three core measurement methods apply. Qualitative methods align neatly with the measurement of beliefs and assumptions. Otherwise known as the interpretivist perspective, safety culture scholars have explored deeply held beliefs through extended research inquiry. Methodologically, social constructivism is most applicable, given the subjective reality formulated through relationships and interactions between people in organizational settings (Antonsen et al., 2017; Guldenmund, 2018). This perspective also recognizes the emerging view regarding the dynamism of safety culture realized in the day-to-day interactions between members of the organization, as they create, destroy and recreate meanings over time through interpretations of events and ongoing sense-making activities such as management communications, team meetings like pre-starts, and the reactions of peers to various safety practices. Grounded theory (Creswell et al., 2007) should be used as the analytical and interpretative strategy, given that discovery of rich descriptions about culture are often likened to the development of organization-specific theories (Geertz, 1973). Data collection should be conducted using a combination of participatory action research (PAR; Baum et al., 2006) and ethnography (Hammersley & Atkinson, 2019). PAR facilitates the iterative discovery and refinement of cultural themes through cycles of data gathering, sense-making through interaction with organizational members, and refinement of understanding. Convergent interviewing (Dick, 2016), which allows a minimally structured and free-flowing approach to qualitative data gathering, might also be considered as a specific data collection method to encourage an emergent and locally relevant understanding of safety culture.

A combination of qualitative and quantitative methods is most appropriate for the measurement of espoused values. Given the established nature of the safety climate field, we recommend a process of adapting and tailoring existing safety climate scales to suit industry and even specific organizational contexts. Focus groups and interviews, largely descriptive in nature and more superficial than the in-depth embedded approach to uncover implicit beliefs, should be used to identify the content of organizationally relevant perceptions of safety's value and priority. Casey and colleagues (under review) articulate a method for developing industry-specific safety climate scales that could be equally applied to an organizational setting. This approach ensures that the quantification of perceptions is locally meaningful and relevant. Metrics such as safety climate level and strength provide data points that may suggest the degree of convergence or differentiation present within the broader safety culture.

At the highest level, that of the manifestation of culture in the form of specific safety behaviors, quantitative measures may be used exclusively. Importantly, we discourage researchers from concentrating solely on behavioral frequencies and inferring safety culture from these observations. Rather, prior qualitative research as discussed above can be used to generate (and confirm) culturally driven practices that are linked to specific situations and conditions. Information about injunctive social norms (i.e., what people generally think should be done) can be used to generate items for specific safety behavior scales that reflect the underlying cultural beliefs. We also recommend that such behaviors are couched within the cultural normative context, such as describing the conditions or situations under which the behavior is being performed. For example, rather than measuring the frequency or effectiveness of behavior such as 'speaking up and asking a worker to stop an unsafe practice', we recommend that methods from social psychology are used to ascertain the appropriateness of such behavior with reference to the workgroup (Fugas et al., 2011).

Table 19.3   Summary of the safety culture research manifesto

Element	Principle	Rationale
1.1	Reflect on and explicitly state how the researchers' own definitions of safety might influence the path of the research and the conceptualization of safety culture.	Surfaces hidden biases inherent within researchers' operating definitions and understandings of safety and culture.
1.2	Explicitly identify the level(s) of safety culture being investigated (i.e., artifacts, values, beliefs).	Clearly shows how the research maps onto established models of organizational culture.
1.3	Align the level(s) of safety culture with corresponding best practice methodology and data gathering techniques.	Reduces the risk of misalignment between definition and method, leading to more valid conclusions.
1.4	Use participatory techniques that involve organizational members in the co-discovery of safety culture.	Increases the validity of qualitative investigations and stimulates growth and change within the organization.
2.1	Avoid the temptation to exclusively quantify safety culture.	Reduces the richness of culture to a single, meaningless number and eliminates important context.
2.2	Avoid the use of generic safety culture surveys.	Reduces the value of the research data obtained and can be difficult to drive meaningful change.
2.3	Provide a clear definition of safety culture avoiding all-encompassing and catch-all terms.	Dilutes the conceptualization of safety culture and may impair measurement and statistical conclusions through content contamination.
2.4	Avoid the use of clichés when describing the nature of safety culture.	Meaningless without explanation.
2.5	Avoid using safety culture and safety climate interchangeably.	Results in conceptual confusion and talking at cross-purposes.

MANIFESTO FOR SAFETY CULTURE RESEARCH

Synthesizing the research presented above, we now develop a manifesto to guide the future of safety culture inquiry. A manifesto is defined as a public declaration of intentions, aims, and policy on a particular issue, which is an approach used to deal with contentious issues or establish a new paradigm (Fowler & Highsmith, 2001). Manifestos have already been used in the discipline of safety science to address the broader (and related) issue of empirical stagnation (Rae et al., 2020). Table 19.3 summarizes our safety culture manifesto and in the sections that follow we describe each commitment in detail. These are divided into two categories (dos and do nots) with best practice recommendations for each.

Dos

1.1 Reflect on and explicitly state how the researchers' own definitions of safety might influence the path of the research and the conceptualization of safety culture. Hidden within the conceptualizations of safety culture is the implicit bias that is brought about by researchers' own beliefs about the nature of safety and culture. For instance, national culture shapes safety-related thinking, which impacts the way it is operationalized and managed (Yorio et al., 2019). Researcher reflexivity is a hallmark of good qualitative research, so investigations of safety culture must require researchers to state the perspective they are adopting and consider how it may be affecting subsequent methods, analysis, and interpretation.

1.2 Explicitly identify the level(s) of safety culture being investigated. Following from Schein's multilayered 'onion' model of organizational culture, safety culture should ideally be measured with reference to all three layers. In the absence of such a comprehensive approach (as reflected in study scope, limits of the specific research questions, or logistical constraints), researchers should at least reference which layer they are measuring, how, and why.

Importantly, regarding the use of Schein's model, researchers should be fully aware that this model provides an outsider's perspective on culture and that this is not the way that insiders experience their culture themselves. On the contrary, they feel their culture makes perfect sense, which is why it is so difficult for them to explain it to the outsider.

1.3 Align the level(s) of safety culture with corresponding best practice methodology and data gathering techniques. As we have demonstrated, one critical problem plaguing safety culture research is misalignment between conceptualization and operationalization. Most commonly, researchers define safety culture as either an all-encompassing construct or narrowly as beliefs and assumptions yet proceed to use quantitative survey tools to measure it. Instead, we strongly recommend that researchers align their definitions of safety culture with corresponding methods. Table 19.4 below shows more specific recommendations about how to align safety culture layers with corresponding methods.

Table 19.4   Aligning safety culture layers with corresponding research methods

Beliefs and assumptions	Espoused values and priorities	Artifacts
Ethnography	Industry and/or organization-specific	Audits and inspections
Convergent interviewing	safety climate surveys	Behavioral observation
Facilitated sense-making workshops	Focus groups	Document review and analysis

1.4 Use participatory techniques that involve organizational members in the co-discovery of safety culture. To fail to involve cultural inhabitants in explorations of safety culture is to neglect a vital sense-making mechanism that ensures validity of the final results. Participatory and cyclical techniques of planning, data gathering, consulting, and reflecting are important to draw out safety culture nuances, confirm emerging hypotheses, and address researchers' own implicit biases and frames of thinking.

Do Nots

2.1 Avoid the temptation to exclusively quantify safety culture. To exclusively reduce the rich nature of safety culture to a single or set of numbers (usually an average across several items) whitewashes the rich descriptions that a qualitative approach brings. At a minimum, if safety culture is quantified, a mixed methods approach should be used to ensure that the numbers are given local relevance and context. Quantification of safety culture also encourages researchers to focus on most easily measured constructs such as frequency of behavior and employee attitudes rather than the more difficult concepts of beliefs, assumptions, and values.

2.2 Avoid the use of generic safety culture surveys. Another heresy that safety culture researchers can commit is to use generic safety culture surveys. Using this approach implicitly suggests that all organizations should adopt carbon copies of the same culture; a potentially dangerous supposition if the existing organizational culture conflicts with the normative template and actually exerts a protective effect over safety-critical activities through shaping employee behavior.

2.3 Avoid defining safety culture using all-encompassing and catch-all terms. Construct contamination and dilution of the safety culture concept results when broad definitions are used. Encouraged by the seminal INSAG definition, there is a tendency across the safety culture literature to reference multiple concepts ranging from beliefs through to practices and policies, through to behavior. However, not all these concepts will be grounded in the local culture. Further, including constructs such as perceptions of safety management system implementation (Job et al., 2020), attitudes (Tear et al., 2020), and risk perceptions (Nævestad et al., 2020) within definitions of safety culture only serves to reduce the psychometric validity of corresponding measurement instruments.

2.4 Avoid the use of clichés when describing the nature of safety culture. There is a preponderance of references to various types of safety culture that connote evaluation; good or bad, healthy, or unhealthy, and weak or strong. Ultimately, such labels are meaningless and empty. Further, what is good or healthy in one industrial setting may be entirely inappropriate or even risky in another. Labels such as these also encourage the homogenization of safety culture across various settings.

2.5 Avoid using safety culture and safety climate interchangeably. Much has been written on the conceptual differences between safety culture and climate (Griffin & Curcuruto, 2016), yet the practice of referring to them interchangeably continues. Safety climate is not a snapshot or momentary picture of the safety culture at a point in time but, rather, a representation of one layer, that being espoused values. More specifically, safety climate represents the intersection between the middle and outer layers of safety culture: the difference between what is espoused versus what is enacted (Zohar, 2010), which collectively infers or signals the value of safety relative to other organizational priorities.

It is our hope that adoption of this manifesto and its commitments will significantly improve the robustness of safety culture research. In the next section we move towards the future of safety culture measurement. To do so, we draw on recent publications in the organizational culture space and articulate methods that could be applied to the safety culture setting with great impact.

INNOVATIONS IN SAFETY CULTURE MEASUREMENT

Conceptual Innovation

It is worthwhile to note that as safety culture research evolves, the definition of what safety is also evolves over time. This development has particular implications for normative conceptualizations of safety culture (by dictating what types of practices are considered 'best') but also permeates across pragmatic and descriptive or interpretivist perspectives by changing the portfolio of behaviors or underlying beliefs that one considers part of a safety culture.

Traditionally, safety is a state achieved by reducing the number of adverse events to as low as possible, which is enshrined in law across many jurisdictions through health and safety legislation. Thus, safety is often equated with the avoidance of negative outcomes, is prevention-oriented, and achieved through top-down control and constraining variability (Rasmussen,1997). Reflecting this school of thought, earlier safety culture ideas (throughout the 1990s) focus on concepts such as compliance and reporting incidents reactively. More recently, as technologies have become increasingly complex and intractable (e.g., the introduction of automation), tasks increasingly interdependent, and operating conditions more dynamic and uncertain, safety scientists have argued for an alternative conceptualization of safety, which should include the presence of positive capacity that creates success (Hollnagel, 2018).

For example, Lingard and colleagues (2014), have embraced this alternative view of safety through the development of capability-based safety culture models. Dimensions and aspects of safety culture that align with this alternative view of safety definition include communication, leadership, teamwork, and other factors that promote the capability to respond and adapt to unexpected surprises and variability. Another example is the work of Bisbey and colleagues (2021) who proposed that safety culture research should focus on the 'enabling conditions' (i.e., tangible practices and situational factors) that enable an underlying safety culture to develop. Safety capability (Casey et al., 2017; Griffin et al., 2014) is similarly conceptualized, and includes the concept of safety culture within a broader construct termed 'social capital'.

It is inevitable that technology and changes in the world of work, such as increased contingent workforces and smaller, more dynamic organizational structures, will change the way we think about and study safety culture (Hu et al., 2020). Automation and the replacement of humans with machines could increase the focus on cultural aspects that promote capabilities in creative or innovative work domains, or tasks such as machine maintenance, and other adaptive behaviors like improvisation when technology fails. It will be fascinating to see how the safety culture concept evolves over time.

New Mixed Methods

Authors such as Guldenmund (2010), and Schein and Schein (2017) have outlined processes for eliciting evidence of deeper beliefs and assumptions through reflecting on cultural artifacts like symbols and behaviors. One practice that is underutilized in safety culture research but has been used somewhat in the related field of safety climate (Hallowell & Yugar-Arias, 2016) is the photovoice technique.

Briefly, photovoice was first developed by Wang and Burris (1997) as a method to record and reflect on a community's concerns, promote open dialogue about important issues, and to ensure a range of stakeholders, particularly the disempowered, can reach decision makers. The photovoice engages people as co-researchers, so it is participatory in nature (Migliorini & Rania, 2017). Over a period of days or weeks, participants visually document artifacts that symbolize a core issue or aspect of their community (Golden, 2020).

Photovoice consists of several phases or sessions (Migliorini & Rania, 2017). First, the researchers engage with the participants to explain the methodology, co-create the process forward, and identify practical changes that are required (also discussing confidentiality and other ethical concerns or issues). Next, participants engage in independent photography to document key issues under investigation. Then, the researchers interview the participants and apply a structured questioning technique called 'SHOWED' (Wang, 2006), which consists of the following lines of inquiry:

1. What do you see here?
2. What is really happening here?
3. How does this relate to your life?
4. Why does this issue exist?
5. What can we do about it?

Alternatively, researchers can vary the level of participation by, for example, engaging in their own independent photography documentation (e.g., as a researcher is shown around a worksite on a tour) and uses these images as prompts to discuss with workers (Hallowell & Yugar-Arias, 2016). Safety climate researchers can even use short scales or bundles of items as interview questions that are used to guide the photovoice process.

Applied to safety culture, photovoice has great potential. Given that Guldenmund (2010) recommended that researchers should begin with artifacts and engage in sense-making with employees to generate hypotheses about the underlying culture, the photovoice technique could be used to expedite this approach. Indeed, in the first author's experience using photovoice to understand a power station's safety culture, participants were asked to take a photo of something that made them feel safe, and provide an explanation of why, as well as any related stories or events that included the artifact and were meaningful to help understand the safety culture. Photos provided by employees stimulated rich and sometimes emotional storytelling; there was the memorial outside the plant that signified the death of a co-worker many years prior, which illuminated the changes in other workers' beliefs regarding the hazard of falls from height and the importance of ensuring adequate controls. Another photo discussed was a picture of a storage tank, and the accompanying story described a previous safety manager who penalized the worker who stood on top of the tank but only after the production job was completed, which led to a further breakdown in trust between workers and managers at the plant. These examples highlight the utility of photovoice in stimulating rich discussion about safety culture, and enable the development of testable hypotheses (e.g., through quantitative survey or focus groups) concerning underlying beliefs and assumptions.

New Data Sources

The proliferation of social media has opened a raft of interesting research opportunities. Even organizations have their own social media platforms, such as Facebook's Workspace, Yammer, and Microsoft Teams. Social media was initially employed by organizations to engage more directly with potential customers and end-users, but increasingly, has been deployed to meet internal objectives such as communication, coordination, and social capital building (Fusi & Feeney, 2018; Khan et al., 2014; Leonardi et al., 2013). Social media data can be used by researchers to map organizational culture and also to chart change in culture due to societal or internal initiatives such as the #MeToo movement (Dolamore & Richards, 2020) or an intervention designed to improve workplace compassion (Clyne et al., 2018).

Another data source that could be a goldmine for organizational culture researchers is employee reviews. Websites such as Glassdoor.com, which offer current and ex-employees the opportunity to rate their employer on various aspects and leave extensive qualitative comments regarding their experiences, have been shown to predict measures of organizational culture and be related to job performance of current employees (Das Swain et al., 2020). As safety becomes more important in organizational priorities and regulators continue to promote it across industry, it is likely that social media and other data sources like employee review sites will include meta-data that could facilitate safety culture research.

Other researchers have explored annual reports and stock market announcements as potential data sources to understand organizational culture. For instance, Pandey and Pandey (2019) used a natural language processing (NLP) algorithm to analyze company annual reports and generate rich descriptions of organizational culture across a predefined taxonomy derived from desktop research. In the safety realm, McDermott and colleagues (2018) manually content analyzed executives' long-term incentive plans for specific safety indicators to inform cross-industry recommendations that would raise the prioritization of safety in Australian construction. Such a method could be easily applied to understand safety culture within and between organizations, for instance, by mapping artifacts such as various safety metrics reported, the types of initiatives undertaken, and even the nature of different words used to describe the organization's safety vision and policy.

New Analytical Technologies

It follows then that the arrival of new data sources also requires new methods to analyze such data efficiently and accurately. Technology stands to revolutionize qualitative research by short-cutting often resource intensive and effortful coding, interpretation, and analysis. Of note, structural topic modeling (STM) is one technique that shows considerable promise and has already been applied to the study of organizational culture.

STM is an automated method (employing machine learning and 'soft' artificial intelligence) for analyzing large volumes of text, usually in the form of documents (Sterling et al., 2019). Across four phases, STM: (1) enables researchers to collect data from larger sources of data, (2) uses inductive exploratory approaches rather than relying on a predefined coding schema, (3) combines both qualitative (generation of themes or topics) and quantitative data (document metadata), and (4) facilitates advanced statistical modeling to explore variable associations (Schmiedel et al., 2019). Regarding the last point, STM is a powerful method because it enables researchers to quantitatively examine associations between document metadata (e.g., organizational department, job tenure) and (a) the prevalence of various topics, and (b) the content contained within various topics.

Applied to organizational culture research, STM is powerful indeed. In addition to mapping the nature of organizational culture at a point in time, STM can be used to identify and describe the dynamics of culture, such as changes in cultural meaning, values, and beliefs over time (Hannigan et al., 2019). Importantly, STM can provide researchers with a less biased method to understand and explore organizational culture, as well as connect organizational culture changes to initiatives and broader societal movements (Hannigan et al., 2019).

Within the safety culture domain, STM is only just starting to be applied (e.g., Goh et al., 2019; Lee et al., 2021; Sujon & Dai, 2021). For instance, STM has been used at a societal level to explore trends regarding patient safety (specifically, changes in issue prevalence) across multiple healthcare settings by analyzing news articles (Kim & Lee, 2019). Goh and colleagues (2019) analyzed existing safety climate and culture published literature to identify six themes or topics regarding avenues that healthcare organizations can explore to establish a safety culture. Yet, the application of STM specifically to the investigation of safety culture at an organizational level is rare. We believe that STM could be particularly useful to analyze the language used in incident reports, company safety bulletins and alerts, and transcribed speech from interactions between employees about safety (e.g., during company pre-start meetings). Future work involving STM and safety culture will likely lead to fruitful insights.

CONCLUSIONS

Although some scholars have called for the 'head' of safety culture (Borys, 2014) we stand poised to block the executioner's blade from coming down and severing decades of empirical inquiry. Granted, many studies within the safety culture portfolio have questionable underpinnings, stemming in large part from the lack of conceptual clarity embedded in definitions such as the highly cited one from INSAG. Perhaps this issue highlights the perils of reverse knowledge transfer, from industry to academia. Given that safety culture has its roots in industry (Glendon, 2008) and was later adopted by academia and shoehorned into existing research on safety and organizational culture, it is no wonder that the field has become so messy. Nevertheless, we believe our attempt to salvage safety culture and bring it back from the brink of irrelevance will contribute to future research in meaningful ways. We encourage researchers to adopt the safety culture manifesto presented here and commit to more robust and rigorous safety culture investigations. Further, we drew on emerging methods from the organizational culture literature to discuss how safety culture research could be innovated and leverage new technologies and tools to enhance its sophistication.

REFERENCES

Adjekum, D. K., & Tous, M. F. (2020). Assessing the relationship between organizational management factors and a resilient safety culture in a collegiate aviation program with Safety Management Systems (SMS). *Safety Science*, 131, 104909.

Antonsen, S. (2009). Safety culture and the issue of power. *Safety Science*, 47(2), 183–191.

Antonsen, S., Nilsen, M., & Almklov, P. G. (2017). Regulating the intangible. Searching for safety culture in the Norwegian petroleum industry. *Safety Science*, 92, 232–240.

Atombo, C., Wu, C., Tettehfio, E. O., Nyamuame, G. Y., & Agbo, A. A. (2017). Safety and health perceptions in work-related transport activities in Ghanaian industries. *Safety and Health at Work*, 8(2), 175–182.

Baum, F., MacDougall, C., & Smith, D. (2006). Participatory action research. *Journal of Epidemiology and Community Health*, 60(10), 854.

Bisbey, T. M., Kilcullen, M. P., Thomas, E. J., Ottosen, M. J., Tsao, K., & Salas, E. (2021). Safety culture: An integration of existing models and a framework for understanding its development. *Human Factors*, 63(1), 0018720819868878.

Borys, D. (2014). Organisational culture: A search for meaning. In *The Core Body of Knowledge for Generalist OHS Professionals*. Tullamarine, VIC: Australian Institute of Health and Safety. Retrieved from https://www.ohsbok.org.au/

Burns, C., Mearns, K., & McGeorge, P. (2006). Explicit and implicit trust within safety culture. *Risk Analysis*, 26(5), 1139–1150.

Busch, C. (2020). Personal communication.

Bye, R. J., Aalberg, A. L., & Røyrvik, J. O. D. (2020). What we talk about when we talk about HSE and culture – A mapping and analysis of the academic discourses. *Safety Science*, 129, 104846.

Casey, T.W., Hu, X., Kanse, L. & Varhammar, A. (under review). A tale of six climates: Reflections and learnings after the development of six industry-specific safety climate scales, *Journal of Safety Research*.

Casey, T., Griffin, M. A., Flatau Harrison, H., & Neal, A. (2017). Safety climate and culture: Integrating psychological and systems perspectives. *Journal of Occupational Health Psychology*, 22(3), 341.

Chen, I. C., & Li, H. H. (2010). Measuring patient safety culture in Taiwan using the Hospital Survey on Patient Safety Culture (HSOPSC). *BMC Health Services Research*, 10(1), 1–10.

Clyne, W., Pezaro, S., Deeny, K., & Kneafsey, R. (2018). Using social media to generate and collect primary data: The #ShowsWorkplaceCompassion Twitter research campaign. *JMIR Public Health and Surveillance*, 4(2), e41.

Cooper, M. D. (2000). Towards a model of safety culture. *Safety Science*, 36(2), 111–136.

Creswell, J. W., Hanson, W. E., Clark Plano, V. L., & Morales, A. (2007). Qualitative research designs: Selection and implementation. *Counseling Psychologist*, 35(2), 236–264.

Das Swain, V., Saha, K., Reddy, M. D., Rajvanshy, H., Abowd, G. D., & De Choudhury, M. (2020, April). Modeling organizational culture with workplace experiences shared on Glassdoor. In Proceedings of the 2020 CHI Conference on Human Factors in Computing Systems (pp. 1–15).

DeBlois, L. A. (1926). *Industrial safety organization for executive and engineer*. McGraw-Hill Book Company, Incorporated.

Dekker, S. (2016). *Drift into failure: From hunting broken components to understanding complex systems*. CRC Press.

Díaz-Cabrera, D., Hernández-Fernaud, E., & Isla-Díaz, R. (2007). An evaluation of a new instrument to measure organisational safety culture values and practices. *Accident Analysis & Prevention*, 39(6), 1202–1211.

Dick, B. (2016). *Convergent interviewing essentials*. Chapel Hill: Interchange.

Dolamore, S., & Richards, T. N. (2020). Assessing the organizational culture of higher education institutions in an era of# MeToo. *Public Administration Review*, 80(6), 1133–1137.

Edwards, J. R., Davey, J., & Armstrong, K. (2013). Returning to the roots of culture: A review and re-conceptualisation of safety culture. *Safety Science*, 55, 70–80.

Edwards, J., Davey, J., & Armstrong, K. (2015). Cultural factors: Understanding culture to design organisational structures and systems to optimise safety. *Procedia Manufacturing*, 3, 4991–4998.

Edwards, J., Freeman, J., Soole, D., & Watson, B. (2014). A framework for conceptualising traffic safety culture. *Transportation Research Part F: Traffic Psychology and Behaviour*, 26(1), 293–302.

Fleming, M. (2005). Patient safety culture measurement and improvement: A 'how to' guide. *Healthc Q*, 8(Spec No), 14–19.

Fleming, M. (2007). Developing safety culture measurement tools and techniques based on site audits rather than questionnaires. Final Project Report, Saint Marys University, 1–63.

Flin, R., Mearns, K., O'Connor, P., & Bryden, R. (2000). Measuring safety climate: identifying the common features. *Safety Science*, 34(1–3), 177–192.

Fowler, M., & Highsmith, J. (2001). The agile manifesto. *Software Development*, 9(8), 28–35.

Fugas, C. S., Silva, S. A., & Meliá, J. L. (2011). Another look at safety climate and safety behavior: Deepening the cognitive and social mediator mechanisms. *Accident Analysis & Prevention*, 45, 468–477.

Fusi, F., & Feeney, M. K. (2018). Social media in the workplace: Information exchange, productivity, or waste? *American Review of Public Administration*, 48(5), 395–412.

Geertz, C. (1973). *Thick description: Toward an interpretive theory of culture*. New York: Basic Books.

Geller, E. S. (1994). Ten principles for achieving a total safety culture. *Professional Safety*, 39(9), 18.

Glendon, I. (2008). Safety culture: snapshot of a developing concept. *Journal of Occupational Health & Safety*, 24(3), 179.

Goh, D. H. L., Zheng, H., Lee, E. W. J., Lee, C. S., & Theng, Y. L. (2019). Information and communication research in promoting workplace safety and health: A topic modeling analysis. *Proceedings of the Association for Information Science and Technology*, 56(1), 658–660.

Golden, T. (2020). Reframing photovoice: Building on the method to develop more equitable and responsive research practices. *Qualitative Health Research*, 30(6), 960–972.

Goncalves Filho, A. P., & Waterson, P. (2018). Maturity models and safety culture: A critical review. *Safety Science*, 105, 192–211.

Goncalves Filho, A. P., Andrade, J. C. S., & de Oliveira Marinho, M. M. (2010). A safety culture maturity model for petrochemical companies in Brazil. *Safety Science*, 48(5), 615–624.

Griffin, M. A., & Curcuruto, M. (2016). Safety climate in organizations. *Annual Review of Organizational Psychology and Organizational Behavior*, 3, 191–212.

Griffin, M. A., Hodkiewicz, M. R., Dunster, J., Kanse, L., Parkes, K. R., Finnerty, D., ... & Unsworth, K. L. (2014). A conceptual framework and practical guide for assessing fitness-to-operate in the offshore oil and gas industry. *Accident Analysis & Prevention*, 68, 156–171.

Guldenmund, F. W. (2000). The nature of safety culture: A review of theory and research. *Safety Science*, 34(1–3), 215–257.

Guldenmund, F. W. (2007). The use of questionnaires in safety culture research – an evaluation. *Safety Science*, 45(6), 723–743.

Guldenmund, F. W. (2010). (Mis) understanding safety culture and its relationship to safety management. *Risk Analysis: An International Journal*, 30(10), 1466–1480.

Guldenmund, F. W. (2018). Understanding safety culture through models and metaphors. In *Safety Cultures, Safety Models* (pp. 21–34). Cham: Springer.

Halligan, M., & Zecevic, A. (2011). Safety culture in healthcare: A review of concepts, dimensions, measures and progress. *BMJ Quality & Safety*, 20(4), 338–343.

Hallowell, M. R., & Yugar-Arias, I. F. (2016). Exploring fundamental causes of safety challenges faced by Hispanic construction workers in the US using photovoice. *Safety Science*, 82, 199–211.

Hammersley, M., & Atkinson, P. (2019). *Ethnography: Principles in practice*. Routledge.

Hannigan, T. R., Haans, R. F., Vakili, K., Tchalian, H., Glaser, V. L., Wang, M. S., ... & Jennings, P. D. (2019). Topic modeling in management research: Rendering new theory from textual data. *Academy of Management Annals*, 13(2), 586–632.

Håvold, J. I. (2010). Safety culture aboard fishing vessels. *Safety Science*, 48(8), 1054–1061.

Heckemann, B., Hahn, S., Halfens, R. J. G., Richter, D. & Schols, J. M. G. A. (2019). Patient and visitor aggression in healthcare: A survey exploring organisational safety culture and team efficacy. *Journal of Nursing Management*, 27(5), 1039–1046.

Hollnagel, E. (2018). *Safety-I and safety-II: The past and future of safety management*. CRC Press.

Hopkins, A. (2019). *Organising for safety*. Wolters Kluwer.

Hu, X., Casey, T., & Griffin, M. (2020). You can have your cake and eat it too: Embracing paradox of safety as source of progress in safety science. *Safety Science*, 130, 104824.

Hudson, P. (2007). Implementing a safety culture in a major multi-national. *Safety Science*, 45(6), 697–722.

IAEA (1991). *Safety culture*. International Safety Advisory Group. Safety Series 75-INSAG-4. Vienna.

Job, A., Silva, I., & Moreira, T. (2020). Test of a safety culture model from a management perspective. *Revista Brasileira de Gestão de Negócios*, 22(2), 250–270.

Kalteh, H. O., Mortazavi, S. B., Mohammadi, E., & Salesi, M. (2021). The relationship between safety culture and safety climate and safety performance: A systematic review. *International Journal of Occupational Safety and Ergonomics*, 27(1), 206–216.

Khan, G. F., Swar, B., & Lee, S. K. (2014). Social media risks and benefits: A public sector perspective. *Social Science Computer Review*, 32(5), 606–627.

Kim, M. K., & Lee, S. M. (2019). The causal relationships among staff nurses' job stress factors, patient safety culture perception and patient safety nursing activities in a university hospital. *Journal of Korean Academy of Nursing Administration*, 25(4), 340–352.

Kirk, S., Marshall, M. N., Claridge, T., Esmail, A., & Parker, D. (2005). Evaluating safety culture. *Patient Safety: Research into Practice*, 173.

Le Coze, J. C. (2019). How safety culture can make us think. *Safety Science*, 118, 221–229.

Le Coze, J. C. (2020). Hopkins' view of structure and culture (one step closer to strategy). *Safety Science*, 122, 104541.

Leaver, M. P., & Reader, T. W. (2019). Safety culture in financial trading: An analysis of trading misconduct investigations. *Journal of Business Ethics*, 154(2), 461–481.

Lee, T., & Harrison, K. (2000). Assessing safety culture in nuclear power stations. *Safety Science*, 34(1–3), 61–97.

Lee, T. W., Kim, P. J., Lee, H. Y., Shin, H. K., Lee, H. S., & Choi, Y. (2021). Factors affecting patient safety culture of clinical nurses: Focusing on authentic leadership and team effectiveness. *Journal of Korean Academy of Nursing Administration*, 27(1), 34–42.

Leonardi, P. M., Huysman, M., & Steinfield, C. (2013). Enterprise social media: Definition, history, and prospects for the study of social technologies in organizations. *Journal of Computer-Mediated Communication*, 19(1), 1–19.

Lingard, H., Zhang, R., Harley, J., Blismas, J. & Wakefield, R. (2014). *Health and safety culture.* Retrieved from https://www.researchgate.net/publication/271589125_Health_and_Safety_Culture.

MacKenzie, S. B. (2003). The dangers of poor construct conceptualization. *Journal of the Academy of Marketing Science,* 31(3), 323–326.

McDermott, V., Zhang, R. P., Hopkins, A., & Hayes, J. (2018). Constructing safety: Investigating senior executive long-term incentive plans and safety objectives in the construction sector. *Construction Management and Economics,* 36(5), 276–290.

McDiarmid, M. A., & Condon, M. (2005). Organizational safety culture/climate and worker compliance with hazardous drug guidelines: Lessons from the blood-borne pathogen experience. *Journal of Occupational and Environmental Medicine,* 47(7), 740–749.

McDonald, N., Corrigan, S., Daly, C., & Cromie, S. (2000). Safety management systems and safety culture in aircraft maintenance organisations. *Safety Science,* 34(1–3), 151–176.

Migliorini, L., & Rania, N. (2017). A qualitative method to 'make visible' the world of intercultural relationships: The photovoice in social psychology. *Qualitative Research in Psychology,* 14(2), 131–145.

Mokarami, H., Alizadeh, S. S., Pordanjani, T. R., & Varmazyar, S. (2019). The relationship between organizational safety culture and unsafe behaviors, and accidents among public transport bus drivers using structural equation modeling. *Transportation Research Part F: Traffic Psychology and Behaviour,* 65, 46–55.

Mustafa, M., Adb Aziz, F.S. & Victor, O. (2017). The influence of safety culture on safety management system. *International Journal of Economic Research,* 14(15), 471–479.

Nævestad, T. O., Blom, J., & Phillips, R. O. (2020). Safety culture, safety management and accident risk in trucking companies. *Transportation Research Part F: Traffic Psychology and Behaviour,* 73, 325–347.

Nævestad, T. O., Phillips, R. O., Størkersen, K. V., Laiou, A., & Yannis, G. (2019). Safety culture in maritime transport in Norway and Greece: Exploring national, sectorial and organizational influences on unsafe behaviours and work accidents. *Marine Policy,* 99, 1–13.

Nævestad, T. O., Vedal Størkersen, K., & Phillips, R. O. (2018). Procedure negligence in coastal cargo: What can be done to reduce the gap between formal and informal aspects of safety? *Safety,* 4(3), 34.

Nowrouzi, B., Gohar, B., Nowrouzi-Kia, B., Garbaczewska, M., Chapovalov, O., Myette-Côté, É., & Carter, L. (2016). Facilitators and barriers to occupational health and safety in small and medium-sized enterprises: A descriptive exploratory study in Ontario, Canada. *International Journal of Occupational Safety and Ergonomics,* 22(3), 360–366.

Olive, C., O'Connor, T. M., & Mannan, M. S. (2006). Relationship of safety culture and process safety. *Journal of Hazardous Materials,* 130(1–2), 133–140.

Oxtoby, C., Mossop, L., White, K., & Ferguson, E. (2017). Safety culture: The Nottingham veterinary safety culture survey (NVSCS). *Veterinary Record,* 180(19), 472–472.

Pandey, S., & Pandey, S. K. (2019). Applying natural language processing capabilities in computerized textual analysis to measure organizational culture. *Organizational Research Methods,* 22(3), 765–797.

Parker, D., Lawrie, M., & Hudson, P. (2006). A framework for understanding the development of organisational safety culture. *Safety Science,* 44(6), 551–562.

Pillay, M., Borys, D., Else, D., & Tuck, M. (2010). Safety culture and resilience engineering–exploring theory and application in improving gold mining safety. *Gravity Gold,* 21, e2.

Podsakoff, N. P., Podsakoff, P. M., MacKenzie, S. B., & Klinger, R. L. (2013). Are we really measuring what we say we're measuring? Using video techniques to supplement traditional construct validation procedures. *Journal of Applied Psychology,* 98(1), 99.

Rae, A., Provan, D., Aboelssaad, H., & Alexander, R. (2020). A manifesto for reality-based safety science. *Safety Science,* 126, 104654.

Rasmussen, J. (1997). Risk management in a dynamic society: A modeling problem. *Safety Science,* 27(2–3), 183–213.

Reason, J. (1996). *Managing the risks of organizational accidents.* Routledge.

Ruan, D., Hardeman, F., & Mkrtchyan, L. (2012). A novel approach for safety culture assessment. *International Journal of Uncertainty, Fuzziness and Knowledge-Based Systems,* 20(supp01), 1–15.

Sari, R. N., & Dewi, D. S. (2021, March). Development models of personality, social cognitive, and safety culture to work accidents in the chemical company. In *IOP Conference Series: Materials Science and Engineering* (Vol. 1096(1), p. 012025). IOP Publishing.

Schein, E. H. (2010). *Organizational culture and leadership* (Vol. 2). John Wiley & Sons.

Schein, E. H., & Schein, P. (2017). *Organizational culture and leadership* (5th ed.). John Wiley & Sons.

Schmiedel, T., Müller, O., & vom Brocke, J. (2019). Topic modeling as a strategy of inquiry in organizational research: A tutorial with an application example on organizational culture. *Organizational Research Methods*, 22(4), 941–968.

Singer, S., Meterko, M., Baker, L., Gaba, D., Falwell, A., & Rosen, A. (2007). Workforce perceptions of hospital safety culture: Development and validation of the patient safety climate in healthcare organizations survey. *Health Services Research*, 42(5), 1999–2021.

Smircich, L. (1983). Concepts of culture and organizational analysis. *Administrative Science Quarterly*, 28(3), 339–358.

Snook, S. A. (2000). *Friendly fire*. Princeton University Press.

Sorra, J. S., & Dyer, N. (2010). Multilevel psychometric properties of the AHRQ hospital survey on patient safety culture. *BMC Health Services Research*, 10(1), 1–13.

Stemn, E., Bofinger, C., Cliff, D., & Hassall, M. E. (2019). Examining the relationship between safety culture maturity and safety performance of the mining industry. *Safety Science*, 113, 345–355.

Sterling, J., Jost, J. T., & Hardin, C. D. (2019). Liberal and conservative representations of the good society: A (social) structural topic modeling approach. *Sage Open*, 9(2), 2158244019846211.

Sujon, M., & Dai, F. (2021). Social media mining for understanding traffic safety culture in Washington State using Twitter data. *Journal of Computing in Civil Engineering*, 35(1), 04020059.

Tear, M. J., Reader, T. W., Shorrock, S., & Kirwan, B. (2020). Safety culture and power: Interactions between perceptions of safety culture, organisational hierarchy, and national culture. *Safety Science*, 121, 550–561.

Turner, B. A. (1978). *Man-made disasters*. London: Wykeham Publications.

Vaughan, D. (1996). *The Challenger launch decision: Risky technology, culture, and deviance at NASA*. University of Chicago Press.

Vogus, T. J., Sutcliffe, K. M., & Weick, K. E. (2010). Doing no harm: Enabling, enacting, and elaborating a culture of safety in health care. *Academy of Management Perspectives*, 24(4), 60–77.

Voss, K. E., Zablah, A. R., Huang, Y. S. S., & Chakraborty, G. (2020). Conjunctionitis: A call for clarity in construct definitions. *European Journal of Marketing*, 54(5), 1147–1159.

Wang, B., Wu, C., & Huang, L. (2018). Emotional safety culture: A new and key element of safety culture. *Process Safety Progress*, 37(2), 134–139.

Wang, C. C. (2006). Youth participation in photovoice as a strategy for community change. *Journal of Community Practice*, 14(1–2), 147–161.

Wang, C., & Burris, M. A. (1997). Photovoice: Concept, methodology, and use for participatory needs assessment. *Health Education & Behavior*, 24(3), 369–387.

Weber, D. E., MacGregor, S. C., Provan, D. J., & Rae, A. (2018). 'We can stop work, but then nothing gets done.' Factors that support and hinder a workforce to discontinue work for safety. *Safety Science*, 108(1), 149–160.

Weick, K. (1987). Organizational culture as a source of high reliability. *California Management Review*, 29(2), 112–127.

Weick, K. E., Sutcliffe, K. M., & Obstfeld, D. (2008). Organizing for high reliability: Processes of collective mindfulness. *Crisis Management*, 3(1), 81–123.

Westrum, R. (1988). Organizational and interorganizational thought. Paper presented to the World Bank conference on Safety Control and Risk Management, Washington, October.

Westrum, R. (2004). A typology of organisational cultures. *BMJ Quality & Safety*, 13(suppl 2), ii22–ii27.

Westrum, R. (2014). The study of information flow: A personal journey. *Safety Science*, 67, 58–63.

Wiegmann, D. A., Zhang, H., Von Thaden, T. L., Sharma, G., & Gibbons, A. M. (2004). Safety culture: An integrative review. *International Journal of Aviation Psychology*, 14(2), 117–134.

Yorio, P. L., Edwards, J., & Hoeneveld, D. (2019). Safety culture across cultures. *Safety Science*, 120, 402–410.

Zohar, D. (1980). Safety climate in industrial organizations: Theoretical and applied implications. *Journal of Applied Psychology*, 65(1), 96.

Zohar, D. (2010). Thirty years of safety climate research: Reflections and future directions. *Accident Analysis & Prevention*, 42(5), 1517–1522.

Index

Printed and bound by CPI Group (UK) Ltd, Croydon, CR0 4YY

16/04/2025

14658397-0001